Smoking

Contemporary Issues
Series Editors: Robert A Baird
Stuart E. Rosenbaum

Other titles in this series:

Smoking
Who Has the Right?

edited by
Jeffrey A. Schaler, Ph.D.
& Magda E. Schaler, M.P.H.

Prometheus Books
59 John Glenn Drive
Amherst, New York 14228-2197

Published November 1998 by Prometheus Books

02 01 00 99 98   5 4 3 2 1

Library of Congress Cataloging-in-Publication Data

Smoking : who has the right? / edited by Jeffrey A. Schaler and Magda E. Schaler.
     p.   cm.
  Includes bibliographical references (p.   ).
  ISBN 1–57392–254–4 (pbk. : alk. paper)
  1. Smoking—United States. 2. Smoking—Law and legislation—United
States. I. Schaler, Jeffrey A. II. Schaler, Magda E.
HV5760.S67   1998
394.1'4—dc21   98–30876
                                                                                    CIP

Printed in the United States of America on acid-free paper

Contents

5

PART II: FOR THE PUBLIC'S HEALTH: JUSTIFYING TOBACCO REGULATION

PART III: LIBERTY AT STAKE: SMOKING AS CHOICE, REGULATION AS COERCION

Introduction

The Smoking Controversy: A Right to Protect versus A Right to Smoke?

Jeffrey A. Schaler and Magda E. Schaler

We begin our introduction to this anthology by asking you to consider the following question: Which is more important to you, health or liberty?

Assume these values are mutually exclusive from a public-policy point of view. Let's phrase the question another way: Which do you value more, freedom from coercion by a paternalistic governmental authority at the possible expense of possible poor health—or freedom from disease or poor health at the expense of being denied pursuit of certain behaviors and activities you find enjoyable despite their risk?

Consider our question in still another way: Is it more noble to secure individual liberty at the risk of harming ourselves than to allow someone else to make decisions about risky activities for us? If this is the case, then we see that liberty and responsibility, again from a public-policy point of view, are positively correlated. To be sure, the more liberty people exercise, the more responsible they must be. The inverse is also true: The more responsible people are, the more liberty they can experience.

If the opposite is true, i.e., if it is more noble to be healthy and protected from increased probability of harm, then the correlation between liberty and responsibility is still a positive one. When we give up our freedom to engage in risky behaviors we must be regarded as less responsible. We become "infantilized" by authority. We assume or are assigned a social role of metaphorical children—even though we are actually adults. Government then becomes our metaphorical parents. We cannot increase liberty by decreasing responsibility and vice versa. While the inverse to our equation is true, the converse is false.

In fact, there is no "right" answer to the question we are posing here. The question is a moral one requiring an answer based on personal values. Individual morality is a heterogeneous quality in the population at large, not a homogeneous one. The answer to our question, it seems to us, is "it depends." It depends on whether one is willing to accept the consequences of one decision or another. We are interested in the arguments supporting one answer or another in light of the different consequences integral to one path or another. We ask you to consider this question in light of the smoking controversy we face today.

THE IMPORTANCE OF STUDYING TOBACCO REGULATION

Smoking policy presents a unique opportunity to study political, economic, legal, and social aspects of health and health behavior. The demonization of the tobacco industry coupled with the medicalization of addiction, and the high financial stakes involved in liabilities cases and revenue losses, are virtual gold mines for analysis and debate. It is on that basis we have assembled this anthology.

The recently proposed regulation of smoking and tobacco products by the U.S. Food and Drug Administration (FDA) takes diverse forms. These include increasing restriction of smoking in public and private domains, requirements of health warnings on cigarette packages, anti-smoking publicity campaigns, prohibitive taxation strategies, age-restrictive vending regulation, and sanctions on advertising. The FDA has asserted that it has a legitimate scientific and legally justifiable basis for regulating nicotine, and thereby all tobacco products containing nicotine. A federal court has upheld this authority: U.S. District Court Judge William Osteen ruled on April 25, 1997, that tobacco products fit the federal definition of a drug, and in so doing he cleared the way for the potential regulation of those products by the FDA. (He also gave the tobacco companies a slight victory, however, in ruling that the government could not restrict cigarette advertising.) Judge Osteen's ruling was reversed by the U.S. Court of Appeals for the Fourth Circuit on August 14, 1998.[1]

Moreover, a plethora of litigation has been launched against the tobacco industry by a conglomerate of state attorneys general successfully seeking compensation for the health care costs incurred by smoking. The tobacco companies have agreed, in part, to pay for such costs, among many other concessions (see on-line, http://www.tobacco resources.com). Public policy is being crafted to reduce mortality and morbidity associated with the use of tobacco. But should the elimination of smoking even be a goal in a free society? Where should the line be drawn between public dissemination of accurate information and the legislation of morality in the form of propaganda?

Tobacco control is the exertion of power by government grounded in the implied health preferences of the nonsmoking majority. By societal nature, we are bound to affect others when we exert our preferences. Rights, depending on ideological perspective, are therefore viewed as either ensured or infringed upon by tobacco control. Various tobacco control initiatives have different goals. Some initiatives aim at reducing public exposure to smoking behavior—protecting "us" from "others." Some strategies attempt to protect "us" from "ourselves," (included here are even the inclinations we may have toward smoking) through tobacco taxation and regulation of tobacco as an addictive substance. Still other regulations are designed to dismantle the tobacco industry's public image by restricting advertising.

Proponents of increased smoking regulation who favor restriction of smoking in public places emphasize the collective right of nonsmokers to be free from the effects of smoking or the behavior of smokers. This position rests on acceptance of the scientific reports of the federal Environmental Protection Agency (EPA) conclusively associating second-hand smoke with adverse respiratory health effects. Economic analysts have addressed second-hand smoke as an externality leading to market failure and tend to steer away from criticism of second-hand smoke regulation. For regulation proponents, it follows, then, that the government should issue regulations protecting the health of nonsmokers and limiting the behavior of smokers. It is further asserted that agencies (especially the U.S. Department of Health and Human Services) should enforce rules governing smoking in what pro-regulationists consider public places, i.e., restaurants, workplaces, and theaters, in an attempt to guarantee the implied health rights of nonsmokers. An example of this approach is the recent prohibition of smoking in private restaurants in California to protect workers from second-hand smoke. Allies in these endeavors include various professional health organizations (e.g., the American Public Health Association) and an array of citizen-action groups.

Anti-regulation advocates, however, have interpreted liberty to imply just the opposite, declaring the rights in question to be those of smokers rather than nonsmokers. Their arguments rely on the constitutional ideal of avoiding government intrusion in, and the restriction of, personal behavior. Anti-regulators claim that especially in the circumstance of restaurants, as private rather than public establishments, government intrusion is unconstitutional. These assertions, voiced most strongly by the tobacco industry and various smokers' rights groups (often funded by the tobacco industry), cite studies rejecting EPA findings that second-hand smoke is a health risk. Accordingly, there is debate over "good" and "bad" science, leaving many people with questions over what to believe (see the article by Morris Chafetz, chapter 14 in this volume). U.S. District Court for the Middle District of North Carolina Judge William L. Osteen rejected the EPA's claim that second-hand smoke was a known carcinogen in an important case decided on July 17, 1998.[2]

THE VOLUNTARY NATURE OF ADDICTION

The debate about smoking rights and regulation also rests on the meaning of addiction. Groups and individuals supporting government regulation of tobacco products contend that nicotine is addictive and that once smokers become addicted they can no longer choose not to smoke. Therefore, they argue, government must intervene to protect citizens from tobacco companies which allegedly enhance the nicotine content of their products to addict smokers. Pro-regulationists assert that smokers are unwittingly "hooked" and can become addicted by smoking.

The claim that addictive behavior is involuntary is a controversial one. Many experts disagree. By definition, addiction refers to behavior. Consequently, it is voluntary. Involuntary "behavior" is not behavior—it is pathological, e.g., an epileptic seizure. The distinction between behavior and disease is important in public policy considerations. Smoking is a behavior. Cancer is a disease. The former refers to mode of conduct, deportment. Behavior is the expression of choice. Disease is defined through signs, tests, physiological lesions, and chemical imbalance.

BEHAVIOR VERSUS DISEASE

The distinction between behavior and disease is also crucial when we consider the difference between what tobacco smoke does to the body and how the smoke gets into the body. The former is concerned with physical and chemical interactions. Tobacco products are inert substances. They cannot purposefully invade a person's body. The latter refers to conduct, volition. People choose to purchase, ignite, and inhale the smoke from tobacco products. We must keep these distinctions in mind throughout the course of our discussion. Smoking policy is fraught with controversy, and we must agree on terms and issues at hand in order to communicate meaningfully.

Again, the facts about smoking behavior do not appear to support the assertion that addictive behavior is involuntary. People quit smoking all the time. Most people quit on their own, without help from others (Fiore et al., 1990). And many people moderate their smoking, i.e., they only smoke one or two cigarettes, at specific times and places, without developing an uncontrollable desire to smoke more (Hennrikus et al., 1996; Gilpin et al, 1997). If adults start smoking because they choose to do so, and moderate their smoking because they choose to do so, and quit smoking—sometimes after fifty years of smoking heavily—because they choose to do so, doesn't it seem reasonable to conclude that people who continue to smoke after many years—even when they know they are suffering health consequences by their behavior—are choosing to do so?

Since smoking is voluntary isn't it accurate to conclude that the controversy surrounding smoking rights and regulation is a political, not a strictly medical one? Smoking is a behavior based on personal choice and values. Thus, the regulation of smoking behavior through institutional control such as government, is, in fact, the regulation of individual choice and behavior.

Since behavior indeed refers to mode of conduct, and the control of conduct can occur in only one of two ways—through internal or external control—then smokers and nonsmokers can either control themselves or be controlled by others. Thomas S. Szasz speaks to this very issue in this volume. How many people would credit the federal government for their personal decision not to smoke? They probably would prefer to take responsibility for not smoking themselves because it is dehumanizing to abdicate their responsibility for not smoking to others.

Formal versus Informal Social Controls

Under what circumstances are institutional forms of social control legally acceptable?

> No matter how carefully rights are drawn and assigned, there remains some potential for conflict. The fact that my preferences extend to your behavior over activities that are well within your defined rights, and vice versa, insures that my satisfaction is influenced by the way that you behave and that your satisfaction is also affected by my behavior. (Buchanan, 1986, pp. 108–109)

James Buchanan's insight reveals a central focus of the debate surrounding tobacco control. Buchanan alludes to the level of interaction inherent in any social environment.

"Liberty" can be viewed as the foundation for either pro- or anti-tobacco regulation arguments. Often the two terms "liberty" and "rights" are used interchangeably, which, to a number of philosophers is a mistake. For the purposes of this discussion, liberty represents either the "preferences" which smokers wish to assert by smoking, or those which nonsmokers wish to assert by being free from smoke. Rights, according to traditional rule of law ideology, are constitutionally appointed entitlements, politically secured by the intentions of the Founding Fathers, and now subject to a great deal of interpretation. Since nowhere in the Constitution was smoking or tobacco explicitly mentioned, there has been an enduring dispute surrounding those issues.

Furthermore, as rights are claimed or established, either for nonsmokers or smokers, it is assumed that the opposing group will accept the responsibility of according the other those rights—either by not smoking or by tolerating smoking. In fact,

> with respect to these debates over competing "rights" to smoke or not smoke, most economists would not pose the issue in this manner. What we are seeking is an efficient outcome, not the preservation of assigned rights in a situation in which there is no market exchange. Determining the optimal smoking rights, outcome involves establishing the benefits and costs of different forms of restriction. This approach takes the problem out of its more strident and inconclusive ideological context in which the debate has been waged. (Viscusi, 1992)

Ultimately, the debate over tobacco regulation continues to challenge any conclusions regarding liberty and rights, pitting the interests expressed through their preferences, of smokers and nonsmokers against each other indefinitely.

Harm to Self versus Harm to Others

We must, for purposes of clarity and accuracy in our discussion, differentiate here between harm to oneself versus harm to others. The primary controversy concerning the right to smoke is focused on whether individuals should be free to harm themselves. Let us agree that no one has the legal right to pursue liberty at the expense of others. Liberty at the expense of others is criminal behavior. Our issue here is this: Do smokers have a right to harm themselves; when they harm no one but themselves? As Lysander Spooner wrote, "vices are not crimes."

The problem we confront next has to do with drawing the line on what constitutes harm. Some argue smokers incur greater health care costs. Who should bear the burden of those costs? If smoking does incur greater costs, and those costs are passed on to nonsmokers in the form of higher health insurance premiums and/or higher taxes to fund Medicare and Medicaid, doesn't that constitute (economic) harm to others? If such is in fact the case, it seems, at first glance, smokers should bear the burden of those expenses.

But that conclusion seems simplistic to us and may set an unfair precedent. If smoking is willful, and responsibility for the consequences of smoking behavior belongs to the smoker, i.e., the health-cost consequences, an equitable health care policy would necessarily discriminate against other people who engage in willful activities incurring greater health care costs. It has been suggested that the health insurance industry could play an integral and interesting role in tobacco regulation. A libertarian approach could advocate the potential for deterrence of smoking by the private sector through assigning smokers to higher risk categories and higher premiums (Halpin and Schauffler, 1993).

Public health advocates have sought allies among the health insurance companies by including smoking cessation benefits in health plans. By shifting the costs of their behavior directly to smokers, it is assumed that economic disincentives would significantly reduce smoking rates. Obviously, the large numbers of un- and underinsured smokers would present a large problem under this model, since they would probably not be subject to the same incentive system, and even more low-income smokers would be priced out of the insurance market altogether.

WHO IS RESPONSIBLE?

If we consider smoking behavior involuntary, then to hold smokers responsible for the consequences of their behaviors seems equivalent to punishing persons for self-inflicted crimes they did not commit. Who is responsible then? Many people today, notably those favoring governmental regulation of nicotine, assert the responsibility belongs to the tobacco industry. The U.S. Department of Health and Human Services ranks tobacco use as the single most preventable cause of mortality in the United States. Tobacco use is a leading cause of diseases of the heart and blood vessels; chronic bronchitis and emphysema; and cancers of the lung, larynx, pharynx, oral cavity, esophagus, pancreas, and bladder, as well as respiratory infections and stomach ulcers. Some argue that smoking behavior is involuntary and that smokers should be held accountable for the greater share of health care costs resulting from smoking. "Sin tax" policies are ways of holding smokers accountable for the consequences of their behaviors and simultaneously are designed to discourage people from smoking. Yet these policies seem contradictory, too.

If smoking is regarded as involuntary, i.e., the result of an addiction that causes an individual to lose the ability to stop smoking, then the attempt to discourage smoking by making smokers pay higher prices for cigarettes and related tobacco products seems to be a cruel and unusual punishment. The Americans with Disabilities Act (ADA) should, at least theoretically, protect smokers against such policies. Obviously, smokers can be discouraged by high prices only if smoking is voluntary behavior. If, on the other hand, smoking is involuntary, high prices will not discourage smoking and will penalize smokers for behaviors they cannot control.

Faced with these apparent contradictions, proponents of tobacco regulation, rallying to the defense of children, assert government must protect children from becoming smokers. This, they often argue, should be done by enforcing age minimums on the sale of tobacco products to minors, eliminating advertising directed toward children, educating children about the dangers of smoking, and so on. Here is a question we must answer in light of these assertions and the policies that are implemented because of them: who are the more appropriate persons to teach children about the possible dangers of smoking, parents or government? Again, this seems to us to be an ethical issue. Most would answer that parents are the proper persons to do so. However, many tobacco regulationists believe they know what is better for children than the children's own parents. Don't parents have the right to teach their children as they see fit?

Clearly the danger in tobacco regulation is the creation of what has come to be known as the "slippery slope": when government mandates personal behavior in one area, what areas of personal conduct can be immune from regulation? Benevolent paternalism has been shown historically to be a road to serfdom. If smoking is banned or regulated because of the dangers it poses, what's next? High-fat diets?

As Morris E. Chafetz has remarked elsewhere, one-third of the population does everything "right," i.e., behaves in health-enhancing ways, complies with recommendations made by health care professionals, and still dies early. One-third of the population does everything "wrong," i.e., behaves in unhealthy ways, refuses to comply with health recommendations, and lives long and meaningful lives. Everyone else seems to fall somewhere in between. We don't know why some people get cancer and others don't. We also don't know what the consequences of tobacco regulation may be. Yet, just as it seems there is a high probability that increased smoking will lead to increased health problems, there seems to be a concomitant risk that increased control of conduct by others, notably government, will lead to abuse of power. Where paternalism, under the masquerade of "public health," imposes formal social controls, informal ones, i.e., relational and self-controls, are the morally, if not legally, appropriate ones.

The validity of some of these conclusions, however, has come under great scrutiny in recent years as confidential tobacco industry files—the Brown and Williamson documents—have been made public, documenting significant differences between public industry statements and private industry knowledge of health risks associated with tobacco use. These documents, released by a "whistle blower" (formerly a Brown and Williamson employee), documented the results of tobacco industry research initiatives and their intentional release of contradictory information.

In this collection we have assembled the best arguments on both sides of the debate. We include the proposals by David Kessler, M.D., former director of the FDA, for FDA regulation of tobacco products and the companies that sell them. These proposals and supporting arguments appeared in the *Journal of the American Medical Association* and the *New England Journal of Medicine,* and have inspired new legislation regarding smoking liberty and regulation and paved the way for liability cases involving the health consequences of smoking.

BACK TO THE FUTURE

In light of the current smoking controversy, which is more important, health or liberty? We have gathered diverse arguments focused on the controversy to assist readers with their answer to our question. Arguments against regulation proposals presented here include historical, sociological, economic, psychological, constitutional, and legal perspectives of the anti-tobacco movement. Arguments supporting consumer sovereignty and the right to cigarettes as property are also presented.

Much has been written to support the medicalization of smoking and the criminalization of the tobacco industry. Most anthologies and books presenting arguments against regulation are dismissed as tobacco-industry apologia, if not funded by the tobacco industry itself. While that is not the case here (we have received no money from the tobacco industry for this book), we believe the soundness of an argument should not be dismissed simply on the basis of who supported the publication of these views. If that were the case, one should simply dismiss the arguments for regulation because they come from the federal government.

We selected David Ryder's and Linda Goldman's chapters on policy analysis to set the stage for analyzing the smoking controversy. We then include historical analyses exposing the "evil" nature of the tobacco industry because those views are instrumental in the proposals for and implementation of tobacco control policies. They include reviews by Peter D. Jacobson, Jeffrey Wasserman, and John Anderson. We balance those with Mark E. Lender's comparison of tobacco regulation proposals with alcohol prohibition, as well as a stunning historical analysis by Robert N. Proctor detailing the Nazi's public health campaign against tobacco that bears striking, if not disturbing, similarity to contemporary efforts. We then frame the controversy from metanalytic and sociological perspectives offered by two of the most respected sociologists in the field, Joseph R. Gusfield and Peter L. Berger.

We begin the section containing arguments against the tobacco industry and in support of government regulation with David Kessler and others' argument for FDA regulation and Lowell Bergman and Oriana Zill's *Frontline* documentation of the "criminal case against the tobacco industry." This is followed by reflections on litigation as cancer prevention by George J. Annas and analysis of tobacco industry tactics by Edward L. Sweda Jr., Richard A. Daynard, and Graham E. Kelder. These experts present erudite arguments supporting regulation to protect public health. Blake D. Poland, while anti-tobacco industry, presents a neutral and balanced assessment in light of these key issues.

We also include rarely heard voices providing evidence that the fundamental assumptions of "regulators" are false. Those include economic arguments based in free-market capitalism and public choice theory by Robert D. Tollison and Richard E. Wagner and property-rights, liberty-based arguments presented by Walter E. Williams, Douglas Den Uyl, and Jeffrey A. Schaler. Rajendra Persaud carefully examines the ethical issues involved in smokers' right to health care. Antony Flew delivers a philosophical *coup de grâce* against the regulationists.

We believe the articles we have selected will be useful to students at all levels of study, and we hope they will enlighten policymakers on both sides of the debate, facilitating a seasoned and balanced understanding of the questions we have raised here. We are each responsible for the consequences of our own actions, whether we favor health at the expense of liberty or vice versa.

NOTES

1. On August 28, 1996, the FDA published a final rule entitled "Regulations Restricting the Sale and Distribution of Cigarettes and Smokeless Tobacco to Protect Children and Adolescents." Cigarette and smokeless tobacco manufacturers, convenience store retailers, and advertisers (the plaintiffs) challenged the FDA's legal authority in the U.S. District Court for the Middle District of North Carolina at Greensboro and Winston-Salem, William L. Osteen Sr., District Judge, to regulate and restrict tobacco products in this manner. Their lawyers argued that Congress has withheld from the FDA the jurisdiction to regulate tobacco products and that the Federal Food, Drug, and Cosmetic Act does not permit the FDA to regulate tobacco products either as drugs or as devices (cigarettes were labeled "nicotine-delivery devices" by the FDA). Judge Osteen held that Congress did not "[intend] to withhold from FDA" the jurisdiction to regulate tobacco products. He also concluded the FDA had the authority to regulate tobacco products under the device provision of the Act and that the FDA lacked the statutory authority to restrict advertising of tobacco products.

Plaintiffs appealed Judge Osteen's ruling. On August 14, 1998, the U.S. Court of Appeals for the Fourth Circuit reversed Judge Osteen's decision stating "For the purposes of these appeals, plaintiffs do not dispute the factual findings of the FDA. Based on our review of the record and the relevant legal authorities, we are of opinion that the FDA lacks jurisdiction to regulate tobacco products. . . . [A]ll of the FDA's August 28, 1996, regulations of tobacco products are thus invalid. . . . This is not a case about whether additional or different regulations are needed to address legitimate concerns about the serious health problems related to tobacco use, and particularly youth tobacco use, in this country. At its core, this case is about who has the power to make this type of major policy decision. As the Supreme Court has previously stated about a different agency and its enabling statute, neither federal agencies nor the courts can substitute their policy judgments for those of Congress. . . . Accordingly, we do not, indeed cannot, pass judgment on the merits of the regulatory scheme proposed by the FDA. . . . [T]he FDA has exceeded the authority granted to it by Congress, and its rulemaking action cannot stand. . . . We are thus of opinion that Congress did not intend to delegate jurisdiction over tobacco products to the FDA. Accordingly, the judgment of the district court is REVERSED" (opinion written by Judge Emory H. Widener Jr., Circuit Judge, U.S. Court of Appeals for the Fourth Circuit, August 14, 1998; *Brown & Williamson Tobacco Corporation et al.* v. *Food & Drug Administration et al.* From 1999 U.S. App. LEXIS 18821). Two FDA regulations are still in effect: Tobacco products may not be sold to anyone under 18 years of age and retailers are required to check photo IDs of purchasers under age 27 (*The Nation's Health* 28, no. 81: 1).

2. In *Flue-Cured Tobacco Cooperative Stabilization et al.* v. *U.S. Environmental Protection Agency* (EPA) (4 F. Supp. 2d 435; 1998 U.S. Dist.), Decided July 17, 1998, the U.S. District Court for the Middle District of North Carolina, Winston-Salem Division, Judge William L. Osteen, lawyers for the tobacco industry argued against the EPA claim that Environmental Tobacco Smoke (ETS) was a Group A carcinogen, a designation meaning there is sufficient evidence to conclude ETS causes cancer in humans. Plaintiffs argued the "EPA exceeded its authority under and violated the restrictions within the Radon Research Act; EPA did not comply with the Radon Research Act's procedural requirements; EPA violated administrative law procedure by making a conclusion regarding ETS before it concluded its risk assessment, and EPA's ETS Risk Assessment was not the result of reasoned decision making" (1998 U.S. Dist. LEXIS 10986). The EPA denied this claim by the Plaintiffs and asserted "the administrative record . . . demonstrates reasoned decision making" (Ibid.).

In his conclusion, Judge Osteen made the following ruling: "In 1988, EPA initiated drafting policy-based recommendations about controlling ETS exposure because EPA believed ETS is a Group A carcinogen. . . . Rather than reach a conclusion after collecting information, researching, and making findings, EPA categorized ETS as a 'known cause of cancer' in 1989. EPA's Administrator admitted that EPA 'managed to confuse and anger all parties to the smoking ETS debate. . . . The Administrator also conceded, 'beginning the development of an Agency risk assessment after the commencement of work on the draft policy guide gave the appearance of . . . policy leading science. . . .' In conducting the Assessment, EPA deemed it biologically plausible that ETS was a carcinogen. EPA's theory was premised on the similarities between MS [mainstream smoke], SS [sidestream smoke], and ETS. In other chapters, the Agency used MS and ETS dissimilarities to justify methodology. Recognizing problems, EPA attempted to confirm the theory with epidemiologic studies. After choosing a portion of the studies, EPA did not find a statistically significant association. EPA then claimed the bioplausibility theory, renominated the a priori hypothesis, justified a more lenient methodology. With a new methodology, EPA demonstrated from the selected studies a very low relative risk for lung cancer based on ETS exposure. Based on its original theory and the weak evidence of association, EPA concluded the evidence showed a causal relationship between cancer and ETS. The administrative record contains glaring deficiencies. . . . In this case, EPA publicly committed to a conclusion before research had begun; excluded industry by violating the Act's procedural requirements; adjusted established procedure and scientific norms to validate the Agency's public conclusion, and aggressively utilized the Act's authority to disseminate findings to establish a de facto regulatory scheme intended to restrict Plaintiffs' products and to influence public opinion. In conducting the ETS Risk Assessment, EPA disregarded information and made findings on selective information; did not disseminate significant epidemiologic information; deviated from its risk Assessment Guidelines; failed to disclose important findings and reasoning; and left significant questions without answers. EPA's conduct left substantial holes in the administrative record. While so doing, EPA produced limited evidence, then claimed the weight of the Agency's research evidence demonstrated ETS causes cancer.

Because EPA exceeded its authority under the Radon Research Act and also failed the Act's procedural requirements, the court will direct the entry of judgment in favor of Plaintiffs' motion for summary judgment and vacate Chapters 1 through 6 of and the Appendices to EPA's *Respiratory Health Effects of Passive Smoking: Lung Cancer and Other disorders*" (Opinion written by Judge William L. Osteen U.S. District Judge, 4 F. Supp. 2d 435; 1998 U.S. Dist.. LEXIS 10986).

This ruling is important for several reasons, however, it is most likely to bear significantly on the authority of government to impose smoking restrictions in public and private places due to alleged carcinogenic effects of second-hand smoke.

REFERENCES

Buchanan, J.M. (1986). "Politics and Meddlesome Preferences." In R. D. Tollison, ed., *Smoking and society: Toward a more balanced assessment* (pp. 333–42). Lexington, MA.: Lexington Books.

Fiore, M. C., T. E. Novotny, J. P. Pierce, G. A. Giovino, E. J. Hatziandreu, P. A. Newcomb, T. S. Surawicz, and R. M. Davis. (1990). "Methods Used to Quit Smoking in the United States: Do Cessation Programs Help?" *Journal of the American Medical Association* 263, no. 20: 2760–95.

Gilpin, E., S. W. Cavin, and J. P. Pierce (1997). "Adult Smokers Who Do Not Smoke Daily." *Addiction* 92, no. 4: 473–80.

Halpin Schauffler, H. (1993). "Health Insurance Policy and the Politics of Tobacco." In R. L. Rabin and S. D. Sugarman (eds.) *Smoking policy: Law, Politics, and Culture.* New York: Oxford University Press.

Hennrikus, D. J., R. W. Jeffery, and H. A. Lando. (1996). "Occasional Smoking in a Minnesota Working Population." *American Journal of Public Health* 86, no. 9: 1260–66.

Viscusi, W. K. (1992). *Smoking: The Risky Decision.* New York: Oxford University Press.

Part I

Tobacco Use and Regulation: Historical Perspectives and Policy Considerations

1

The Analysis of Policy: Understanding the Process of Policy Development*

David Ryder

One of the gravest errors which can be made by the novice social policy analyst is to assume that policy making is in any way a rational process. (Stockwell, 1993, p 53S)

INTRODUCTION

Responses to the recent book *Alcohol Policy and the Public Good* (Edwards et al., 1994) suggest that there is much support, at least among those who work in the alcohol arena, for more rational policies that will reduce the harm associated with this most popular beverage. However, the key question left unanswered is why, in the face of a wealth of research demonstrating the public health benefits to be gained by the policies recommended in this book, adoption of such policies is the exception rather than the rule (Hawks, 1995). An emerging discipline, that of policy analysis, if applied to examples of successful policy adoption, can provide some guidance on this dilemma.

The purpose of this chapter is to describe one model of policy analysis, the components of the model being illustrated by examples from a range of

D. Ryder, "The Analysis of Policy: Understanding the Process of Policy Development," *Addiction* 91 (1996): 1265–70. Copyright © 1996. Reprinted by permission of Carfax Publishing Ltd.

*I would like to thank John Clark, Visiting Fellow, Department of Health Studies, Edith Cowan University, Perth, Western Australia; Professor David Hawks, Director, National Centre for Research into the Prevention of Drug Abuse, Curtin University, Perth, Western Australia and Associate Professor Alan Peachment, School of Management and Marketing, Curtin University, Perth, Western Australia, for their valuable comments on an earlier draft of this chapter.

Table I. The Stages of the Policy Process	
Stage	**Description**
Agenda setting	Government decides that action is (or is not) required on a particular issue
Issue filtration	Government decides the means by which options for action will be generated
Issue definition	The problems, options and opportunities that the government needs to consider are clarified
Forecasting	Government considers what the probable consequences are should a given policy be adopted
Options analysis	Government reviews the various options that will achieve the desired goal, and selects the most appropriate
Objective setting	Government sets objectives to measure the effectiveness of the policy chosen
Monitoring	The consequences of the chosen policy are monitored against the objectives. Unintended consequences may also be monitored
Maintenance/ succession termination	Government decides to continue with the policy (maintenance), replace it with an alternative policy (succession) or discontinue the policy (termination)

alcohol and tobacco policies. By understanding policy in this manner, it is suggested that advocates of particular policy options will be able to raise the probability that their policy is the one that will be adopted.

The discipline of policy analysis has its genesis in President Kennedy's 'New Frontier' and President Johnson's 'Great Society' programs of social change in America in the 1960s, where it was apparent that mechanisms for evaluating the effectiveness of these programs were inadequate (Wildavsky, 1985). Initially conceived as an evaluation system at the institutional level, policy analysis has developed into a discipline concerned with microanalysis of the policy process, with 'the analysis of the determinates, characteristics and implications of public policies and programs' (Poister, 1979, p. 5). In other words, it is the study of how and why governments choose to act on some issues and not on others; with the form and stated intent of policies; and with the effects of policies, both intended and unintended. A distinction has to be drawn between policy analysis and policy advocacy, the former being descriptive of what is, and the latter being proscriptive of what should be. It is intended that the descriptive analysis undertaken in this chapter will strengthen proscriptive advocacy for public health policies. An interesting descriptive model of the process of policy development has been proposed by Hogwood & Gunn (1984) and the following is a summary of this, using where possible illustrative examples from Australia and briefly indicating some of the ways researchers may be able to influence the policy process.

The model assumes that government policy can be best understood as an eight-stage process. It is important to note that these processes do not necessarily occur in a linear fashion, and indeed more than one stage may be in operation at the same time. In practice it is difficult to differentiate some stages from others, and so for clarity in this chapter some case examples are used to illustrate more than one stage at a time. Descriptions of each of the stages are provided in Table 1.

Agenda Setting

The first stage is *agenda setting,* or deciding that action has or has not to be taken. This is essentially a political decision, which may or may not be based upon a scientific analysis of evidence. The decision by the then Australian prime minister, Bob Hawke, to call a "Drug Summit," from which the National Campaign Against Drug Abuse arose, is often ascribed to the personal drug-related problems within his family, but there are grounds for also believing that previous Royal Commissions that directly or indirectly investigated drug use in Australia had produced a momentum for change, and that the problems in the prime minister's own family acted as the catalyst that served to release that energy (Hawks, 1993).

Researchers can influence the policy process at this stage by taking every opportunity to provide evidence to politicians, public servants, Royal Commissions and so on, in a form that is readily understood by these various groups. Consideration can also be given to providing the evidence under the auspices of groups that carry more political credibility than the individual, high-profile expert panels being an example of this.

Issue Filtration and Issue Definition

The second stage of the model is *issue filtration,* which concerns the means by which government decides what should be done. It may be decided that options will be generated within the bureaucracy, or submissions and discussion be conducted externally through contracting of consultants, public meetings, or other such means. This is followed by a third stage of *issue definition,* involving a process of clarifying both the problem or opportunities government is wishing to address, and the options that are to be considered. In practice it is often difficult to separate activities into either issue filtration or issue definition, and for clarity the two are discussed together. The processes occurring prior to the adoption of standard drink labeling on alcoholic beverage containers in Australia are used for illustrative purposes. This issue was first considered by the Ministerial Council on Drug Strategy, comprising the ministers for health and justice/attorney's general from each of the six state governments and the federal government of Australia, in 1990. They referred it to the National Food Authority (NFA) for discussion and recommendation in 1991 (Stockwell & Beel, 1994).

On the basis of research evidence and the advice of the medical profession that such a move would be an effective public health measure, the NFA recommended that standard drink labeling be mandatory on all alcoholic beverage containers from July 1993. Such a recommendation requires the approval of the National Foods Standards Council (NFSC), to whom it was thus referred. In tandem with these developments, brewing and distilling interests had conducted a counter campaign, which deterred sufficient ministers that the NFSC stalled on making a decision and, at a meeting in March 1994, postponed any decision. In this instance issue definition and issue filtration lead to the political conclusion that the policy option should proceed no further.

The next steps taken by advocates of the policy are illustrative of the way in which an understanding of the policy process can be effectively utilized. These steps included intensive lobbying of relevant ministers by groups and individuals within the health sector and media campaigns to raise awareness of the issue with the general public. Clear communication between the various groups advocating the policy meant that the campaign was coordinated and efficient. It is also of interest that the Winemakers' Federation were supportive of the policy, and some winemakers in Western Australia and South Australia voluntarily adopted the policy (Stockwell, 1993). This initiative was praised by the health lobby demonstrating that, as in war, policy advocacy can make for unusual alliances. It is also noteworthy that the federal minister for health, who was opposed to the standard drink labeling policy, was replaced at this time by a much more sympathetic minister. Also of interest is the fact that the policy was thought to have a greater chance of success if it was marketed as a measure to inform the public rather than as a health warning system. Unfortunately, NFA guidelines stipulate that information labels are to be 1.5 mm in height, while warning labels have to be 3 mm in height. In order to ensure the speedy adoption of the policy, this was a compromise that had to be accepted. The campaign was successful, and standard drink labeling of alcoholic beverages became mandatory in Australia as of 22 December 1995. It is noteworthy that a justification given by the federal minister for health for the adoption of the policy was the evidence of public support for standard drink labeling (Stockwell & Beel, 1994).

What this example illustrates is that policy development is not solely a scientific process but involves lobbying, the development of alliances, and the selling of the policy in a manner that will have the best chance of success. It can also be influenced by political factors, including the change of a key minister, and compromise solutions can be better than no solution at all. In many ways it can be seen as a battleground, in which the politically most powerful alliance will win. However, there is also a clear role for research in the process, which in this case example illuminated the value of standard drink labeling but also provided ammunition for the battle, in the form of evidence to counter the claims of the brewers and distillers, and the support that there was for the policy among the general public.

Researchers can thus influence the process at this stage by lobbying (either directly or through others) and providing evidence, in a readily understandable form, to refute the arguments of the opposition.

FORECASTING AND OPTIONS ANALYSIS

The fourth stage, that of *forecasting,* and the fifth, that of *options analysis,* have particular importance for those wishing to have policy adopted, as it is at this stage that much policy founders. Forecasting involves a consideration of how the situation will develop should the policy option or options be adopted in their proposed form. It can be argued that the watering down of the Australian National Policy on Alcohol, specifically those aspects relating to control policies, came about as a result of the forecast effect such policies would have on the South Australian wine industry, and on the profitability of the alcohol industry as a whole (Cornwall, 1989). It is perhaps wise for the expert to also indulge in a little 'crystal ball' forecasting, to attempt to assess the probable outcome of the policy option proposed, and modify the proposal as required. A clear example of this is provided by Secker (1993) who, when chief executive officer of the Totalisator Agency Board in Western Australia, wished to ban smoking in all the betting venues under the control of the board. In the realization that suggesting such a policy from the point of view of public health would not convince key players in the decision making process, the policy was marketed (a term used deliberately) in business terms, as a move that would attract customers because of the smoke-free atmosphere. The policy was adopted with little problem. A clear distinction can be made between means and ends, and consideration has to be given to means that have the greatest probability of achieving the desired end.

If policy advocates fail to successfully forecast outcomes for a range of policy options, and the policy they advocate is not adopted, an understanding of the reasons for failure can be utilized effectively in reformulating the policy

(Peachment, 1984). The failure of the Western Australian government to achieve a ban on the sponsorship of sport by tobacco companies in 1982 and 1983 was in large part due to the reduced revenue that would result for sporting bodies (Daube, 1993). In 1987, therefore, similar legislation in Victoria included an increase in tobacco taxation, a proportion of which was hypothecated (i.e., solely dedicated to) the funding of sport (Galbally, 1993). Similar legislation was also enacted in Western Australia in 1991 (Carroll, 1993).

To have influence at this stage, researchers need to consider the probable costs and benefits that will accrue from adoption of a given policy, and market the policy in terms of the benefits that will have most importance for key players in the political process. They can also use research findings to refute where possible the potential costs of the policy, which are sure to be emphasized by the opposition. If all else fails, an analysis of the reasons why a policy was not adopted can generate creative modifications which, by removing the objections of opponents, raises the probability that the policy will be adopted in the future.

OBJECTIVE SETTING AND MONITORING

Researchers, reputed to have an objective frame of mind, may well see themselves as having a particular role to play in the next two stages, those of setting objectives to measure whether a policy achieves what it is meant to achieve, and monitoring the policy once implemented. While this is an appropriate view it misses the complexity of policy outcomes, of which two are of particular note. First, there are many instances whereby a government policy will achieve outcomes seen as desirable by one department but negative by another. Raising the real price of alcoholic beverages by increasing taxation has been shown to reduce per capita consumption and consequent alcohol-related problems (Edwards et al., 1994), a public health gain one would expect to be viewed positively by departments of health; but if there is a subsequent loss of tax revenue, then the outcome may be viewed negatively by treasuries. In order to give support, or reduce resistance, to particular policies advocates need to address the concerns of other powerful players in the political process. To this end, consideration of public health outcomes are necessary but not sufficient. If attention is paid to the concerns of these other groups, and outcomes measured to allay those concerns, then the longevity of a given policy may be enhanced, and resistance to similar policies under consideration in other jurisdictions reduced. Again a distinction between means and ends is useful.

A second consideration is that most policies have both intended and unintended effects, and that the unintended can be utilized by policy advocates. The rise in the real price of alcohol in the United Kingdom in 1981 came about as a result of an increase in the excise applied to alcoholic beverages. An unintended effect of this increase was that total per capita consumption of alcohol fell by 18 percent and consequent alcohol-related problems by 16 percent (Kendell, DeRoumainie & Ritson, 1983). Neither the reduction in consumption nor alcohol-related problems was an intended effect of the policy, but their occurrence has been effectively utilized by those concerned with public health, such that a policy of raising the real price of alcoholic beverages by taxation increases is advocated, with reduced alcohol consumption and related problems as intended effects (Edwards et al., 1994).

Researchers can thus support policy by providing evidence not only in terms of public health, but also on issues that are of concern to other key players in the political process. This will almost certainly include economic considerations. In addition, an objective analysis of a range of policy outcomes, both intended and unintended, may well lead the researcher to new insights, new lines of research, and new policies to advocate.

POLICY MAINTENANCE, SUCCESSION, AND TERMINATION

The end game of the policy process is where the government has to decide to maintain the policy; replace it with an alternative, or terminate the policy, which can be seen in some senses as a return to the initial phases of the policy process. Government has to decide whether to place the issue back on the agenda or not and, if placed on the agenda, deciding what to do about it. For policy maintenance and policy succession, the principles of agenda setting and issue filtration discussed previously will once again apply, but it is useful to discuss policy termination in its own right. Terminating policy is often seen as a most difficult exercise for governments, who generally prefer to be seen to be doing something rather than stopping doing something, and thus may well decide to simply let the policy continue (Hogwood & Gunn, 1984). This option is eliminated if termination is built into the policy at the beginning in the form of a sunset clause, although it is important to note that such a clause only ensures that the legislation is reviewed and not necessarily terminated. Those wishing to ensure that public policy serves the public good could consider lobbying for a sunset clause in policies that are perceived as being contrary to that good. An example of this in practice concerned the liberalization of liquor licensing regulations during the America's Cup defense in Fremantle in 1986–1987. Lobbying by the WA Alcohol and Drug Authority ensured that the liberalization policy terminated soon after the conclusion of the Cup defense, regulations returning to the status quo (D. V. Hawks, pers. comm., 1995).

The role of the researcher at this stage of the process can be to provide policy advocates with evidence to be used in lobbying for maintenance, succession, or termination, but this is only possible if this stage has been anticipated earlier in the policy process, at least as early as options analysis, and the evidence collected accordingly.

DISCUSSION

This analysis of policies in the alcohol and tobacco arena has several important lessons for policy advocacy. By viewing the policy process as a series of stages researchers can match their strategy to the stage of the policy's development, raising the probability that the policy advocated will eventually be adopted. Policy analysis also suggests that a military metaphor is appropriate. Consideration of policy options is akin to warfare, with competing armies attempting to either have the policy adopted or prevent such adoption from occurring. To extend the metaphor, the winner of the battle is the army with the most power, in this case political rather than military, although in the real world (of politics and the military) the outcome of conflict is most often pragmatic compromise. The key players in the conflict, as far as alcohol and tobacco policy are concerned, are on one side academic researchers, representatives of medical and other professions, and nongovernment agencies, sharing a concern for public health. On the other side are representatives of the alcohol and tobacco industries, concerned with their own economic viability. How then can researchers enhance their power and win the battle? The above analysis of successful policy adoption suggests three fruitful approaches. First, researchers can form alliances with others holding similar aims. The allies can and often do include representatives of "the health lobby." The alliance of this lobby with the Winemakers' Federation in successfully advocating the adoption of standard drink labeling on beverage containers, demonstrates that those who may be "enemies" in one battle can be allies in another. Secondly, researchers can provide evidence that can be used as "ammunition" in the battle. The use of research evidence in the standard drink labeling campaign is a clear example of this in practice. It is also important that such ammunition is in a form that other allies can utilize, requiring, for example, that data be presented in a form that is understandable to those with little or no understanding of statistics. Thirdly, battles are best fought on grounds of one's own choosing, and where the opposition's ammunition is less effective. The banning of smoking in Western Australian betting shops (Secker, 1993) is a good example of this. Arguing the case from a public health perspective was seen as an unwinnable approach. Choosing to fight from a business perspective proved successful.

An important caveat is that while it is legitimate, indeed necessary, for researchers to engage in the battle, it is important that this not be at the expense of those ethical principles to which research must adhere.

The adoption of policies in the public arena is essentially a political process. This is often not scientific, but neither does it exclude science. By understanding the politics of the policy process, and that this is a process with discernible stages, researchers can learn to work with it, thus raising the probability that alcohol and other policies will contribute to "the public good."

REFERENCES

Carroll, A. (1993). "The Western Australian Health Promotion Foundation—Healthway." *Health Promotion Journal of Australia* 3: 42–43.

Cornwall, J. (1989) *Just For the Record: The Political Recollections of John Cornwall.* Adelaide, South Australia, Wakefield Press.

Daube, M. (1993). "Health Promotion Foundations in Australia." *Health Promotion Journal of Australia* 3: 3.

Edwards, G., P. Anderson, T. Babor, et al. (1994). *Alcohol Policy and the Public Good.* Oxford, Oxford Medical Publications.

Galbally, R. (1993). "The Victorian Health Promotion Foundation—Vic Health." *Health Promotion Journal of Australia* 3: 4–5.

Hawks, D. V. (1993). "The Formulation of Australia's National Health Policy on Alcohol." *Addiction* 88 (suppl.): 19S–20S.

Hawks, D. V. (1995) "Why Do So Many Administrations Persist with Unintelligent Alcohol Policies?" *Addiction* 90: 199–201.

Hogwood, B. W., & L. A. Gunn. (1984). *Policy Analysis for the Real World.* Oxford, Oxford University Press.

Kendell, R. E., M. de Roumainie, & E. B. Ritson. (1983). "Effect of Economic Changes on Scottish Drinking Practices." *British Journal of Addiction* 78: 365–80.

Peachment, A. (1984). "Learning from Legislative Disasters." *Medical Journal of Australia* 145: 482–85.

Poister, T. H. (1979). *Public Program Analysis: Applied Research Methods.* Baltimore, Md.: University Park Press.

Secker, A. (1993). "The Policy Research Interface: An Insiders View." *Addiction* 88 (Suppl.): 115S–20S.

Stockwell, T. (1993). "Influencing the Labeling of Alcoholic Beverage Containers: Informing the Public." *Addiction* 88 (suppl.): 53S–60S.

Stockwell, T. & A. Beel. (1994). *Public Support for the Introduction of Standard Drink Labels on Alcohol Containers* (Perth, WA: National Centre for Research into the Prevention of Drug Abuse).

Wildavsky, A. (1985). "The Once and Future School of Public Policy." *Public Policy International* 79: 25–41.

2

Tobacco: The Road to Litigation

Linda Goldman*

The evidence that physical harm is caused by smoking increases daily. The effects are not confined to those who practice the habit, but are spread to the sharers, passive smokers. The public are becoming aware that tobacco inhalation leads not only to potentially lethal diseases of the lung but may also be implicated in cardiovascular pathology of passive and active smokers.[1] As those damaged become aware of the problems, so litigation is becoming an increasingly powerful means of achieving recompense for plaintiffs and restriction on smoking in public places and at work.

Cases cover diverse interests: states sue by reason of their involvement in the cost of health care for what appears to be avoidable disease; individuals and groups of passive and voluntary smokers now seek compensation for the harm which they have suffered. In the public field, injunctions to prevent misleading tobacco advertising have been ordered by the Australian Courts.[2] Thus the industry was prevented in that country from claiming there is no link between passive smoking and ill health.

There is a current wave of cases now being brought by individuals and groups against manufacturers for their failure to warn of the risks of smoking, including the risk of addiction, and to take steps to reduce the risks. In one American case, documents have been produced showing that Lorillard Tobacco Company was alerted to the risk of cigarettes containing carcinogens as long ago as 1946[3] and failed to offer any warnings. Passive smokers are also bringing actions against those who caused or permitted them to remain in situations, including the workplace, where they could not avoid

Society for the Study of Addiction to Alcohol and Other Drugs. (1995). "Tobacco: The Road to Litigation." *Addiction* 90: 1581–86. Reprinted by permission of Carfax Publishing Ltd.

*Additional research was carried out by Amanda Goff.

inhaling environmental tobacco smoke (ETS). In the area of employment law, the emphasis is shifting in favor of employers imposing smoking bans albeit with correct procedures to ensure fairness.[4-6]

NOT QUITE A CRIME

U.K. law bans smoking in connection with the specific health risks of fire, as in several regulations, including the *Highly Flammable Liquids and Lique-fied Petroleum Regulations 1972*[7] and the *Gas Safety (Installation and Use) Regulations 1994*.[8] Moving toward a more general concept of health promotion, Transport Regulations prevent smoking on public transport. The widest safety concept is in the Health and Safety at Work Act 1974 which imposes a general duty on employers to take reasonably practicable steps to ensure the health, safety, and welfare of employees and the *Management of Health and Safety at Work Regulations 1992* (MHSWR)[9] require employers to carry out risk assessments and take steps to reduce significant risks. These branches of the criminal law could be applied to limit or eliminate smoking in the workplace and the effect of MHSWR remains to be seen.

BREACH OF CONTRACT

Civil cases involving illness caused at work rely on breach of the implied term of the contract of employment not to damage the health of the employee in accordance with the principle set out in *Johnstone* v. *Bloomsbury Health Authority*[10] where a junior doctor successfully challenged his employer's contractual right to require him to work extended overtime which in fact caused damage to his health. Further, the Unfair Contract Terms Act 1977 applies to employment situations, so that a clause in a contract purporting to avoid liability for the effects of risk is void.

NEGLIGENCE

A whistle-stop tour of the law of negligence shows us that, in order for a claim for damages to succeed, the plaintiff must prove that there was a duty of care which was breached and that significant harm resulted which was reasonably foreseeable. Although the tobacco industry has provided voluntary warnings since 1971 on U.K. products and by regulatory control since 1991,[11] it is resisting claims that it has long known of the risks of smoking and breached its duty of care by failing to warn or take steps to reduce addictive or carcinogenic constituents. Since *Donoghue* v. *Stevenson* (1932),[12] the case concerning a snail found in a bottle of ginger beer (the plaintiff drank the contaminated ginger beer and became ill), it has been settled law that a manufacturer owes a duty of care to persons who are likely to use the product. Thus, users of cigarettes who have suffered injury need to prove that the manufacturers knew that tobacco products were and are dangerous and that it was reasonably foreseeable that significant harm would result from their use.

It is arguable that the tobacco companies ought to have known of the risk inherent in their products. The law clearly recognizes the situation where the defendant ought to have known of a potential danger. In *Stokes* v. *Guest Keen and Nettlefold (Bolts and Nuts) Ltd.* (1968),[13] the employers were liable for the occupational disease suffered by the plaintiff who contracted scrotal cancer as a result of being exposed to certain mineral oils. The company doctor had failed to warn that such a risk existed as he did not wish to spread alarm among the staff. The court held that the employer was required to take positive steps to ensure the health of its staff in view of the knowledge which it ought to have.

CLASS ACTION

Smoking litigation is no longer the province solely of the affected individual. The original situation of "smoke and the world smokes with you; sue and you sue alone" (with apologies to Ella Wheeler Wilcox) has changed as the 1990s are fast becoming the decade of the class action, with groups of people affected by tobacco combining to take legal action against the manufacturers or employers. This does not preclude the individual, who may still proceed in their own right, as the passive smokers tend to, but allows for the large mass of affected individuals to combine legal resources in order to save duplication of effort and thereby ultimately save costs.

In the United States, the February 1995 decision of the New Orleans court in the Castano case permitted a class action to be brought by up to 40 million present smokers and 50 million former smokers in addition to actions on behalf of those who have died as a result of smoking. This "test" case, *Castano* v. *The American Tobacco Company,* has been brought by Mrs. Diane Castano on behalf of her late husband who died of smoking-related disease after a life-time of smoking, and "all other nicotine-dependent persons". If it crosses the various hurdles of the legal system, the case will be the largest industrial liability suit ever brought to trial with anticipated damages on an almost unimaginable scale.

Damages awarded to date to victims of asbestos-related disease are thought to be in the region of $10 billion. In comparison, if only 10 million of the 90 million or so American smokers of the last fifty years were to join the action, and were only to be awarded damages of $10,000 each, total damages would amount to $100 billion.[14] The claim at present is for punitive damages as well as compensation for economic loss, emotional distress, and medical costs arising out of the tobacco companies' concealment of their knowledge of the addictive capacity of nicotine.[15]

The plaintiffs will not necessarily have taken heart from the U.S. Food and Drug Administration's Drug Abuse Advisory Committee's unanimous conclusion in August 1994 that nicotine is addictive, as the tobacco companies, who deny all knowledge of addictive properties and in any case say the FDA is wrong, will say that even if the FDA is right, that knowledge was not available until the present day and cannot be used retrospectively. That will be a matter of evidence which it is the responsibility of the plaintiffs to bring before the court.

THE INDUSTRY FIGHTS BACK

The U.S. Environmental Protection Agency (EPA) released figures in May 1994 showing that 3,000 passive smokers a year die of lung cancer caused by inhaling ETS [environmental tobacco smoke]. R. J. Reynolds Tobacco promptly responded by placing full-page newspaper advertisements claiming that the EPA's figures were based on defective research and asserting that a nonsmoker living with a smoker inhales no more than the equivalent of 1.5 cigarettes.[16]

Philip Morris, a leading US cigarette manufacturer, said in a statement:

> In order for the alleged class in *Castano* to recover, millions of individual trials around the country will be necessary. In each such trial, the plaintiffs will have to prove, on an individual basis, injury in fact, causation and reliance. And, in each such case, the industry's affirmative defenses will be resolved by a jury.[17]

Prior to the *Castano* case, claims for damages against the tobacco industry have failed in the American courts where juries have accepted the argument that people who smoke go voluntarily to the risks which have been well known for many years, even before publication of clinical data and the use of warnings. The Castano lawyers do not pursue the simple fact of health damage resulting from the use of tobacco. Instead, they seek compensation for the results of addiction to tobacco, claiming that the tobacco industry were aware of the addictive nature of nicotine and knowingly used it to encourage customers into dependency. Philip Morris is reported as saying through its lawyers: "We are not going to be settling any cases. We never have and there is no reason for us to settle. The only people who will benefit are the plaintiffs' lawyers."

THE CASE FOR PASSIVE SMOKERS

In general, passive smokers have brought individual cases which have some-times settled behind the scenes and are sometimes successful in the courts. Two well-known cases against employers who permitted smoking in the workplace in England and Australia, respectively, are those of Veronica Bland (her passive smoking claim was settled out of court for £15,000 in 1993) and Liesel Scholem (in 1992 she was awarded A$85,000). In 1994 Terry Hurlstone, the father of an English hospital patient, was awarded £50 against the hospital who permitted smoking in the private rooms, which made him uncomfortable while visiting his daughter.[18]

An unusual class action is currently running in the United States on behalf of thirty nonsmoking airline cabin crew, representative of 60,000 fellow employees, who were obliged to inhale ETS on flights where smoking was per-mitted. The medical conditions from which they suffer are attributed to passive smoking and include lung cancer, asthma, and other diseases. In 1994 a Florida judge approved the continuation of their class action which could lead to awards of up to $5 billion.[19] The case is of interest as it is the first time that the American courts have recognized possible harm from passive smoking.

CLASS LITIGATION IN THE UNITED KINGDOM

A group of some three hundred English smokers who believe that their var-ious illnesses are related to smoking wish to sue the English tobacco compa-nies for negligence,[20] claiming that the companies knew or ought to have known of the risks of smoking. The main element of their claim is that the manufacturers failed to take any or any sufficient steps to reduce the risks, nor did they give adequate warnings of them. The plaintiffs say that from the 1950s at least, the tobacco industry knew or ought to have known that smoking caused many diseases and that the early printed warnings misled the public about the risks, merely saying "smoking can damage your health."

The group sought legal aid to pursue their claims which, if successful, could result in damages of over £20 million. Legal Aid is needed in the first instance to obtain expert opinion on the effect of advertising and warnings and other matters connected with failure to reduce the nicotine content of cigarettes before taking Counsel's opinion on the likelihood of a successful outcome to litigation.

In the first instance and on appeal, the Legal Aid Board refused to grant the necessary initial funding as it was satisfied that the manufacturers were in breach of their duty to minimize risk to smokers, but "was not persuaded that any individual in the group action could establish that they fell ill as a result of that breach of duty."[21] After judicial review in 1994 (in which the court directed that there were general issues relating to what the industry knew about the risks of smoking and what the companies did once they knew the risks), those issues were then put before a different committee, and in February 1995, legal aid was granted to the group of 27 representative plaintiffs. At present, the claim is couched in terms that the group suffered foreseeable harm when cigarette manufacturers failed to act upon knowledge which it is alleged that they had, namely, that smoking was harmful and that the risk could be lessened by reducing the level of tar and nicotine in their products.

THE STATE VERSUS INDUSTRY

In the United States, Mississippi, Minnesota, Florida, and West Virginia have started litigation naming all the American tobacco companies as defendants. The claims are for punitive damages, reimbursement of past health care of victims of smoking-related disease, compensation for future cost of health care for current and future victims, and an injunction forbidding the promotion of cigarettes to minors.[22]

The reason for bringing these cases is that the cost of treating smoking-related disease to the individual states and insurance agencies is enormous and increasing. For example, West Virginia's health budget for smoking-related illness runs currently at $500 million per year. The cost of litigation is also huge, and partly to offset their legal costs and partly to avoid repetition of matters which are common to both plaintiffs, the State of Minnesota has joined with the Blue Cross Health Insurance Company to recover welfare and health insurance expenditure arising from smoking-related illnesses. They allege that the tobacco industry illegally hid the health hazards of cigarettes and manipulated nicotine levels to ensure that customers would become addicted.[23] The conspiracy is further alleged to constitute a breach of the state's antitrust laws.

Mississippi and Florida have pending litigation against the tobacco manufacturers, claiming recompense for the cost of medical treatment and welfare programs for victims of smoking-related disease. The Mississippi case was the first of its kind, with the other states following their example. Their attorney general is quoted as saying that the lawsuit is based on a simple notion: "You caused the health crisis; you pay for it."[24]

Mississippi has had a progressive record in smoking litigation since 1993 when circuit judge Eugene Bogen ruled in *Wilks* v. *The American Tobacco Company* that:

> . . . cigarettes are, as a matter of law, defective and unreasonably dangerous for human consumption. Cigarettes are defective because when used as intended, they cause cancer, emphysema, heart disease, and other illnesses . . . [the appropriate standard in tobacco liability cases is that of] absolute liability. . . .[25]

THE COSTS WEAPON

When judicial pronouncements such as that of Judge Bogen are made, to the lay person it would seem that the battle is over, only the terms of the victory need be set out. However, the massive resources of the tobacco industry have hitherto been used as a means to defeat intended actions by potential plaintiffs. In America in 1992 there were claims by Cipollone and Haines against the Liggett Group of Tobacco Companies. The plaintiffs came up against the problem of the contingency fee system wherein their legal representatives are required to take a case through to trial without any fee on account. The very nature of these cases is that there is likely to be huge expenditure which could bankrupt them while the client is not required to contribute anything unless and until the plaintiff prevails at trial.

In the Haines case, which commenced in 1983 as a test case on behalf of smokers who had contracted lung cancer allegedly arising out of smoking, the judge has recently been removed on the defendants' application[20] which means that, if the case is to continue, the plaintiff's lawyers must bear the repeated cost of beginning again: that arose out of the first judge ordering the defendants to produce certain documents which they were reluctant to disclose. In Cipollone, the plaintiff voluntarily withdrew his claim, and in Haines, the plaintiff lawyer sought to withdraw from the case because litigation against the tobacco industry "has become an unreasonable financial burden."

SHOULD THE INDIVIDUAL GO IT ALONE?

In Scotland, the widow of Alfred McTear was planning in February 1995 to reapply for legal aid to pursue her claim for damages on behalf of her late husband who died in 1993 of lung cancer attributed to smoking. The climate is probably right for a further attempt to gain legal aid, particularly in view of the recent grant for the mass English action. The Scottish legal system is separate from the English system, so the McTear case could not join with the English group action, but perhaps this might be the time for the Scots to consider a group action of their own of which McTear could form a part.

DAVID AND GOLIATH

Further afield, Dr. Sarah Hodson is set to make legal history in New South Wales: she is claiming A$1000 from WD & HO Wills, the cost of overcoming her nicotine addiction. The matter was to have been heard in a Consumer Claims Tribunal, the equivalent of the English small claims system, but the tobacco company disputed the claim and succeeded in their application for the matter to be heard in a higher court. This forces up the costs of the action. The outcome will be known later this year, if Dr. Hodson can afford to continue her case. This is similar to the American case of *Deskiewickz* v. *Philip Morris* which started in 1993 and is also for a relatively small amount: $1153 to cover the cost of medical treatment for nicotine patches and health club membership fees. Mr. Deskiewicz claims that Philip Morris owed him a duty of care to warn him that nicotine is addictive and he would require treatment to enable him to stop smoking.

CONCLUSION

From the manufacturers' point of view, success for any plaintiff, whether on the small or large scale of damages, or whether a group or individual action, will open the floodgates of litigation. In a civil case, the plaintiff is required to prove their case to the standard of "the balance of probabilities" which means that it is more likely than not that events happened in the way the plaintiff alleges. Although this is a lower standard than is required in the criminal courts where the jury has to be sure of the reasons for its decision, proof may continue to be difficult in many cases as the defendants will always have a few intervening factors on which they will rely to show that smoking was not the main cause of a plaintiff's illness.

As medical research improves and evidence becomes more and more damning, it is likely that defense experts will have to be somewhat creative in their interpretation of medical conditions. A Finnish doctor who gave evidence to support the defendants in a smoking case is now being charged with perjury.[26] He seems to have forgotten that an expert's duty is to the court, no matter whether he is instructed by one "side" or the other. The duty of an expert is clear. His evidence should be impartial and not biased toward the party who instructs him.

In the English courts, civil matters are tried with the plaintiff having to bear the burden of proof and being required to prove their case on the balance of probabilities. Criminal matters are required to be proved so that the jury are sure of the guilt of the accused. Such a standard is higher than that which would be required in any smoking case brought in the United Kingdom or any common law jurisdiction, such as Australia or the United States, but the tobacco companies are implacable legal foes and present greater difficulties for plaintiffs than defendants in the cases which are now commonplace against those who permit passive smoking.

When these cases begin to come to court, the judges will need to see documentary evidence showing the state of knowledge at the time it is alleged the industry should have warned of risks or taken steps to reduce the risks. After that, a battle of experts as to how the illnesses came into being and what steps could and should have been taken will give the judge sufficient information on which to base his decision. At present, Mr Hurlstone's £50 award is the flagship decision in English civil litigation.

REFERENCES

1. Glanz, S. A., & W. W. Parmley. (1995). "Passive Smoking and Heart Disease: Mechanisms and Risk." *Journal of the American Medical Association* 273: 1047–53.

2. *AFCO* v. *Tobacco Institute* (1991) 98ALR670.

3. The *Cipollone* case, reported *GLOBALink News Bulletin,* October 27, 1995.

4. Howard, G. (1990). "Some Legal Issues Relating to Passive Smoking in the Workplace." *British Journal of Addiction* 85: 873–82.

5. Howard, G. (1992). "Passive Smoking: Some Further Legal Issues for Employers." *British Journal of Addiction* 87: 695–701.

6. Goldman, L. (1993). "The Effect of Implementation of Nonsmoking Policies in the Workplace: An Update on the Law." *Addiction* 88: 1321–25.

7. SI 1972 No 917 (London, HMSO).

8. SI 1994 No 1886 (London, HMSO).

9. SI 1992 No 2051 (London, HMSO).

10. [1991] 2A11ER 293.

11. *Tobacco Products Safety (Labelling) Regulations 1991* (SI 1991 No 1530).

12. AC 562.

13. 1 WLR 1776.

14. *The Times,* February 21, 1995.

15. *Guardian,* May 30, 1994.

16. *The Times,* May 25, 1994.

17. *The Times,* February 21, 1995.

18. *Nuffield Hospital* v. *Hurlstone* (1994) unrep.

19. *The Times,* December 14, 1994.

20. Day, M., and C. Hopkins (1993). "Smoke Signals." *Law Society Gazette* 90: 32–33.

21. *The Independent,* June 21, 1994.
22. *The Times,* February 21, 1995.
23. *Wall Street Journal,* August 19, 1994.
24. *The Times,* May 25, 1994.
25. *Tobacco Products Litigation Reporter,* May 12, 1993.
26. Aurejarvi, E. (1994). *The Battle in Finland against the Tobacco Industry.* Paris, 9th World Conference.

3

Historical Overview of Tobacco Legislation and Regulation

Peter D. Jacobson, Jeffrey Wasserman, and John R. Anderson

The use and regulation of tobacco is one of the most controversial topics at all levels of government. From a regulatory perspective, the principal conundrum is how to regulate a product that is lethal when used as intended, but remains legal for most people over eighteen years of age. As a consequence, tobacco control reveals some of the most salient tensions in American political theory: under what circumstances can government limit individual freedoms to protect citizens from the consequences of their personal and lifestyle choices? What is the relationship between the federal, state, and local governments as the locus of regulatory responsibility for controlling tobacco use? How can conflicting rights and interests (i.e., the right to avoid cigarette smoke versus the right to smoke) best be resolved? And what role does the concept of civil norms play in discouraging smoking in public places relative to tobacco control laws?

Even today, when smoking in public places is highly regulated in many states, the debate over the scope of that regulation is far from settled. The tension between individual liberties and governmental intervention to protect the public's health is at issue. That the state has the right to regulate smoking to secure the public's health is beyond question. The policy debate is about when, how, and under what circumstances the state should exercise that power (Jacobson, Wasserman, & Raube,1993).

In this chapter we will trace the history of tobacco control at all levels of government, and discuss the various ways in which the debate over tobacco control has been framed. Many other sources can provide a recitation of cur-

Reprinted from the *Journal of Social Issues* 53, no. 1 (1997), with the permission of Blackwell Publishers.

rent federal, state, and local laws and regulations (see, e.g., CDC, 1995; Coalition for Smoking Or Health [CSOH], 1995; CDC, 1995; Americans for Non-smokers' Rights [ANR], 1996). While we will summarize the current regulatory structure based on those sources, we will also raise the broader questions that animate the continuing debate over tobacco control, and offer some observations about the future role of tobacco control laws and regulations.

HISTORICAL ANTECEDENTS

Despite a few seventeenth-century restrictions, significant anti-smoking legislation was not enacted until the second half of the nineteenth century, primarily in response to the fire hazard created by smoking. Two themes characterized this early legislation: One theme focused on the fire hazard created by smoking (e.g., an 1847 Boston ordinance prohibited smoking on public streets because of the extreme fire danger to wooden structures), while the other concentrated on the morality of smoking. Eventually, opposition to smoking on moral grounds was swept aside by the economic benefits associated with tobacco production and consumption. As the popularity of smoking grew, states realized that cigarette taxes were an important source of revenue, so early anti-smoking legislation was repealed. In fact, by 1927, all state statutes were repealed and the anti-tobacco movement was legally, as well as practically, dead. The political tide did not begin to turn again until the 1960s and lacked momentum until the 1980s.

ARGUMENTS IN FAVOR OF REGULATING SMOKING IN PUBLIC PLACES

In recent years, the primary argument justifying regulation of tobacco products has been the associated health costs and risks. As noted above, early anti-smoking regulations also contained a moral opposition to tobacco use.

Opposition to Smoking on Moral Grounds

In 1856–57, the British medical journal *Lancet* featured an issue in which fifty doctors expressed their views on "The Great Tobacco Question." Various doctors associated tobacco with increases in crime, nervous paralysis, loss of intellectual capacity, and vision impairment. But the *Lancet* editors argued that, since tobacco was so widespread, it must have some good or at least pleasurable effects. If the evil effects of tobacco were as dreadful as these doctors claimed, the journal's editors concluded that the human race would have ceased to exist (Wagner, 1971; Kluger, 1996).

By the late 1800s, many observers thought cigarettes were corrupt and morally repugnant. For example, in 1884, the *New York Times* warned that smoking could "ruin the republic." Women who smoked were considered promiscuous, and were warned they could become sterile, mustachioed, or tuberculous. In the 1890s, Lucy Page Gaston led a Chicago-based anti-tobacco campaign modeled on the anti-alcohol campaign. Similarly, Henry Ford spoke against smoking, and Thomas Edison refused to hire smokers (Wagner, 1971; Kluger, 1996).

At the beginning of the twentieth century, fourteen states had passed laws banning the production, sale, advertisement, or use of cigarettes within their boundaries. For example, in 1897, Tennessee adopted a statute to prohibit the sale of cigarettes. The statute was upheld by the Tennessee and United States Supreme Courts as a valid exercise of a state's police power to protect public health (*Austin* v. *Tennessee,* 179 U.S. 472 [1900]). In 1901, New Hampshire made it illegal for any person, firm, or corporation to produce, sell, or store for sale, any form of cigarette. A 1907 Illinois law made the manufacture, sale, or gift of a cigarette punishable by a fine of not more than $100 or imprisonment for not more than thirty days. In New York, women were forbidden to smoke in public. Progressive reformers in the early twentieth century were particularly concerned about the "demoralizing" effects of tobacco on children, leading to laws prohibiting tobacco sales (primarily cigarettes) to children under the age of eighteen (or twenty-one) in many states (IOM, 1994).

As smoking grew in popularity, the laws were not enforced and, in many instances, were ultimately repealed. By 1909, when the last of these early state laws were passed, national cigarette sales were twice what they had been five years earlier. Cigarette smoking increased dramatically from 1930 on, with the greatest percentage gains during and immediately following World War II. In 1945, 267 billion cigarettes were sold, 12 percent more than in 1944, 48 percent more than in 1940, and 124 percent more than in 1930 (Wagner, 1971).

Opposition to Smoking on Health Grounds

Accompanying this growth in smoking popularity, scientific evidence regarding its ill effects began to be published. In the 1930s, the medical community began to investigate the increase in lung cancer. By the 1940s, scientific reports began to associate smoking with cancer, heart disease, and other adverse health effects. Evidence mounted in the 1950s (Kluger, 1996).

In 1964, the first Surgeon General's Report on Smoking and Health was published. The report concluded that smoking was causally related to lung cancer; that it was the most important cause of chronic bronchitis; that it increased the risk of dying from chronic bronchitis and emphysema; and that it caused coronary disease. Since then, other Surgeons General's Reports have provided additional scientific and quantitative support for these conclusions, and have focused on the particular need to reduce youth access to cigarettes. For example, a recent Surgeon General's Report was devoted entirely to preventing tobacco use among young people (USDHHS, 1994). The focus on teenagers is due, in part, to the fact that about one-half of adult smokers had become regular smokers by age eighteen (CDC, 1993). In a summary of the Surgeon General's Report, Elders, Perry, Eriksen, and Giovino (1994) note that nearly all first use of tobacco occurs prior to high school graduation. Just as troubling, the report noted that the rate of increase in teenage smoking has not declined in the past few years, despite substantial declines in smoking in the population at large. A recent report (CDC, 1994) confirms that smoking among teenagers has actually increased during the past decade, especially among black youths. One policy implication of these reports is that smoking morbidity and mortality can be reduced significantly if teenagers' access to cigarettes is limited (IOM, 1994).

The most recent scientific debate on smoking concerns the effects of passive smoking. In 1990, the Environmental Protection Agency (EPA) released a draft report that reviewed twenty-four epidemiological studies. The EPA concluded that passive smoking causes 3,800 lung cancer deaths each year (EPA, 1992), corroborating an earlier report on passive smoking from the surgeon general (USDHHS, 1986).

Passive smoking appears to be a particular risk to infants and children. In a study on lung cancer and exposure to tobacco smoke in the household, Janerich and Thompson (1990) concluded that 17 percent of lung cancers among nonsmokers can be attributed to high levels of exposure during childhood and adolescence. Passive smoking has also been found to be a risk factor for other cancers. For example, a case-control study of women in Utah found that exposure to passive smoking three or more hours a day almost tripled the relative risk of cervical cancer in nonsmokers (Slattery et al., 1989).

ARGUMENTS QUESTIONING SMOKING REGULATIONS

The above arguments have largely propelled recent regulatory restrictions, but they are not universally accepted as a justification for intervening in the market. For instance, Rabin (1991) argued that current anti-smoking legislative efforts lack a coherent underlying justification, in part because the health risks are primarily borne by the smoker, and in part because the harm threshold for many nonsmokers (such as restaurant patrons) has not been shown to be substantial. Further, Rabin and Sugarman (1993) argue that changing civil norms, rather than regulations, will lead to reductions in smoking in public places. It is important to note that these commentators, while noting certain conceptual limitations in the current regulatory regime, do not oppose smoking regulations.

Other commentators, especially libertarians and those associated with the law and economics movement, argue that the market should determine where and how smoking should be regulated (see, e.g., Tollison & Wagner, 1991; Zycher, 1990). These commentators actively oppose smoking regulations on conceptual grounds as unjustified government paternalism. Supporters of the tobacco industry also argue that smokers retain certain rights in pursuing personal social behavior and cannot be discriminated against for their tobacco use (Jacobson, Wasserman, & Raube, 1993).

Much of the opposition to tobacco control laws is for philosophical reasons. A few commentators nonetheless challenge certain aspects of the scientific evidence and regulations based on that evidence. For instance, Gori (1995) challenges the EPA results on passive smoke.

ANTI-SMOKING LEGISLATION AND REGULATION

As the scientific evidence of tobacco's harmful effects mounted, legislative activity grew on both the state and federal levels. In states without laws preempting stronger local ordinances, municipalities also have been active in restricting public use of cigarettes.

Federal

Federal activity to regulate smoking has a mixed heritage. Along with providing subsidies for tobacco farmers, Congress has limited federal regulatory oversight and has been largely stymied in restricting smoking by tobacco industry lobbying pressure. At the same time, the emergence of the surgeon general as a moral and scientific spokesperson against smoking has added a significant federal voice to smoking reduction efforts.

In response to the 1964 Surgeon General's Report on Smoking, Congress enacted the Cigarette Labeling and Advertising Act in 1965, which required health warnings on all cigarette packages. The act superseded proposed Federal Trade Commission (FTC) rules requiring that manufacturers disclose on all packaging and advertisements that "cigarette smoking is dangerous to health" and "may cause death from cancer and other diseases." Instead, the act mandated the following warning on cigarette packaging: "Caution: cigarette smoking may be hazardous to your health." Equally important, the act preempted states from imposing more stringent health warning requirements and prohibited federal agencies from requiring more stringent health warnings.

In 1967, the Federal Communications Commission (FCC) ruled that the "fairness doctrine" applied to cigarette commercials. As a result, all broadcasters who carried cigarette advertising were required to provide equal time to warn the public about cigarettes. In 1968, 1300 anti-smoking messages were aired by the three major networks (Lewit, Coate, & Grossman, 1981). A year later, Congress passed the Public Health Cigarette Smoking Act of 1969, banning all cigarette advertising from television and radio, eliminating the need for broadcasters to provide equal time for anti-smoking messages. The ban was enacted with the acquiescence of the tobacco industry, which was beginning to be affected adversely by the anti-smoking advertisements, and feared greater regulatory activity (Kagan & Vogel, 1993). The act also amended the health warning on cigarettes to: "Warning: The Surgeon General Has Determined That Cigarette Smoking Is Dangerous to Your Health." Additionally, Congress restricted the FTC from requiring manufacturers to include health warnings in print advertising, and barred states from imposing "any requirement or prohibition based on smoking and health" on advertising and promotion of cigarettes packaged with labels conforming to the statute.

In 1972, the FTC and cigarette manufacturers agreed upon consent orders requiring all cigarette advertising to display the same warning required for cigarette packaging. Subsequently, the Comprehensive Smoking Education Act of 1984 (CSEA) required four rotating health warnings on all cigarette packages and advertisements. More recently, the Comprehensive Smokeless Tobacco Health Education Act of 1986 required three rotating health warnings for all smokeless tobacco product packaging and advertising. In 1989, Congress voted to ban smoking on airline flights of less than two hours (later extended to flights under six hours).

In recent years, Congress has become more active in legislating tobacco controls where children are involved. Perhaps most significantly, the federal government enacted the 1992 Alcohol, Drug Abuse and Mental Health Agency Reorganization Act requiring states to enact and enforce laws against the sale and distribution of tobacco products to individuals under eighteen years of age. Known as the Synar Amendment (42 U.S.C. 300x-26), the law conditions Alcohol, Drug Abuse, and Mental Health block grant allocations to the states on compliance with these provisions. If a state fails to enact or enforce such laws, its block grant allocations can be reduced by 10 percent in the first year, and by up to 40 percent by the fourth year of noncompliance. The Synar Amendment took effect for all states in 1995. Congress also enacted the Pro Children Act of 1994, prohibiting smoking in indoor facilities that are routinely used for the delivery of certain services to children, including schools, libraries, day care, health care, and early childhood development centers.

However, the tobacco industry continues to be a strong opponent, particularly on the federal regulatory level. To a large extent, the tobacco industry has successfully limited the extent of federal regulatory oversight. As Kluger (1996, p. 740) observes, it has been a ". . . long-standing travesty that [has] allowed society's most dangerous consumer product to escape serious regulation." For example, the agency most likely to oversee tobacco products, the Food and Drug Administration (FDA), was effectively limited in 1938 by congressional language that failed to define tobacco as a food or drug that should be regulated (Kluger, 1996).

Since the 1960s, few federal agencies have attempted to promulgate tobacco use restrictions because of expected opposition from Congress or outright congressional prohibition of regulatory authority. Cigarettes have been specifically exempted from coverage under the Fair Labeling and Packaging Act of 1966, the Controlled Substances Act of 1970, the Consumer Product Safety Act of 1972 (establishing the Consumer Product Safety Commission), and the Toxic Substances Act of 1976. Other nonexempted regulatory agencies, including the Environmental Protection Agency (EPA) and the Occupational Safety and Health Administration (OSHA), have considered, but abandoned, efforts to regulate smoking. EPA has determined that environmental tobacco smoke should be treated as a dangerous carcinogen, but has yet to promulgate regulations that would implement its finding. Likewise, OSHA has proposed standards for regulating indoor air at private worksites, including restrictions on smoking, also without being able to implement the regulations.

In 1995, the FDA announced a series of regulations aimed at restricting youth access to tobacco. The proposed FDA rule, in outline, would: ban cigarette sales in vending machines, ban tobacco billboard advertisements within 1,000 feet of schools or playgrounds; restrict ads in publications with more than 15 percent youth readership to black and white, text-only format; require the tobacco industry to fund a $150-million-per-year anti-smoking media campaign; ban brand-name sponsorship of sporting events and concerts; and permit the FDA to regulate tobacco products. Absent a shift in congressional sentiment or reaching a "grand bargain" with the tobacco industry (Kluger, 1996), there is little likelihood that the regulations will be implemented as proposed.

Despite the relative absence of federal regulation of tobacco products, the importance of the surgeon general's reports on tobacco cannot be understated as a contributing factor in the emergence of a policy environment receptive to various tobacco control strategies (Jacobson, Wasserman, & Raube, 1993; Kagan & Vogel, 1993). As Kagan and Vogel (1993) point out, the authority of the surgeon general's office and the meticulous accumulation of the scientific evidence have allowed the various surgeons general to "advocate interventionist governmental policies." In particular, the 1986 Surgeon General's Report on the dangers of environmental tobacco smoke undermined libertarian arguments that anti-smoking laws were unnecessary to protect third parties from tobacco's harms, and facilitated the expansion of state and local anti-smoking laws (Jacobson, Wasserman, & Raube, 1993; Kagan & Skolnick, 1993).

State Involvement

Trends

Four trends capture state legislative developments since 1989: (1) the expansion of the number of states enacting some smoking restrictions; (2) a legislative focus on enacting laws to restrict access to teenagers, including vending machine and point-of-sale restrictions; (3) the enactment of some form of nondiscrimination against smokers (thirty states between 1989 and 1995, according to CSOH, 1995); and, (4) the continued enactment of state laws preempting stronger local ordinances (twenty-seven states according to CSOH, 1995; seventeen according to CDC, 1995). Taken at face value, these trends appear to be somewhat contradictory. In all likelihood, the legislative results represent the shifting balance between the tobacco industry and tobacco control proponents as various arguments, i.e., science versus individual freedoms, gain in the legislative debate. The trends also reflect the trade-offs demanded as the price of legislation. For example, the only way to enact statewide Clean Indoor Air Act restrictions in Florida and Illinois was to accede to preemption (Jacobson, Wasserman, & Raube, 1993).

The Legislative Debates

Most of the state legislative debates from the late 1970s through the mid- to late 1980s centered on the sufficiency of the scientific evidence to justify legislative intervention. When the debate was on the scientific evidence, the tobacco industry was on the defensive. Beginning in the mid- to late 1980s, there appeared to be a shift in the nature of the debate—away from science and toward consideration of personal freedoms issues—largely resulting from the tobacco industry's strategy to emphasize individual rights (Jacobson, Wasserman, & Raube, 1993). This strategy met with some success, particularly in generating legislation to protect smokers from discrimination in employment, such as that enacted in Illinois, but was generally not sufficient to overcome the weight of the scientific evidence.

In the early to mid-1990s, the terms of the debate shifted once again, this time toward a focus on children. For many anti-smoking advocates, the focus on children was likely to become an effective strategy because of its general political attractiveness to legislators and because it is difficult for the tobacco industry to publicly oppose restrictions on youth access. So far, largely to comply with the federal Synar Amendment, all states have enacted youth access restrictions. Even so, one prominent anti-smoking activist recently objected to the youth access strategy as derogating from a more comprehensive attack on smoking (Glantz, 1996).

Restricting Smoking in Public Places

For the most part, statutes limiting smoking in public places were relatively rare prior to 1970. At that time, only fourteen states[1] had laws that limited smoking. In 1977, 392 smoking control bills were introduced in the various state legislatures, and twenty-eight states enacted forty-four bills into law (Christoffel & Stein, 1979). Although most of these bills involved matters such as taxation of cigarettes or control of transport, a considerable number sought to limit cigarette smoking in one way or another.

Today, forty-nine states restrict smoking in some manner in public places. These laws range from nominal restrictions, such as public buildings and schools in Indiana and Kentucky, to very extensive restrictions, such as prohibitions on smoking in many public places in Utah and Vermont. Only a few states have enacted comprehensive clean indoor air laws that restrict or prohibit smoking in a wide variety of public places. In addition, forty-three states restrict smoking at public worksites, and twenty-three states restrict smoking in private worksites (CSOH, 1995). In Table 1, we combine 1995 published data from the Centers for Disease Control and the Coalition on Smoking Or Health to show state laws on several dimensions: clean indoor air restrictions at government worksites, private worksites, and restaurants; youth access restrictions on vending machines and vendor licensing; advertising restrictions; and preemption and nondiscrimination provisions.

Two items stand out from Table 1. First, the sheer volume of tobacco control legislation suggests that tobacco remains a subject that legislators are willing to confront. Second, the tobacco industry has had considerable success at the state level in enacting legislation that preempts more stringent local ordinances and prohibits discrimination against smokers, especially in employment. As many as twenty-seven states have some form of preemptive legislation, often prohibiting stronger local ordinances than the provisions of state law (CSOH, 1995). As part of Washington State's Synar Act, for example, the tobacco industry was able to include a provision that preempts local licensure or regulating tobacco sales in retail stores. Except for legislation in a few states, such as Minnesota, the tobacco industry has also been successful in preventing stringent Clean Indoor Air Act restrictions and in diluting enforcement authority.

Table 1. Summary of State Laws by Type of Restriction and State

State	Smoke-Free Indoor Air			Youth Access to Tobacco Products			Preemption		Non-Discrimination
	Gov't worksites	Private worksites	Restaurants	Vending machine restrictions	Licensing	Advertising of tobacco products	CSOH	CDC	
Alabama					X				
Alaska	X	(a)	X	X	X				
Arizona	X								X
Arkansas	(a)			X	X				
California	X	X	X	(a)		X	X	X	
Colorado	X			X					X
Connecticut	X	X	X	X	X		X	X	X
Delaware	X	X	X		X		X	X	
Florida	X	X	X	X	X		X	X	
Georgia				X	X				
Hawaii	X		X	X					
Idaho	X		X	X					
Illinois	X	X	X	(a)		X	X	X	X
Indiana	X			X					X
Iowa	X	X	X	X	X		X	X	
Kansas	X		X		X				
Kentucky	(a)			X	X	X	X	X	X
Louisiana	X(b)	X(b)		X(b)	X	X	X	X	X
Maine	X	X	X	X			X		X
Maryland	(a)	(a)	X	X	X				
Massachusetts	X		X	X	X		X		
Michigan	X		X	X	X	X	X	X	
Minnesota	X	X	X	X				X	
Mississippi				X			X		X
Missouri	X	X	X	X					X
Montana	X	X	X	X	X		X		X
Nebraska	X(b)	X	X	X	X				
Nevada	X		X	X	X		X	X	X
New Hampshire	X	X	X	(a)	X				X
New Jersey	X	X		X	X		X		X
New Mexico	X			X			X		X
New York	X	X	X	X	X		X		X
North Carolina	(a)				X		X	X	X
North Dakota	X		X		X				X
Ohio	X			X	X				
Oklahoma	X		X	X	X		X	X	X
Oregon	X		X	X			X		X
Pennsylvania	X	X	X		X	X	X	X	
Rhode Island	X	X	X	(a)	X				X
South Carolina	X				X			X	X
South Dakota	X			X			X		X
Tennessee				X			X	X	X
Texas					X	X			
Utah	X	X	X	X	X	X	X		
Vermont	X	X	X	X	X				
Virginia	X		X	X (b)			X	X	X
Washington	X	(a)	X	X	X		X		
Washington, DC	X	X	X	X	X				X
West Virginia						X			X
Wisconsin	X	X	X	X	X		X		X
Wyoming	X			X					X
Total									

Sources: Centers for Disease Control, 1995; Coalition on Smoking Or Health, 1995.

(a) = CSOH, not CDC

(b) = CD, not CSOH

Youth Access Restrictions

As of 1993, forty-seven states had enacted laws that prohibited the sale of tobacco products to persons under eighteen years of age (Bierig, Weber, & Scarborough, 1994). By 1995, all states had restricted minors' access to tobacco products in one form or another. But as the IOM (1994) report on preventing nicotine addiction in children points out, these laws have gone largely unenforced since their enactment in the early part of the twentieth century. "Despite increased national interest in curtailing underage smoking, minors still have virtually unimpeded access to tobacco products" (IOM, 1994, p. 201). Indeed, it was not until the late 1980s that public attention to youth access restrictions became an integral part of the policy agenda. Since then, local communities have shown a greater willingness to enact and enforce ordinances limiting minors' access to cigarettes.

Local Involvement

At the local level, the number of ordinances restricting smoking has also increased. In 1985, approximately ninety local communities restricted smoking in public places (CDC, 1989). By 1993. over five hundred counties or cities had enacted anti-smoking ordinances (Coalition on Smoking Or Health, 1993; see also Rigotti & Pashos, 1991). Currently, 782 communities have enacted clean indoor air ordinances, 281 have enacted youth access ordinances, and 273 have enacted both (ANR, 1996). Further growth in local ordinances restricting smoking behavior is limited by statewide laws that preempt local ordinances and protect smokers' rights against discrimination for smoking behavior.

Despite these restrictions, a growing number of local anti-smoking laws have targeted teenagers. For example, according to the Surgeon General's Report on preventing tobacco use among young people, at least thirty cities in Minnesota, New York, California, Maryland, New Jersey, and Louisiana have outlawed the use of cigarette vending machines. Moreover, many other cities have adopted laws that limit teenage access to cigarette vending machines by requiring that such machines be placed in view of an employee, restricting the use of the machines to certain types of businesses and/or private facilities, or requiring the use of locking devices on the machines (USDHHS, 1994; IOM, 1994).

For a variety of reasons, including more stringent regulation of vending machines, minors now purchase most cigarettes at convenience stores and gas stations. Thus, local ordinances permitting license removal from vendors who sell cigarettes to minors is a more powerful law than laws requiring cigarettes to be sold from behind the counter.

In addition to federal advertising regulations, several localities have restricted advertising for tobacco products. For example, Boston and San Francisco each have banned tobacco advertising in their mass transit systems (Bierig, Weber, & Scarborough, 1994). In 1994, Baltimore banned publicly visible cigarette and alcohol billboards, with some minor exceptions (Garner, 1996). Cincinnati has also prohibited cigarette advertisements near schools, playgrounds, and parks. As Garner (1996) recounts, Baltimore's ad ban was upheld by the Fourth Circuit Court of Appeals, *Penn Advertising of Baltimore, Inc.* v. *Mayor of Baltimore,* 63 F.3d 1318 (4th Cir., 1995). The ban was reaffirmed in *Anheuser-Busch* v. *Schmoke,* #94-143 (4th Cir., 1996), despite a recent U.S. Supreme Court case overturning restrictions on alcohol advertising based on First Amendment commercial speech freedoms.

JUDICIAL INVOLVEMENT

Until recently, courts have played a decidedly secondary role in regulating tobacco products, generally permitting states and localities wide-ranging authority to regulate tobacco products. The courts' reluctance to overturn laws regulating smoking was succinctly summarized by the U.S. Supreme Court in *Austin* v. *Tennessee,* 179 U.S. 343 (1900) in holding that the regulation of cigarette sales was within the powers of the states: "Without undertaking to affirm or deny their evil effects, we think it within the province of the legislature to say how far [cigarettes] may be sold or to prohibit their sale entirely . . . and there is no reason to doubt that the act in question is designed for the protection of the public health." (179 U.S. 348-349).

As a result, there actually have been only a few challenges to state or local tobacco control laws. On the other hand, juries have been reluctant to hold cigarette manufacturers responsible for the free choices an adult smoker makes, and courts have not imposed strict liability on the manufacturers, thus limiting the incidence of litigation (see, e.g., Schwartz, 1993). The tobacco industry's defense that the smoker assumes the risk has meant that ". . . tort liability has contributed virtually nothing to the array of strategies employed to control tobacco use" (Rabin, 1991, p. 494).[2] Recently, however, a jury in *Carter* v. *Brown & Williamson Tobacco Corp.* (Florida, August 1996) ruled in favor of a plaintiff who had started smoking before warnings were required on packs of cigarettes. Whether this is a harbinger of future verdicts remains to be determined, but it at least suggests that the tobacco industry may not be invulnerable to legal challenges regarding the dangerousness of its products and to challenges about its veracity.

It seems unlikely that courts will intervene to block tobacco control regulations. Indeed, the Florida Supreme Court recently upheld a local ordinance that required applicants for public employment in North Miami to refrain from smoking for one year prior to their application (*City of North Miami* v. *Kurtz*, 1995 Lexis 568, [Florida, 1995]). Likewise, courts have upheld total bans on vending machines as a means of restricting youth access to cigarettes (Bierig, Weber, & Scarborough, 1994).

With the emergence of class-action litigation challenging nicotine addiction and the smoking-related costs of Medicaid coverage, courts may yet become an important forum for regulating tobacco products by imposing damages for resulting harms (see Kelder et al. 1997). Nevertheless, while promising as a means of protecting many regulatory provisions, reliance on a judicial strategy to go beyond what the regulators or legislators are willing to enact has inherent limitations. Recently, for instance, a major class-action lawsuit against tobacco manufacturers was thrown out by the Fifth Circuit Court of Appeals. Other challenges await a much-publicized strategy of states suing tobacco firms for recovery of Medicaid health care costs. Showing net economic harm from cigarettes, given savings in entitlements from earlier death, may be difficult. Nevertheless, the recent verdict noted above may indicate that the industry is starting to be held to higher standards of disclosure on the hazards of smoking. Thus, the legal situation is fluid, and it remains to be seen whether courts will act as a regulatory constraint on tobacco sales and consumption.

Studies of Effectiveness and Implementation

Accompanying the increase in state and local tobacco control legislation and regulation, researchers have attempted to study empirically how effective these various approaches are for reducing both smoking in public places and youth smoking initiation rates. These results are important for understanding what works and for understanding the gaps in legislation that need to be addressed.

An important gap in the literature is the availability of an accurate measure of regulatory stringency. At present, it is very difficult to compare the effectiveness of state legislative provisions across jurisdictions (that is, to determine which laws work best). Current indices of regulatory stringency, including Wasserman et al. (1991) and Warner (1981), essentially assign numeric values to particular regulatory provisions, and total the resulting figures to arrive at a set of index values, often using a range of Minimal, Moderate, Extensive, and Comprehensive (see, e.g., CSOH, 1995). Absent certain adjustments, these indices can be misleading. A stringency index must also take into account: whether state law preempts local ordinances; the level of enforcement authority contained in the legislation; the locus of enforcement authority (state versus local); the existence of smokers' rights provisions;

whether smoking is prohibited in certain locations or only restricted; whether private worksites are covered; and which party has the burden of showing that smoking is permitted or prohibited.

Effectiveness of Regulations Limiting Smoking Behavior

The literature on the effectiveness of clean indoor air restrictions demonstrates the inherent conundrum underlying these laws. To be effective, some continuing enforcement presence is needed, but most clean indoor air laws lack a strong enforcement component and are perceived to be self-enforcing. If, in fact, they are not self-enforcing, the laws are unlikely to be particularly effective.

For example, Rigotti et al. (1988), Rigotti et al. (1992), Rigotti et al. (1993), and Rigotti, Stoto, and Schelling (1994) have conducted a significant amount of research regarding the compliance of businesses with anti-smoking laws, in particular the self-enforcement approach. Results from these studies, conducted in Cambridge, Massachusetts, indicate that awareness of the local no-smoking ordinance in workplaces declined from 92 percent to 73 percent over the two years after passage. Eighty percent of companies surveyed restricted smoking [between] three and twenty-four months after passage, but only half the businesses fully complied with the law at either date. Based on this work, Rigotti, Stoto, and Schelling (1994) conclude that business size is important in determining compliance, with small businesses less likely to rely on self-enforcement; that the anti-smoking laws led to a high level of smoking restrictions; and that reminders to business are needed to avoid erosion in compliance over time.[3]

Effectiveness of Regulations Restricting Minors' Access to Tobacco Products

Several studies have shown how easily minors can purchase cigarettes (see, e.g., DiFranza & Brown, 1992; Radecki & Zdunich, 1993; and DiFranza, Savageau, & Aisquith, 1996). Other studies have demonstrated that merchant education has failed to produce sustained refusal to sell cigarettes to minors (Feighery, Altman, & Shaffer, 1991). The literature on enforcement of youth access restrictions is less extensive, but demonstrates generally the ability and need to enforce these laws. Unlike the Clean Indoor Air Act restrictions, youth access restrictions are not susceptible to self-enforcement.

For example, Feighery, Altman, and Shaffer (1991) examined the effects of combined community education and enforcement efforts in four Northern California communities. They found that the combined enforcement and education approach resulted in reduced tobacco sales to minors, but that education efforts alone had only a limited effect. Similarly Feighery et al. (1991) examined the enforcement of laws against selling cigarettes to minors. They found that aggressive enforcement and follow-up compliance checks led to 96 percent compliance by cigarette vendors against sales to minors, and a substantial reduction (50 percent) in tobacco use among local junior high school students.

As a followup to the 1991 study, Jason et al. (1996) studied the accessibility of cigarettes to "older" minors. The ability of minors aged fifteen through seventeen to purchase cigarettes from merchants in Woodridge, Illinois, was compared with the same ability of minors aged thirteen and fourteen. The results from sixteen compliance checks revealed that sales rates to the thirteen- and fourteen-year-olds were below 13 percent. Sales rates to the fifteen- and sixteen-year-olds were below 20 percent, while sales rates to the seventeen-year-olds were 25 percent. Based on these results, the authors suggest that interventions designed to restrict minors' access to cigarettes must address the differing abilities of minors of differing ages to purchase cigarettes.

DISCUSSION

Taken together, the current state of regulatory, judicial, and legislative pressure on the tobacco industry presents a concentrated, perhaps unprecedented, assault on a legal product. Along with continuing educational efforts, the current activity represents a comprehensive approach to tobacco control. Two questions, however, remain unanswered. First, in view of the recent increase in smoking rates, how effective are regulations restricting smoking? The fact remains that a certain portion of the population, perhaps as much as 20 percent, remains impervious to efforts to reduce smoking. And second, what are the consequences if the tobacco industry emerges relatively unscathed, and hence deadlier than ever, from this regulatory assault? In short, it is timely to ask where anti-smoking advocates go from here.

The first issue is to determine where and how to allocate anti-smoking resources. As Rabin and Sugarman (1993) note, there is an undetermined relationship between cultural change and the enactment of laws and regulations. To the extent that cultural norms lead to reductions in tobacco use, continued pressure for additional restrictions may be counterproductive by stimulating a backlash against governmental or paternalistic policies. But, to the extent that laws and regulations stimulate or validate changing cultural norms, it is important not to abandon the force of law in maintaining the desired goal of reduced tobacco use. The issues Rabin and Sugarman raise are whether gains from additional restrictions are worth the costs, and whether the rights-based approach is the most effective way to resolve the underlying conflicts between smokers and nonsmokers.

While recognizing the potential costs of seeking additional regulations, as well as the unanswered question of how effective the laws and regulations are in reducing tobacco use, we strongly believe that abandoning the effort to obtain additional laws would be a mistake. In all likelihood, changes in civil norms facilitate the enactment of legislation which, in turn, codifies civil norms. Given their symbolic authority, laws serve to institutionalize nascent civil norms (Kagan & Skolnick, 1993). Legislation therefore acts to express the government's public policy concern that tobacco use is dangerous to health, contributes to a social climate that discourages smoking in public places, and legitimizes attempts to bring additional public pressure to reduce cigarette consumption. Tobacco control legislation also shifts control from the smoker to the nonsmoker and places the burden of showing that smoking is permitted on the smoker. These provisions are important because most people obey the law voluntarily. Just as civil norms, absent legislative support, may not last, legislation alone, absent evolving social norms that render tobacco control laws more effective, will not achieve the goals of reducing cigarette consumption, a lesson learned in the early 1900s. Indeed, previous research demonstrates that nonsmokers will not ask smokers to refrain from smoking, unless such reinforcing support is present and clear (Gibson & Werner, 1992, 1994).

Thus, it would be a mistake for anti-smoking advocates to abandon a legislative strategy. Instead, advocates need to clarify the rationale for additional legislation and regulations, specify the areas where laws are needed, and participate in implementing these laws. Public policy should be designed to discourage smoking in public places and prevent cigarette sales to minors. Legislation restricting those activities is the strongest message the government can send to protect the public's health.

A subsidiary question for anti-smoking advocates is whether to concentrate their resources at the state or local level. As previous studies have shown, the tobacco industry is considerably more powerful at the state than at the local level (Jacobson, Wasserman, & Raube, 1993; Samuels & Glantz, 1991; Samuels et al., 1992). While the political dynamic will differ across states, it is important for tobacco control advocates to recognize that they can be more effective at the local level. They also face the danger of having their resources exhausted by contesting the tobacco industry at the state level.

One of the unresolved issues in the literature is the extent to which the vagueness of most statewide anti-smoking legislation and concomitant limitations in enforcement authority render clean indoor air act restrictions more of a symbolic statement of the desire to control smoking than an easily enforceable mandate. An issue that is often ignored in legislative battles is the locus of responsibility for enforcing and implementing tobacco control legislation. Relatively few studies have addressed directly the question of how laws restricting smoking in public places and youth access restrictions are implemented and enforced (Burns et al., 1992).[4]

Several other directions seem promising, based on preliminary empirical findings, and should be pursued. First, the California anti-smoking advertisements, funded by Proposition 99 funds, have been successful (see Siegel & Biener, 1997) and should be replicated in other states. Research by Pierce and others (Pierce, Lee, & Gilpin, 1994; Evans et al., 1995; DiFranza & Aisquith, 1995) shows that the tobacco industry's advertisements have a powerful effect on youth. Fashioning an equally devastating portrait of the harms from tobacco should remain an anti-smoking imperative.

Second, despite Glantz's (1996) concerns that the focus on youth access restrictions will impede a more comprehensive anti-smoking effort, the fact remains that few people choose to initiate smoking in their twenties or beyond. If so, it makes sense to concentrate resources on school-based and other youth programs to determine what additional approaches would be effective in reducing smoking initiation rates (Brownson et al., 1995; Hine et al., 1997). We now know, for example, that until recently, smoking initiation rates for black youths were far less than for white youths. According to CDC that trend has been reversed. What can we learn about why rates for black youths have fluctuated so rapidly? How can those lessons be extrapolated to other groups?

Third, as our current work will demonstrate (Jacobson & Wasserman, 1996), state and local efforts to enforce anti-smoking laws (both clean indoor air and youth access restrictions) are woefully inadequate. Anti-smoking advocates and coalitions need to pay more attention to the admittedly less scintillating tedium of enforcement. For example, coalitions might focus part of their legislative activities on strengthening enforcement provisions, including local licensure removal and suspension authority.

CONCLUSIONS

No matter how successful the anti-smoking campaign has been in recent years in generating legislative and regulatory scrutiny, in changing civil norms that have led to generally lower cigarette consumption, and in putting the tobacco industry on the defensive, at least regarding youth access to tobacco, the tobacco industry remains a strong, creative, and relentless opponent. In a democracy, the relationship between the right of the government to protect the public's health constantly collides with the equally powerful right of the individual to determine how to live his or her own life, free from governmental interference. Striking the proper balance is never easy, particularly when the economic survival of politically powerful interests is at stake. Absent a consistent, comprehensive, and committed effort from anti-smoking advocates, legislators and regulators are likely to subordinate public health interests to the tobacco industry's narrow economic claims.

This historical overview suggests how far anti-smoking advocates have come in reducing the public's exposure to cigarette smoke and the harms from tobacco. It also suggests how much more needs to be done to limit those health risks and harms. In our view, the anti-smoking gains over the past two decades have been substantial. But they are also fragile and not irreversible, subject to the tobacco industry's creative abilities to reglorify smoking.

NOTES

1. For convenience, we include the District of Columbia as a state.
2. As many have noted, there is a certain irony in the way that the health warnings from the 1960s, enacted over tobacco industry opposition, have virtually insulated the industry from tort liability.
3. For similar conclusions in other settings and areas, see Nordstrom and DeStefano, 1995; Patten et al., 1995; and Brownson et al., 1995.
4. The authors are currently conducting a Robert Wood Johnson Foundation-funded study of tobacco control enforcement and implementation in seven states.

REFERENCES

Americans for Nonsmokers Rights. Berkeley. Calif.. "Counts of Local Smoking Control Ordinances," data provided to this project, May 1996.

Bierig. J. R., S. A. Weber, & T. R. Scarborough. (1994). Legal analysis of approaches to state and local regulation of tobacco advertising and sales in the U.S. Analysis prepared by Sidley and Austin at the request of the American Medical Association.

Brownson. R. C., J. R. Davis, J. Jackson-Thompson, & J. C. Wilkerson, (1995). "Environmental Tobacco Smoke Awareness and Exposure: Impact of a Statewide Clean Indoor Air Law and the Report of the U.S. Environmental Protection Agency." *Tobacco Control* 4: 132–44.

Burns, D. M., R. Axelrad, D. Bal, et al. (1992). "Report of the Tobacco Research Study Group on Smoke-Free Indoor Air Policies." *Tobacco Control* 1 (Suppl.): S14–S18.

Centers for Disease Control (CDC). (1989). *The Surgeon General's 1989 Report on Reducing the Health Consequences of Smoking: 25 Years of Progress* (Executive Summary). CDC, 38 (Suppl. no. 2).

———. (1993). *Minors' Access to Tobacco—Missouri, 1992, and Texas, 1993.* CDC, 42, 125–28.

———. (1994). *Cigarette Smoking among Adults—United States, 1992, and Changes in the Definition of Current Cigarette Smoking.* CDC, 43, 342–46.

——— (1995). *State Laws on Tobacco Control—United States, 1995.* CDC, 44 (Suppl. no. SS–6).

———. *Minors' Access to Smokeless Tobacco—Florida, 1994.* CDC, 44.

Christoffel, T. & S. Stein. (1979). "Using the Law to Protect Health: The Frustrating Case of Smoking." *Medicolegal News* 7, no. 4.

Coalition on Smoking Or Health (CSOH). (1993). *State Legislative Actions on Tobacco Issues.* Washington, D.C.

— — —. (1995). *State Legislative Actions on Tobacco Issues* (Jessica Bartelt, Ed.), Washington, D.C.

DiFranza, J. R. & B. F. Aisquith. (1995). "Does the Joe Camel Campaign Preferentially Reach 18- to 24-Year-Old Adults?" *Tobacco Control* 4: 367–71.

DiFranza, J. R. & L. J. Brown. (1992). "The Tobacco Institute's 'It's the Law' Campaign: Has It Halted Illegal Sales of Tobacco to Children?" *American Journal of Public Health* 82: 1271–73.

DiFranza, J. R., J. A. Savageau, & B. F. Aisquith. (1996). "Youth Access to Tobacco: The Effects of Age, Gender, Vending Machine Locks, and "It's the Law" Programs." *American Journal of Public Health* 86: 221–24.

Elders, J. M., C. L. Perry, M. P. Eriksen, & G. A. Giovino. (1994). "The Report of the Surgeon General: Preventing Tobacco Use among Young People." *American Journal of Public Health* 84: 543–47.

Evans, N., A. Farkas, E. Gilpin, C. Berry, & J. P. Pierce. (1995). "Influence of Tobacco Marketing and Exposure to Smokers on Adolescent Susceptibility to Smoking." *Journal of the National Cancer Institute* 87: 1538–45.

Feighery. E., D. G. Altman, & G. Shaffer. (1991). "The Effects of Combining Education and Enforcements to Reduce Tobacco Sales to Minors." *Journal of the American Medical Association* 266: 3168–71.

Garner. D. W. (1996). "Banning Tobacco Billboards: The Case for Municipal Action." *Journal of the American Medical Association* 275:1263–69.

Gibson, B., & C. M. Werner. (1992). "The Decision to Attempt Interpersonal Control: The Case of Nonsmoker-Smoker Interactions." *Basic and Applied Social Psychology* 13: 269–84

Gibson, B., & C. M. Werner. (1994). "Airport Waiting Areas as Behavior Settings: The Role of Legibility Cues in Communicating the Setting Program." *Journal of Personality and Social Psychology* 66: 1049–60.

Glantz, S. A. (1996). "Editorial: Preventing Tobacco Use—The Youth Access Trap." *American Journal of Public Health* 86: 156–57.

Gori, G. B. (1995). "Policy against Science: The Case of Environmental Tobacco Smoke." *Risk Analysis* 15: 15–22.

Hine, D. W., C. Summers, K. Tilleczek, & J. Lewko. (1997). "Expectancies and Mental Models as Determinants of Adolescents' Smoking Decisions." *Journal of Social Issues* 53, no. 1: 35–52.

Institute of Medicine (IOM). (1994). *Growing Up Tobacco Free.* Washington, D.C.: National Academy Press.

Jacobson, P. D., J. Wasserman, & K. Raube. (1993). "The Politics of Anti-Smoking Legislation: Lessons from Six States." *Journal of Health Policy and Law* 18: 787–819.

Janerich, D. T., & D. W. Thompson. (1990). "Lung Cancer and Exposure to Tobacco Smoke in the Household." *New England Journal of Medicine* 323: 632.

Jason. L. A., W. D. Billows, D. L. Schnopp-Wyatt, & K. King. (1996). "Long-Term Findings from Woodridge in Reducing Illegal Cigarette Sales to Older Minors." *Evaluation and the Health Professions* 19: 3–13.

Jason, L. A., P. Y. Yi, M. D. Anes, & S. H. Birkhead. (1991). "Active Enforcement of Cigarette Control Laws in the Prevention of Cigarette Sales to Minors." *Journal of the American Medical Association* 266: 3159–61.

Kagan, R. A. & J. H. Skolnick. (1993). "Banning Smoking: Compliance without Enforcement." In *Smoking policy: Law, politics, and culture,* ed. R. L. Rabin and S. D. Sugarman, 69–94. New .York: Oxford University Press.

Kagan, R. A. & D. Vogel. (1993). "The Politics of Smoking Regulation: Canada, France, the United States." In *Smoking policy: Law, politics, and culture,* eds. R. L. Rabin and S. D. Sugarman, 22–48. New York: Oxford University Press.

Kelder, G. E., R. A. Daynard, & R. C. Porfiri. (1997). "Judicial Approaches to tobacco Control: The third Wave of Tobacco Litigation as a Tobacco Control Mechanism." *Journal of Social Issues* 53, no. 1.

Kluger, R. (1996). *Ashes to Ashes: America's Hundred-Year Cigarette War, the Public Health, and the Unabashed Triumph of Philip Morris.* New York: Alfred A. Knopf.

Lewit, E. M., D. Coate, & M. Grossman. (1981). "The Effects of Government Regulation on Teenage Smoking." *Journal of Law and Economics* 24: 545–70.

Nordstrom, D. L., & R. DeStefano. (1995). "Evaluation of Wisconsin Legislation on Smoking in Restaurants." *Tobacco Control* 4: 125–28.

Patten. C. A., J. P. Pierce, S. W. Cavin, C. C. Berry, & R. M. Kaplan. (1995). "Progress in Protecting Nonsmokers from Environmental Tobacco Smoke in California Workplaces." *Tobacco Control* 4: 139–44.

Pierce, J. P., L. Lee, & E. A. Gilpin. (1994). "Smoking Initiation by Adolescent Girls, 1944 Through 1988: An Association with Targeted Advertising." *Journal of the American Medical Association* 271: 608–11.

Rabin, R. L. (1991). "Some Thoughts on Smoking Regulation." *Stanford Law Review* 43: 475–96.

Rabin. R. L. & S. D. Sugarman. (1993). "Overview." In *Smoking Policy: Law, politics, and culture,* eds. R. L. Rabin and S. D. Sugarman, 3–21. New York: Oxford University Press.

Radecki, T. E. & C. D. Zdunich. (1993). "Tobacco Sales to Minors in 97 U.S. and Canadian Communities." *Tobacco Control* 2: 300–305.

Rigotti, N. A., M. A. Stoto, M. Kleiman, & T. Schelling. (1988). *Implementation and Impact of a City's Regulation of Smoking in Public Places and the Workplace: The Experience of Cambridge, Massachusetts.* Institute for the Study of Smoking Behavior and Policy, JFK School of Government, Harvard University. Publication No. S-88-17.

Rigotti, N. A. & C. L. Pashos. (1991). "No-Smoking Laws in the United States: An Analysis of State and City Actions to Limit Smoking in Public Places and Workplaces." *Journal of the American Medical Association* 266: 3162–67.

Rigotti, N. A., D. Bourne, A. Rosen, J. A. Locke, & T. Schelling. (1992). "Workplace Compliance with a No-Smoking Law: A Randomized Community Intervention Trial." *American Journal of Public Health* 82: 229–35.

Rigotti, N. A., Stoto, M. A., Brier, M. F., Rosen, A., & Schelling, T. (1993). "Retail Stores Compliance with a City No-Smoking Law." *American Journal of Public Health* 83: 227–56.

Rigotti, N. A., M. A. Stoto, & T. Schelling. (1994). "Do Businesses Comply with a No-Smoking Law? Assessing the Self-Enforcement Approach." *Preventative Medicine* 23: 223–29.

Samuels, B. E., M. E. Begay, A. Hazan, & S. A. Glantz. (1992). "Phillip Morris's Failed Experiment in Pittsburgh." *Journal of Health Politics, Policy, and Law* 17: 329–51.

Samuels, B. E. & S. A. Glantz. (1991). "The Politics of Local Tobacco Control." *Journal of the American Medical Association* 266: 2110–17.

Schwartz, G. T. (1993). "Tobacco Liability in the Courts." In *Smoking policy: Law, politics, and culture,* eds. R. L. Rabin and S. D. Sugarman, 131–60. New York: Oxford University Press.

Siegel, M. & Biener, L. (1997). "Evaluating the Impact of Statewide Anti-Tobacco Campaigns: The Massachusetts and California Tobacco Control Programs." *Journal of Social Issues* 53: no. 1.

Slattery, M. L., L. M. Robison, T. K. French, T. M. Abbott, J. C. Overall Jr., & J. W. Gardner. (1989). "Cigarette Smoking and Exposure to Passive Smoking Are Risk Factors for Cervical Cancer." *Journal of the American Medical Association* 261: 1593.

Tollison, R. D. & R. E. Wagner. (1991). "Self-Interest, Public Interest, and Public Health." *Public Choice* 69: 323–43.

U.S. Department of Health and Human Services. (1986). *The Health Consequences of Involuntary Smoking.* A report of the Surgeon General. Rockville, Md.: U.S. Department of Health and Human Services, No. 87–8309.

U.S. Department of Health and Human Services. (1994). *Preventing Tobacco Use among Young People.* A report of the Surgeon General. Atlanta, Georgia, U.S. Department of Health and Human Services.

U.S. Department of Environmental Protection (EPA). (1992). *Respiratory Health Effects of Passive Smoking: Lung Cancer and Other Disorders.* Washington, D.C.

Wagner, S. (1971). *Cigarette Country: Tobacco in American History and Politics.* New York: Praeger Publishers.

Warner, K. E. (1981). "State Legislation on Smoking and Health: A Comparison of Two Policies." *Policy Sciences* 13: 139–52.

Wasserman. J., W. G. Manning, J. P. Newhouse, & J. D. Winkler. (1991). "The Effects of Excise Taxes and Regulations on Cigarette Smoking." *Journal of Health Economics* 10: 43–64.

Zycher, B. (1990, June). "Insurance Markets, Smoking, and the Coase Theorem." Paper presented at Annual Meeting of the Western Economic Association International, San Diego, Calif.

4

A Sociological View of the Anti-Smoking Phenomenon

Peter L. Berger

A famous professor at a German medical school in the nineteenth century is said to have opened a lecture with the following statement: "Gentlemen: I will now expound to you the omnipotence of God on the basis of the anatomy of the louse." The theological assumptions of this proposition, alas, cannot be pursued here. The professor, however, was also expressing an important insight about the character of scientific inquiry, namely, that reality is all of one piece and that looking at any slice of it can give us a sense of the whole. This is as true of social reality as it is of the physical universe. It also describes both the motive and the quality of my own interest in the anti-smoking phenomenon. That phenomenon, frankly, is only of limited interest to people who are not either members of an anti-smoking movement or employees of the tobacco industry. In an age of apocalyptic anxieties, most of us have many other things to worry about than the allegedly nefarious consequences of smoking. So do I.

The anti-smoking phenomenon is something I stumbled on by accident a few years ago and it has remained very marginal to my interests as a sociologist (which are centered on problems of modernization and Third World development). I have found, though, that this particular phenomenon is interesting, not so much in itself, but in terms of the light it sheds on wider social and cultural trends in our society. I might, then, open this chapter with a slight paraphrase: "Ladies and gentlemen: I will now expound to you certain features of Western advanced industrial societies on the basis of the anatomy of the anti-smoking phenomenon."

Originally published in *Smoking and Society: Toward a More Balanced Assessment,* edited by R. D. Tollinson (Lexington, Mass.: Lexington Books, 1984). Reprinted by permission of University Press of America.

Put differently, this chapter is an attempt to use sociological categories to place the anti-smoking phenomenon in a wider context. Some principal features of such a sociological approach will be spelled out in the next section. From the outset, however, the reader is entitled to some answers to the following questions: What is the evidence on which the author is basing his observations? What is the author's bias? Does he have any vested interests of his own in the matter under discussion?

I first noticed the anti-smoking phenomenon through the increased aggressiveness of some of its activists in the United States. Irritated by this, I wrote a brief article about this.[1] This article was brought to the attention of some individuals in the tobacco industry and subsequently I did a moderate amount of consulting with that industry. My most intensive contact with the anti-smoking phenomenon was attendance, as a consultant for the tobacco industry, at two international conferences on smoking and health held under the auspices of the World Health Organization (Stockholm 1979 and Winnipeg 1983). Although I have not undertaken primary research of my own on the subject, since about 1978 I have read a good deal of anti-smoking literature and have conversed with a considerable number of individuals engaged on both sides of this issue. I have used an unpublished study, Michael Thompson et al., "The Political Culture of Anti-Smoking Groups," which compares such groups in the United States and Britain.[2]

Sociology has always purported to be a "value-free" science (the phrase was coined by the classical sociologist Max Weber). This means that, insofar as sociological propositions are scientifically valid, individuals with different, even contradictory values can agree on them. In this precise sense, the present chapter will also seek to be "value-free." Concretely this means that the analysis presented here could, in principle, be accepted or rejected by people on either side of the current controversy over smoking.

At the same time, sociologists in particular are sensitive to the fact that one's own biases and vested interests inevitably color one's perceptions of evidence. For this reason it is good practice to be very up-front about these, allowing readers to decide for themselves whether one's analysis is or is not as "value-free" as it purports to be. My bias, then, is against the anti-smoking phenomenon (I might say, paraphrasing again, that I'm an "anti-anti-smoking" person). This bias is political: I perceive the anti-smoking movement as tending toward further intrusion by government into private life, and I don't like such intrusion. Do I have vested interests in the matter? I'm not employed by the tobacco industry and would not have served as a consultant to it if it had not been for the aforementioned bias; my consulting fees have been an exceedingly small fraction of my income and would hardly be a reasonable motive (indeed, I wonder if I might not have a pecuniary motive to switch sides on this issue). I *do* have one vested interest in the matter that should be avowed: I am myself a smoker and as such have been personally annoyed by anti-smoking activism. Obviously, no one likes a habit one derives pleasure from to be castigated as a cosmic pestilence. On the other hand, this particular vested interest is lessened by the fact that I smoke pipes and cigars rather than cigarettes—the principal villains in the anti-smoking campaign.

There is one further and important point to be made about the status of this chapter: no competence is claimed here on the scientific controversy regarding smoking and health, and the sociological analysis presented is not dependent on any conclusions regarding this controversy. This point is important enough to be spelled out a little more. Very few people are professionally qualified to evaluate the scientific evidence on smoking and health. Let it be stipulated that medical researchers, physiologists, biochemists, and perhaps statisticians can arrive at an independent judgment on the weight of this evidence. The rest of us, having no independent access to "the truth of the matter," must take our opinions second-hand and on the basis of some sort of faith. This faith (which, of course, must also be very largely faith in this or that authority) is precisely what can be analyzed sociologically— regardless of what an independent scientific judgment might finally be. Nothing in what follows, then, is to be construed as implying that the scientific evidence cited by anti-smoking advocates either is or is not as valid as they suppose it to be.

A SOCIOLOGICAL APPROACH

Sociology, of course, always seeks to place specific human phenomena in a broader context of societal structures and change. The approach employed here, however, is somewhat more specific. It is the approach commonly called that of the "sociology of knowledge." While the assumptions and implications of this approach can be and have been elaborated to a vast extent,[3] the basic thrust of the sociology of knowledge can be stated rather simply: ideas are plausible to people in specific social contexts. Put a little differently, ideas do not float around in some Platonic heaven detached from social forces, but rather, they link up with specific and empirically researchable groups in society, and ipso facto with the interests of these groups.

This root proposition of the sociology of knowledge is expressed by the concept of "plausibility structure." This refers to whatever social context is required for an idea to be credible to people. For example, there is the idea that witches cast spells that cause disease. If I were to propose this idea in Boston [today], it is very unlikely that I would find a responsive audience, except perhaps in this or that occultist subculture. On the other hand, people who put forth this proposition in New England in the seventeenth century found a very responsive audience indeed (much to the inconvenience of the alleged witches). This historical difference can be described by saying that contemporary Boston lacks the plausibility structure for a belief in witchcraft, while colonial Salem, Massachusetts, did provide this plausibility structure. It further follows that an individual in the latter location in time and space had no difficulty whatever taking a proposition about disease-causing witches very seriously—perhaps even taking the underlying worldview for granted—while I and my contemporaries would have to invest considerable effort before we could even entertain such an idea as a hypothesis. Indeed, we very probably would have to immerse ourselves in the aforementioned occultist underworld before we could bring ourselves to the point of taking the matter seriously. Conversely, I and my contemporaries readily explain this or that pathological condition by the categories of psychoanalysis, which to a citizen of colonial Salem would appear as crazy as witchcraft appears to us. It should be noted that these statements do not hinge on any final judgments as to whether witchcraft or psychoanalysis are or are not scientifically valid; they refer to *socially defined* reality, not to reality as it may be deemed to be by this or that science. Thus let it be imagined that, sometime in the future, scientists might decide that witchcraft is an empirical phenomenon after all; this interesting discovery would not force us to revise the statement that witchcraft had a plausibility structure in New England in 1692 and lacked it in [1998]. History, sad to say, is not governed by scientific truth, and the period when people did not believe in witches will just have to be put down as another of those ages of superstition to which the human race seems prone.

Some ideas take the form of norms: they enjoin us to do this or to refrain from doing that. All norms, however, rest upon cognitive presuppositions. Thus someone may proclaim a crusade against witches: "Witches are evil: They must be driven out." This *normative* program, however, rests on the *cognitive* presuppositions that (1) there *are* witches and (2) that they are bad news. It may be assumed that an anti-witchcraft crusader, especially one who has been crusading for a long time and derives power, prestige, or income from anti-witchcraft activities, will not take kindly to the proposition that witches are a figment of his or her imagination or that witches perform a commendable community service.

This last observation leads to a central concern of the sociology of knowledge, namely, the relation between ideas and vested interests. It is possible to distinguish two different kinds of vested interests, already alluded to in what has just been said about the cognitive defensiveness of the anti-witchcraft crusader. There are material and ideal interests. When people speak of vested interests, they usually mean the material ones: I am an anti-witchcraft specialist, and by virtue of this fact I have a fulltime appointment as an officer of the Inquisition (we are now, let us assume, in Seville rather than Salem), a powerful and prestigious job that also supplies me with a considerable, reasonably secure livelihood. It is obvious in this case that I will have a vested interest in the crusade against witches—and, by the same token, in the ideas about witchcraft on which the crusade is predicated. But there can also be vested interests of a nonmaterial sort: I'm *not* an employee of the Inquisition and I derive my livelihood from a professorship at the University of Seville; but I have written two books on witches (perhaps books that established my reputation as a scholar), my notions about witches are connected with a lot of other ideas that I have espoused (religious ideas, political ideas, and perhaps others), and in any case I have reached the age at which one is reluctant to revise ideas that one has held for many years. Such ideal interests will also affect the way in which I look at the issue of witchcraft.

A moment's reflection about a phenomenon as remote from one's own context as witchcraft will lead to the insight that vested interests of either sort are never limited to one party only; they always build on both sides of any disputed issue. The alleged witches themselves, needless to say, have vested interests in the matter—of a particularly pressing, material variety. But so do the employees of (let us imagine) the Witches Antidefamation Society and so does that other professor, who has written several books arguing that witches do not exist. This particular sociology-of-knowledge insight can be formulated in precise scientific prose by saying that, when it comes to vested interests, what is good for the goose is always good for the gander as well. Another point that should be very clearly made in this connection is this: to say that people's thinking is affected by their vested interests in no way implies that people are insincere. On the contrary, the great majority of people believe with the utmost sincerity that their vested interests coincide with the truth. Most Inquisitors sincerely believe that witches are wicked and most witches, equally sincere, believe that they are innocent. The reason for this is probably quite simple too: insincerity always requires a considerable effort, which most people are unwilling or unable to make (the great Machiavellians are a very small minority of the human race); it is much easier to hold one's beliefs sincerely.

Probably the concept that has passed most widely from the vocabulary of the sociology of knowledge into general usage is that of "ideology." An ideology, in its simplest definition, is an idea that expresses a vested interest. It follows that not all ideas are ideological; it follows further that just about any idea can, under certain circumstances, take on ideological functions, and some ideas start off that way. The most commonplace of ideologies is in politics—that is, in activities that have to do with the acquisition and the wielding of power. In politics, ideologies are part and parcel of the power game: "ideas as weapons." Once again, at the risk of being repetitious, one must stress that to describe an idea as ideological says nothing about whether this idea may be judged to be true or false, or a mixture of truth and error, by an objective observer standing outside this particular political fray.

The preceding, and necessarily sketchy, description of this particular sociological approach has deliberately avoided any reference to the anti-smoking phenomenon. It is applicable to just about any situation in which ideas enter into conflicts between social groups. The reader will have had no difficulty, however, in applying it mentally to the phenomenon at issue. The anti-smoking phenomenon, too, has a particular plausibility structure, and one of the tasks of sociological analysis must be to delineate its boundaries. The normative messages of the anti-smoking campaign intended to restrain or remove smoking must be understood as based on cognitive presuppositions, about the allegedly nefarious consequences of smoking, that most people are poorly equipped to evaluate. Most importantly, there are vested interests on *both* sides of the issue, and *both* sides take ideological stances— that is, use ideas as weapons in the conflict.

The anti-smoking movement uses the phrase "smoking interests," which refers, of course, to the tobacco industry. Fair enough: the tobacco industry obviously has enormous vested interests in the outcome of the current conflict, and these interests have an ideological aspect. Thus the tobacco industry has an obvious interest in questioning propositions about the negative effects of smoking. One might speculate that, if some scientist appeared who produced alleged evidence to the effect that smoking is a sure cure for leprosy, the tobacco industry would be sympathetically inclined, while the anti-smoking group would take a dim view of the hypothesis. And these predispositions would be at least relatively independent of the eventual scientific outcome of this particular argument, though in the end the weight of evidence would probably compel either side to draw back from its predispositional attitude. When leprosy disappears, say, from the Republic of Bongobongo in precise correlation, year by year, with the increase in smoking among its citizens, the anti-smoking movement might concede that perhaps smoking is good for lepers, though it may still point out that the causal connection can only be established once the cause of leprosy is known. In short, there are smoking as well as anti-smoking interests. The smoking interests are not difficult to identify. They consist of the tobacco industry, its political allies, especially in tobacco-producing areas, and, although only in a passive and politically unreliable manner, those portions of the public who smoke and are annoyed by those who want to stop or penalize the habit. The ideological predisposition of this group, obviously, is negative or at least skeptical toward allegations that smoking is inimical to health. But what is good for the smoking goose is also good for the anti-smoking gander. Thus the politics and the ideology of the anti-smoking interests must also be the subject of sociological analysis.

THE POLITICS OF ANTI-SMOKING

Broadly speaking, the anti-smoking interests are constituted by all those who derive power, prestige, or income from the anti-smoking campaign. While correct, this statement is too broad, and a further differentiation is useful.

Looking at the anti-smoking phenomenon, one is impressed by its bifurcation into two distinct, though increasingly related, segments—the anti-smoking *movement* and various organizations constituting an anti-smoking *bureaucracy*. Thompson et al., looking at the phenomenon both in the United States and in Britain, have referred to the same bifurcation, using the slightly awkward terms "sects" and "castes," the former being voluntary activist groups campaigning against smoking, the latter various "establishment" groups who have taken up the anti-smoking cause. In the American case, groups such as ASH (Action on Smoking and Health) and GASP (Group Against Smokers' Pollution) represent the movement, while the Office on Smoking and Health represents the anti-smoking cause within the federal government; the bureaucratic aspect of the phenomenon is also represented by nongovernmental agencies such as the American Cancer Society and the American Lung Association in the United States and the Royal College of Physicians in Britain. This distinction, of course, is at first purely formal, but it has significant implications.

The movement groups are, by their very nature, democratic and to some extent charismatic; they live by the enthusiasm of their voluntarily committed membership, and their leaders retain credibility only as long as they can enlist members' enthusiasm. In consequence, this sort of group tends to be highly activist and "single issue" in orientation. By contrast, bureaucracies are hierarchically organized, and authority rests not on charismatic appeal (there are no "members") but on formal credentials. The politics of bureaucracy tend to be cautious, multiple-issue in orientation, and ipso facto more inclined toward the politics of compromise. These characteristics are reflected in the literature emanating from these two camps within the anti-smoking campaign.[4] There are differences in all this between the United States and Britain, but they are of only marginal interest to the matter at hand.

It is, of course, the movement groups that think of anti-smoking in terms of a crusade. Anti-smoking is not only their sole ideological interest, it is the very reason for their existence. Absolutist, aggressive attitudes toward smoking follow logically. By contrast, the bureaucratic agencies concerned with the issue are *also* concerned with many other issues; they do not depend on smoking or nonsmoking for their existence; and they can afford to be more relaxed about the matter. Indeed, one might make the case that such bureaucratic agencies are not so much interested in the abolition of smoking as in its regulation. It follows that these bureaucratic agencies are more amenable to rational negotiations and compromises with the tobacco industry, while the movement portrays the industry as an evil force with which no morally acceptable dealings are possible. This difference appears to be borne out in the experience of tobacco industry people.

One sociological generalization that is widely supported empirically is that movements, qua movements, do not last.[5] There are several reasons for this; an underlying one is that enthusiasm is a fugitive emotion and a group that wants to survive over time has to find a more durable foundation. Thus, movements either disappear after a while as their adherents take up another, new and more exciting cause, or change into more structured groups which, under modern conditions, means that they become bureaucratized. Thompson et al. have put this in their own terms by saying that sects become castes. One would, therefore, hypothesize as Thompson et al. did that the movement and the bureaucratic components of the anti-smoking phenomenon would, over time, tend to amalgamate.

This hypothesis is strongly supported by what could be observed at the Winnipeg conference. The symbiosis, again as one would expect, is both organizational and ideological. Organizationally, the movement has become itself much more bureaucratized and has entered into complex relationships with the existing bureaucracies, especially in government. Parallel to this development there has been, if not an amalgamation, at least an approximation of the two ideological constellations: the ideology of the movement has become somewhat less aggressive (less "sectarian") as the bureaucratic agencies have officially espoused the anti-smoking point of view. This will be discussed again in the final section of this chapter; it is a development of considerable significance.

The anti-smoking phenomenon is originally and to a large extent still a phenomenon of Western advanced industrial societies, strongest in North America and in Northern Europe (one is almost, at least in a metaphorical sense, tempted to call it a phenomenon of "cultural Protestantism"). In these countries, the anti-smoking movement is one of many voluntary groupings banded together to push a cause, while the bureaucratic agencies that have taken up the anti-smoking cause are embedded in the vast structures of the Western welfare state. In recent years, however, the phenomenon has been internationalized and has become worldwide in its intended strategy. The major vehicle for this internationalization has been the World Health Organization (WHO), not the most prestigious of United Nations' (UN) bodies, but still one with great resources and prestige. The injection of the anti-smoking cause into the UN universe of discourse has had ideological as well as organizational ramifications. The UN is, above all, an organization of Third World governments. Logically enough, the anti-smoking cause has here become entangled with other strands of Third World ideology, notably hostility to multinational corporations. The tobacco industry has thus become targeted as yet another nefarious manifestation of multinational capitalism. There has been an important brake on this development, though—the simple but far-reaching fact that tobacco is an important component in the economies of many Third World societies.

One other way of looking at the internationalization of the anti-smoking campaign is in terms of the vested interests of the Western as well as international bureaucracies involved. Just as international capitalism has created networks of power that transcend national boundaries, so there now exist international networks of bureaucrats. It is tempting to speak here of "welfare state imperialism": just as capitalists have pushed into new areas of the world in search of markets, so do the international bureaucrats—not only those of the UN but also of the agencies of Western governments with concerns for Third World development. Thus, Third World participants at both the Stockholm and the Winnipeg conferences were brought there at the expense of the Scandinavian development agencies. Third World ideologists, in talking about the relation between multinationals and local economic interests, like to use the term "dependency" to describe this relationship. "Welfare state imperialism," it seems, establishes very similar relationships, by which power and privilege are distributed in the Third World by institutions centered elsewhere.

There is another important point to be made about the politics of anti-smoking: its class-specified character. In Western countries, especially in the United States, there are sharp class differences in terms of smoking behavior: lower-income people smoke more than upper-income people. This is important, not just because the anti-smoking movement is largely upper-middle-class in its constituency—that, after all, is characteristic of most organized movements rallied around causes (the upper-middle-class, for reasons that cannot be pursued here, is most prone to enlist in cause-related campaigns). But this particular movement targets a component of lifestyle—one which is particularly concentrated in the working class now. Thus the anti-smoking campaign stands in a long tradition of movements that have sought to impose upper-middle-class values and lifestyles on the lower strata of the class system and to use government power to enforce this imposition. The temperance movement in the United States is a perfect earlier example. That particular experiment was a failure, but it would be rash to predict similar failure in this instance.

The conventional phrase "upper middle class" may no longer suffice in describing the class dynamics in play here. A category used recently is that of the "new class" or "knowledge class." Put simply, this class is composed of all those people who derive their livelihood, not from the production and distribution of material goods and services, but from the production and distribution of symbolic knowledge. These are all the people employed in education, the media, the therapeutic and counseling agencies, and the institutions engaged in planning and administering the "quality of life."

Though obviously a minority of the population, this class exercises considerable power due to its access to the major communication channels of the society. Its interests are often in conflict with those of the old middle class, or "bourgeoisie," which is centered in business and industry. A very important fact about this class is that a major part of it depends directly or indirectly upon government subsidization. Accordingly, it has a strong vested interest in the expansion of government services, especially in the expansion of the welfare state. In this perspective, the anti-smoking campaign is a small part of a much larger process—namely, the process whereby this new class seeks to enlarge its power in society. The wider ramifications of this, however, go beyond the limits of this chapter; the matter of class interests will, however, be taken up once more in the discussion of ideology.

THE IDEOLOGY OF ANTI-SMOKING

The anti-smoking campaign, especially in its movement form, is charged with strong moral sentiment: here is a great evil that must be combatted. Indeed, very strong language is customary in the anti-smoking rhetoric—smoking is supposed to be "the single most important preventable cause of death," an "epidemic," a "pestilence," and the tobacco industry is given such attractive epithets as "merchants of death." In other words, the campaign is strongly normative in tone. As previously indicated, however, normative injunctions make no sense without the appropriate cognitive premises. The most important of these premises—indeed, in some ways the only one—is that smoking is unhealthful. The anti-smoking campaign, therefore, is a battle for health against disease and death.

Within anti-smoking circles, it is assumed that scientific evidence on this matter is conclusive, and that anyone denying this is motivated either by vested interests (the spokesmen for the tobacco industry) or by wishful thinking (recalcitrant smokers). As previously stated, the present analysis must bracket the question of the weight of this scientific evidence. Two observations, however, can be made. First, the evidence is clearly complex, and much of it is statistical in nature; therefore, it is important, from the viewpoint of the anti-smoking cause, that the cognitive presuppositions be frequently and emphatically—even ritually—repeated. Second, there is a considerable degree of defensiveness (one may say, "cognitive defensiveness") about the evidence on *both* sides of the issue; that is, there is nervousness about any data that might throw doubt on one's own position. This is easily understandable in the case of the tobacco industry. The defensiveness of the anti-smoking camp, however, is somewhat more difficult to understand, and, to an outside observer, suggests that the evidence may not be as conclusive as that camp would have one believe. Anti-smoking is a theme that is not isolated; inevitably, it is located within a wider ideological and cultural configuration. This configuration in turn can be located within the class system of Western societies. Further research would be required to make this latter location definitive, but it may be hypothesized that it is primarily in the upper middle class, more narrowly in that portion of it that has been called the new knowledge class. If so, one would expect that anti-smoking will show strong linkages to other ideological themes popular in this class; one would also look for class interests in the matter. As far as the available evidence goes, the linkages are fairly prominent; the matter of class interests must remain more speculative—all one can really do is to point to the *general* interest of this class in the expansion of the welfare state (this general interest being distinct from the specific vested interests of anti-smoking staffs in the promotion of their cause).

The strongest linkage, of course, is with what may be called an overall "health cult." Here health becomes an ultimate, virtually sacral, goal. One should be careful here: if smoking is indeed the peril that these people purport it to be, then it is rational to be against it. What is suggestive, though, is the extravagant claims made in the anti-smoking literature not only against smoking, but, by implication, in favor of a healthful lifestyle liberated from smoking. The point here is that the anti-smoking cause is not alone in this view. Western cultures, with America probably in the lead, are replete with various health movements which all suggest that, if only one does this and avoids that, one will attain a joyful, wholesome, and (above all) long life. The enormously powerful place attained by the medical establishment is a logical consequence of this cultural theme: doctors are the priesthood of this cult, hospitals are the sanctuaries, and government is urgently expected to support and universalize this new "established religion." It is likely that this emphasis on health and longevity is related to secularization—that is, to a decline in plausibility among many people, especially in the knowledge class, of older religious beliefs. Be this as it may, the emotional violence of the anti-smoking movement becomes more understandable in the light of this particular linkage: if health is a quasi-religious goal, then any threat to health must take on a devilish quality. Once more, the analogy with the temperance movement is striking (the liquor industry, of course, played the villain role then).

There are also clear linkages with the environmentalist and the consumer movements. Ecological imagery abounds in the anti-smoking literature. Smoking is a form of pollution; indeed, smokers are polluters. Conversely, the ideal of a "smoke-free world" (now the official slogan of the anti-smoking movement) is portrayed in the imagery of ecological soundness. The linkage with the consumer movement is explicit, and in a number of countries consumer groups have taken up the anti-smoking cause: here is a hazardous product being marketed by allegedly unscrupulous businesses, and consumers band together to combat this danger. In the UN context, as already remarked upon, there is also a linkage with the wider anti-capitalist ideology: the tobacco industry is supposed to be a particularly clear case of the evils of multinational corporations, especially as they allegedly dump harmful products on the innocent peoples of the Third World. This theme is muted in the anti-smoking literature within Western countries, and one can only speculate on the place it has in the thinking of people who belong to a class with generally left-leaning political opinions.

Crusades not only mobilize people against an evil, but they also conjure up utopian visions of a world freed from this particular evil. Some of this, no doubt, is a functional requirement of political mobilization: people will not make much of an effort on behalf of a cause deemed trivial or minor. But one may surmise that in this case more is involved than political tactics. The linkage with the cult of health suggests that there is a real utopia—one that is actually plausible to the people who evoke it rhetorically. As already indicated, it is a utopia of a joyful, long life, a sort of eternal youth. Allied to this is the vision of a life in which risks have been reduced to a minimum—especially by way of government action. The utopia, then, implies not only energetic health and youth, but a careful protection against all threats to the same by a benevolent and powerful government. One senses a certain contradiction here, a strange symbiosis of liberationism and hypochondria. But then utopias have never been exercises in logic.

There is one more very interesting ideological point to be made. At least in terms of Anglo-Saxon political culture, there is the general assumption and value that individuals have the right to do whatever they want unless they harm others; while government is obligated to protect one individual against the harm that others might do to him, it is not the function of government to protect an individual against himself. This political value creates an obvious problem for the anti-smoking campaign: after all, people smoke voluntarily and, if they become ill in consequence, they only harm themselves. It is precisely this logic that lies behind the campaigns to "decriminalize" drug abuse, sexual deviance among consenting adults, and other "victimless crimes." The anti-smoking movement, however, is precisely intent on (so to speak) "criminalizing" smoking—at least to the extent of increasingly "stigmatizing" it (the term is actually used in anti-smoking literature). The strategy, quite overtly, is to progressively stigmatize smoking, segregating the smoker in all public places, and eventually to eliminate smoking as a socially acceptable custom.

How is this to be made politically palatable? The answer is clear: by suggesting that smoking harms, not only the smoker, but various categories of "innocent bystanders." For this reason, there are three pivotal issues in the anti-smoking campaign: the issue of "passive smoking," the issue of "children," and the issue of "social costs." "Passive smoking" is the term (a very imaginative one) used to describe the claimed effect of an individual's smoking on others in his or her immediate environment. The anti-smoking literature uses two arguments in this connection: that passive smoking is an annoyance and that it actually causes disease. The former is a point not dependent on scientific evidence; undoubtedly there are people irritated by smoke and they can be mobilized to insist on their right to be freed of this irritation in public places. The second argument is based on rather sparse and apparently disputed evidence to the effect that, for example, spouses of smokers are more susceptible to a number of diseases.

Whatever the state of the scientific evidence, the issue of passive smoking is important for the anti-smoking demand that smoking be at least segregated if not banned in public places, which increasingly is so defined as to include the workplace. Children, of course, are "innocent bystanders" par excellence. Therefore, the alleged harm of smoking to children is much emphasized in the literature (again, this involves passive smoking as well as children smoking themselves). It is interesting that in some of the literature the term "children" includes all teenagers. Contrast this with the terminology employed by advocates of abortion: a sixteen-year-old will be a "young woman" if she seeks an abortion; here she appears as a "child" if she smokes. There is also much emphasis on the alleged harm to fetuses ("unborn children," as prolife advocates might put it) from the smoking of their mothers.

The most ample, and elegant, extension of the notion of the "innocent bystander" is undertaken by means of the concept of "social costs." Here we all become "innocent bystanders." The concept refers to any costs accruing to society as a whole from the actions of individuals. For example, it is argued that an individual driver who fails to buckle up his safety belt and is seriously injured in an accident because of this failure harms not only himself but society as a whole, because others have to pay more to take care of his medical costs or, if he dies, to support his family. Thus, everyone's insurance or tax rates will go up, and society may also be partially or totally deprived of his own productive contribution. The same argument is made here in the case of the smoker. To buttress this argument, allegedly scientific econometric calculations are brought forth to show the aggregate costs of smoking to society. Not surprisingly, the tobacco industry has been parading its own calculations to demonstrate what its elimination would cost society. Whatever the merits of these competing econometrics, the concept of "social costs" is very useful to the anti-smoking movement in calling for government interventions in what most people still think of as an area of private behavior.

FROM STOCKHOLM TO WINNIPEG

The anti-smoking movement has been around for many years now. It has its veterans, its hero figures (such as Sir George Godber of England), even its martyrs (such as Joseph Califano, former head of the U.S. Department of Health, Education and Welfare, supposedly driven from his post because of his opposition to smoking). When anti-smoking veterans meet, they have common battles to reminisce about and common biographical reference points to recognize each other by. The WHO conferences, meeting in four-year intervals, are important as reference points of this sort, signposts for the progress of the movement. It is, therefore, appropriate to conclude this chapter by a comparison of the Stockholm and Winnipeg conferences (1979 and 1983).

There were, of course, considerable continuities. One significant change was in the relative emphasis on scientific information and advocacy techniques. The Stockholm program contained a larger number of scientific papers; the Winnipeg program was dominated by "how to" sessions—how to organize campaigns, how to lobby, and so on. The implication is clear: the scientific evidence is all in; the agenda now is a practical one. There continues to be a bifurcation between movement and bureaucratic elements within the anti-smoking camp, but the impression obtained is one of much greater amalgamation. In striking support of the thesis presented earlier by Thompson et al., what has emerged now is a sort of international anti-smoking conglomerate. Bureaucrats from governmental and international agencies happily spout the rhetoric of the movement. More important, the various movement groups appear to have become much more professionalized. Their staffs appear to be much more technically competent, matter-of-fact in their approach to strategy, and exhibit remarkable political know-how. One might sum all this up by saying that the anti-smoking movement presented itself as having come of age at Winnipeg. It is no longer a small voluntary crusade fighting against the odds for its cause, but a large and self-confident array of organizations enjoying wide support from government and other prestigious institutions.

Another interesting validation of the Thompson thesis comes from a shift in tactics. Thompson et al. had concluded from their content analysis that the anti-smoking "sects" stressed a punitive approach to smokers, while the "castes" stressed health and adopted a more benign attitude toward smokers, seeing them as victims rather than villains. Therefore, as "sects become castes" (in our terminology, as the movement becomes bureaucratized), one would expect that the rhetoric within the movement groups would also become more positive and benign. This is exactly what came out at Winnipeg. Vilification was pretty much limited to the tobacco industry. The approach to smokers, recommended in paper after paper, was benevolent, "user-friendly." In Stockholm the favored "educational" tool still appeared to be fear—images of people coughing their lungs out, and the like. Winnipeg was aglow with imagery of healthy, young people cavorting in blissful surroundings, and the like. In the words of one speaker, the goal should be not frightening people but "selling a lifestyle." Nonsmoking, in other words, is to be presented as part and parcel of a desirable lifestyle. Some of this new imagery was literally visual, through films, TV programs, and posters; it also permeated the verbal presentations.

There is a curious aspect to this tactical shift. The shift is, in effect, from an ascetic to a hedonistic stance. Nonsmoking used to be, almost by definition, abstemious, while smoking, by contrast, was always suggestive of enjoyment, relaxation, living well. Needless to say, the latter imagery has been very prominent in tobacco advertising. The new lifestyle approach of the anti-smoking movement expropriates, as it were, the hedonistic theme for its own ends. It remains to be seen how successful this shift will be.

Two new themes surfaced in the Winnipeg program—feminism and religion. There was one very well-attended session led by a British feminist and anti-smoking activist which tried to define smoking as a women's issue. This was not altogether easy, not only because the feminist movement has until now shown little interest in the subject, but because data indicate that women smoke more as they enter the labor force—placing the anti-smoking feminist in an ideological double bind. The religion session was poorly attended and probably of little significance, except for one point: the discussion of data indicating that anti-smoking has become an important emphasis of fundamentalist movements in various Muslim countries. An Egyptian physician who served as chairman of the session expressed the opinion that anti-smoking might become an important cause for the "Muslim masses." If he is right, and given the strength of Islamic fundamentalism in large portions of the globe, this could become significant in the near future.

As it presented itself in Winnipeg, the anti-smoking movement is confident in itself, its future prospects, and its ultimate victory. One may be skeptical as to whether ultimate victory is ever possible for this kind of cause. It remains true that the movement can look back on impressive successes, both in the decline in smoking in Western countries (outside the West, to its chagrin, the story is very different) and in the increasing willingness of government to take measures against smoking as well as against the tobacco industry. Official pronouncements of the movement confidently refer to further steps in the direction of the situation already existing in several Scandinavian countries (the promised land of the movement) where, as was repeatedly and proudly stated, smoking is well on the way to being a disreputable activity engaged in by consenting adults in private.

There is much reason for giving credence to this confidence. One growing problem in Western countries, however, may well be the aforementioned class distribution of both smoking and anti-smoking. The working classes of Western societies have shown strong resistance to the imposition of upper-middle-class values in other areas of life, and they may show comparable resistance to the anti-smoking campaign. As long as Western societies are democracies, this may mean political problems for the movement. A further problem may be the growing sentiment in the same countries that government regulation over the lives of individuals has gone too far. In both these problem areas the prospects of the anti-smoking phenomenon would seem to be linked to the prospects of the new knowledge class, which is its principal protagonist. To the extent that this class succeeds in consolidating and expanding its position in society, especially via the mechanisms of the welfare state, the future of the anti-smoking cause will indeed be bright.

NOTES

1. "Gilgamesh on the Washington Shuttle," *Worldview,* November 1977.
2. Michael Thompson et al., "The Political Culture of Anti-Smoking Groups," unpublished study, Institute for Policy and Management Research, 1979.
3. See Peter L. Berger and Thomas Luckman, *The Social Construction of Reality* (Garden City, N.J.: Doubleday, 1966), and Peter L. Berger, Brigitte Berger, and Mansfreid Kellner, *The Homeless Mind: Modernization and Consciousness* (New York: Random House, 1973).
4. Thompson et al. engaged in a content analysis of these materials. See their "Political Culture."
5. Max Weber developed this idea in his well-known theory of the "routinization of charisma."

5

A New Prohibition?: An Essay on Drinking and Smoking in America*

Mark Edward Lender

PROHIBITION'S MODERN PARALLEL

Prohibition took root early in the United States. It flowed logically from the ideology of the Revolutionary generation, which fostered the ideal of a republic blessed with virtuous citizens and cleansed of Old World corruptions. This desire to build a pristine new order led easily to perfectionism, an absolutist moral outlook which took full flower in the reform movements of the early nineteenth century. To a major extent, the perfectionist world view lay behind National Prohibition and, ultimately, much of the anti-smoking crusade of the 1990s.

American reform has always encompassed a large measure of charity and benevolence. Prohibitionists, including temperance and anti-tobacco activists, have cared genuinely and deeply about the well-being of their fellow citizens. Ultimately, however, issues such as smoking and drinking became (and remain) symbolic evils that served as targets for movements with much broader social and political agendas. Many reformers, following the dictates of perfectionist logic, have displayed a marked aversion to compromise or moderation. Rather, they have preferred their own anti-pluralist vision of the good society—a society predicated on common standards and behaviors.

*This work was undertaken with a grant from the Brown & Williamson Tobacco Corporation, for which I want to express my appreciation. A number of colleagues provided helpful criticisms of my various drafts, and in particular I would like to thank Penny Booth Page, at Rutgers University, and Jack Kamerman, Mary Lewis, and Jacki Walker, at Kean College of New Jersey, for their comments. I would also like to thank Diana Dean, at the University of Houston, for her invaluable research assistance.

The reform faithful have seldom brooked opposition lightly. Indeed, they have tended to demonize those accused of impeding the perfectionist agenda: if opponents stood in the way of virtue and "progress," they were evil. In the past, the temperance movement had frequently characterized drinkers and the alcohol beverage industry this way; now, smokers and the tobacco industry increasingly are accorded similar treatment. In the perfectionist view, one cannot morally obstruct the abolition of social evil. In short, prohibitionism was—and, I think, *is*—a serious business, with implications reaching far beyond whether or not someone could find a legal drink or buy a cigarette. Prohibition is about the nature of society and about who determines that nature.

America's defining experience with prohibition occurred from 1920 to 1933, the era of National Prohibition. The "noble experiment," as Herbert Hoover termed it, sought the abolition of the manufacture and sale of beverage alcohol and, by implication, of drinking itself. Important as it was, however, the "liquor question" was only part of the story. Prohibitionists also targeted tobacco. Indeed, the movements to abolish alcohol and tobacco actually were intertwined as part of the same perfectionist crusade.

Coercion in the Guise of Policy

There are also modern parallels to all of this. While alcohol remains a real social issue, certainly a compelling phenomenon is the recent movement to restrict the use of tobacco products. Americans are witnessing a surge of anti-smoking sentiment, and feelings are strong enough to raise the prospect of government intervention—and perhaps even coercion—in matters of personal conduct considered beyond the reach of political policy since the repeal of National Prohibition in 1934.

With apologies to George Santayana and Thomas Carlyle, history does not repeat itself. But it can be instructive, and it will be my intention to use the history of prohibition to draw attention to certain of the more important aspects of today's debate over smoking in America. I do not believe that the similarities between the anti-liquor and anti-smoking reformers are coincidental. If I am right, then the question of prohibition, with all of its wider social and ideological implications, is as interesting and germane to the late 1990s as it was a century ago.

TEMPERANCE ALL OVER AGAIN

The question of a new prohibition is not academic. It is quite real. No one (at least no one other than fringe political groups) has proposed another constitutional amendment to outlaw alcohol or tobacco products; nor has anyone seriously suggested banning all smoking or drinking. But during the 1980s, and into the early 1990s, popular concern over aspects of drinking behavior and smoking have raised serious policy issues.

Alcohol was the first to draw heavy fire. During the 1980s, the personal and public health implications of alcoholism and, especially, drunken driving provoked a number of legislative initiatives. Prodded by such grass-roots pressure groups as Mothers Against Drunk Driving, state and federal authorities variously took steps to raise the minimum age for the legal purchase of alcohol, enact host-liability laws, and provide for stricter curbs against alcohol-related mayhem on the roads. It was an effective campaign for public sympathy and awareness.

At the same time, much of the public changed its drinking habits. With minimal legal prompting, many Americans simply began drinking less alcohol. While available statistics (as of 1986) are insufficient for precise comparisons with prior decades, it is clear that alcohol beverage consumption leveled off nationally. At least one survey (conducted for *Time* magazine in 1985) reported that, among Americans eighteen or older, only 67 percent drank alcohol beverages, one of the lowest estimates in some time. A third of those polled indicated that they were drinking less than they had before, while "only 6 percent said they were drinking more."[1]

Yuppies Embrace Temperance

There is no simple explanation of these phenomena, and we can only speculate on why Americans moderated their drinking. In the early 1980s, the personal health and self-image concerns of young professionals ("yuppies") may have played a role. Concerned with fitness and "looking good," some were supposedly leery of the health complications or calories associated with excessive drinking. "There's no such thing as a fat yuppie," one wag noted in *Time*. Whatever their motivations, most Americans took an increasingly dim view of heavy drinking. Fewer enjoyed "happy hour" or the three-martini lunch, while many businesses discouraged any drinking at all during the working day. To be sure, many heavy drinkers altered their behavior not at all, but their conduct and its consequences now attracted more critical comment. Attitudes had indeed changed.[2]

All of this hardly constituted a new prohibition crusade. Yet, for the first time in almost fifty years, there was enough concern over alcohol to attract considerable attention in the national media. A surprising number of journalists discerned the rise of a nascent temperance movement or "neoprohibitionism." In 1985, *Time* devoted a cover story to the issue, asking whether Americans were not embarking on a "new temperance" crusade.

More subtly, columnist George Will suggested that concerns over drinking behavior reflected a return to more conservative and communitarian social values. Dwight Heath, an anthropologist, saw a growing public interest in "law and order" behind some of the focus on alcohol.[3] Whatever the explanation, the fact was that reasonable observers saw a stiffening public posture toward alcohol-related problems, and a willingness to use legal remedies accordingly.

Michael Gartner went farther still. The title of his column in *USA Today* said it all: "Bring back Prohibition." He noted the dubious history of enforced abstinence in the 1920s, yet he insisted that "something must be done." The destructiveness of alcohol abuse had reached unbearable levels, Gartner held, and only government intervention offered any chance of relief.[4] Gartner's was a minority position. But one need not agree with him to conclude that, during the 1980s and early 1990s, prohibition had reentered the vocabulary of serious public discourse.

A Debate Rekindled by Government Reports

If anything, the debate over smoking has brought the prohibition issue into sharper focus. Many of the health risks associated with smoking have been common knowledge for over a century. Indeed, even as it crusaded against alcohol, the old temperance movement had directed considerable fire at tobacco; and between 1895 and 1927, fifteen states had tried to ban cigarettes on health and moral grounds. But current concerns about smoking are a more recent phenomenon. By the 1940s, polls indicated that perhaps half of all smokers thought that cigarettes were unhealthy, and by the 1950s, as much as ninety percent of the American public was aware of claims that smoking caused lung cancer.[5] Still, perhaps half of the American populace puffed on.

But the 1964 report of Surgeon General Luther Terry began a sea-change in attitudes and in smoking behavior. The report explicitly identified smoking as a cause of lung cancer in men and firmly established the dangers of tobacco in the popular mind. Since then, subsequent reports have further stirred popular concern. In 1986, Surgeon General C. Everett Koop alleged that second-hand smoke causes lung cancer in nonsmokers, and a 1993 Environmental Protection Agency report classified tobacco smoke as a class-A carcinogen.[6] The influence of these reports on public awareness would be hard to overestimate; virtually no one growing up in America since the turn of the century could seriously claim not to understand—or at least to have heard about—the health risks associated with smoking.

Behavior Sways Under Social Pressure

Legislative and regulatory actions to control smoking paralleled rising popular concern. Through the early 1980s, relatively mild initiatives at the federal, state, and local levels focused on restricting sales to minors; placing warning labels on tobacco products; and providing nonsmoking sections in aircraft, public buildings, and restaurants. At the same time, government and private groups maintained a vigorous public education effort on the hazards of tobacco. None of these measures was a step toward prohibition, but they gripped public attention.

Beginning in 1964, and most dramatically between 1974 and 1991, the number of smokers in America has declined by half, to approximately 40 million people, or 26 percent of the population. Though at any given time the actual numbers might vary within different groups, the point is clear: the vast majority of Americans no longer smoke, and the unpopularity of smoking has steadily increased. Only among high school seniors and African Americans, for example, has the proportion of smokers edged upward since 1993.[7] Most of the nation, including most former smokers, voluntarily elected abstinence from tobacco.

Despite the substantial reductions in smoking, however, many anti-smoking reformers remain unsatisfied. They object to all smoking, and especially to smoking among the young. In addition, they find alarming the fact that the number of smokers has stabilized instead of continuing a progressive decline. The reformers are legion and articulate, although their arguments have only come into boldest relief in mid-1994. In virtually simultaneous attacks on the tobacco industry, Dr. David Kessler, commissioner of the federal Food and Drug Administration, and Congressman Henry Waxman of California captured national headlines. Kessler, in a well-orchestrated media blitz, charged tobacco companies with manipulating nicotine levels in cigarettes in order to deliberately assure the addiction of consumers. "It is our understanding," Kessler alleged, "that manufacturers commonly add nicotine to cigarettes to deliver specific amounts of nicotine." His goal was to extend FDA regulatory authority over tobacco, which would then be dealt with as a dangerous drug.[8]

Waxman's agenda was every bit as ambitious. In a series of congressional hearings, he also charged that manufacturers had covered up the addictive nature of nicotine; Waxman then rode roughshod over tobacco executives when they tried to explain manufacturing and marketing practices. His objective was enactment of the proposed Smoke-Free Environment Act, certainly the most stringent congressional effort against tobacco. it would mandate smoke-free areas in all buildings entered by more than ten people per day; the alternative for building owners would be fines of up to $5,000 per day.[9]

(While Waxman was probably unaware of it, the "five" and "ten" aspects of the Smoke-Free Act—the $5,000 and ten-person provisions—struck a note of historical irony. In 1929, in a virtual last-gasp effort to enforce National Prohibition, Congress passed the draconian Jones Act. It set penalties of five years and $10,000 for most first-time offenders of the prohibition laws—and thus became popularly known as the "Jones 5 & 10 Law." Most Americans hated it. No doubt Waxman would find little comfort in the analogy.[10])

Kessler and Waxman, it should be noted, were not working alone. Other federal initiatives were fully in accord with theirs, if not so boldly in the headlines. Proposals to discourage smoking through heavy taxation, bans in the workplace, the schools, and at public functions, further restrictions on sales and by various other means all had (and still have) their proponents. In a demonstration symbolic of the entire modern crusade, President Clinton and his wife, Hillary Rodham Clinton, banned smoking from the White House. It was not the first such gesture on the part of a First Lady: over a century earlier, Lucy Webb Hayes, wife of President Rutherford B. Hayes and a staunch temperance advocate, stopped serving alcohol at White House functions. Instead, guests received lemonade, earning her immortality among reformers as "Lemonade Lucy."[11]

Even Opponents Are Surprised by Bitterness

How far, then, are reformers willing to go in their war against tobacco? Unsurprisingly, representatives of the tobacco industry fear the worst, with some claiming that anti-smoking advocates are pursuing the *de facto* prohibition of cigarettes. If we can discount the fears of the tobacco companies, however, we must also concede that feelings are not confined to the industry, or even to smokers.

In fact, the bitter rhetoric of the debate has raised eyebrows among even some nonsmokers and public health advocates. Dr. David C. Lewis, editor of the *Brown University Digest of Addiction Theory and Application,* and a long-standing foe of smoking, has seen a drift toward zealotry in the 1990s crusade. Wondering "how much will we rely on prohibitionist solutions" in the anti-tobacco reform, Lewis cautioned against repeating the mistakes of a century ago. "Our challenge," he warned his readers, "is to find ways to preserve public health without resorting to failed prohibition strategies."[12]

Richard Klein, author of *Cigarettes Are Sublime* (1993), has noted that cigarettes are indeed bad for individual and public health. But the developments of the early 1990s, he insisted, offered a "direct analogy" to the events surrounding National Prohibition. In Klein's view, the legal abolition of smoking would only recreate the societal turmoil that accompanied efforts to enforce the Volstead Act.[13]

The Ring of an Earlier Rhetoric

As it did when alcohol came under fire in the 1980s, the press again raised the prohibition issue. In April 1994, *U.S. News & World Report* ran a cover story that framed the question bluntly: "Should Cigarettes Be Outlawed?" The same month, *Time* ran a similar lead: "Threatening to snuff out smoking for good, the crusade against tobacco shifts into high gear." With some hyperbole, the magazine asked if "the crusade" had "turned into a witch hunt."[14] Headlines, of course, often play to the most dramatic aspects of a public issue. Yet the media had recognized a significant point, and repeated coverage made it part of the public question: even if a de jure prohibition was not the goal of many opponents of smoking, many reformers did want to see its eventual demise—no matter what individual smokers thought—and much of their rhetoric clearly had the ring of the old anti-liquor crusaders.

However, even if (for the sake of argument) we might discount the possibility of a latter-day prohibition of alcohol or tobacco, another issue remains: there seems little denying the persistence of a prohibitionist mentality in many American reformers. Putting the matter in its simplest terms, there are those who, upon deciding that a substance or a behavior was harmful, would ban it. In the cases of smoking or drinking, not only would they give up the practices themselves, they would take action to compel the rest of society to follow suit. In the past, such a decision implied a broader social agenda than the abolition of specific problems. Rather, the elimination of particular evils supposedly would open the doors to a better world—or, more precisely, a better world as defined by the reformer—which can be quite a different matter.

Does this kind of thinking lie behind some of the reform activity of the 1990s? At least in the case of smoking, there are some suggestive hints that it does. Dr. Faith T. Fitzgerald, of the University of California at Davis Medical Center, is distinctly uneasy in this regard. As she sees it, one of the chief problems is the concept of "wellness." The term, which combines physiological and psychological health in a wider context of "social well being," has grown in popularity since the 1980s. Wellness promises "potential perfection," and it has become a serious matter with increasing popular acceptance of social responsibility for health care.

Beware a Mandate to Control Behavior

When individual health becomes a social responsibility, Fitzgerald points out, then conduct detrimental to personal health, by definition, becomes socially irresponsible. If society has to pay for the costs, then "failures of self-care," such as drinking and smoking, become "crimes against society." Fitzgerald warned against "developing a zealotry" that could lead to a "mandate to control people's behavior for the sake of their mortal bodies." Such a step would be perverse, she concluded, "in a nation founded on the belief that one should not legislate behavior even for the sake of the immortal soul."[15] This would be a wide social agenda indeed.

Fitzgerald is no Cassandra. Some anti-tobacco activists have argued their case on precisely the social grounds she feared. Professor John Banzhaf, who teaches law at George Washington University, has long tried to use the courts as agents of social change. Capable and aggressive, Banzhaf has been a scourge of the tobacco industry, but he has readily conceded that his interests in smoking are only part of a much wider agenda for social change. The war on cigarettes is only an opening gambit.[16]

Dr. Jonathan Fielding, a former Massachusetts health commissioner and currently (1994) a professor of public health at UCLA, takes a similar view. Smoking is dividing America along class lines, Professor Fielding has claimed. Most smokers are poorer and less educated than nonsmokers, a situation he has labeled wrong in and of itself. "In a country where we have too many things that divide people," he charged, "this is another thing dividing us."[17] Thus has the cigarette become an affront to social justice.

Ardent Spirits, Republican Ardor

There is ample precedent for Dr. Fielding's perspective. American reform has a long history of using specific issues or, more precisely, the battle against particular evils, to advance a broader vision of social reform. If the abolition of smoking, for example, were to contribute to "wellness" for all, or to lessening the gap between rich and poor, generations of earlier crusaders would have recognized the strategy. Given its contemporary resurgence, however, it is worth asking where this linkage of reform and social idealism got its start.

In fact, it dated from the birth of the republic. Until the late eighteenth century, few voices had challenged the problems of alcohol abuse. But the Revolution changed all of that. To a generation concerned over social stability and virtue, few things seemed to have more disruptive potential than intemperance. This unsteadying fear lay behind America's classic early stricture of drunkenness: *An Inquiry into the Effects of Ardent Spirits on the Human Mind and Body* (1784), by Dr. Benjamin Rush of Philadelphia. Rush commanded attention. An ardent republican, he had been active in Revolutionary politics, signed the Declaration of independence as a Pennsylvania delegate, and served for a time as a surgeon general of the Continental army. Rush enjoyed a reputation as perhaps the new nation's foremost physician and one of its most influential social reformers. Indeed, he was arguably the key man in the history of prohibition: for the next two centuries, crusades against alcohol and tobacco played out largely within the medical and political contexts he had defined in the 1780s and 1790s.[18]

Rush had decried the use of hard liquor for years, but his masterpiece was the *Inquiry*. The tract was radical. It was the first serious work to describe alcoholism as a disease, and it insisted that alcohol was addicting. Rush described a subtle but inexorable addiction process; once an "appetite" for spirits had become fixed, the victim was helpless to resist. In fact, Rush deserves major credit for establishing the modern paradigm of addiction, which has survived into the 1990s.[19]

Menace of the Drunken Voter

Rush's ideological concerns were equally significant. He saw in drinking what others had only hinted at: alcohol problems threatened civic virtue and the life of the republic itself. Allow drunkenness to flourish, Rush cautioned, and the Revolution would have been fought in vain. The nation would soon "be governed by men chosen by intemperate and corrupted voters," men who would rule through demagoguery instead of virtue. Worse, the Almighty would never look favorably on a people who preferred to drink whiskey rather than build a golden edifice dedicated to liberty and a moral republican order.

Such a threat cried out for a vigorous response. To avert calamity, Rush advocated not only personal abstinence from hard liquor, but the adoption of strict communal sanctions against drunkards. Drunkards, he warned, were the antithesis of virtuous citizens; they were incapable of managing their own affairs and certainly could not be responsible enough to vote. He also urged that "good men of every class unite and besiege" their leaders with demands for fewer taverns and heavy taxes on "ardent spirits" as further means to stem the tide of intemperance.[20] For Rush, then, the stakes of temperance involved far more than drinking.

Vices That Corrupted the Virtuous

Nor, we should note, did Rush confine his attention to alcohol. He also considered tobacco an "intoxicant" and felt that smoking and snuff presented the young republic with an evil only somewhat less dangerous than drunkenness. In 1798, over a decade after he published the *Inquiry,* Rush brought out his *Observations upon the Influence of the Habitual Use of Tobacco upon Health, Morals and Property.* Smoking and chewing, he exclaimed, were disgusting practices, as dangerously habituating as alcohol and as damaging to health. Equally horrid was the link between tobacco and alcohol; drinkers, Rush held, were usually smokers as well. Both vices were antisocial, reason enough to warrant the obloquy of the virtuous. Significantly, Rush urged reformers to consider drinking and smoking in the same light.[21]

Finally, in assessing the impact of Benjamin Rush, it is impossible to overemphasize one point. For Rush, and for many after him, the implications of addiction were as much matters of politics and ideology. His various warnings about the dangers of "craving" and "habituation" were based on what he thought was good medicine; he placed on record the addictive natures of alcohol and tobacco. But he used those arguments vociferously to make a political point. The future welfare of the republic, Rush believed, depended heavily upon how vigorously succeeding generations would grapple with his message.

DRINKERS, SMOKERS, AND PASSIVE REFORM

As the nineteenth century dawned, the drinking habits that had so worried Dr. Rush continued unabated. In fact, the years spanning the 1790s and 1830s probably saw the heaviest drinking in American history. Consumption estimates tell the story: from an annual average of 5.8 gallons of absolute alcohol per capita (for people aged fifteen or older) in 1790, mean absolute alcohol intake rose to 7.1 gallons a year by 1810. With minor fluctuations, it remained at about that level through the 1830s.[22] American drinking had reached unparalleled levels.

Drinking at such levels provoked a deepening chorus of alarm. Significantly, these criticisms took their place amid a widening context of national reform, and, during the early 1800s, any condition labeled a social evil generated an effort to set it right. Temperance, however, which included a vocal anti-tobacco component, became one of the most popular causes. By 1826, after a series of local reform initiatives, the American Society for the Promotion of Temperance (the basis of the later American Temperance Union) had emerged as the spearhead of a national anti-liquor crusade. Leadership rested firmly in the hands of socially prominent clergy and laymen, whose proclaimed purpose was the reformation of the nation through abstinence from ardent spirits. The early temperance movement, then, was not a prohibitionist crusade.

Temperance to Total Abstinence

By the late 1830s, however, the movement was evolving. The fear of alcohol addiction, the enslavement to drink that Rush had described, was instrumental in the process. The change was crucial: temperance was no longer abstinence from distilled beverages; gradually, it came to mean total abstinence. In 1836, a national temperance convention formally endorsed total abstinence as the movement's official position. There was still some resistance among the rank and file, but by the end of the decade the issue was virtually closed. Temperance reform, for the first time, had gone fully "dry." Yet total abstinence did not translate immediately into prohibition. Compulsory reform would come, but for the time being, most reformers were content with "moral suasion." That is, they expected appeals to morality, common sense, civic virtue—anything but government intervention—to persuade citizens to lay down the bottle voluntarily. Personal choice was still the key.

Equally remarkable was the extent to which moral suasion succeeded. In 1835, almost a generation before America saw its first prohibition laws, temperance leaders estimated that two million people had renounced distilled liquor (causing some four thousand distilleries to close), while nearly a quarter of a million persons had become total abstainers. Membership in temperance organizations had climbed to about 1.5 million. Thousands of others, without any temperance affiliation or signing any pledge, also moderated their drinking. The cumulative effect sent national liquor consumption plummeting. From a high of just over seven gallons of absolute alcohol per capita annually in 1830, consumption estimates fell to slightly more than three gallons by 1840—the largest ten-year drop in American history.[23] Drinking, in sum, no longer enjoyed its traditional status.

Drinking Diminished Well before Prohibition

The example of bringing the worst excesses of drinking behavior under control *before* legal prohibition is worth noting. Millions of Americans, having accepted that drinking was a national problem, responded by *voluntarily* abstaining or by moderating consumption. This occurred without prohibitory laws, without paying for any governmental enforcement effort, and without violating libertarian democratic values. Drinking problems did not disappear, but they were significantly reduced, and society was not burdened by a governmental effort to compel uniform standards of public and personal behavior. In light of subsequent events, one can only speculate on the wisdom of some of the compulsory reform efforts that came shortly thereafter.

Partisans in the modern debate over tobacco might learn from the nineteenth-century experiment with moral suasion. Arguably, the fates of drinking in the mid-1830s and smoking since the 1960s are comparable. After thirty years of warnings about the health hazards inherent in smoking, millions of Americans concluded that the risks were not worth any enjoyment derived from tobacco. They stopped smoking, or never started, based on personal choice. No enforcement effort—unless one includes warning labels on cigarette packages and restrictions on advertising—compelled individual action. As in the 1830s, the major reductions in "problem behavior," in the cases of smoking as well as drinking, occurred before restrictive legislation or any compulsory social policy.

PROHIBITION'S GOAL: ABSOLUTE PERFECTION

During the 1830s and 1840s, however, as in the 1990s, reform was adopting a more zealous tone. For many, the mitigation of social problems was no longer enough. Ultimately, reformers set their sights on "legal suasion"—that is, on legislated prohibition. The step marked a crucial juncture in American history. It not only put reform on a new and more strident course, but it broke a path for future generations of reformers. The early prohibitionists pioneered the absolutist posture that has characterized much of American reform well into the twentieth century, including much of the modern anti-smoking crusade.

There was a powerful logic at work in prohibition, one which blended Rush's addiction theory with perfectionist reform. If a substance was addictive, then by definition, as legions of reformers explained, there was no room for moderation. It could lead only to personal and social ruin. Moreover, a zealous perfectionism argued that mere improvement was not enough; problems must be eliminated in order to fully reform—to "perfect"—society.

A Crusade to Cleanse Society

Over time, perfectionism would prove a remarkably durable aspect of American reform. There always had been this element in republicanism, the various reform movements, and in the evangelical religious sects of the antebellum years; but perfectionist sentiments attained real influence in prohibitionism.

The sense of mission would allow no halfway measures: if alcohol, tobacco, or anything else was evil, then citizens had a duty to abolish it in defense of the common good. If society was to be cleansed, prohibition seemed necessary and logical; and abstinence, once a voluntary personal decision, would now come through legislation to save society as a whole. Perfectionism helped put coercion in the arsenal of reform.

Tobacco Was a Smaller Target

While alcohol was at the center of the prohibitionist storm, tobacco played a smaller, but still revealing role. Following Rush's lead, a number of other reformers denounced snuff and smoking with genuine enthusiasm. They had a litany of indictments, which virtually repeated complaints against alcohol: tobacco use was addicting; it impoverished the smoker or "snuffer," it was a poison; it caused cancer; it induced dissolution and dissipation; it was an affront to God and to society. A Dr. Joel Shew found no fewer than eighty-seven conditions linked to tobacco, including hemorrhoids.[24] Other physicians, reporting in the quite respectable *Journal of Health,* announced that tobacco was a "narcotic" that frequently drove smokers and snuff users to drink. Indeed, reformers often charged that tobacco was so caustic to the throat that water could not soothe the irritation; the smoker had to use alcohol to deaden the pain.[25] In sum, the anti-tobacco crusaders proclaimed the weed an evil as dangerous as the demon rum.

Perhaps the most zealous antebellum crusader was the Reverend George

Trask, of Fitchburg, Massachusetts. Trask was a former smoker, "a tremulous, haggard clergyman, on the verge of the grave." The reverend described himself as a "radical" bent on the destruction of the "enormous evil" of tobacco.[26] In 1852, borrowing directly from the temperance movement, Trask even circulated an anti-tobacco pledge in which subscribers resolved to abstain from all forms of tobacco use "totally and forever."[27] Later, he became editor of the *Anti-Tobacco Journal,* which assiduously reported on any and all efforts against tobacco. The man was nothing if not dedicated.

Trask's most famous publication was the widely-distributed *Thoughts and Stories on Tobacco for American Lads, or Uncle Toby's Anti-Tobacco Advice to His Nephew Bill Bruce* (1852), in which he warned his fictive young relative of the dangers of "the filthy habit." Presented in the morality-play format of temperance fiction, "Uncle Toby" offered a revealing glimpse of the reform mentality. Trask followed total abstinence doctrine to the letter: tobacco was as addicting as alcohol, and thus moderation had no credence. Progressively, the smoker lost control over tobacco until the weed had enslaved him. Crime, poverty, and broken health followed inexorably. This was only logical, for in Trask's view, alcohol and tobacco were "Siamese Twins"; a cigar, like rum, would turn a boy "drunk as a Toper."[28]

Like their temperance brethren, Trask and most other anti-tobacco reformers also were prohibitionists. By the early 1850s, the small but noisy American Anti-Tobacco Society had concisely stated the reform position: crusaders would "break up a death-like, prevalent stupidity in relation to the evils of tobacco," and "create a public conscience, which, we trust in God, will lead to the removal of so great a curse."[29] Trask agreed, proclaiming that his anti-tobacco efforts were part and parcel of the legislative war against demon rum. Neal Dow, perhaps America's quintessential prohibitionist and the father of "legal suasion," returned the compliment and publicly applauded anti-tobacco reformers as fellow crusaders. Other reformers, including Horace Greeley, Horace Mann, and Edward Norris Kirk issued similar endorsements.[30]

New Voices Based on Old Themes

None of this came as a surprise. Anti-liquor and anti-tobacco sentiments derived from the same ideological roots, and they adopted the same tactics and prohibitionist goals. It is important to note that these were not parallel movements: reformers who fought alcohol and tobacco were part of the same movement. Alcohol, vastly more popular, captured more public (and thus historical) attention; but tobacco had provoked its share of wrath, and it would remain a candidate for more. If the antebellum reform experience had shaped the contours of future attacks on alcohol, it had done the same for tobacco. Indeed, if modern anti-smokers are enthusiastic, they are not original: their battles are a reprise of themes defined generations ago.

Through the 1850s, however, support for prohibition of any sort was often haphazard. Most drys, including anti-tobacco advocates, knew that coerced abstinence was many steps ahead of popular opinion, despite widespread sympathy for more moderate temperance ideas. To press the question too soon, they feared, could provoke an unfavorable reaction, particularly if an unwilling public saw prohibition as an invasion of civil rights. It was a dilemma for drys, but the stakes, a sober republic and all its consequent moral and civil blessings, seemed worth the gamble. Theodore Parker of New England, one of the greatest of the antebellum reformers, admitted that prohibition indeed seemed "an invasion of private rights." But he reasoned that it was "an invasion . . . for the sake of preserving the rights of all."[31] In another age, Congressman Waxman and Dr. Kessler would say much the same thing.

Yet by the early 1850s, the outlook for prohibition had changed. Except for abolition, the temperance crusade had emerged as the most powerful and politically potent antebellum reform effort. In 1846, temperance forces in Maine, under the leadership of Neal Dow, persuaded the legislature to ban the manufacture and sale of distilled liquors. It was a halfway measure, and it lacked penalties sufficient to compel full compliance; but the partial victory was a clear sign of things to come.

Grappling with Political Morality

On the other hand, many political leaders, including some with dry loyalties, remained appalled at the prospect of thrashing out temperance questions in the political arena. There was no national consensus on prohibition, as millions of Americans still prized their right to drink. The possibility existed that a drive for prohibition would evoke determined resistance, further rending a republic already being torn asunder by the slavery question.

This fear proved well founded as opposition appeared on a number of fronts. The beverage industry, formerly respected, fought back in desperation. Brewers counterattacked with genuine hatred, feeling especially wronged. Until the rise of total abstinence, the brewers had considered themselves temperance allies. They saw beer, as Rush had suggested, as a wholesome substitute for ardent spirits. Teetotalism, however, drove them to common cause with the distillers. Immigrants also formed a major opposition block. Initially, the reformers had found considerable sympathy in some ethnic communities; however, when presented with total abstinence, most immigrants clung stubbornly to their wet heritage. Nor did the South have much use for prohibition. The movement never fully died in the slave states, but it declined quickly as Southerners found that many drys also were firm abolitionists. As political and social policy, then, Prohibition was a real problem, destined to upset as many people as it pleased.

Legislators Bowed to Tireless Lobbying

But the prohibitionists were tireless. They incessantly lobbied state legislatures and often allied themselves with other reform factions that sought dry votes for their own ends. As their strength grew, drys commanded the attention, if not the admiration, of major political leaders. Matters came to a head in 1851. Rectifying its ineffectual statute of 1846, Maine passed the nation's first truly comprehensive, and seemingly effective, prohibition law. It was a genuinely historic moment, and dry reformers hailed the Maine Law as the great legislative breakthrough it was.

Temperance workers moved quickly to follow up their victory. In August 1851, another temperance convention issued a battle cry for the passage of Maine Laws throughout the nation. Lobbying at the state level redoubled, and prohibition became the goal of what was now clearly one of the most comprehensive political efforts the nation had ever seen. Massachusetts went dry less than a year later, and Maine Laws next carried the day in Vermont, Minnesota Territory, and Rhode Island (1852), Michigan (1853), Connecticut and Ohio (1854), and in Indiana, New Hampshire, Delaware, Illinois, Iowa, and New York (1855). Similar measures almost won in Wisconsin, Pennsylvania, and New Jersey. In Canada, the provinces of Nova Scotia and New Brunswick also outlawed booze. Such a legislative domino effect is not unlike the march of state and local anti-smoking laws being enacted today.

Politicized morality thus seemed well on its way to rolling back the tide of over two hundred years of American drinking habits. By the mid-1850s, many dry reformers were congratulating themselves on having destroyed the old consensus on drinking as a positive good, and they eagerly looked forward to national prohibition. They were sure that the day was almost at hand when the purified republic would no longer tolerate demon rum anywhere within its borders.

THE PRICE OF PERFECTION

The early reformers had won, but it was a costly and, in some respects, a questionable triumph. During the contests for prohibition, they had claimed the high moral ground, routinely invoking patriotic and religious sentiments as they flayed "King Alcohol" and, to a lesser extent, tobacco. But the struggle had been bitter, and it revealed a grim side of the reformers: in the heat of battle, they proved willing to attack opponents in the most brutal of terms. The tenacity of the opposition had infuriated prohibitionists, and dry frustrations honed a deep invective. One result was the virtual demonization of drinkers and smokers, a sentiment expressed in countless tracts, sermons, broadsides, and lectures. Actual alcoholics were "slaves" to their habit, broken down in health, worthless and corrupted as citizens, and threats to society. Moderate drinkers were *worse* in that they set a bad example that lured others into trouble.[32] In either case, drinkers were not erring brethren; they were an affront to morality and to the social order. There was little to forgive in such miscreants.

Thus the stigma attached to drinking was not just medical; the matter went far beyond questioning the drinker's regard for his own health. Rather, it struck at the individual's status in the community and as a citizen. His behavior made him a threat to everyone, and thus placed him outside the pale of "acceptable" norms. In effect, reformers had successfully defined drinking as deviant behavior and drinkers, therefore, as deviates. This was powerful stuff indeed.

Stigma Erodes the Middle Ground

Exasperation with the liquor industry took reformers down other questionable paths. They were utterly convinced that the liquor industry acted only from the basest of motives. Reformers believed that avarice alone moved liquor men, as well as a disdain for the public good. The only moral course for anyone in the business, they believed, was to resign or close. Some did. But most did not and in fighting for their livelihoods convinced drys that the alcohol beverage industry was leagued in a conspiracy against reform. The "Liquor Power"—the business and its allies—was evil. If drinkers were deviates, then the industry itself was a virtual outlaw.

Such sentiments, whether directed at drinkers or the industry, produced rhetoric to match, and it was hardly calculated to elicit rational (or even polite) debate. Thus the middle ground in the controversy disappeared; neither could see any redeeming features in the other. Invective had replaced discourse, and even civility. Having won their point under such circumstances, prohibitionists were not prepared to be magnanimous in victory. Rather, they saw their new majority status as grounds to compel obedience to the social standards they had fought for. We might call their posture "benign intolerance" out of deference to their sincerity, but it was intolerance nevertheless.

If perfectionists could not see this trait in themselves, others certainly did. Indeed, much earlier, one particularly acute observer had all but predicted it. This was a visiting French aristocrat, Alexis de Tocqueville, whose *Democracy in America* afforded a penetrating look at antebellum society and mores. Tocqueville was impressed with Americans. They were convinced of the "perfectibility of man," he noted, and they had an unparalleled propensity to organize on behalf of causes. In this regard, the burgeoning temperance reform struck him worth watching. "The first time I heard in the United States," he wrote, "that a hundred thousand men had bound themselves publicly to abstain from spirituous liquors, it appeared to me more like a joke than a serious engagement."[33] He soon learned differently. Temperance men would not be content "With drinking water by their own firesides," he predicted; rather, they would join together to convince others of their position. Tocqueville considered this remarkable, an event virtually without precedent in conservative Europe.

"Tyranny of the Majority"

Yet the Frenchman was uneasy with aspects of this reforming zeal. America had relatively few institutional checks on popular passions, he noted, and he was pointed in his observation that majority opinions did not lightly tolerate opposition. In fact, the many were likely to run roughshod over the few, and Tocqueville already had discerned what he considered "formidable barriers around the liberty of opinion." Consequently, he warned of a potential "tyranny of the majority." Such a tyranny could crush liberty as surely as any monarchy. He did not see the threat as particularly serious in the early 1830s, but he maintained "that there is no sure barrier against it."[34] Tocqueville was right; perfectionism had its dark side.

The experience of the 1990s bears comparison, for some of the key characteristics of the early reform movements have endured. Certainly reform has retained much of its zealous aspect. Much of the zeal and self-righteousness of reformers is common to any era. Some of it is even necessary. In part, movements define themselves by their opponents, and demonizing them—as in the cases of smokers and drinkers—is essential in rallying the faithful and in fixing their common identity and purpose. Accordingly, the process of stigmatizing behaviors and individuals has stood the test of time; "demonization" is alive and well, with smokers largely replacing drinkers as the targets of reforming ire. Anti-tobacco advocates have labored mightily to define smoking as a deviant behavior, and many smokers see themselves as an embattled minority (as even some drinkers did during the 1980s).

Nor do modern reformers concede anything to the motives of the opposition. Charges of conspiracy and avarice still dog reform targets. This sort of posturing, an effective tactic in the arsenal of antebellum crusaders, remains a fixture among the zealous. Such anti-smoking champions as Dr. Kessler and Congressman Waxman, for examples, have found it well nigh impossible to see anything but the basest of motives at work in the tobacco industry. There is a significant point here: like the alcohol prohibitionists, many reformers in the 1990s have gone beyond warning of the dangers of the product itself. They have charged manufacturers with deliberately endangering public health and well-being in the advertising and marketing of their product. This they have said in a press campaign carefully orchestrated to influence popular opinion. Neal Dow would have understood the approach and the purpose; American reformers, as Tocqueville noted, have seldom been amateurs in the business of reaching the public. This sense of mission has maintained much of the fire of perfectionism. Given their druthers, many of those who today fight for a "risk free" society would offer opponents as little quarter as their antebellum predecessors.

The Dry Movement Almost Crumbles

There were other lessons as well. The experience of the 1850s also demonstrated the perils of enacting prohibitionist policies without a clear popular mandate. As the 1850s advanced, it became obvious that no such mandate existed; those who prophesied a dry millennium were wrong. In fact, the Maine Laws marked the high tide of temperance influence in the antebellum years, a tide that ebbed quickly with the approach of the Civil War. By the late 1850s, the nation faced a crisis over slavery and the preservation of the Union. Most Americans, including the major political parties, and even some important temperance leaders, increasingly gave the impending sectional struggle a higher priority than they did the battle against alcohol or tobacco. Under the circumstances, dry forces lost much of their hard-won political influence. Also aiding the disenchantment with prohibition were a number of European medical reports that concluded that alcohol, while undeniably dangerous in excess, was not deleterious in moderation. All this caught reformers off guard, and opponents of prohibition took heart.

Indeed, political prohibition fell apart at a speed that astonished even its enemies. By the 1860s, bereft of major political allies, Maine Laws crumbled to dust in state after state. Legislatures either repealed them outright, modified them to permit liquor sales with minimal interference, or allowed them to languish virtually unenforced. For the time being, the crusade was over.

Yet the legacy of the prohibition struggle remained. The movement had indelibly etched total abstinence on much of the popular mind. It had convinced many that the dry doctrine held the key to the stability and prosperity of the republic. And if its political manifestation, prohibition, had fallen on hard times, thousands remained loyal to the idea nonetheless. In fact, the antebellum movement set an important precedent: Few temperance advocates in subsequent years would seriously advance any other method than legal prohibition as a solution to the liquor question.

PROHIBITION TAKES THE NATION

The movement that secured the Eighteenth Amendment to the Constitution was a more potent and successful reprise of the antebellum temperance crusade. There were some important differences: women, largely under the aegis of the Woman's Christian Temperance Union, became major participants with an agenda of their own; and the Anti-Saloon League deployed novel political tactics. But reform fundamentals remained: perfectionism sustained an absolutist and antipluralist world view; the general welfare justified over-riding individual values; and opponents of reform were still demonized. Temperance workers were more willing than ever to impose their views on society for its own good, regardless of the opposition.

In fact, the perfectionist impulse to cleanse society overshadowed the battle against drinking itself. This reflected the success of the antebellum crusade in reducing alcohol consumption. By the 1850s, Americans were drinking only some two gallons per person annually, a figure close to modern consumption estimates (the 1978 level was close to 2.8 gallons).[35] Thus postwar temperance assaults focused not on consumption per se, but against drinking as a symbol of rampant pluralism and social disorder.

Such symbols were everywhere. Immigration, alcohol-related crime, poverty and family problems, concerns over industrial efficiency and disorder, and social drinking among the middle and upper classes all offended temperance sensibilities. Most offensive of all were the urban saloons. Too many were simply ginmills, and the worst catered to drunkenness, crime, profanity, smoking, tobacco chewing, prostitution, gambling and political corruption. Their patrons, frequently immigrants and unskilled industrial workers, held few values in common with temperance advocates. Indeed, the saloon seemed to mock temperance conceptions of public virtue and stood starkly at odds with traditional American mores. It constituted, as one historian aptly noted, a "counterculture," dangerous and inherently evil.[36]

But the liquor business worried little about its image. In fact, with ample funds to assure political support, it insolently faced down complaints. Large brewers owned most of the saloons and used them as outlets for their beers. They openly encouraged heavy drinking. New patrons often received free drinks and, as one industry spokesman explained, this tactic extended even to children. A few cents spent on free drinks for boys was a good investment; the money would be amply recovered as these youths became habitual drinkers. Many Americans, and by no means just temperance workers, regarded such practices much the same as our own generation would consider a drug-pusher giving children "free samples." Such conduct accorded temperance workers a perfect target.

It took time to rebuild dry strength, however. The first real resurgence came in the early 1870s, with the founding of the Woman's Christian Temperance Union [WCTU]. Members viewed drink and the saloon as dangers to their families and to their status as women, and they organized nationally with zeal and intelligence. Some initiatives were fairly novel. Using Ohio's Adair Law, for instance, which held taverners responsible for some of the actions of drunken patrons, women helped pioneer litigation as a reform device. But victories came slowly. By the late 1880s, only five states were back in the prohibition column, and national prohibition seemed a remote dream.

Temperance Propaganda Prevails

Yet the slow pace of dry political activity was deceptive. Popular opinion *was* turning against the demon, reacting to decades of temperance propaganda, including alcohol education in the schools and health warnings from physicians and scientists. It was a sophisticated effort, and Americans heard a consistent anti-liquor message. By the 1890s, grassroots reform efforts had generated enough strength for a renewed temperance surge, including an organization with enough political savvy to capitalize on dry numbers.

This was the Anti-Saloon League, the brain-child of Reverend Dr. Howard Hyde Russell of Ohio.[37] With skilled leadership, the league became the most influential political pressure group of its day. National and state offices, with paid staff and thousands of motivated volunteers, brought out the vote and linked grass-roots drys with elected officials at all levels. League speakers traversed the country, speaking in front of church, civic, labor, and business groups. An information clearing house at league headquarters in Westerville, Ohio, sent out millions of tracts for political, public information, and educational purposes. The message was clear and consistent, and represented perhaps the most sophisticated public relations effort any reform organization had ever mounted. Politicians simply could not ignore such massive expressions of dry sentiment; while the alcohol beverage industry, its forces divided over how to respond, never learned to deal with the dry propaganda barrage or the league's vigorous local organizing. It gave the league, and prohibition, the initiative.

National Prohibition loomed ever closer. By 1903, over a third of the nation, or 35 million people, lived under some type of prohibitory law. That figure rose to 46 million, or about half of the populace, by 1913.[38] Thus, prohibition had won hundreds of small battles at the local and state levels well before Congress formally considered a prohibitory amendment to the Constitution. Yet in 1916, after a tremendous push from all dry organizations, the general elections sent so many League-endorsed candidates to Congress that National Prohibition was virtually assured. The Eighteenth Amendment easily received congressional approval in December 1917 and, by January 1919, the necessary thirty-six states had voted to ratify. No previous amendment had ever passed so quickly and with so clear a mandate. The nation thus became constitutionally dry in January 1920.

Yet even in dying (for that is how matters looked in 1920), drink served a vital national purpose. Alcohol had been the enemy to generations of Americans wedded to the venerable ideals of republican virtue and stewardship.

Indeed, the anti-liquor reformers saw themselves fulfilling the perfectionist dreams of their predecessors. The temperance wars, in their view, had been every bit as crucial as other conflicts—including the Revolution and the Civil War—that had shaped the contours of American history. Thus the death of liquor symbolized the fruition of dreams unfolding since the late 1780s, the passing of the last hurdle on the path to the virtuous republic. Drinking in America now seemed only a part of an imperfect past.

Tobacco Remained a Target for Reformers

As alcohol prohibition reached high tide, reformers did not neglect their argument with tobacco. As in the antebellum years, the assault on the weed was a smaller affair, but it remained an integral and interesting part of the broader prohibitionist impulse. In fact, the smoking controversy ultimately revealed a good deal about the outside limits of prohibition as social and political policy. Reformers had no use for any tobacco product, but the focus of their attack was the cigarette. For decades, cigarettes were not especially popular with smokers; but when the development of cigarette manufacturing machines made them cheap and convenient, they caught on. By the turn of the century, cigarettes had surged in popularity among smokers, and after the First World War, when they became a favorite of the troops, cigarettes were an established part of the American scene. But the popularity of the cigarette marked it for the special attention of reformers.

For reformers, the real problem was young smokers. They maintained that cigarette manufacturers overtly marketed to boys and young men (although many women smoked as well). In the reform atmosphere of the late nineteenth and early twentieth centuries, this was the equivalent of waving the proverbial red flag in front of the bull. The WCTU and other groups responded predictably and vigorously, and from the same motivations that prompted their hatred of the demon rum. Cigarette smoking, like alcohol, was a matter of "home protection."

Temperance doctrine on tobacco had not changed since the days of Benjamin Rush, thus the WCTU in particular saw the cigarette as a threat to their children, their homes, to health, and to social standards. Indeed, anti-cigarette rhetoric was virtually indistinguishable from the reform jeremiads against alcohol. "The ruin of the republic is close at hand," warned an editorial in the *New York Times,* if cigarette use ever became general.[39] This was a classic republican philippic.

However, the war on smoking differed from the dry crusade in at least one important respect. Most reformers never seriously considered a constitutional solution to smoking. Tobacco would remain the focus of statute law, up to and including any national legislation reformers considered necessary. This was also the case with opiates and other drugs, which fell under the purview of the 1914 Harrison Act. Amending the Constitution, the basic charter of the nation, was the great moral and symbolic statement, and that was reserved for the true archenemy of the republic, alcohol.

There were some important exceptions to this general view. From time to time, the WCTU and other reformers considered a drive for constitutional action against tobacco. This was especially the case in the immediate aftermath of the victory over alcohol. The crusader with the highest hopes was WCTU veteran Lucy Page Gaston. By 1890, Gaston was campaigning full time against cigarettes, and until her death in 1924 she was a formidable agitator and a thorn in the side of the tobacco industry.[40] Nevertheless, most dry leaders argued against another constitutional amendment. The Anti-Saloon League stressed the enforcement of the Volstead Act, and feared that a drive for a tobacco amendment would push popular support for all prohibition too far. The league saw tobacco as a worthy target of reform, but considered the timing wrong for another constitutional crusade. It was a key tactical decision, and most reformers, including anti-tobacco advocates, agreed.[41]

Smoking as a 100-Year-Old Issue

At the same time, reformers understood that the lack of an anti-tobacco amendment posed little practical barrier to effective tobacco prohibition. Anti-smoking forces modeled their efforts directly on the locality-by-locality and state-by-state tactics pioneered by the Anti-Saloon League; and, at almost the same time that the league began to score dry victories, tobacco's foes started winning some rounds of their own. Indeed, by the 1890s, anti-smoking had become a major public issue.[42]

The specific lines of attack varied, although virtually all of them have a very modern ring. Local and state law was a staple. By the turn of the century, virtually every state legislature, and many municipalities, had considered placing restrictions on cigarette sales; and in keeping with WCTU concerns, there was particular attention to preventing tobacco sales to minors. There were various proposals to impose heavy taxes on tobacco products, or to require merchants to pay expensive licensing fees, in order to discourage sales. Many municipalities, including some of the nation's largest cities, also outlawed smoking in public places.[43] Virtually all of these tactics were venerable temperance weapons; Rush, for example, had suggested taxation as an anti-drinking measure as early as the 1780s. The similarity of techniques further illustrated the intertwined relationship of the anti-alcohol and anti-tobacco reformers.

Science was another club shared by alcohol and tobacco prohibitionists. Over time, both had produced an impressive roster of medical and scientific authorities to warn against smoking and drinking, and many of these warnings were sincere and based on the best information available from research and statistics. On the other hand, reformers were often more concerned with marshaling popular support for prohibition than with the accuracy of particular statistics. Reverend Trask was a case in point. As one historian has pointed out, Trask was among the first to play fast and loose with health statistics. He insisted, for example, that upward of twenty thousand Americans died annually from tobacco, including many from cancer. German doctors, Trask also reported, blamed tobacco for half the deaths among young men between eighteen and twenty years old. The reverend wasted little time on derivation of such figures, but he happily used them to beat the drums for prohibition.[44] Other reformers would use numbers in similar fashion through the 1920s (and, as we will see, into the 1990s).

FDA Regulation Failed Once Before

There were also some interesting policy initiatives. In early 1929, Senator Smoot, of Utah, called for the regulation of tobacco by the Food and Drug Administration. The senator's intent was directly comparable to Dr. Kessler's interest in FDA regulation of tobacco today. It would provide federal authority to set the terms and conditions of the contents of tobacco products as well as their sales. In effect, Smoot, like Kessler and former Congressman Mike Synar, was seeking government authority to determine in what form tobacco products would reach the public and under what circumstances, if at all. It was a clear attempt at de facto prohibition.[45] Congress was having none of it, however, and Smoot's gambit went nowhere. The fate of its modern incarnation remains an open question.

Individually, none of these anti-tobacco initiatives would have prohibited smoking. Together, however, they probably would have gone far toward an informal prohibition. Occasionally, they aroused enough anti-tobacco sentiment to permit the actual prohibition of cigarettes. Between 1895 and 1897 the legislatures of three states—North Dakota, Iowa, and Tennessee—prohibited cigarette sales or the sale of cigarette papers. The cause picked up momentum in 1900, when the United States Supreme Court found the Tennessee law constitutional, and by 1909, nine additional states or territories (Oklahoma Territory, Wisconsin, Nebraska, Indiana, Arkansas, Illinois, Kansas, Washington, South Dakota, and Minnesota) had enacted prohibitory laws. Idaho and Utah passed similar laws in 1921. These victories encompassed neither the more populous states nor (as we will see) the base of popular support enjoyed by alcohol prohibition. Nevertheless, the crusaders had accomplished a great deal. It was enough, at least, to prompt one national magazine to ask a pointed question: "Is tobacco going to have its scalp added to the belt of the prohibitionist beside that of the lamented, but as yet not altogether late, alcohol?"[46]

TOBACCO ATTACK FAILS

In fact, the answer was a resounding no. While satisfying to reformers, restrictions on tobacco proved unpopular with most citizens. Even in the most ardently anti-smoking states, sizeable minorities (perhaps they were awakened majorities) protested vigorously; and if they did nothing else, such objections demonstrated the danger inherent in prohibition laws not based on overwhelming popular support. Most states abandoned cigarette prohibition even before the framing of the Eighteenth Amendment; and in states that did not, the issue remained disruptive. In Kansas, for example, the debate turned ugly. Cigarette prohibition fell (1927), but only after reformers and their opponents—notably veterans of World War I, who felt they had earned the right to make their own decisions on whether or not to light up—traded nasty recriminations. The crusade also suffered as wild medical claims against tobacco failed to muster credible scientific support. Thus, even as the tide of alcohol prohibition was cresting, the fate of tobacco prohibition was questionable at best.[47]

Consumers Preferred Choice

It was enough to cause some reformers to reassess their goals. Between 1919 and 1921, three major anti-cigarette organizations, convinced that over-zealous reformers were actually hurting the cause, expelled Lucy Page Gaston and reverted to working through moral suasion.[48] In state after state, legislators found anti-tobacco laws increasingly unpopular, difficult and expensive to enforce, and not particularly effective in reducing smoking. While many crusaders soldiered on, they fought a losing battle; cigarette prohibition was gone by the late 1920s, and so were many other restrictions against smoking. By the end of the decade, tobacco prohibition was no longer a serious public question.[49]

It is difficult to identify precisely why the anti-tobacco crusade ended so abruptly. Certainly the failure of prohibition laws to effectively prohibit was a factor, as was the consequent inability of reformers to sustain a popular mandate. The effective political opposition of the powerful tobacco industry, which never shared the pariah status of the liquor traffic, was also telling. But broader cultural factors also played a role.

By the 1920s, a more pluralistic and consumer-oriented society had emerged; Americans were more hedonistic and less inclined to appreciate appeals for single standards of behavior or to accept intrusions into personal lifestyles.[50] The tobacco crusade, not rooted in a constitutional amendment, and without benefit of lobbying groups of the stature of the Anti-Saloon

League, was unable to adjust to such cultural and political vagaries. Popular support evaporated. These same forces took a bit longer to catch up with National Prohibition—a bit longer, but not much.

Profits in the Pockets of Criminals

In fact, by the late 1920s, time was also running out for the Eighteenth Amendment. This was true despite the fact that prohibition could point to some real successes. After the Volstead Act became law in 1920, even wet studies conceded that drinking had fallen to its lowest levels in history (probably under a gallon per capita annually), and that alcohol-related traffic accidents, industrial injuries, and health problems of all kinds had declined as well. Social workers also reported fewer cases of drinking-related family problems and poverty.[51] All of this was genuinely impressive, but it was only part of the picture.

Drinking did not disappear, however. Moderate drys were willing to take a long view, arguing that continued public education and persuasion would foster respect for the Volstead Act and, over time, lead to the final extinction of Demon Rum. That did not happen. A sizeable minority continued to drink and alcohol consumption gradually climbed toward pre-prohibition levels. The growing illicit market kept bootleggers at work; and, if prohibition did not give rise to organized crime (and we cannot blame it for that), it did foster the expansion of criminal enterprise and vastly increase its profits.

While drys were shocked at such developments, they should not have been surprised. There were too many precedents. Antebellum prohibition had loosed a steady flow of illegal alcohol which found its way to willing customers. This happened even in Maine, where all of the efforts of Neal Dow himself failed to eradicate bootlegging. Indeed, the phenomenon may be relatively impervious to time and place, for there are modern examples as well. In 1993, for example, in an overt effort to discourage smoking, Canada imposed prohibitory tax increases on cigarettes. This triggered major smuggling operations which quickly supplied about a third of all Canadian cigarette sales; the problem disappeared when Canada rescinded the taxes. In 1994, Michigan also used taxation as a prevention measure, and quickly saw its citizens turn to cheaper cigarettes in neighboring states or to bootlegged products.[52] Thus, the pattern has been remarkably consistent over time: prohibitory policies, including taxation with a prohibitory intent, create demands readily supplied by illicit sources.

Only a Police State Could Guarantee Abstinence

A truly massive law enforcement effort might have dried up America, just as it might have prevented illegal cigarette sales in Canada. But such an effort would have entailed a monumental police presence in everyday life, and very few citizens would have tolerated it. State and national authorities realized as much, and no consistent enforcement drive ever materialized. Consequently, the nation witnessed a massive disregard for the law of the land, a process accompanied by the corruption of law enforcement itself. At the same time, many of those who ignored the law openly disparaged prohibitionist values, which they considered intrusive, anti-libertarian, and, in the more hedonistic 1920s, inconvenient and silly. While millions still supported the Noble Experiment, thoughtful observers, including many moderate reformers, understood that things had not worked out as planned.

This state of affairs was intolerable to most drys. Rather than compromise, they elected coercion. Ira Landrith, a national lecturer for the Anti-Saloon League, put their case in grand perfectionist style: "Democracy Must Be Decent or Die! Republicanism Must Be Respectable or Ruined! Progressivism Must Be Pure or It Is Pre-ordained to Perish!" Landrith, who could turn a phrase, then called for "A saloonless nation by 1920," a line prescient of former Surgeon General C. Everett Koop's call for a "smoke-free America by 2000."[53] It was this outlook that impelled increasingly harsh enforcement measures. A suggestion that drinkers be sent to work camps in the Aleutian Islands went nowhere, but in 1929, Congressional drys did pass the draconian Jones Act—the infamous "5 & 10" law. Far from the liberating social panacea its supporters had intended, prohibition had become oppressive.

During the 1920s, for example, illegal liquor production and marketing became commonplace; smuggling liquor from foreign sources became too profitable to stop, even with the combined and progressively more expensive efforts of federal, state and local authorities. In 1923, the treasury secretary told Congress that his department needed a staggering $28 million to fund the Prohibition Unit adequately (so much for the $5 million that had been estimated), while a few years later one enforcement official suggested an annual figure of $300 million.

Speakeasies and other illegal distribution operations routinely made "protection" payments to local police. Widespread media coverage of consequent scandals at least gave the appearance (however mistaken) of a society thrown into turmoil. Moreover, illegal alcohol, like illegal cigarettes, was not taxed and yielded nothing to the public coffers. Finally, zealous prohibition enforcement exacted a human toll. In 1929, to cite only one illustration, dry agents clubbed a suspected bootlegger unconscious, then shot his unarmed wife as she came to his aid. By then, relatively few Americans saw drinking as a clubbing or shooting offense. This incident was hardly representative of the prohibition enforcement effort, but it made for vivid headlines and a nasty impression on the public.

Bad Science Couldn't Save the Cause

Even as they sought to coerce public behavior, drys fought tenaciously for popular opinion. Ultimately, even in this they were heavy-handed. Attempts to buttress the dry cause with medical and scientific evidence was a case in point. Temperance doctrine had long stressed the dangers of addiction and other health problems linked to alcohol, and properly so. But the reformers went too far and allowed policy concerns to override the limits of available research. The WCTU, for example, through its Department of Scientific Temperance, and the independent Scientific Temperance Association tried to place the mantle of scientific objectivity on claims that ethyl alcohol was invariably a poison and always addicting.[54] This was demonstrably ridiculous: millions of moderate drinkers never became alcoholics or suffered any deleterious effects from drinking, and most of the public knew it.

So did most doctors and scientists. There was never any question that alcohol use carried health risks, but any number of prominent physicians weighed in against dry exaggerations of the "poisonous" nature of alcohol. Moreover, they also took drys to task for publishing skewed interpretations of experimental results. By the late 1920s, virtually all temperance statistics on the dangers of alcohol and on the alleged benefits of prohibition had come under careful scrutiny and were found wanting or questionable. Wets made the most of dry exaggerations, but attorney Clarence Darrow scored a particularly telling point. If a clear scientific verdict emerged against alcohol, he wrote, even sensible opponents of prohibition would urge others to abstinence. "But prophecy is not science," and there was no such verdict; and Darrow was convinced that national policy should not rest on such a questionable base when the rights of others were involved.[55]

The politics of Repeal grew steadily from the chorus of discontent. Prohibition was still enshrined in the Constitution, and most wets discounted outright repeal. Yet popular alarm was palpable, and Anti-Saloon League gaffes, carefully exploited by wet organizations, set the stage for a denouement. Weakened by declining membership and leadership changes, the league misread the popular mood. In 1928, it abandoned nonpartisanship in order to oppose wet Democrat Alfred E. Smith; then, in the face of the Depression, it insisted that prohibition was still the key national issue. Americans saw this for the absurdity it was. Thus, tied to the Republicans and unable to prevent Democrats from adopting a wet platform, the once mighty league could only watch as Franklin D. Roosevelt's landslide victory swept away the barriers to Repeal. On December 5, 1933, when the Twenty-first Amendment repealed the Eighteenth, it was almost an anticlimax.

CYCLES OF PROHIBITION

America has experienced prohibition, or at least prohibitionist sentiments, in cycles.[56] From the late eighteenth to the late twentieth centuries, reformers periodically have proposed to eliminate problems attributed to drinking and smoking by eliminating beverage alcohol and tobacco products. The logic and motives behind these reform cycles have been remarkably consistent, and so have many of the results. These are worth considering in the context of today's controversy over smoking.

Certainly prohibition has not lent itself to civil discourse. The perfectionist strain has remained a central part of prohibitionist thinking, and has cast the debate over smoking in stark terms of good and evil. If the temperance movement excoriated drinking in terms unlikely to foster compromise, many anti-smoking crusaders also have crossed the same line of invective. Until very recently, most smokers and nonsmokers had accommodated one another; common courtesy generally prevailed in such matters as where to smoke in restaurants or whether one smoked in another's home. New efforts to drive smokers from public places, however, have added an edge to the debate entirely reminiscent of earlier attacks on social drinking. In any case, it appears that government regulation will now increasingly determine what most citizens used to settle among themselves.

Smokers Are Targets Again

Intentionally or not, restrictions on smoking have prompted a growing disparagement of individual smokers. Alcohol prohibitionists slipped easily from attacks on alcohol to demonizing those who drank it. Over time, reformers carefully shaped popular opinion to view drinking as unacceptable, antisocial, even deviant, behavior. This was part and parcel of building support for prohibitory legislation. Increasingly, smokers now find themselves in a similar situation, blamed for inconveniencing others, setting a poor example to nonsmokers, and overburdening the health care system. If the old temperance experience offers any guide, smokers can expect to bear the brunt of even greater personal criticism as the anti-smoking movement gathers steam.

This is *not* a prediction, for it is already fact. I cite only one illustration, but it is revealing. Only recently, the Daut family was refused the only available room at a Missouri motel because Mr. Daut admitted that he was a smoker. Motel policy barred giving nonsmoking rooms to smokers, even if they agreed not to smoke. But Daut agreed to more than that: he successively volunteered to leave his cigarettes at the front desk, and then to sleep in his car if his wife and two small children could stay in the room. The answer was still no, and the entire family slept in the car.[57] The situation was one of the more unfortunate legacies of our prohibitionist heritage, and we can probably expect to hear more of the same.

Absolutist convictions have led prohibitionists in other questionable directions. Building public policy on inconclusive or even questionable information has been a prominent case in point. As I noted earlier, justifiable concerns over health risks inherent in drinking helped shape policy in the nineteenth and early twentieth centuries. But exaggerated and even specious claims helped destroy the credibility of National Prohibition. Are we about to make a similar mistake? No one questions the health risks associated with smoking. But various governmental bodies have also considered anti-smoking initiatives based on the supposed dangers of environmental or "second-hand" smoke. This is a murky point, for the issue remains the subject of real contention. Both sides dispute the other's data—sometimes pointedly—and it is not my intention to evaluate scientific evidence. The point, however, is that while the debate continues, policy planning moves apace. We might recall Clarence Darrow's caution about setting policy before reaching a clear scientific "verdict." Ultimately, such a course may risk the credibility of the cause it purports to serve.

Addiction as a Subjective Issue

The matter of addiction also poses a problem. Addiction has been a staple of temperance concerns since the time of Benjamin Rush. Alcoholism has afflicted millions, a fact with staggering social, economic, and cultural consequences. Yet the overwhelming majority of drinkers do not become addicted, a fact which put the lie to grossly exaggerated dry claims on the subject. Nineteenth- and early twentieth-century claims against cigarettes foundered for much the same reason. Dire warnings simply did not jibe with daily observation.

Addiction remains a tricky matter. In 1964, the surgeon general's report labeled tobacco (actually nicotine) habituating, but not addicting in the sense of alcohol or other drugs. Yet the latest FDA anti-smoking posture derives specifically from the 1988 surgeon general's claim that tobacco is addicting on the model of cocaine and heroin. Clearly, addiction has become a broader and less rigorously defined conception over the years, and now includes a much wider variety of behaviors and habits. Even so, tens of millions of Americans have voluntarily quit smoking, and the vast majority have done so without outside help and without government interference with their personal behavior. Arguably, the FDA, and others who issue dire warnings on the addictive dangers of cigarettes, are on the same slippery ground as the Scientific Temperance Association. Will daily observation again belie exaggerated predictions?

Reformers Have Already Won

Such questions prompt others. One can reasonably ask, for example, if certain agencies and reformers have not embarked on an exercise of reform or regulatory over-kill. The nation has not stopped smoking, but most of it has, and trends still appear downward. Public opinion overwhelmingly accepts the view that smoking is dangerous; smokers frequently go out of their way to avoid making nonsmokers uncomfortable. In effect, reformers have already *won*. Moreover, they have done so on a pattern established years ago: We should recall that among drinkers, the most substantial modifications of problem behavior occurred well *before* the Maine Laws or National Prohibition. Since 1964, the story of smoking has been roughly the same. Yet calls for the virtual, if de facto, abolition of smoking continue.

Under the circumstances, we must ask again why anti-smoking advocates remain so zealous. What, in fact, do they really want? We have noted that prohibitory legislation has previously covered broader social and political agendas. There was, of course, the old perfectionist vision of a social nirvana that would emerge after the death of Demon Rum. Now the goals may be somewhat different: "wellness," some overall health care policy, even a variation (as some conservatives think) on venerable anti-corporate reform themes.[58] In any case, if today's anti-smoking campaigns are strictly about smoking, reformers should say as much. If they are part of a broader agenda—and some clearly are—then reformers should say that.

On the Brink of a Reforming Rampage?

If comprehensive health-care policy is a goal among some anti-tobacco activists (as it most certainly is), then there is every reason to proceed with caution. The current focus of reform is smoking, but the same logic that would regulate tobacco for health reasons would impel regulation of other things as well. Alcohol, for all of the time-honored reasons, would be a natural target once again, with all of the complications such a step would entail. Red meat, of course, is a leading source of cholesterol, and heart attack kills more Americans every year than any other disease. Should we not regulate the consumption of beef and pork? This is not completely speculative. In late 1994, Yale University professor Kelly D. Brownell called for "sin" taxes on unhealthy foods, as we already have on alcohol and tobacco, to pay for the health complications of "low-nutrition" eating habits.[59] His column brought an immediate counterattack: one respondent, a former smoker, noted that "Americans should be concerned about having government define sin."

> I quit smoking many years ago, but I despise the self-righteous smugness of some nonsmokers. Is it a sin to smoke but not a sin to be rude, confrontational

and just plain cruel to those who do smoke? . . . How long after " unhealthy" foods are taxed will we see the spectacle of fellow diners in restaurants pointing fingers, literally, at someone eating an eclair? Will there be special areas in buildings . . . for those who want to have a Twinkie with lunch?[60]

If reactions to Brownell were pointed, however, so was his logic. Indeed, aggressive regulators could well make a case for extending alcohol and tobacco controls and taxes to other products.

Whatever their motives—and there is no doubting the good intentions of most—many who would restrict smoking would strenuously object to being called prohibitionists. Yet prohibition has never depended entirely on national legislation or even on actual prohibition laws. Prohibitory policies have relied on local laws to control alcohol and tobacco use, age and locational restrictions, selective taxation, litigation, and regulatory policy. Virtually all of the control techniques mentioned today have antecedents in earlier prohibition campaigns. Implemented singly, their impact would have been (and has been) limited; but combined, they have the potential to produce de facto prohibition. These were precisely the tactics employed to such startling effect by the Anti-Saloon League; they were intended to lay the foundation for a much broader, but later, legislative attack. They did just that.

Still Ripe for Illegal Trade

In some important respects, however, there is little practical difference between de facto and de jure prohibition. Over time, the strict enforcement of prohibitory laws, regulations, taxes, or whatever has generated fairly consistent difficulties. Alcohol and tobacco prohibition has fostered the growth of illegal markets for both commodities, has often led to widespread disrespect for the law, has strained law enforcement resources, and has even corrupted the criminal justice system. The recent Canadian experience with prohibitory taxation, for example, only replicated many of the problems associated with the history of American prohibition. Ultimately, some of the worst social costs came not from drinking or smoking, but from the enormous social, political, economic, and moral consequences of going too far in limiting behavior. I do not suggest that a ban on smoking would fully replicate such distressing states of affairs, but it is worth asking reformers how far they would be willing to go in dealing with the almost inevitable violations of any tobacco prohibition.

Finally, we do need to carefully consider the libertarian questions inherent in prohibitionist policies. Americans have prohibited certain behaviors in the past, and they may well again; I have never argued that Americans cannot ban something they find objectionable. My point is that if they do, they should undertake it with their eyes open, and perhaps honestly and openly call it what it is: prohibition. As we proceed, we should bear in mind that earlier policies aimed at the complete elimination of behaviors have led the nation down some unintended paths. As de Tocqueville warned, the "tyranny of the majority" can be a very pernicious tyranny, even when imposed in the name of the general welfare; it limits thought as well as conduct. Prohibition invites these intrusions into private lives; and if the past is any guide, prudence has always been the better course when considering any such invitation.

NOTES

1. The *Time* article is quoted and summarized in Mark Edward Lender and James Kirby Martin, *Drinking in America: A History,* rev. ed. (New York: Free Press/Macmillan, 1987), 191. The trend toward moderation has continued into the 1990s. By 1992, annual average per capita consumption—measured in gallons of absolute alcohol (that is, ethyl alcohol alone, not including water or other substances in a beverage)—had fallen to its lowest level since 1967, and more Americans were turning from alcohol to soft drinks, coffee, and other nonalcoholic beverages. See "More Americans Choosing Not to be a Part of the Drinking Scene," *The Bottom Line* [Alcohol Research Information Service], 14 (Winter 1993): 4-8; "Absolute Alcohol Consumption," *Ibid.,* 23-26; U.S. Dept. of Health and Human Services, Eighth Special report to the U.S. Congress on Alcohol and Health (Washington, DC: 1993), 3-5.

2. Quoted in Lender and Martin, *Drinking in America,* 191-92. Scholarship has also reflected the heightened public interest in alcohol-related questions. In particular, a growing number of historians have turned their attention to the temperance movement, often concluding that the anti-liquor crusade had produced some beneficial results. It was the first time in generations that disinterested scholars had found much to admire in dry reform. See especially John C. Burnham, "New Perspectives on the Prohibition 'Experiment' of the 1920s," *Journal of Social History* 2 (1968): 51-69, and Norman H. Clark, *Deliver Us from Evil—An Interpretation of American Prohibition* (New York, 1976). Some careful studies even found that the repeal of the Eighteenth Amendment was a mixed blessing, and that it was hardly the progressive measure described in earlier scholarship; e.g., David E. Kyvig, ed., *Law, Alcohol, and Order: Perspectives on National Prohibition* (Westport, CT, 1985). Other disciplines, notably those touching on public health issues, also put alcohol under scrutiny. If alcohol was a dangerous chemical, they asked, should government regulators not deal with it as such? See, for example, Dan E. Beauchamp, *Beyond Alcoholism: Alcohol and Public Health Policy* (Philadelphia, 1980). Opinion was anything but unanimous on such questions, nor did it have to be. The point was that these matters had engaged academe as they had not for decades, and that temperance and criticisms of beverage alcohol emerged from the 1980s with a vastly enhanced scholarly credibility.

3. The issue of the "new temperance" movement or "neoprohibitionism" is discussed in Lender and Martin, *Drinking in America,* 191-201.

4. Michael Gartner, "Bring back Prohibition," *USA Today,* May 1994.

5. "Cigarette Smoking and Health Risks: Four Centuries of Information and Public Awareness," Report, Section 2.2, Nov. 1988, Brown & Williamson Tobacco Corp.; U.S. Dept. of Health and Human Services, *The Health Consequences of Smoking: Nicotine Addiction, a Report of the Surgeon General* (Washington, D.C., 1988), 9-11; John A. Meyer, "Cigarette Century," *American Heritage,* 43, No. 8 (1992): 76-79.

6. Christopher John Farley, "The Butt Stops Here," Time, 18 Apr. 1994, 60.

7. Associated Press, "Smoking Among Women Increases, Reversing Trend," *Washington Post*, 4 November 1994.

8. "Should Cigarettes Be Outlawed?" *U.S. News & World Report*, 28 Apr. 1994, 35.

9. Christopher John Farley, "The Butt Stops Here," Time, 18 Apr. 1994, 58.

10. The Jones Act (also called the Jones-Stalker act) specifically forbid courts from discriminating between "slight or casual" and serious violations of prohibition laws when imposing sentences; see Ernest Hurst Cherrington, ed., *The Anti-Saloon League Year Book*, 1931 (Westerville, OH, 1931), 17. On reactions to the law, see Lender and Martin, *Drinking in America*, 163-64. The act was amended in 1931 to reduce the severity of punishments for "petty offenses."

11. Mark Edward Lender, *Dictionary of American Temperance Biography: From Temperance Reform to Alcohol Research, the 1600s to the 1980s* (Westport, CT, 1984), 221.

12. David C. Lewis, "For Health but Against Prohibition," *Brown University Digest of Addiction Theory and Application* 13, No. 9 (1994): 11-12.

13. Richard Klein, *Cigarettes Are Sublime* (Durham, NC, 1993); Klein quoted in Christopher John Farley, "The Butt Stops Here," *Time*, 18 Apr. 1994, 58-64.

14. Shannon Brownlee, Steven V. Roberts et al., "Should Cigarettes Be Outlawed?" *U.S. News & World Report*, 18 Apr. 1994, 32-38; Christopher John Farley, "The Butt Stops Here," *Time*, 18 Apr. 1994, 58-64.

15. Faith T. Fitzgerald, "The Tyranny of Health," *New England Journal of Medicine* 331, No. 3 (1994): 12-13.

16. "Changing the World, Cigarette Foe Banzhaf Sees the Law as Tool to Attack Social Ills," *The Wall Street Journal*, 17 Apr. 1969.

17. For a discussion of Rush's influence, and especially his ideological convictions, see Lender and Martin, *Drinking in America*, 34-40; an overview of his temperance activities is in Lender, *Dictionary of Temperance Biography*, 421-24; unless noted otherwise, my treatment of Rush follows these sources.

18. Fielding quoted in Farley, "The Butt Stops Here," 64.

19. Harry G. Levine, "The Discovery of Addiction: Changing Conceptions of Habitual Drunkenness in America," *Journal of Studies on Alcohol* 39 (1978): 143-74; Mark Edward Lender and Karen R. Karnchanapee, "Temperance Tales: Antiliquor Fiction and American Attitudes toward Alcoholics in the Late 19th and Early 20th Centuries," *Ibid*. 38 (1977): 1347-70.

20. Rush quoted in Lender and Martin, *Drinking in America*, 38.

21. Benjamin Rush, *Observations upon the influence of the Habitual use of Tobacco upon Health, Morals and Property* (Philadelphia, 1798); Gordon L. Dillow, "The Hundred Year War Against the Cigarette," *American Heritage*, Feb./Mar. 1981.

22. For statistics on alcohol consumption, and their implications, see W. J. Rorabaugh, *The Alcoholic Republic: An American Tradition* (New York, 1979).

23. Lender and Martin, *Drinking in America*, 71-72.

24. Gordon L. Dillow, "The Hundred Year War Against the Cigarette," *American Heritage*, Feb./Mar. 1981, 6.

25. "Tobacco," *Journal of Health* [Philadelphia], Vol. 1, No. 3, 7 Oct. 1829, 36-38, Arents Collection, No. 3191, New York Public Library; "M'Allister's Dissertation on Tobacco," *Ibid.*, Vol 1, No. 21, 14 July 1830, 329-31.

26. *Anti-Tobacco Journal* [Fitchburg, MA], Vol 1, No. 1 (1859): 2.

27. *Ibid.*, Vol 2, Nos. 10-12 (Oct., Nov., Dec. 1873): 183.

28. [George Trask], *Thoughts and Stories on Tobacco for American Lads: Or Uncle Toby's Anti-Tobacco Advice for His Nephew Billy Bruce* (Boston, 1852), 9-10, *passim.*

29. "*Anti-Tobacco Journal*," Vol. 1, No. 5 (Aug. 1860): 135.

30. Trask, *Thoughts and Stories on Tobacco*, 10; Dillow, "The Hundred Year War," 6; Lender, *Dictionary of Temperance Biography*, 202-203, 280-82, 320-22.

31. Parker quoted in Lender and Martin, *Drinking in America*, 73.

32. Denunciations of moderate drinking were staples of the temperance literature; some of the best examples are in Daniel Dorchester's comprehensive dry history, *The Liquor Problem in All Ages* (Cincinnati, OH, 1884). See also Lender and Karnchanapee, "Temperance Tales."

33. Alexis de Tocqueville, *Democracy in America*, ed. by Richard D. Heffner (New York, 1956, orig. 1835 and 1840), 201.

34. Ibid., 116-117.

35. The figure for 1992 was 2.34 gallons, a further decline but still slightly ahead of the 1850 estimate of 2.10 gallons; see "Absolute Alcohol Consumption," *Bottom Line*, 25-26.

36. This was the conclusion of Clark, *Deliver Us from Evil*; for a particularly revealing study, see Perry R. Duis, *The Saloon: Public Drinking in Chicago and Boston, 1880-1920* (Urbana, 1983). A dry view is in George M. Hammell, ed., The Passing of the Saloon (Cincinnati, OH, 1908).

37. Russell advocated three operational tenets. The first was the direct involvement of the pulpit in prohibition politics. Working first through Methodist churches (and thereafter through other denominations as well), the league effectively urged Ohio congregations to vote dry. The second technique was "local option," which began to dry up Ohio on a county-by-county or town-by-town basis. Finally, there was a nonpartisanship: The league proved that it could marshall votes for anyone—Republican or Democrat—who was willing to vote dry. The major parties rapidly awoke to the electoral power of the league, and it soon became apparent that the political fortunes of the antiliquor crusade did not depend on any single party, and certainly not on the small and ineffectual Prohibition Party. Throughout the 1890s, then, the Anti-Saloon League gathered momentum as it duplicated its Ohio successes elsewhere, forming state chapters and a national organization (1895) along the way. The best treatment of the league is K. Austin Kerr's *Organized for Reform: a New History of the Anti-Saloon League* (New Haven, CT, 1985); still useful is a contemporary study by Peter Odegard, *Pressure Politics: The Story of the Anti-Saloon League* (New York, 1928).

38. Lender and Martin, *Drinking in America*, 129.

39. Quoted in Dillow, "The Hundred Year War," 7.

40. "Plan Amendment to outlaw Tobacco," *New York Times*, 3 Aug. 1919; for a contemporary view of the question, see L. Ames Brown, "Is a Tobacco Crusade Coming?" *Atlantic Monthly*, Oct. 1920, 446-55; on Gaston, see "Lucy Page Gaston," *Herald*, Passaic, NJ, Editorial Digest, 23 Sept. 1924; and "Miss Gaston, Cigarette Foe, Passes Away," *Chicago Tribune*, 21 Aug. 1924.

41. "Dry League Not to join Tobacco Fight," *Scranton [PA] Times*, 27 Feb. 1925.

42. Despite its failure to formally endorse tobacco prohibition, the indirect influence of the Anti-Saloon League in the anti-cigarette movement was considerable. Reformers specifically noted their debt to techniques developed by the League. For examples, see "National Drive to Be Launched Upon Tobacco: Attack on 'Filthy Weed' Based on Tactics of Anti-Saloon League," *Akron [Ohio] Journal*, 26 Mar. 1925; interview statement by Wilbur Crafts, International Reform Bureau, Summer 1919, 3.

43. Dillow, "The Hundred Year War," 10-13; Brown, "Is a Tobacco Crusade Coming?" 450, 454. The Pennsylvania chapter of the WCTU wanted the firing of teachers who smoked. "W.C.T.U. Meeting Assails Cigarettes," *Philadelphia Inquirer*, 19 Oct. 1927.

44. Dillow, "The Hundred Year War," 6; *Anti-Tobacco Journal*, Vol 1, No. 2 (Jan. 1869): 31.

45. Sen. Reed Smoot, "Extension of Food and Drugs Act to Tobacco and Tobacco Products," *Congressional Record*, Vol. 71, No. 45, 10 June 1929, 2687-91.

46. Garrett Smith, "Is Tobacco Doomed," *Leslie's*, 14 May 1921, 1.

47. Brown, "Is a Tobacco Crusade Coming?" *passim*.

48. "Lucy Page Gaston Ousted By League," *New York Telegraph*, 27 Aug. 1921.

49. Dillow, "The Hundred Year War," 15.

50. Jack S. Blocker, Jr., *American Temperance Movements: Cycles of Reform* (Boston, MA, 1989), 110; Lender and Martin, *Drinking in America*, 152-53, 166, 172, further develop this point.

51. Burnham, "New Perspectives on Prohibition," *passim*; Clark Warburton, *The Economic Results of Prohibition* (New York, 1932); Martha Bensley Bruere, *Does Prohibition Work?* (New York, 1927); Evangeline Booth, *Some Have Stopped Drinking* (Westerville, OH, 1928); Lender and Martin, *Drinking in America*, 136-39.

52. "Report Says Interstate Smuggling of Tobacco Products May Be Approaching Epidemic Levels," PRNewswire [Detroit], 20 Oct. 1994.

53. Landrith quoted in Lender, *Dictionary of Temperance Biography*, 288. Koop was not the first to turn such a phrase; in 1920, the International Anti-Cigarette League, a creation of Lucy Page Gaston, launched its crusade with the optimistic slogan, "A smokeless America by 1925." "Smokeless U.S. by 1925, Cigarette League's Slogan," *Sioux Falls [SD] Press*, 9 Mar. 1920.

54. E.g., Cora Frances Stoddard, *Science and Human Life in the Alcohol Problem* (Westerville, OH, 1930), and, by the same author, *Alcohol in Experience and Experiment* (Evanston, IL, 1934).

55. Clarence Darrow and Victor S. Yarros, *The Prohibition Mania: A reply to Professor Irving Fisher and Others* (New York, 1927), 20. This volume also provides a convenient survey of dry statistical and scientific claims.

56. The cyclical nature of prohibition is pointed out in Blocker, *American Temperance Movements*.

57. Jonathan Welsh, "If You Really Need a Hotel Room, Don't Ever Ask for an Ashtray," *Wall Street Journal*, 14 Dec. 1994.

58. E.g., Jeffrey St. John, "The New Terrorism: The Cancer Crusade, and the Political Corruption of Science," The Tobacco Institute, Winter Meeting, 29 Feb. 1980, Marco Island, FL.

59. Kelly D. Brownwell "To Trim the Fat, Tax the Rich," *New York Times*, Op-Ed, 15 Dec. 1994.

60. Karen Ruta to the editor, 15 Dec. 1994, *New York Times*, Op-Ed, 21 Dec. 1994.

6

The Anti-Tobacco Campaign of the Nazis: A Little Known Aspect of Public Health in Germany, 1933–45

Robert N. Proctor

Medical historians in recent years have done a great deal to enlarge our understanding of medicine and public health in Nazi Germany. We know that about half of all doctors joined the Nazi party and that doctors played a major part in designing and administering the Nazi programs of forcible sterilization, "euthanasia," and the industrial scale murder of Jews and gypsies.[1,2] Much of our present day concern for the abuse of humans used in experiments stems from the extreme brutality many German doctors showed toward concentration camp prisoners exploited to advance the cause of German military medicine.[3]

TOBACCO IN THE REICH

One topic that has only recently begun to attract attention is the Nazi anti-tobacco movement.[4-6] Germany had the world's strongest anti-smoking movement in the 1930s and early 1940s, supported by Nazi medical and military leaders worried that tobacco might prove a hazard to the race.[1-4] Many Nazi leaders were vocal opponents of smoking. Anti-tobacco activists pointed out that whereas Churchill, Stalin, and Roosevelt were all fond of tobacco, the three major fascist leaders of Europe—Hitler, Mussolini, and Franco—were all nonsmokers.[7] Hitler was the most adamant, characterizing tobacco as "the wrath of the Red Man against the White Man for having been

Robert N. Proctor, "The Anti-Tobacco Campaign of the Nazis: A Little Known Aspect of Public Health in Germany, 1933–45." This article was first published in the *British Medical Journal* 313 (1996): 1450–53, and is reproduced by permission of the *BMJ*.

given hard liquor." At one point the Führer even suggested that Nazism might never have triumphed in Germany had he not given up smoking.[8]

German smoking rates rose dramatically in the first six years of Nazi rule, suggesting that the propaganda campaign launched during those early years was largely ineffective.[4,5] German smoking rates rose faster even than those of France, which had a much weaker anti-tobacco campaign. German per capita tobacco use between 1932 and 1939 rose from 570 to 900 cigarettes a year, whereas French tobacco consumption grew from 570 to only 630 cigarettes over the same period.[9]

Smith et al. suggested that smoking may have functioned as a kind of cultural resistance,[4] though it is also important to realize that German tobacco companies exercised a great deal of economic and political power, as they do today. German anti-tobacco activists frequently complained that their efforts were no match for the "American style" advertising campaigns waged by the tobacco industry.[10] German cigarette manufacturers neutralized early criticism—for example, from the SA (Sturm-Abteilung; stormtroops), which manufactured its own "Sturmzigaretten"—by portraying themselves as early and eager supporters of the regime.[11] The tobacco industry also launched several new journals aimed at countering anti-tobacco propaganda. In a pattern that would become familiar in the United States and elsewhere after the Second World War, several of these journals tried to dismiss the anti-tobacco movement as "fanatic" and "unscientific." One such journal featured the German word for science twice in its title (*Der Tabak: Wissenschaftliche Zeitschrift der Internationalen Tabakwissenschaftlichen Gesellschaft*, founded in 1940).

We should also realize that tobacco provided an important source of revenue for the national treasury. In 1937–38 German national income from tobacco taxes and tariffs exceeded 1 billion Reichsmarks.[12] By 1941, as a result of new taxes and the annexation of Austria and Bohemia, Germans were paying nearly twice that. According to Germany's national accounting office, by 1941 tobacco taxes constituted about one twelfth of the government's entire income.[13] Two hundred thousand Germans were said to owe their livelihood to tobacco—an argument that was reversed by those who pointed to Germany's need for additional men in its labor force, men who could presumably be supplied from the tobacco industry.[14]

CULMINATION OF THE CAMPAIGN: 1939–41

German anti-tobacco policies accelerated toward the end of the 1930s, and by the early war years tobacco use had begun to decline. The Luftwaffe banned smoking in 1938 and the post office did likewise. Smoking was barred in many workplaces, government offices, hospitals, and rest homes. The NSDAP (Nationalsozialistische Deutsche Arbeiterpartei) announced a ban on smoking in its offices in 1939, at which time SS chief Heinrich Himmler announced a smoking ban for all uniformed police and SS officers while on duty.[15] The *Journal of the American Medical Association* that year reported Hermann Goering's decree barring soldiers from smoking on the streets, on marches, and on brief off duty periods.[16]

Sixty of Germany's largest cities banned smoking on street cars in 1941.[17] Smoking was banned in air raid shelters—though some shelters reserved separate rooms for smokers.[18] During the war years tobacco rationing coupons were denied to pregnant women (and to all women below the age of 25) while restaurants and cafes were barred from selling cigarettes to female customers.[19] From July 1943 it was illegal for anyone under the age of eighteen to smoke in public.[20] Smoking was banned on all German city trains and buses in 1944, the initiative coming from Hitler himself, who was worried about exposure of young female conductors to tobacco smoke.[21] Nazi policies were heralded as marking "the beginning of the end" of tobacco use in Germany.[14]

German tobacco epidemiology by this time was the most advanced in the world. Franz H. Müller in 1939 and Eberhard Schairer and Erich Schöniger in 1943 were the first to use case-control epidemiological methods to document the lung cancer hazard from cigarettes.[22,23] Müller concluded that the "extraordinary rise in tobacco use" was "the single most important cause of the rising incidence of lung cancer."[22] Heart disease was another focus and was not infrequently said to be the most serious illness brought on by smoking.[24] Late in the war nicotine was suspected as a cause of the coronary heart failure suffered by a surprising number of soldiers on the eastern front. A 1944 report by an army field pathologist found that all thirty-two young soldiers whom he had examined after death from heart attack on the front had been "enthusiastic smokers." The author cited the Freiburg pathologist Franz Büchner's view that cigarettes should be considered "a coronary poison of the first order."[25]

On June 20, 1940, Hitler ordered tobacco rations to be distributed to the military "in a manner that would dissuade" soldiers from smoking.[24] Cigarette rations were limited to six per man per day, with alternative rations available for nonsmokers (for example, chocolate or extra food). Extra cigarettes were sometimes available for purchase, but these were generally limited to fifty per man per month and were often unavailable—as during times of rapid advance or retreat. Tobacco rations were denied to women accompanying the Wehrmacht. An ordinance on November 3, 1941, raised tobacco taxes to a higher level than they had ever been (80–95 percent of the retail price). Tobacco taxes would not rise that high again for more than a quarter of a century after Hitler's defeat.[26]

IMPACT OF THE WAR AND POSTWAR POVERTY

The net effect of these and other measures (for instance, medical lectures to discourage soldiers from smoking) was to lower tobacco consumption by the military during the war years. A 1944 survey of one thousand servicemen found that, whereas the proportion of soldiers smoking had increased (only 12.7 percent were nonsmokers), the total consumption of tobacco had decreased—by just over 14 percent. More men were smoking (101 of those surveyed had taken up the habit during the war, whereas only seven had given it up) but the average soldier was smoking about a quarter (23.4 percent) less tobacco than in the immediate prewar period. The number of very heavy smokers (thirty or more cigarettes daily) was down dramatically—from 4.4 percent to only 0.3 percent—and similar declines were recorded for moderately heavy smokers.[24]

Postwar poverty further cut consumption. According to official statistics German tobacco use did not reach prewar levels again until the mid-1950s. The collapse was dramatic: German per capita consumption dropped by more than half from 1940 to 1950, whereas American consumption nearly doubled during that period.[6,9] French consumption also rose, though during the four years of German occupation cigarette consumption declined by even more than in Germany[9]—suggesting that military conquest had a larger effect than Nazi propaganda.

After the war Germany lost its position as home to the world's most aggressive anti-tobacco science. Hitler was dead but also many of his anti-tobacco underlings either had lost their jobs or were otherwise silenced. Karl Astel, head of Jena's Institute for Tobacco Hazards Research (and rector of the University of Jena and an officer in the SS), committed suicide in his office on the night of April 3–4, 1945. Reich Health Führer Leonardo Conti, another anti-tobacco activist, committed suicide on October 6, 1945, in an allied prison while awaiting prosecution for his role in the euthanasia program. Hans Reiter, the Reich Health Office president who once characterized nicotine as "the greatest enemy of the people's health" and "the number one drag on the German economy"[27] was interned in an American prison camp for two years, after which he worked as a physician in a clinic in Kassel, never again returning to public service. Gauleiter Fritz Sauckel, the guiding light behind Thuringia's anti-smoking campaign and the man who drafted the grant application for Astel's anti-tobacco institute, was executed on October 1, 1946, for crimes against humanity. It is hardly surprising that much of the wind was taken out of the sails of Germany's anti-tobacco movement.

THE FLIPSIDE OF FASCISM

Smith et al. were correct to emphasize the strength of the Nazi anti-smoking effort and the sophistication of Nazi era tobacco science.[4] The anti-smoking science and policies of the era have not attracted much attention, possibly because the impulse behind the movement was closely attached to the larger Nazi movement. That does not mean, however, that anti-smoking movements are inherently fascist[28]; it means simply that scientific memories are often clouded by the celebrations of victors and that the political history of science is occasionally less pleasant than we would wish.

REFERENCES

1. Proctor, R. N. (1988). *Racial Hygiene: Medicine under the Nazis.* Cambridge, Mass.: Harvard University Press.

2. Kater, M. H. (1989). *Doctors under Hitler.* Chapel Hill: University of North Carolina Press.

3. Annas G, & M. Grodin. (1992). *The Nazi Doctors and the Nuremberg Code.* New York: Oxford University Press.

4. Smith G. D., S. A. Ströbele, & M. Egger. (1995). "Smoking and Death." *BMJ* 310:396.

5. Borgers, D. (1995). "Smoking and Death." *BMJ* 310:1536.

6. Proctor, R. N. (In press). "Nazi Cancer Research and Policy." *J. Epidemiol. Community Health.*

7. Bauer D. (1937). "So lebt der Düce." *Auf der Wacht* 19–20.

8. Picker H. (1951). *Hitlers Tischgespräche im Führerhauptquartier.* Bonn: Athenäum-Verlag.

9. Lee P. N., ed. (1975). *Tobacco Consumption in Various Countries.* 4th ed. London: Tobacco Research Council.

10. Reid, G. (1939). "Weltanschauung, Haltung, Genussgifte." *Genussgifte* 35:64.

11. Kosmos. (1933). *Bild-Dokumente unserer Zeit.* Dresden: Kosmos.

12. Reckert, F. K. (1942). *Tabakwarenkunde: Der Tabak, sein Anbau und seine Verarbeitung.* Berlin-Schöneberg: Max Schwabe.

13. "Erkennung und Bekämpfung der Tabakgefahren." (1941). *Dtsch. Artzebl.* 71:183–85.

14. Klarner, W. (1940). *Vom Rauchen: Eine Sucht und ihre Bekämpfung.* Nuremberg: Rudolf Kern.

15. "Rauchverbot für die Polizei auf Strassen und in Diensträumen." (1940). *Die Genussgifte* 36:59.

16. "Berlin: Alcohol, Tobacco and Coffee." (1939). *JAMA* 113:1144–45.

17. "Kleine Mitteilungen." (1941). *Vertrauensarzt* 9:196.

18. "Mitteilungen." (1941). *Off. Gesundheitsdienst* 7:488.

19. Charman, T. (1989). *The German Home Front 1939–1945.* London: Barrie & Jenkins.

20. Fromme, W. (1948). "Öffentlicher Gesundheitsdienst." In: E. Rodenwaldt, ed. *Hygiene.* Part 1. *General Hygiene.* Wiesbaden: Dietrich'sche Verlagsbuchhandlung, 36.

21. *Informationdienst des Hauptamtes für Volksgesundheit der NSDAP.* (1944) April–June:60–61.

22. Müller, F. H. (1939). "Tabakmissbrauch und Lungencarcinom." *Z. Krebstforsch.* 49:57-85.

23. Schairer E, & E. Schöniger. (1943). "Lungenkrebs und Tabakverbrauch." *Z. Krebsforsch* 54:261-9.

24. Kittel, W. (1944). "Hygiene des Rauchens." In: S. Handloser and W. Hoffmann, eds. *Wehrhygiene.* Berlin: Springer-Verlag.

25. Goedel, A. (1944). "Kriegspathologische Beiträge." In: A. Zimmer, ed. *Kriegschirurgie.* Vol 1. Vienna: Franz Deuticke.

26. Pritzkoleit, K. (1961). *Auf einer Wege von Gold: Der Triumph der Wirtschaft.* Vienna: Verlag Kurt Desch.

27. (1939). "Werberat der deutschen Wirtschaft." *Volksgesundheit und Werbung.* Berlin: arl Heymanns.

28. Peto, R. (1995). "Smoking and Death." *BMJ* 310:396.

Suggestions for Further Reading

Gostin, L. O., P. S. Arno, and A. M. Brandt. (1997). "FDA Regulation of Tobacco Advertising and Youth Smoking: Historical, Social, and Constitutional Perspectives." *Journal of the American Medical Association* 277, no. 5: 410–18.

Heischman, S. J., L. T. Kozlowski, and J. E. Henningfield. (1997). "Nicotine Addiction: Implications for Public Health Policy." *The Journal of Social Issues* 53: 13–33.

Kiernan, V. G. (1991). *Tobacco: A History.* London: Random Century.

Leventhal, H., and P. D. Cleary. (1980). "The Smoking Problem: A Review of the Research and Theory in Behavioral Risk Modification." *Psychological Bulletin* 88: 370-405.

Proctor, R. N. (1997). "The Nazi War on Tobacco: Ideology, Evidence, and Possible Cancer Consequences." *Bulletin of History of Medicine* 71: 435-88.

Part II

For the Public's Health: Justifying Tobacco Regulation

7

The Legal and Scientific Basis for FDA's Assertion of Jurisdiction over Cigarettes and Smokeless Tobacco

David A. Kessler, Philip S. Barnett, Ann Witt, Mitchell R. Zeller, Jerold R. Mande, and William B. Schultz

On August 28, 1996, President Clinton announced the final regulations of the U.S. Food and Drug Administration (FDA) restricting the sale and promotion of cigarettes and smokeless tobacco.[1] The FDA's assertion of jurisdiction over tobacco products under the Federal Food, Drug, and Cosmetic Act (the Act) was the culmination of an exhaustive, two-and-a-half-year investigation of tobacco products. This chapter explains the legal and scientific basis for this assertion of jurisdiction.

In asserting jurisdiction over cigarettes and smokeless tobacco, FDA relied on its authority to regulate drugs and devices. Under the relevant portion of the Act, a product is a "drug" or "device" if it is an article (other than food) "intended to affect the structure or any function of the body."[2] When FDA last considered this issue, it declined to assert jurisdiction over cigarettes because it lacked evidence that cigarettes were intended to affect the structure or function of the body.[3] Since that time, however, substantial new evidence became available to FDA. This evidence included the emergence of a scientific consensus that the nicotine in cigarettes and smokeless tobacco causes and sustains addiction, as well as the disclosure of thousands of pages of internal tobacco company documents revealing that the tobacco manufacturers know that nicotine causes significant pharmacological effects, including addiction, and design their products to provide pharmacologically active doses of nicotine.

This new evidence demonstrated to FDA that (1) nicotine in cigarettes and smokeless tobacco does "affect the structure or any function of the body"

Reprinted with permission from the *Journal of the American Medical Association* 277, no. 5 (February 5, 1997): 405–408. Copyright © 1997, American Medical Association. Reprinted with permission.

and (2) these effects on the structure and function of the body are "intended" by the manufacturers. These findings, which are explained below, provided the basis for the agency's determination that cigarettes and smokeless tobacco are subject to FDA jurisdiction as products that contain a "drug," nicotine, and a "device" for delivering this drug to the body.[4]

EFFECTS ON STRUCTURE AND FUNCTION

The scientific evidence before FDA established that the nicotine delivered by cigarettes and smokeless tobacco has significant pharmacological effects on the structure and function of the body. First, this evidence showed that nicotine in cigarettes and smokeless tobacco causes and sustains addiction. As the surgeon general has reported, nicotine exerts psychoactive (or mood-altering) effects on the brain that motivate repeated, compulsive use of the substance. These pharmacological effects create dependence in the user. The pharmacological processes that cause this addiction to nicotine are similar to those that cause addiction to heroin and cocaine.[5]

Second, scientific studies showed that nicotine in cigarettes and smokeless tobacco produces other important pharmacological effects on the central nervous system. Under some circumstances and doses, for instance, the nicotine has a sedating or tranquilizing effect on mood and brain activity. Under other circumstances and doses, the nicotine has a stimulant or arousal-inducing effect on mood and brain activity.[6]

Third, as the surgeon general also documented, nicotine in cigarettes and smokeless tobacco affects body weight.[7]

The FDA found that these effects on the structure and function of the body are significant and quintessentially druglike. They are the same as the effects of other drugs that FDA has traditionally regulated, including stimulants, tranquilizers, appetite suppressants, and products, such as methadone, used in the maintenance of addiction. For these reasons, the agency concluded that cigarettes and smokeless tobacco "affect the structure or any function of the body" within the meaning of the Act.

THE ISSUE OF INTENT

Having established that nicotine in cigarettes and smokeless tobacco affects the structure and function of the body, the central question before FDA became whether these effects of nicotine on the structure or function of the body are "intended" by the manufacturers. To answer this question, FDA was required to evaluate objectively all the relevant evidence of intent before the agency.

This evidence fell principally into three categories: (1) evidence that the pharmacological effects and uses of cigarettes and smokeless tobacco are foreseeable to a reasonable manufacturer; (2) evidence that consumers actually use cigarettes and smokeless tobacco predominantly for pharmacological purposes; and (3) evidence of the statements, research, and actions of the manufacturers themselves. The agency determined that, whether considered independently or cumulatively, this evidence demonstrated that cigarettes and smokeless tobacco are in fact "intended" to be used for pharmacological purposes.

NICOTINE'S FORESEEABLE PHARMACOLOGICAL EFFECTS

Before 1980, when FDA last considered its jurisdiction over tobacco products, no major public health organization had determined that nicotine was an addictive drug. Today, however, all major public health organizations in the United States and abroad with expertise in tobacco or drug addiction recognize that the nicotine delivered by cigarettes and smokeless tobacco is addictive. Since the 1980s, nicotine in tobacco products has been recognized as addictive by the American Psychiatric Association (1980),[8] the U.S. surgeon general (1986 and 1988),[9] the American Psychological Association (1988),[10] the Royal Society of Canada (1989),[11] the World Health Organization (1992),[12] the American Medical Association (1993),[13] and the Medical Research Council in the United Kingdom (1994).[14] This scientific consensus is based on a wealth of epidemiologic and laboratory data establishing that tobacco users display the clinical symptoms of addiction and that nicotine has the characteristics of other addictive drugs.[15]

It is also now well established that the nicotine in cigarettes and smokeless tobacco will cause, and be used for, other significant pharmacological effects, including its psychoactive or mood-altering effects in the brain.[16] In addition, it is widely recognized today that nicotine plays a role in weight regulation, with substantial evidence demonstrating that cigarette smoking leads to weight loss.[17]

The FDA found that this new scientific consensus made it foreseeable to any reasonable manufacturer that cigarettes and smokeless tobacco would cause addiction to nicotine and be used by consumers for pharmacological purposes, including satisfying their addiction. In light of the overwhelming scientific data and consensus, FDA concluded that the tobacco industry's public assertions that nicotine is not addictive were simply not credible.

The agency's finding that cigarettes and smokeless tobacco have foreseeable pharmacological effects has important legal significance. When Congress expanded the current definition of "drug" in 1938 to include products "intended to affect the structure or any function of the body," it was well understood that "[t]he law presumes that every man intends the legitimate consequences of his own acts."[18] Consistent with this well-accepted legal principle, FDA's regulations provide that a product's intended pharmacological use may be established by evidence that the manufacturer "has knowledge of facts that would give him notice" that the product will be widely used for pharmacological purposes, even if the product is not promoted for this purpose.[19] Thus, the agency concluded that the tobacco manufacturers must be held to "intend" the foreseeable pharmacological uses of their products.

CONSUMER USE OF TOBACCO PRODUCTS

A second and related basis for establishing that a product is intended to affect the structure or-function of the body is evidence showing that consumers actually use the product for pharmacological purposes. In fact, courts have recognized that even in the absence of any evidence that the manufacturer has promoted the product for a pharmacological purpose, the product's intended use as a drug or device may be established solely by evidence showing that consumers use the product predominantly for pharmacological purposes.[20]

In the case of cigarettes and smokeless tobacco, studies conducted since 1980 demonstrated to the agency that consumers do use these products "predominantly" for pharmacological purposes, including satisfying an addiction to nicotine. Major recent studies have concluded that 77 to 92 percent of smokers are addicted to nicotine in cigarettes.[21] Similarly, the U.S. Department of Health and Human Services recently estimated that 75 percent of young regular users of smokeless tobacco are addicted to nicotine.[22] A recent survey by the Centers for Disease Control and Prevention also showed that the majority of young consumers who use cigarettes or smokeless tobacco daily do so for mood alteration.[23]

Thus, this evidence of actual consumer use provided an independent basis for FDA's conclusion that cigarettes and smokeless tobacco are intended to affect the structure and function of the body.

MANUFACTURER STATEMENTS, RESEARCH, AND ACTIONS

The third category of evidence considered by the agency was newly disclosed evidence showing that tobacco companies expect their products to be used by consumers for pharmacological purposes and have designed their products to be pharmacologically active. Although this evidence included three decades of tobacco industry statements, research, and actions, virtually all of it became available only recently as the result of FDA's investigation, congressional hearings, and other sources.

The evidence of the tobacco manufacturers' statements, research, and actions in the administrative record led FDA to make two central findings regarding the manufacturers' actual intent. First, FDA found that "[m]anufacturers of cigarettes and smokeless tobacco know that nicotine in their products causes pharmacological effects in consumers, including addiction to nicotine . . . , and that consumers use their products primarily to obtain the pharmacological effects of nicotine.[24]

This finding was based in part on evidence that showed that senior officials and researchers working for the tobacco manufacturers had for decades consistently described nicotine as a pharmacologically active drug. For instance, the record showed that in internal documents tobacco company officials and researchers called nicotine "a very remarkable beneficent drug" (1962),[25] "addictive" (1963),[26] "a potent drug with a variety of . . . physiological effects . . . [and] a habit-forming alkaloid" (1972),[27] "a narcotic, tranquilizer, or sedative" (1976),[28] "pharmacologically active in the brain" (1976),[29] "the physiologically active component of smoke having the greatest consequence to the consumer" (1978),[30] "a powerful pharmacological agent with multiple sites of action" (1980),[31] "an extremely biologically active compound capable of eliciting a range of pharmacological, biochemical and physiological responses" (1980),[32] "a 'drug' " (1981),[33] and "a physiologically active . . . substance . . . [that] alters the state of the smoker by becoming a neurotransmitter and a stimulant" (approximately 1992).[34]

The agency's finding was also supported by repeated acknowledgments in the internal company documents that consumers use tobacco products to obtain the pharmacological effects of nicotine. These documents showed, for instance, that tobacco company researchers recognized that "the confirmed user of tobacco products is primarily seeking the physiological 'satisfaction' derived from nicotine"[35] and that "[w]ithout any question, the desire to smoke is based on the effect of nicotine on the body."[36] The documents also showed that the tobacco company researchers' knowledge of the importance of nicotine was communicated to the highest levels of the companies. Thus, as early as 1969, Philip Morris' vice president for research and development told the Philip Morris board of directors that "the ultimate explanation for the perpetuated cigarette habit resides in the pharmacological effect of smoke on the body of the smoker."[37]

Second, FDA found that "[m]anufacturers of cigarettes and smokeless tobacco design their products to provide consumers with a pharmacologically active dose of nicotine."[38] The FDA based this finding in part on industry documents that disclosed internal research to determine the dose of nicotine that must be delivered to provide "pharmacological satisfaction for the smoker,"[39] as well as estimates by industry scientists of the minimum and optimum doses of nicotine that tobacco products must deliver.[40] As one former senior official at Philip Morris put it, "a key objective of the cigarette industry over the last twenty to thirty years" was "maintaining an acceptable and pharmacologically active nicotine level" in low-tar cigarettes.[41]

The record before the agency showed that several methods enhancing nicotine delivery are commonly used in the manufacture of commercial cigarettes. Tobacco blending to raise the nicotine concentration in low-tar cigarettes is common. According to the vice chairman and chief operating officer of Lorillard Tobacco Co., for instance, "the lowest 'tar' segment is composed of cigarettes utilizing a tobacco blend which is significantly higher in nicotine."[42] Another common technique for enhancing nicotine delivery in low-tar cigarettes is the use of filter and ventilation systems that by design remove a higher percentage of tar than nicotine.[43] Yet a third type of nicotine manipulation is the addition of ammonia compounds that increase the delivery of "free" nicotine to smokers by raising the alkalinity or pH of tobacco smoke. These ammonia technologies are widely used within the industry.[44]

In the case of smokeless tobacco, the evidence before the agency showed that nicotine manipulation is accomplished through the use of chemicals that alter the pH of the smokeless tobacco. The FDA found that moist snuff brands that are marketed as "starter" brands have a low pH and consequently deliver a low level of "free" nicotine to the user, limiting the absorption of nicotine in the mouth. The low nicotine deliveries allow the new user to develop a tolerance to nicotine without experiencing adverse reactions such as nausea and vomiting. In contrast, moist snuff brands that are marketed to experienced users have a high pH and consequently deliver a high level of "free" nicotine to the user, increasing the amount of nicotine available for absorption. The increased nicotine deliveries provide sufficient nicotine to sustain the user's addiction.[45]

Consistent with this evidence, the internal company documents actually described tobacco products as vehicles for the delivery of nicotine. In these documents, for example, senior officials and researchers for the tobacco manufacturers expressly conceived of tobacco products as "a dispenser for a dose unit of nicotine,"[46] "[n]icotine delivery devices,"[47] "a vehicle for delivery of nicotine, designed to deliver the nicotine in a generally acceptable and attractive form,"[48] and "the means of providing nicotine dose in a metered fashion."[49]

Under the Act, these findings of the manufacturers' actual knowledge and product design provided a third independent basis for establishing that the manufacturers "intend" to affect the structure and function of the body. The plain meaning of "intend" includes "to have in mind" or "to design" for a particular use.[50] As the agency's investigation of the tobacco company documents revealed, the manufacturers did both (1) "have in mind" the use of cigarettes for the particular purpose of delivering the pharmacological effects of nicotine and (2) "design" their products to provide these effects.

TOBACCO PRODUCTS ARE COMBINATION PRODUCTS

Under the Act, products such as cigarettes and smokeless tobacco that are intended to affect the structure and function of the body can be either a "drug" under section 201(g)(1)(C) or a "device" under section 201(h)(3).[51] The principal difference between a drug and a device is that a device "does not achieve its primary intended purposes through chemical action within or on the body . . . and . . . is not dependent upon being metabolized."[52] Since enactment of the Safe Medical Devices Act of 1990, products can also be regulated as "combinations" of a drug and a device.[53] Examples of combination products include drug delivery systems such as nebulizers used by persons with asthma and transdermal patches.[54]

Based on the agency's findings regarding the pharmacological effects and intended uses of nicotine in cigarettes and smokeless tobacco, FDA concluded that the nicotine in these products is a "drug" under the Act.

The FDA further found that cigarettes and smokeless tobacco are not simply packaged nicotine. The agency found that cigarettes are "a highly engineered product" with components such as the tobacco blend, the filter, and the ventilation system that "have been carefully designed to deliver controlled, pharmacologically active doses of nicotine to the smoker."[55] Likewise, FDA found that the processed tobacco in smokeless tobacco functions "to deliver the nicotine to the cheek and gum tissue for absorption into body."[56] The FDA determined that these components of cigarettes and smokeless tobacco meet the statutory definition of a "device." Thus, FDA concluded that cigarettes and smokeless tobacco products are "combination products" under the Act.

THE TOBACCO INDUSTRY'S ARGUMENTS

The tobacco industry made two principal arguments contesting FDA's assertion of jurisdiction. First, the industry asserted that the agency was barred from regulating tobacco products because FDA had previously taken the position that it did not have jurisdiction over tobacco products, causing Congress to enact alternative approaches to regulating these products, such as the Federal Cigarette Labeling and Advertising Act and the Comprehensive Smokeless Tobacco Health Education Act.

Historically, FDA has asserted jurisdiction over tobacco products when there is sufficient evidence before the agency to establish that the products in question are "intended" to affect the structure and function of the body. Over thirty years ago, for instance, FDA asserted jurisdiction over a brand of cigarettes that were intended to reduce body weight.[57] In that case, the weight-reduction claims made by the manufacturer were sufficient evidence to allow the court to conclude that the cigarettes at issue were "obviously an article intended to affect the structure and/or function of the body."[58] In the past, however, FDA did not regulate cigarettes and smokeless tobacco as a class of products, because in the absence of advertising promoting cigarettes and smokeless tobacco for weight loss or other pharmacological uses, FDA could not establish that these products were intended to affect the structure or function of the body. The FDA's recent assertion of jurisdiction is consistent with this approach. The reason FDA is now regulating cigarettes and smokeless tobacco as a class of products is that for the first time the evidence before the agency is sufficient to show that these products are in fact "intended" to affect the structure or function of the body. None of the statutes cited by the tobacco industry bar FDA from regulating cigarettes or smokeless tobacco once this intent has been demonstrated. For example, the narrow preemption provision in the Federal Cigarette Labeling and Advertising Act only restricts federal agencies from requiring "statement[s] relating to smoking and health . . . on any cigarette package."[59]

Second, the tobacco industry argued that the intended use of a product must be determined exclusively on the basis of the promotional claims made by the manufacturer. Under the industry's legal theory, unless tobacco products are labeled and advertised for sustaining nicotine addiction, altering mood, or regulating weight, they are not "intended" as drugs or devices. Thus, the industry urged FDA to disregard the evidence from internal company documents, as well as the evidence of the foreseeable and actual consumer uses of cigarettes and smokeless tobacco.

The FDA rejected this interpretation of the Act for several reasons. First, the industry's position is contrary to the plain language of the Act. The Act does not provide that only products "promoted" to affect the structure or function of the body are drugs or devices. Rather, the Act provides that products "intended" to affect the structure or function of the body are drugs or devices. The ordinary meaning of "intend" permits a wide range of evidence to be considered in determining intent, including the types of evidence relied upon by the FDA.

Second, consistent with the plain meaning of "intend," the courts have concluded that FDA is "free to pierce . . . a manufacturer's misleading . . . labels to find actual therapeutic intent on the basis of objective evidence."[60] The courts have thus recognized that FDA may consider many categories of evidence beyond the manufacturer's promotional claims, including evidence of the pharmacological effects of the product,[61] the purposes for which consumers actually use the product,[62] the medical use of the product,[639] and how the product was formulated.[64]

Third, preserving FDA's authority to consider evidence of the pharmacological effects and uses of a product, as well as evidence of the manufacturer's knowledge and actions, is necessary for the protection of the public health. If promotional claims alone determined the intended use of a product, virtually any manufacturer of drugs or devices could avoid being required to demonstrate the safety and effectiveness of its product under the Act by simply refraining from making pharmacological claims for the product. For instance, under the tobacco industry's interpretation, a company could market a potent tranquilizer or an antidepressant for its "pleasurable" effect and thereby avoid FDA regulation. To protect the public from the unregulated distribution of products with pharmacologically active ingredients, the agency must be able to look beyond a manufacturer's promotional claims when determining whether to regulate such products.

CONCLUSION

For the reasons summarized above, FDA concluded that (1) the evidence before it demonstrated that cigarettes and smokeless tobacco are intended to sustain addiction and produce other pharmacological effect and (2) these products should therefore be regulated as "devices" intended to deliver the "drug" nicotine. This assertion of jurisdiction is the basis for one of the most important regulations in the agency's history: the Children's Tobacco Rule, a comprehensive approach to reducing cigarette and smokeless tobacco use by children by restricting their access to tobacco products and limiting the appeal of tobacco advertising to youth.[65]

NOTES

1. The regulations were published in the *Federal Register* on August 28, 1996. 61 *Federal Register* 44396.

2. 21 USC 321(g)(1)(C), 321(h)(3).

3. *Action on Smoking and Health v Harris*, 655 F2d 236 (DC Cir 1980).

4. FDA's assertion of jurisdiction is currently being challenged in four lawsuits filed in the U.S. District Court for the Middle District of North Carolina by cigarette and smokeless tobacco manufacturers and groups representing advertising and convenience store interests. *Coyne Beahm, Inc.* v. *U.S. Food and Drug Administration*, No. 2:95CV00591 (filed August 10, 1996); *American Advertising Federation* v. *U.S. Food and Drug Administration*, No. 2-95CV00593 (filed August 10, 1995); *U.S. Tobacco Co.* v. *U.S. Food and Drug Administration*, No. 6:95CV00665 (filed September 19, 1995); *National Association of Convenience Stores* v. *Kessler*, No. 2:95CV00706 (filed October 4, 1995).

5. U.S. Department of Health and Human Services, Public Health Service. *The Health Consequences of Using Smokeless Tobacco: A Report of the Advisory Committee to the Surgeon General* (Bethesda, Md.: Public Health Service, 1986), pp. 182–83; U.S. Department of Health and Human Services, Office of Smoking and Health, *The Health Consequences of Smoking: Nicotine Addiction, A Report of the U.S. Surgeon General.* (Washington, D.C.: U.S. Government Printing Office, 1988), pp. 7–8, 334–35.

6. Norton, R., K. Brown, and R. Howard, "Smoking, Nicotine Dose and the Lateralisation of Electrocortical Activity," *Psychopharmacology* 108 (1992): 473–79.

7. U.S. Department of Health and Human Services, Office of Smoking and Health, *The Health Consequences of Smoking,* pp. 431–32.

8. American Psychiatric Association, *Diagnostic and Statistical Manual of Mental Disorders,* 3d ed. (Washington, D.C.: American Psychiatric Association, 1980), pp. 159–60, 176–78.

9. U.S. Department of Health and Human Services, Public Health Service, *The Health Consequences of Using Smokeless Tobacco*; U.S. Department of Health and Human Services, Office of Smoking and Health, *The Health Consequences of Smoking,* pp. 431–32.

10. American Psychological Association, statement in *Hearing before the Subcommittee on Health and the Environment of the Committee on Energy and Commerce, U.S. House of Representatives,* 100th Cong. 1st Sess., July 29, 1988.

11. Royal Society of Canada, Health Protection Branch, *Tobacco, Nicotine, and Addiction: A Committee Report* (Ottawa, Ontario: Health and Welfare Canada, August 13, 1989), pp. v–vi.

12. World Health Organization, *International Statistical Classification of Diseases and Related Health Problems, 10th Revision (ICD-10)* (Geneva, Switzerland: World Health Organization, 1992), p. 76.

13. American Medical Association, "Ethyl Alcohol and Nicotine as Addictive Drugs," In *1993 AMA Policy Compendium* (Chicago: American Medical Association, 1993), p. 35.

14. Medical Research Council, *MRC Field Review of Drug Dependence* (London: Medical Research Council, 1994), p. 11.

15. J. C. Anthony, L. A. Warner, and R. C. Kessler, "Comparative epidemiology of dependence on tobacco, alcohol, controlled substances and inhalants: Basic findings from national comorbidity survey," *Experimental Clinical Psychopharmacology* 2 (1994): 244–68; L. T. Kozlowski, A. Wilkenson, W. Skinner, et al., "Comparing Tobacco Cigarette Dependence with Other Drug Dependencies," *JAMA* 261 (1989): 898–901; Centers for Disease Control and Prevention, "Cigarette Smoking among Adults—United States," *MMWR Morbidity and Mor-*

tality Weekly Report 43 (1993): 924–30; T. E. Novotny, J. P. Pierce, M. C. Flore, et al., "Smoke-less Tobacco Use in the United States: The Adult Use of Tobacco Surveys," *Monographs of the National Cancer Institute* 8 (1989): 25–28; H. H. Severson, "Enough Snuff: ST Cessation from the Behavioral, Clinical, and Public Health Perspectives," in *Smokeless Tobacco or Health: An International Perspective* (Bethesda, Md.: National Institutes of Health, 1993), monograph 2, NIH publication No. 93–3461; W. A. Corrigall and K. M. Coen, "Nicotine maintains robust self-administration in rats on a limited access schedule," *Psychopharmacology* 99 (1989): 473–78; W. A. Corrigall, K. B. J. Franklin, K. M. Coen, et al., "The mesolimbic dopanimergic system is implicated in the reinforcing effect of nicotine," *Psychopharmocology* 107 (1992): 285–89; M. J. Marks, J. B. Burch, and A. C. Collins, "Effects of Chronic Nicotine Infusion on Tolerance Development and Nicotine Receptors," *J. Pharmacol. Exp. Ther.* 226 (1983): 817–25; M. E. M. Benwell, D. J. K. Balfour, and J. M. Anderson, "Evidence that tobacco smoking increases the density of (–) [3H] nicotine binding sites in the human brain," *Journal of Neurochemistry* 50 (1988): 1243–47.

16. Norton et al., "Smoking, Nicotine Dose and the Lateralisation of Electrortical Activity"; Pritchard, "electroencephalographic Effects of Cigarette Smoking"; J. Golding and G. L. Mangan, "Arousing and De-arousing Effects of Cigarette Smoking under Conditions of Stress and Mild Sensory Isolation," *Psychophysiology* 19 (1982): 449–56.

17. U.S. Department of Health and Human Services, Office of Smoking and Health, "The Health Consequences of Smoking," pp. 431–32.

18. *Agnew v. United States,* 165 US 36, 53 (1897).

19. 21 CFR 201.128, 801.4.

20. *Action on Smoking and Health* v. *Harris,* pp. 239–40.

21. J. R. Hughes, S. W. Gust, and T. F. Pechacek, "Prevalence of Tobacco Dependence and Withdrawal," *American Journal of Psychiatry* 144 (1987): 205–208; G. E. Woody, L. B. Cottler, and J. Cacciola, "Severity of Dependence: Data from the DMS-IV Field Trials," *Addiction* 88 (1993): 689–96; K. L. Hale, J. R. Hughes, A. H. Oliveto, et al., "Nicotine Dependence in a Population-Based Sample," in L. Harris, ed., *Problems of Drug Dependence, 1992* (Washington, D.C.: U.S. Government Printing Office, 1993), NIDA Research Monograph 132.

22. U.S. Department of Health and Human Services, Office of Smoking and Health, *Spit Tobacco and Youth* (Washington, D.C.: U.S. Government Printing Office, 1992), p. 8.

23. Centers for Disease Control and Prevention, "Reasons for tobacco use and symptoms of nicotine withdrawal among adolescents and young adult tobacco users—United States, 1993," *MMWR Morbidity and Mortality Weekly Report* 43 (1994): 745–50.

24. U.S. Food and Drug Administration, "Nicotine in cigarettes and smokeless tobacco is a drug and these products are nicotine delivery devices under the Federal Food, Drug, and Cosmetic Act: Jurisdictional determination," *Federal Register* 61 (August 28, 1996): 44619, 44630.

25. C. Ellis, science adviser to BATCO board, "The Smoking and Health Problem," in *Smoking and Health—Policy on Research,* Proceedings of a BATCO Research Conference (Southampton, England, 1962). BAT Industries PLC, formerly the British-American Tobacco Company (BATCO), is the corporate parent of Brown & Williamson Tobacco Corp., the third-largest cigarette manufacturer in the United States.

26. A. Y. Yeaman, general counsel of Brown & Williamson Tobacco Corp, "Implications of Battelle Hippo I and II and the Griffith filter," July 17, 1963, memorandum that is now part of FDA's administrative record to docket 95N-0253.

27. C. E. Teague, assistant director of research for R.J. Reynolds Tobacco Co., "Research planning memorandum on the nature of the tobacco business and the crucial role of nicotine therein," April 14, 1972, memorandum that is now part of FDA's administrative record to docket 95N-0253.

28. A. Udow, researcher for Philip Morris Inc., "Why People Start to Smoke," June 2, 1976, 141 *Congressional Record* H7663, July 25, 1995.

29. Minutes of BATCO Group R&D conference on Smoking Behavior at Southampton, England, October 11–12, 1976, minutes that are now part of FDA's administrative record to docket 95N-0253.

30. Philip Morris Inc., "Research and Development Five-Year Plan, 1978," memorandum that is now part of FDA's administrative record to docket 95N-0253.

31. J. L. Charles, researcher for Philip Morris Inc., "Nicotine Receptor Program-University of Rochester," March 18, 1980, memorandum that is now part of FDA's administrative record to docket 95N-0253.

32. BATCO Group R&D, "Method for Nicotine and Cotinine in Blood and Urine," May 21, 1980, memorandum that is now part of FDA's administrative record to docket 95N-0253.

33. Tobacco Advisory Council, a trade association representing United Kingdom tobacco manufacturers, monograph on the pharmacology and toxicology of nicotine, 1981, monograph that is now part of FDA's administrative record to docket 95N-0253.

34. Philip Morris Inc., draft report regarding a proposal for a "safer" cigarette code-named Table, approximately 1992, report that is now part of FDA's administrative record to docket 95N0253.

35. Teague, research planning memorandum on the nature of the tobacco business.

36. M. Senkus, researcher for R.J. Reynolds Tobacco Co, "Some Effects of Smoking," 1976/77, talk delivered to R.J.R. Tobacco Marketing and Marketing Research personnel, attached to comment No. 96181 to FDA's administrative record to docket 95N-0253.

37. H. Wakeham, vice president for research and development for Philip Morris Inc., "Smoker Psychology Research," November 26,1969, memorandum that is now part of FDA's administrative record to docket 95N-0253.

38. U.S. Food and Drug Administration, "Nicotine in cigarettes and smokeless tobacco is a drug . . ." p. 44630.

39. BATCO Group R&D conference at Duck Key, Fla., January 12–18, 1974, memorandum that is now part of FDA's administrative record to docket 95N-0253.

40. Senkus, "Some Effects of Smoking"; notes of BATCO Group R&D conference at Duck Key, Fla.; W. L. Dunn, researcher for Philip Morris Inc., "Motives and Incentives in Cigarette Smoking," 1972, industry internal paper on FDA's administrative record to docket 95N-0253.

41. W. A. Farone, "The manipulation and control of nicotine and tar in the design and manufacture of cigarettes: A scientific perspective," March 8, 1996, memorandum that is now part of FDA's administrative record to docket 95N-0253.

42. A. W. Spears and S. T. Jones, "Chemical and Physical Criteria for Tobacco Leaf of Modern-day Cigarettes," *Recent Adv. Tobacco Sci.* 7 (1981): 22.

43. U.S. Food and Drug Administration, "Nicotine in cigarettes and smokeless tobacco is a drug . . ." pp. 44963–69.

44. Ibid., pp. 44970–75.

45. Ibid., pp. 45110–16.

46. Dunn, "Motives and Incentives in Cigarette Smoking."

47. Philip Morris Inc., draft report regarding a proposal for a "safer" cigarette code-named Table."

48. Teague, research planning memorandum on the nature of the tobacco business and the crucial role of nicotine therein.

49. Proceedings of BATCO Group R&D Smoking Behavior-Marketing Conference, session 1, July 9-12, 1984, document that is now part of FDA's administrative record to docket 95N-0253.

50. W. Morris, *The American Heritage Dictionary of the English Language,* 2d ed. (Boston, Mass.: Houghton Mifflin Co., 1991), p. 668.

51. 21 USC 321 (g)(1)(C), 32 1(h)(3).

52. Ibid.

53. 21 USC 353(g).

54. U.S. Food and Drug Administration, intercenter agreement between the Center for Drug Evaluation and Research and the Center for Devices and Radiological Health, 1991.

55. U.S. Food and Drug Administration, "Nicotine in cigarettes and smokeless tobacco is a drug . . . ," p. 45209.

56. Ibid., pp. 45213–14.

57. *United States* v. *Bulk Cartons . . . Trim Reducing-Aid Cigarettes,* 178 F Supp. 847 (DNJ 1959).

58. Ibid., p. 851.

59. 15 USC 1334(a).

60. National Nutritional Foods Association v. FDA, 504 F2d 761, 789 (2d Cir., 1974).

61. *United States* v. *Undetermined Quantities ... 'Pets Smellfree,'* 22 F3d 235, 240 (10th Cir., 1994).

62. *Action on Smoking and Health* v. *Harris,* pp. 239–40.

63. *United States* v. *An Article of Device . . . Toftness Radiation Detector,* 731 F2d 1253. 1257 (7th Cir., 1984).

64. *American Health Products Co.* v. *Hayes,* 574 F supp. 1498, 1508 (SDNY, 1983).

65. See note 1.

8

The Criminal Case against the Tobacco Industry

Lowell Bergman and Oriana Zill

THE TARGET LETTERS

The tobacco industry won some important battles during the summer of 1998, including derailing congressional efforts to pass national tobacco legislation and a recent federal appeals court decision to overturn a lower court's ruling giving the Food and Drug Administration (FDA) the power to regulate tobacco. Despite recent gains, the industry still faces upcoming court battles from the state Medicaid cases and the threat of the looming criminal case. It now appears that the U.S. Department of Justice [DOJ] criminal case against the tobacco industry is reorganizing, and certain companies may be better off than originally thought.

Frontline has learned that the criminal case against Philip Morris has stalled and the prosecutors are having difficulty proving criminal misconduct against the giant of the tobacco industry. Sources close to the investigation have told *Frontline* that Philip Morris has so carefully relied upon internal lawyers that many of the potential claims against them simply cannot be proven. The case against R.J.R. Tobacco is still proceeding, but prosecutors may have difficulty bringing charges before the statute of limitations expires [in 1999]. The case against Brown & Williamson Tobacco remains the strongest case at Justice and indictments will most likely appear before the end of [1998].

This article originally was published in FRONTLINE ONLINE's web site report, "Inside the Tobacco Deal" at www.pbs.org/frontline/shows/settlement, in May 1998. Reprinted with permission.

In early July [1998], the attorney general assigned John C. Keeney, seventy-six, to head the DOJ Special Task Force on Tobacco. Keeney is a long-term veteran of the Justic Department who has extensive experience with organized crime cases. This change could signal a new approach to the tobacco case at the Justice Department, although Keeney has not yet implemented any major changes in strategy. Keeney replaces Mary Spearing, former head of the Fraud Division, who left in June [1998] for private practice. He will take over the nearly four-year-old investigation of the tobacco industry that has remained a thorny issue for the companies.

In the spring of 1998, target letters went out from the Special Task Force on Tobacco of the Department of Justice to the attorneys representing Brown & Williamson Tobacco, the corporation, and to a number of the corporation's senior executives. Attorneys familiar with the "target letter" procedure told PBS *Frontline* that the letters are a notification to the nation's third largest cigarette company that it could expect to be indicted by the federal grand jury, and was being afforded an opportunity to present evidence prior to the prosecutor actually asking for formal charges.

Sources close to the investigation tell PBS *Frontline* that actual indictments are not expected for some time, probably by the end of [1998]. The notification of the Brown & Williamson executives and attorneys is seen by some observers as an invitation for them to cooperate with the Department of Justice before they are charged. That's exactly what DNA Plant Technology Corporation (DNAP), the company which worked with Brown & Williamson (B & W) to develop genetically engineered tobacco plants with an artificially high nicotine content, chose to do. In exchange for pleading to a minor charge and paying a fine, DNAP has been cooperating in the ongoing investigation of B & W, providing testimony that has in part led to the issuance of the "target letter."[1]

The investigation of B & W and its officials is said to be focused on the company's statements to the FDA about both allegedly boosting the impact of nicotine with additives; and with statements they made in person as well as written comments to the FDA concerning the genetic engineering of tobacco plants (Y-1 Tobacco). The individuals who have been notified are said to have participated in meetings at the FDA that were tape recorded and participated in preparing official B & W submission—document—to the FDA during the agency's comment period on its proposal to regulate the tobacco industry.

The FDA was first informed of the "impact boosting" technology and the genetic engineering project back in 1994 by a then-secret source, Dr. Jeffrey Wigand. Later Dr. Wigand—the former vice president of Research and Development of B & W—repeated those charges in a deposition in the Mississippi Medicaid suit in November of 1995.[2]

FOUR-YEAR-OLD CRIMINAL INVESTIGATION

These new events represent a watershed in the now almost four-year-old Washington-based federal criminal investigation of the tobacco industry. It began as a pro forma inquiry that was assigned to several Justice Department prosecutors who were between cases. Today it is a growing Special Task Force in the Fraud Section of the Criminal Division of the Department of Justice (DOJ), occupying a suite of offices that includes over a dozen attorneys and an equal number of full-time senior FBI agents. The task force became one of the DOJ's major criminal cases in March of 1997, when senior FBI officials offered to provide a full time squad of experienced agents. The FBI's commitment of personnel was a signal that the DOJ management believed that there was in fact criminal conduct that might be proven in court.

The Justice Department originally initiated the investigation in response to a prosecution memo drafted by the office of Congressman Marty Meehan (Dem.-MA). Initially, the investigation focused on the statements of the tobacco CEOs in April of 1994 that they did not 'believe' that nicotine was addictive.[3] While the DOJ Task Force explored the possibility of perjury charges, that option has been abandoned because of the difficulty of prosecuting anyone for their "belief."

The task force is now focusing on allegations of conspiracy to defraud; violations of "1001"—false statements to the U.S. government; tax violations related to the Council on Tobacco Research; illegally targeting children and adolescents in advertising; and the degree to which the industry's lawyers conspired to deceive trial courts and the U.S. government when it came to revealing what it knew about the health effects of tobacco.

THE TOBACCO INDUSTRY LAWYERS

Sources tell PBS *Frontline* that the role of the attorneys—both inside and outside counsel—is a constant subject of interest to the investigators. Rulings in Minnesota's Medicaid case, and similar rulings in Florida's Medicaid case citing the "crime fraud exception" have stripped away the use of the attorney/client privilege by tobacco's lawyers. Simply, you cannot use the confidentiality granted to attorneys to shield what appears to be criminal conduct.

Millions of documents have been released as a result of these findings. In fact, it was the first such finding by a federal judge [in 1992] that would lead to the first serious criminal investigation of the industry.

Prosecuting lawyers for aiding and abetting a criminal conspiracy is a relatively new development. Task force lawyers are looking at a recent ruling in Florida as they consider charges against the tobacco lawyers. In a recent Cali Cartel Case, the lawyers who were involved in assisting the drug lords were charged for being part of the conspiracy. They claimed their role was that of an attorney, a counselor, and that they are protected by their privileges. However, the federal judge ruled that whether or not the attorney/client privilege applied was a matter that would be decided by the jury. The jury heard the case and came back deadlocked. Prosecutors in the tobacco investigation have been contemplating a similar approach.

Dr. Gary Huber, for example, has been interviewed extensively by FBI agents and federal prosecutors. Dr. Huber, for many years a favorite scientist of the tobacco defense firm of Shook, Hardy & Bacon, maintains in an interview with *Frontline* that he was told by David Hardy, the late senior partner and architect of the tobacco industry's defense strategy, that the purpose of their sponsorship of medical research was to delay regulation.[4]

RICO

Initially (see "Development of RICO Argument" section below) some of the Justice Department personnel— especially the FBI—recommended using the RICO, or racketeering, statutes. This was rejected in part because the Fraud Section of the Criminal Division of the Justice Department rarely uses the RICO Act as opposed to the Drug or Organized Crime Sections. The failure to use RICO limits some aspects of the case that could be made against the industry both in terms of the extent of the conspiracy and the severity of the charges.

Without using RICO, the task force is operating under a deadline of April of 1999 due to the five-year statute of limitations. Charges could be brought based on a starting point of April 1994—the appearance of the CEOs of the industry before Congressman Waxman's committee, and the Marty Meehan memorandum. Professor Robert Blakely and others believe that a move by the prosecutors to consider RICO charges—Blakely wrote the RICO law— would relax that deadline, and would allow them to include the historic roots of the tobacco industry's strategy to keep information from the surgeon general and other government entities involved in protecting the public health.

Documents

With the exception of parts of the B&W investigation, much of the tobacco industry case is a document case. Investigators regularly peruse the Internet for documents that have emerged from cases around the country, especially Minnesota. "Minnesota saved us a lot of time. They litigated all the issues raised by the industry to block discovery, and we are benefiting as a result," explained one task force member.

One veteran investigator remarked that it has to be a document case because " . . . we get more informants from the Mafia than we do from inside tobacco."

The FBI has even established a web site inviting individuals with knowledge of the industry to contact them. There is no indication that it has been a great success. One source says that the lack of witness/informants, and the extensive lawyering "especially by Philip Morris makes this a very difficult case."

THE ROOTS OF THE INVESTIGATION

On the roster of the prosecutors involved in the Task Force is a Ms. Elisa Liang. While she has an office in Washington at 1500 New York Avenue with the rest of the Justice Department Tobacco Task Force, her real home is in the Eastern District of New York (Brooklyn). Ms. Liang has inherited, and is passing on the results of, the first serious criminal investigation of the tobacco industry. Her particular focus is the Council on Tobacco Research, the non-profit tax-exempt entity established by the industry (see below) to fund and find answers to the questions surrounding tobacco and health.

The initial probe in Brooklyn started [in 1992] when a federal judge wrote a scathing opinion about the conduct of the industry. In February 1992, U.S. District Judge H. Lee Sarokin wrote these words in the case of Susan Haines against the tobacco industry:

> ". . . [O]ne wonders when all industries will recognize their obligation to voluntarily disclose risk from the use of their products. All too often in the choice between the physical health of consumers and the financial well-being of business, concealment is chosen over disclosure, sales over safety, and money over morality. Who are these persons who knowingly and secretly decide to put the buying public at risk solely for the purpose of making profits and who believe that illness and death of consumers is an appropriate cost of their own prosperity! As the following facts disclose, despite some rising pretenders the tobacco industry may be the king of concealment and disinformation.[7]

Judge Sarokin's opinion was the result of years of tobacco and health litigation that he presided over, including the famous Cipollone case.[8] He was ruling in this matter on a motion by the same lawyers involved in that case. The idea was to unseal and reveal the documents which the industry had claimed were protected by the attorney/client privilege. Sarokin's conclusion, given his opening remarks, was a given: "The court concludes that the evidence overwhelmingly favors applying the crime/fraud exception in this case. . . ."

Sarokin ruled that the documents had to be handed over. But his scathing, emotional opinion gave the industry an opening, and they applied to the Third Circuit Court of Appeals and Sarokin eventually was removed from the case for bias.[9] Some who agreed with him lamented his outburst because it removed a strong, knowledgeable jurist from the case.

THE EASTERN DISTRICT AND THE COUNCIL ON TOBACCO REGULATION

The removal of the judge did nothing to stop the impact of his decision. Rarely, if ever, has a federal judge suggested that the mountains of documents should be made public because they were really part of a massive fraud, and that the lawyers were guilty of a potentially criminal cover-up.

In Brooklyn, back at the headquarters of the U.S. Attorney for the Eastern District, prosecutors and investigators read about Sarokin's blast, and reacted. One told *Frontline*: "If a federal judge is saying the [tobacco] attorneys could not have documents held privileged because of the crime/fraud exception, you assume there is a crime or a fraud there."

And so an investigation, a criminal investigation, of possible fraud by the industry was initiated. The Brooklyn federal probe approved by U.S. Attorney Andrew Maloney and supervised by one of his deputies, Matthew Fishbein, immediately set off a cascade of memos from inside the industry as subpoenas for documents arrived.

The investigation focused on areas already prepared by the plaintiffs in *Cipollone* and *Haines,** and memorialized by Judge Sarokin: that the tobacco industry had created an institution, the Council on Tobacco Research, that promoted allegedly objective scientific research into the health effects of tobacco. In reality, that research was controlled to make sure it either disproved any causation between tobacco and disease, or the research was stopped before it could reach a conclusion.

OTHER CRIMINAL INQUIRIES

There were other criminal investigations of the tobacco industry popping up around the country. Cigarette smuggling on a massive scale from low tax

---

*http://www.pbs.org/wgbh/pages/frontline/shows/settlement/timesline/haines:html (Eds.)

tobacco states to high tax states like New York had long been a favorite activity of organized crime. And smuggling cigarettes into countries in Europe and Asia to avoid taxes or undermine a national tobacco monopoly was a big business that could only go on if U.S. tobacco manufacturers were supplying the cigarettes that are then smuggled. While the FBI launched a number of preliminary inquiries, none bore fruit.

In New Orleans, a U.S. Customs undercover operation picked up a massive smuggling operation involving Brown & Williamson Tobacco. The New Orleans case revealed a conspiracy to transport untaxed cigarettes into Canada, which had recently jacked up its tobacco tax. While that case would result in arrests and at least one guilty plea (by a regional manager for the tobacco company), B & W successfully employed well-financed, hardball legal maneuvers. They even got the Justice Department to remove the lead prosecutor in the case and filed lawsuits (later dropped) against individual officers of U.S. Customs.

Meanwhile, the U.S. Attorney for the Southern District of New York was examining the failure of Phillip Morris to disclose its potential liabilities to stockholders in its SEC [Securities and Exchange Commission] filings. And in Washington, the Anti-Trust Division of the Justice Department was beginning to look at an industry-wide conspiracy to keep a "fire safe" cigarette off the market. Both probes appear to have concluded without resolution.

THE COUNCIL ON TOBACCO RESEARCH

The Eastern District (Brooklyn) investigation had the advantage of all the work done by the Cipollone lawyers, and the fact that the industry had claimed a reported $500 million in charitable contributions to its Council on Tobacco Research. Those contributions were tax deductible, and so the theory became that if it could be shown that the contributions were not for real research, but in essence public relations material designed to defeat lawsuits and regulation, then there might be tax fraud.

In fact, documents now available from the tobacco companies' files—many concealed from the public and the government by the use of the attorney/client privilege—state that the CTR was in fact a "public relations front" whose research grants were guided by attorneys. But, according to one senior investigator in the Eastern District of New York case, the investigation got bogged down in document production. "We didn't get to the heart of the case fast enough, since there are so many documents that we were trying to go through."

But the theory that attracted the Eastern District is still active today in the current investigation, and in many of the Medicaid suits brought by the state attorneys general. It is based on the industry's public relations response to the first health scare over tobacco nearly forty-five years ago.

THE FRANK STATEMENT

In 1954, when the first allegations emerged about smoking and cancer, the industry responded by issuing an advertisement in hundreds of national newspapers, a "Frank Statement to Cigarette Smokers."[10] In it, the industry promised to be honest with the public. "We accept an interest in people's health as a basic responsibility, paramount to every other consideration in our business."

They also founded a new "independent" research organization, called the "Tobacco Industry Research Committee." The name was later changed to the Council on Tobacco Research. They pledged that this group would be independent and staffed with scientists of "unimpeachable integrity and national repute."

In addition, the industry and its lawyers sponsored what were called "Special Projects," that were supervised by a coordinating Committee of Counsel. The Haines lawyers alleged that the "Special Projects" were aimed at obfuscating the debate on smoking and health and hiding evidence that smoking was addictive and caused diseases.

"We started looking at the Council on Tobacco Research, the Committee of Counsel and the Tobacco Institute because these were the only places where the industry crossed paths, and the natural place where they would set industry-wide policy," said a source familiar with the New York case. The investigation became overwhelmed with documents. This source reveals that while the Brooklyn case hit all the major points being made today, they simply lacked focus: "The bottom line is that we should have been looking smaller, to prove that specific things are crimes, rather than trying to go through one million documents and get the big picture."

TOBACCO EXECUTIVES TESTIFY

While the Brooklyn case eventually landed on the back burner, a seminal event in April 1994 would result in setting off the current special tobacco investigation. That event was the testimony of the seven tobacco executives before Henry Waxman's Congressional Committee.[11] Among the witnesses were William Campbell of Philip Morris, James Johnston of RJR, Andrew Tisch of Lorillard, and Thomas Sandefur of Brown & Williamson. All the executives, along with their colleagues from Liggett, U.S. Tobacco and others, would testify that they did not believe nicotine to be addictive. Those statements, combined with an avalanche of publicity around an ABC News broadcast about nicotine manipulation, created a controversy that still plagues Big Tobacco today.

That day, the tobacco executives also testified that they do not manipulate the levels of nicotine in their products in order to addict smokers. Several months earlier, the FDA had announced plans to consider regulation of nicotine as a drug. The tobacco executives vehemently opposed the regulation of nicotine. They claimed nicotine levels were simply linked to tar levels, and that nicotine was merely one component of the "taste" experience in smoking.

DAY ONE STORY AND THE MEEHAN MEMO

The testimony that they "believe that nicotine was not addictive," combined with the roiling public controversy over an ABC News *Day One* story that described the alleged manipulation of nicotine, focused the public on the issue and the industry's willingness to dissemble.[12] But this broadcast and other events were taking place during a period when Big Tobacco—the major companies—only played hardball. They sued ABC News, eventually intimidating its corporate management into forcing a settlement and retraction onto the News Division. But the suit against ABC was a short-lived victory for Big Tobacco.

Many Americans were shocked by the tobacco executives' statements and their confrontational attitude. Congressman Marty Meehan (Dem.-MA), a former federal prosecutor, was especially offended and began drafting a letter to Attorney General Janet Reno. Meehan and his staff followed up in December 1994 with a draft of what is known as a "prosecution memo" or a "pros memo" in DOJ vernacular—a document that outlines the law and the instances of alleged crime. It was part of the custom and policy of the Department of Justice to prepare a response, including an "investigation" by one or more department attorneys. It is a courtesy that the Justice Department affords to members of Congress or the White House staff.[13]

Meehan focused on several main legal issues: *Perjury,* or lying to Congress; *1001,* or Deception of federal officers or agencies; *Fraud,* a scheme to lie or mislead, especially through the mail or wires; and Criminal Conspiracy, or RICO, a conspiracy to commit criminal acts. He outlined some of the evidence and encouraged the Justice Department to seek out more from the mountains of secret industry documents they could subpoena.

One of Meehan's advisors and co-authors, Clifford Douglas, an attorney and dedicated anti-tobacco activist, made sure that the letters and the memo got to the *Wall Street Journal*. They published an article in July of 1995 announcing that the Department of Justice would convene a grand jury to investigate perjury, lying to federal officers and agencies, and other activities by the industry.

In point of fact, few at the Department of Justice took the situation seriously. The industry executives' testimony that they did not "believe" that nicotine was addictive might have been laughable back in the spring of 1994, but it was unlikely that anyone could prove perjury. "Belief" was a lawyer's word that no doubt was inserted in their statements on advice of counsel. It is nearly impossible to prove someone lied willfully and materially about a belief.

JIMMYE WARREN, SENIOR TRIAL ATTORNEY, DOJ

The Meehan memo and letter wound up on the desks of two attorneys assigned to the Fraud Section of the Department of Justice. This branch of the Criminal Division specializes in industry misbehavior, and many of the attorneys assigned to it have made their mark prosecuting defense contractors. But one of the lawyers who received the assignment to look into the tobacco industry's possible criminal conduct had a long career prosecuting complex drug and gang cases. Unlike many of her colleagues, Ms. Jimmye Warren was used to dealing with recalcitrant witnesses who would stop at nothing to conceal their crimes.

Warren's experience and her dogged focus would prove crucial in the early stages of the probes. Her colleagues would often express chagrin that they were assigned to the case simply to write a letter back to the congressman saying there was no evidence of criminal wrongdoing that might result in a conviction. After all, their supervisor, Mary Spearing, chief of the Fraud Section, was known for being extremely conservative in her approach to cases. Unlike the organized crime or drug sections of the department where Warren had spent most of her career, the Fraud Section rarely, if ever, used the expansive powers of the RICO, or racketeering, statute. Crimes in this part of the Justice Department were usually prosecuted one by one, and never perceived in the overall matrix that made RICO so effective.

THE MERRELL WILLIAMS DOCUMENTS

In the spring of 1994, another event took place that would invigorate the criminal case, and give the DOJ prosecutors a lot of reading material. Merrell Williams had been a paralegal for a law firm working with Brown & Williamson Tobacco. His job was to sort through industry documents. While reading documents, Williams began to understand the depth of industry deception and began secretly copying documents and taking them out of the building. By the time he was fired, he had copied four thousand pages of internal documents.

Among the documents was a memorandum by Brown & Williamson general counsel, Addison Yeaman, which states that "we are in the business of selling nicotine, an addictive drug."[14] That document remains today one of the most damaging ever to emerge from inside the industry.

The Merrell Williams documents were crucial to the developing criminal investigation. They contain evidence that the industry had known about the dangers of cigarettes and kept it hidden from the public. Justice Department officials got copies of the documents and added them to the growing pile of evidence which included another cache of memorandums from inside Phillip Morris that were leaked to the press, as were the B & W files.

THE FIRST WITNESS, JEFFREY WIGAND

Around this time, a whistleblower emerged named Dr. Jeffrey Wigand.[15] Wigand had been a Vice President of Research for Brown & Williamson until he was fired in March of 1993. He provided the invaluable resource of an insider's knowledge of a major tobacco company. It was Wigand who could bring to life and bring up to date the documents that Williams had liberated.

Wigand testified in November 1995 in a sealed deposition in Pascagoula, Mississippi, for the Mississippi state attorney general's lawsuit against the industry. Wigand had already been contacted by the Justice Department prosecutors and Ms. Jimmye Warren attended his deposition. Her mere presence at the anti-trust deposition that morning and the attorney general's proceeding that afternoon changed the course of the criminal case. Wigand's testimony would provide a road map that would later reach fruition in the target letters that were sent recently to B & W.

WIGAND'S TESTIMONY

Wigand testified that Brown & Williamson edited out sections of documents that might prove damaging in future litigation. He told of shipping documents out of the country so they would be unavailable for examination in the United States if subpoenaed.

He described the process of treating nicotine with ammonia in order to boost its impact on the brain. "The primary method of managing or manipulating nicotine delivery," said Wigand, "is by use of the ammonia compound." He testified that his boss Thomas Sandefur had lied under oath to the United States Congress when he stated that "I believe that nicotine is not addictive."

Finally, he described how Brown and Williamson had genetically engineered a special tobacco plant named Y-1, which was twice as high in nicotine as regular tobacco. They then illegally exported the tobacco seeds to Brazil to grow and imported the tobacco back to the United States for use in B & W cigarettes.

Wigand's testimony would jump-start the Justice Department's investigation.[16] They now had someone to explain the documents and bring them to life. DOJ prosecutor Jimmye Warren quckly moved to stay in contact with Wigand's then criminal lawyer, Ephriam Margolin. The two worked out a cooperation agreement and proceeded to prepare Wigand for further debriefing by the Department of Justice so that his information could be presented to a grand jury in Washington. Warren and Margolin then approached a federal judge in Washington, D.C., to stop Brown & Williamson Tobacco's attorneys from deposing Wigand until such time as the Justice Department had finished debriefing him. This was a crucial move in helping to preserve Wigand's survival as his former employer launched a nationwide effort in the media and through investigators and public relations operatives to smear the whistleblower.

Y-1 TOBACCO AND THE FDA

B & W was suing Wigand in part for his public disclosures, but also because they no doubt suspected that he was behind the trouble they were having with the FDA. More than a year earlier, Wigand had begun secret meetings with the FDA to help in their attempts to prove that nicotine is an addictive drug that should be regulated. During these meetings, Wigand explained in detail the Y-1 tobacco story, including the fact that Brown & Williamson Tobacco had hired a genetic engineering firm called DNA Plant Technology to develop the high-nicotine plants. He also told them to look for the patent for Y-1 in Portuguese in Brazil.

Armed with this information, ten FDA investigators, including Special Investigator Jack Mitchell, traveled to the Brown & Williamson offices in Louisville, Kentucky, to question the company. Without letting on that he knew about Y-1, Mitchell questioned the Brown & Williamson officials and asked them about genetic engineering and plant breeding.

"One of our party of ten FDA people asked the question to whether Brown & Williamson engaged in any genetic engineering or genetic changing of the nicotine in the plants," said Mitchell during his interview with *Frontline*. "And, at first, the answer we got was no. But then [they], as I recall, clarified that answer by saying Brown & Williamson indeed did fund some research on that project at private universities, but they did not do the genetic engineering research themselves."

Mitchell also asked them many questions about manipulating nicotine, and the answers to his questions were not straightforward. "I think there were executives at the companies who have been, to be kind, less than candid about some of these key issues," Mitchell told *Frontline*. This is important because producing Y-1 is not, itself, a crime under United States law. However, as Mitchell pointed out, "You have an affirmative obligation as a company to provide accurate and honest information to the government, even if you're not a regulated industry."

After this session with the FDA, B & W appeared to realize their mistake. Representatives from DNAP, the company that conducted their genetic research, and B & W descended on the FDA as the administrator, David Kessler, was preparing to testify. According to sources, those meetings with Kessler's chief deputy—Mitch Zeller—now provide some of the statements that are part of the grand jury investigation. Those statements, combined with statements made in B & W's filings with the FDA by their executives, have also triggered some of the target letters that make up the first substantive criminal prosecution of the industry.

DEVELOPMENT OF THE RICO ARGUMENT

In the midst of the state attorneys general Medicaid cases, a Florida judge suggested that given the massive nature of the fraud he was learning about in the courtroom, that the RICO statute might apply to the industry. That hint led the Florida attorney general, Bob Butterworth, and the lead plaintiff's attorney, Ron Motley, to go in search of an expert in the racketeering law and its use.[17] They recruited the former federal prosecutor G. Robert Blakey, who had written the RICO law.

After initial skepticism, Blakey developed an analysis of the tobacco industry based on RICO.[18] Central to his argument is his allegation that the industry conspired to destroy evidence that would be damaging to it in court. While this theory has not been adopted by the Department of Justice, it has been the subject of internal discussions.

Frontline has received various documents from lawyers involved in the RICO litigation in the Florida and Texas Medicaid cases. These documents support Blakey's theories and would have been part of the court cases had those states not settled their suits. Two of those documents are especially on point. In a 1977 Philip Morris memo from a Mr. Dunn to Dr. Thomas Osdene (PM Director of Research), Dunn says: "I have given Carolyn approval to proceed with this study. If she is able to demonstrate, as she anticipates, no withdrawal effects of nicotine, we will want to pursue this avenue with some vigor. If however, the results with nicotine are similar to those gotten with morphine and caffeine, we will want to *bury it*. Accordingly, there are only two copies of this memo. . . ."

Another document, a 1972 Committee of Counsel memo from Fred Panzer to Horace Kornegay, outlines the basic strategy of the industry:

> For nearly twenty years, this industry has employed a single strategy to defend itself on three major fronts—litigation, politics and public opinion. While the strategy was brilliantly conceived and executed over the years helping us win important battles, it is only fair to say that it is not, nor was it intended to be, a vehicle for victory. On the contrary, it has always been a holding strategy, consisting of:
> - creating doubt about the health charge without actually denying it;
> - advocating the public's right to smoke, without actually urging them to take up the practice;
> - encouraging objective scientific research as the only way to resolve the question of the health hazard.

The document goes on to discuss setting up more projects and releasing the results in book form only if favorable, especially directing the "favorable" research to their allies in Congress.

The RICO argument has continued to be used in other third party cases against the tobacco industry. In fact, there was a recent decision in a New York District Court to accept the RICO argument in the Taft-Hartley Act Funds case against the tobacco companies.

ANOTHER WHISTLEBLOWER EMERGES

Ron Motley developed a witness who would be invaluable to his RICO argument, which had been accepted by the federal court in Texas as well as Florida's state court. The witness emerged because internal industry documents revealed that one of the many projects they supported was, in fact, a sham. It was called "The Havard Project," and it was run by a scientist named Dr. Gary Huber. Motley contacted Dr. Huber and showed him many of the documents, eventually convincing Huber to become a whistleblower for the state Medicaid cases.

Frontline interviewed Dr. Huber in March 1998 to hear his story.[19] Huber described to us, from an insider's perspective, how the industry had used him, manipulated his research and wasted his career. "Every scientist that the industry had any contact with had a keeper, within the industry, a lawyer." Huber was visited repeatedly by tobacco executives and he briefed them on his research. But he was never left alone with the executives, there was always a lawyer present, to protect any conversation under attorney/client privilege.

Huber's entire research program had been centered on the attempt to create emphysema in animals, to study whether there were links between smoking and emphysema. Huber worked for years in the lab, exposing rats and pigeons to cigarette smoke. Then, when he finally achieved some results and produced emphysema in animals, his research was cut off by the industry and his lab shut down.

When Motley contacted Huber, he showed him a document, which *Frontline* also has, which indicates the industry had created emphysema in animals as early as 1969. But they never shared this research with Huber.[20] "We worked night and day for years and we did develop emphysema in animals," Huber says. "And then I learned, twenty-five years later that they had already done this within the industry. And done it before the Harvard Project started and didn't tell us about it."

When asked why the industry would do this, Huber is clear in his opinion. "From all I've seen it was to buy time. To buy time to pass the liability from the manufacturer to the consumer with the labels, to buy time to avoid regulation for greater profit. To buy time to diversify their markets overseas. To buy time to diversify their enormous profits into other industries. To buy time."

Huber discovered that his career had been squandered to a grand design and he decided to come forward. He has been interviewed extensively by the Justice Department as part of their case.

THE MINNESOTA STATE MEDICAID CASE

It was in a Minnesota courtroom in February of 1996 that prosector Jimmye Warren again appeared representing the United States government. This time she raised the heat in the state's lawsuit against the industry by informing the court that the Criminal Division was interested in all the documents being disgorged by the state's lawyers in that case.

THE TASK FORCE

By the spring of 1996, the complexion of the DOJ's case was transformed. No longer a pro forma letter-writing exercise, the case was becoming a high priority of the department. The earlier investigation in Brooklyn that had come to a virtual standstill was incorporated into the Tobacco Task Force. Attorneys like Randall Eliason, who worked in the U.S. Attorney's office in Washington, D.C., joined in. Warren's partner in the probe, Richard Wiedis, was given his own little team on Philip Morris, while another DOJ veteran, Marie O'Rourke, headed a team looking at R. J. Reynolds.

The task force's importance was marked in March of 1998 by the addition of a full-time squad of FBI agents who were veterans of complex investigations. Their supervisor is Duncan Wainwright. Providing a full-time FBI squad to an investigation is a recognition by the FBI's administrative hierarchy that the case is a top priority that will in fact result in real action.

Duncan Wainwright's background included being the lead agent ten years earlier in the Department of Justice's RICO civil action against the Teamsters Union. Brought in the Southern District of New York, the Teamster's RICO case resulted in a court-appointed trusteeship that continues in part to this day. It was a phenomenal success, ending decades of open corruption in the union and leading directly to the first democratic election of its leadership. Since then, Wainwright had supervised a number of complex FBI probes into fraud by major defense contractors.

THE LANDSCAPE CHANGES

Since 1996, the DOJ prosecutors have been bringing witnesses before several separate grand juries considering various aspects of alleged tobacco company crimes. Tobacco industry executives such as Nick Brookes of Brown & Williamson have been called in to testify. The Justice Department has used the tactic of encouraging lower-level employees to "turn" on their bosses and reveal criminal wrongdoing. And Big Tobacco is taking the threat seriously enought to hire a heavy-duty criminal defense team, including former Whitewater prosecutor Robert Fiske.

After the DNAP charges and plea bargain and the notification to Brown & Williamson that it and some of its executives were targets, the landscape around the case changed dramatically. Armed now with all the documents that are on the Internet, including the millions made available in the Minnesota case, the Department of Justice Task Force is organizing its approach.

With evidence piling up, it was logical that the FBI would propose that the tobacco criminal investigation take on the RICO statute as its model. The argument about RICO has been ongoing throughout the probe, but in late 1997, Fraud Chief Mary Spearing rejected the notion. Without RICO, the prosecutors have only until April 1999 before the statute of limitations expires. Some of the most senior FBI agents who have been working on the case are being pushed into retirement since they have reached the age of fifty-five. This could also damage the continuity of the investigations.

Mary Spearing left for private practice in June 1998 and John Keeney is heading the department's Task Force and the Fraud Section.

JOHN KEENEY

At seventy-six, Keeney is the oldest and most experienced employee at the Department of Justice headquarters. John "Jack" Keeney has worked for the DOJ since 1951. He worked on organized crime for Robert Kennedy in the early 1960s and became a fixture at the DOJ, rising in the career ranks to run the Crime Division, and then to being a perennial special assistant to the attorney general. Keeney is rarely quoted in the press, and the fact that his son recently emerged as the defense attorney for a prominent figure in the campaign finance investigations of the DOJ raised questions about conflict of interest.

Keeney is known as a keeper of the department's deepest secrets and a master of working out ways of avoiding potential problems for his bosses. His appointment to run the Fraud Section and to supervise its most high-profile investigation may be a reflection of the political minefields that surround the probe.

LIGGETT BECOMES AN INFORMANT

The recent DOJ agreement with Liggett and its owner, Bennet LeBow, is likely to help the investigation, but not reveal any dramatic new evidence.[21] This company was in the inner circle of the tobacco industry for years and may provide some clues to inter-company agreements that would help to prove the conspiracy if a RICO case should be started. Liggett attempted to negotiate immunity from criminal prosecution, but was unable to get it. Liggett has waived the attorney/client privilege, which will force its attorneys and others to provide evidence to the task force.

CONCLUDING NOTES ON THE JUSTICE DEPARTMENT'S CURRENT CASE

The tobacco industry has recently won some major battles, demonstrating their strength in congressional politics and in the courts. It now appears that Philip Morris is no longer a prime target of the Justice Department investigation due to the expertise of their in-house council at "lawyering" the documents. Yet the Department of Justice investigation could lead to dramatic challenges for the rest of the industry in the year to come. The Justice Department, unlike Congress, needs no concessions from the industry to prosecute, yet could demand huge concessions in any plea agreement. And the DOJ investigation includes the parent companies, who are likely to "give up" the tobacco companies to prevent the parent companies from suffering damage. The criminal case against the tobacco industry may become the greatest hazard yet on Tobacco Road.[22,23,24,25,26]

NOTES

1. FOR IMMEDIATE RELEASE
FRIDAY, JANUARY 23, 1998

PLANT COMPANY PLEADS GUILTY IN TOBACCO FRAUD INVESTIGATION
WASHINGTON, D.C.—DNA Plant Technology Corporation (DNAP) pleaded guilty today to one misdemeanor count of conspiracy to violate the Tobacco Seed Export law, the Department of Justice announced. Sentencing was set for a later date.

The plea is the first criminal conviction in the Department's continuing investigation of the tobacco industry. As part of its plea agreement, DNAP agreed to cooperate with the government's investigation.

The Department's Fraud Section and the U. S. Attorney's office for the District of Columbia said DNAP pleaded guilty before Chief Judge Norma Holloway Johnson to a criminal information filed in U.S. District Court for the District of Columbia charging it with conspiring to send tobacco seed to several foreign countries without a federal permit (18 U.S.C., Sec. 371).

DNAP, based in Oakland, California, is a biotechnology company that develops and improves various plant varieties through genetic engineering and advanced breeding technique.

According to the information, DNAP entered into a contract in 1983 with a United States tobacco company (which, as an unindicted co-conspirator, the government declined to name as a matter of policy), to grow and improve high-nicotine lines of tobacco.

The information charged that DNAP conspired with the tobacco company and its Brazilian affiliate to violate a law that prohibited the export of tobacco seed from the United States without a permit. It charged that employees of DNAP and the tobacco companies, from 1984 through 1991, conspired to illegally export tobacco seeds to Brazil and a number of other countries to develop tobacco with a high nicotine content. The law prohibiting such exports was repealed in 1991.

The government said employees of DNAP and the tobacco company illegally shipped the seed by air express or courier and hid it on themselves to smuggle into Brazil while traveling.

One of the tobacco company's goals, said the information, was to develop a reliable source of high-nicotine tobaccos that could be used to control and manipulate the nicotine levels in the company's cigarettes. The government also charged that during an investigation of the tobacco industry by the Food and Drug Administration in 1994, DNAP knowingly concealed from the FDA information about its contract with the tobacco company and the export of tobacco seeds.

The maximum penalty for the misdemeanor violation is a fine of $200,000 or twice the pecuniary gain to DNAP under the contract.

The Justice Department praised the work of the Federal Bureau of Investigation (FBI) squad dealing with the tobacco investigation. [Source unknown. See http://www.pbs.org/wgbh/pages/frontline/shows/settlement/timelines/dna.html]

    2. Deposition of Jeffrey Wigand: http://www.gate.net/~jcannon/documents/wigand.html

    3. http://www.pbs.org/wgbh/pages/frontline/shows/settlement/timelines/april94.html

    4. http://www.pbs.org/wgbh/pages/frontline/shows/settlement/interviews/huber.html

    5. http://www.fbi.gov/majcases/tobacco/wfo.htm

    6. http://www.pbs.org/wgbh/pages/frontline/shows/settlement/timelines/meehan.html

    7. U.S. District Judge H. Lee Sarokin, Newark, N.J. 1992. http://www.pbs.org/wgbh/pages/frontline/shows/settlement/timelines/haines.html

    8. 1983—Rose Cipollone and Judge Lee Sarokin: Rose Cipollone was fifty-seven years old and dying of lung cancer when she filed a product liability suit against three cigarette makers—Liggett Group, Philip Morris and Lorillard. Cipollone had averaged a pack and a half a day since she was sixteen years old and was accusing the tobacco companies of failing to warn her adequately of the potential lethal effects of cigarettes and their addictive nature. Cipollone died in October 1994, but her lawyer Marc Edell pursued the lawsuit. District court judge Lee Sarokin presided over the case and ruled a number of times to open up the discovery process. The documents obtained represented the first glimpse by an outsider into the internal documents of the tobacco companies. Judge Lee Sarokin ruled that Liggett was to pay $400,000 in damages to Cipollone's family—the first time a tobacco company had to pay damages to the family of a stricken smoker. Liggett was held to have been negligent for its failure to warn smokers properly of the health risks prior to 1966 and for advertising that could be interpreted as a warranty for safety. Philip Morris and Lorillard were let off completely because Cipollone had started smoking these brands after the warnings began in 1966. Sarokin's opinion in this case, and in the Haines case, were extremely critical of the tobacco companies and formed the basis for a Justice Department investigation.

    http://www.pbs.org/wgbh/pages/frontline/shows/settlement/timelines/cippolone.html

    9. http://www.pbs.org/wgbh/pages/frontline/shows/settlement/timelines/haines.html

  10. http://www.pbs.org/wgbh/pages/frontline/shows/settlement/timelines/frank.html

  11. http://www.pbs.org/wgbh/pages/frontline/shows/settlement/timelines/april94.html

  12. http://www.pbs.org/wgbh/pages/frontline/shows/settlement/timelines/1995.html

  13. http://www.pbs.org/wgbh/pages/frontline/shows/settlement/timelines/meehan.html

  14. This memo was one of the documents stolen by Merrell Williams when he worked for a Brown & Williamson law firm. His documents were leaked to Congress by Dick Scruggs and Mike Moore and ended up on the Internet after being delivered to anti-tobacco activist, Professor Stan Glantz at the University of California, San Francisco. He received the documents from an unknown source 'Mr. Butts.'

The document is an internal Brown & Williamson memo from July 17, 1963. It is written by Addison Yeaman, General Counsel for Brown & Williamson. He is summarizing the soon-to-be-released surgeon general's report and assessing potential damage to the cigarette industry. The document is critically important; it indicates that top-level executives in the tobacco industry knew about the dangers of smoking back in the early 1960s, but they continued to deny them for over thirty years.

In this paragraph, Yeaman is responding to the upcoming surgeon general's Report and concluding that it's highly likely that cigarettes will be shown to cause cancer:

> Whatever qualifications we may assert to minimize the impact of the Report, we must face the fact that a responsible and qualified group of previously noncommitted scientists and medical authorities have spoken. One would suppose we would not repeat Dr. Little's oft reiterated "not proven." One would hope the industry would act affirmatively and not merely react defensively. We must, I think, recognize that in defense of the industry and in preservation of its present earnings position, we must either (a) disprove the theory of causal relationship or (b) discover the carcinogen or carcinogens, co-carcinogens, or whatever, and demonstrate our ability to remove or neutralize them. This means that we must embark—in whatever form of organization—on massive and impressively financed research into the etiology of cancer of the lung. Certainly one would hope to prove there is no etiology of cancer as it relates to the use of tobacco; what constituents or combination of constituents in cigarette smoke cause or are conducive to cancer of the lung. Certainly one would hope to prove there is no etiological factor in smoke but the odds are greatly against success in that effort. At the best, the probabilities are that some combination of constituents of smoke will be found conducive to the onset of cancer or to create an environment in which cancer is more likely to occur.

In [the following] paragraph, Yeaman is describing what will likely occur after the surgeon general's Report is released and the cigarette industry comes under attack. All of these measures are now (1998) being attempted, but were not attempted in 1963, when the memo was written.

> Thus to accept its responsibility would, I suggest, free the industry to take a much more aggressive posture to meet attack. It would in particular free the industry to attack the surgeon general's Report itself by pointing out its gaps and omissions, its reliance on statistics, its lack of clinical evidence, etc., etc. True, we might worsen our situation in litigation, but that I would risk in contemplation of the greater benefits to be derived from going on the offensive. My record of advice in this area may well justify the charge of inconsistency, but let me say that so long as the industry does not assume its research responsibility my long-held position would remain unchanged and I would oppose either outright attacks on the surgeon general's Report or the giving of assurance to the smoking public not supported by research evidence.
>
>   There is, however the problem of what to do until the doctor comes and this leads me to the second of the two measures I would urge the industry to take:
>
> 2. The surgeon general's Report will, of course set off attacks all along the line. Our harsher critics—Senators Moss and Neuberger, the American Cancer Society, et al.—will immediately press for all sorts of restrictive and repressive programs:
>   a) Public education directed particularly at the young.
>   b) Much harsher FTC rules in respect of cigarette advertising, with restriction of the scope and control of content thereof. One might anticipate rules seeking to prevent the use of "glamour situations," endorsements including those of athletes, prominent entertainment figures, etc., and quite likely an effort to bar tobacco advertising from television and radio.
>   c) "Content" labeling or cautionary legends.
>   d) FTC to be given power of preliminary injunction in respect of cigarette advertising.
>   e) Repressive taxation.

Next, Yeaman suggests that the industry attempt to deter criticism by voluntarily agreeing to warning labels on cigarette packs:

To accomplish anything effective, the Institute needs the leadership of a strong tobacco figure, e.g., Albert Clay, Paul Hahn, etc., a highly expert trade association staff including experienced and respected lobbyists and, lastly, such adornments of public figures as appearance and occasion warrant.

The question immediately arises: how would such aggressive posture affect litigation? With one exception (*Green* v. *American Tobacco Co,*), those actions which have gone to judgment were won by the defendants on the defense of assumption of risk. The issuance of the surgeon general's Report will, in my opinion, insure the success of that defense as to causes of action arising in the future *if the industry can steel itself to issuing a warning.* I have no wish to be tarred and feathered, but I would suggest the industry might serve itself on several fronts if it voluntarily adopted a package legend such as "excessive use of this products may be injurious to health of susceptible persons": and would embody such a legend in pica in its shocking [*sic*]—that I would rather not try to anticipate the arguments against it in this note but reserve my defense.

It is difficult to assess the effect of the report on causes of action arising prior to its issuance. Logically, it would be argued, the report does no more than to collate pre-existing knowledge, knowledge as available to the buyer as the seller. But logic might—in the minds of a jury—yield to the emotional reaction that if this knowledge was available to the seller it was up to him, *having the means to do so,* to make the product safe. A jury might, whether instructed or not, operate on the theory of comparative negligence: "True the buyer was negligent in smoking a product he knew was dangerous, but he was lulled by the seller and the seller's negligence was the greater in failing to make his product safe."

In [the following] section, Yeaman seems to be suggesting that the industry admit that nicotine is addictive and that the industry sells nicotine. He also admits that cigarettes cause lung cancer and may cause emphysema. He suggests that they challenge these claims, but also offer better filters to calm smoker's health worries:

Our investigation definitely shows that both kinds of drugs (Rauwolfin alkaloids and nicotine) act quite differently, and that nicotine may be considered (its cardiovascular effects not being contemplated here) as more 'beneficial'—or less noxious—than the new tranquilizers, from some very important points of view.

The so-called beneficial effects of nicotine are of two kinds:
1. Enhancing effect on the pituitary-adrenal response to stress;
2. Regulation of body weight.

These effects do not seem to be shared by reserpine, which on the contrary shows undesirable side actions that are not given by nicotine, i.e. a nearly complete blockade of gonadic and thyroid activities, reflecting most probably a general blockade of the hypothalamo-pituitary system, which normally controls all the endocrine activities.

Moreover, nicotine is addictive.

We are, then, in the business of selling nicotine, an addictive, drug effective in the release of stress mechanisms. But cigarettes—we will assume the surgeon general's committee to say—despite the beneficent effect of nicotine, have certain unattractive side effects:
1) They cause, or predispose to, lung cancer.
2) They contribute to certain cardiovascular disorders.
3) They may well be truly causative in emphysema, etc. etc.

We challenge those charges and we may have assumed our obligation to determine their truth or falsity by creating the new Tobacco Research Foundation. In the meantime (we say) here is our triple, or quadruple or quintuple filter, capable of removing whatever constituent of smoke is currently suspect while delivering full flavor—and incidentally—a nice jolt of nicotine. And if we are the *first* to be able to make and sustain that claim, what price Kent? Dare we as a matter of policy make such claims? If they are true and if we make no claim of freedom from danger—indeed, if we cry caution—why should we not? I would submit that the FTC in the face of (1) the industry's research effort, (2) the truth of our claims, and (3) the "public interest" in our filter, cannot successfully deny us the right to inform the public.

As for litigation, it would be my opinion that we would not put ourselves in substantially worsened position and in any event a successful Avalon [*sic*] could be expected to satisfy a number of judgments for damages.

Have we an obligation to make our knowledge available to our competitors? If the Griffith claims stand up and when we have perfected the Griffith filter and stocked, the necessary machinery, etc., then I suggest there is strong moral obligation on us to make our knowledge public and free. And think of the kudos. I will be vastly surprised if such disclosure markedly adds to our competitors' knowledge, but that is beside the point.

The point is: On this new terrain, permitting strong offensive action, *we get there fastest with the mostest.*

15. http://www.pbs.org/wgbh/pages/frontline/shows/settlement/timelines/wigand.html
16. http:://www.gate.net/~jcannon/documents/wigand.html
17. http://www.pbs.org/wgbh/pages/frontline/shows/settlement/interviews/motley.html
18. http://www.pbs.org/wgbh/pages/frontline/shows/settlement/interviews/blakey.html
19. http://www.pbs.org/wgbh/pages/frontline/shows/settlement/interviews/huber.html
20. http://www.pbs.org/wgbh/pages/frontline/shows/settlement/case/bergmandoc.html
21. http://www.pbs.org/wgbh/pages/frontline/shows/settlement/interviews/lebow.html
22. SMOKING HOWITZERS:

These were released as a result of the ongoing state Medicaid lawsuits. From these and many other documents, lawyers in the Medicaid suits have developed various theories to show the tobacco industry committed a fraud against the American public. The documents have contributed to the idea that the tobacco industry lawyers controlled scientific research in an attempt to hide data that was damaging to the industry. In other words, they covered up evidence that smoking is addictive and causes diseases. They also used or "misused" the attorney/client privilege to try to keep this evidence from the public.

AUERBACH DOG STUDY:

This document shows that as early as 1970 cigarette companies had medical evidence that smoking causes lung cancer in animals.

This document, written on April 3, 1970, is from a British tobacco company, Gallaher Limited. The document is a memo that summarizes the results of a smoking study conducted on dogs. It is very important: it shows that cigarette companies had medical evidence that smoking causes lung cancer in animals as early as 1970.

Gallaher Limited
From: General Manager, Research
To: Managing Director
Your Ref. — — —
Sub. Ref. VOT/JR Date: 3rd April, 1970
Subject: Auerbach/Hammond Beagle Experiment
CONFIDENTIAL:

Recently, you asked me to prepare some brief notes on our views on the Auerbach/Hammond work with some beagles.

I have set down our views on this research , which are partly taken from a memorandum to Mr. Pritchard dated 25th February. I also attach for your information documents H465, which has been prepared by Dr. Brian Davis, on the implications of the Auerbach work for Harrogate research.

Our views are as follows: —

(1) We have had an opportunity of seeing both the Auerbach work and the work at Battelle North West. Both research groups are using beagles which are made to inhale fresh whole cigarette smoke. The main difference is that in Auerbach's dogs a tracheostomy has been carried out and a tube inserted into the trachea. This means that smoke can be involved directly through the trachea into the lungs, thus bypassing the mouth and upper part of the trachea. In contrast, the dogs at Battelle North West have no surgical treatment and are trained to inhale the smoke from a smoking mask. Given the right animal handler and a reasonable period of acclimatization (usually about a month), the dogs appear to inhale the smoke without undue stress and the minimum of restraint. The only obvious outward evidence of smoking is that they tend to salivate. Those two contrasting methods are described because ideally most biological research workers would prefer an animal model which does not resort to surgery and therefore fairly severe trauma, with the possible risk of introducing infection into a part of the body adjacent to that under test. However, even when we bear this in mind, Auerbach's research is undoubtedly a significant step forward and we have to remember that the control animals also tolerated a tracheostomy without undue discomfort and trauma and there was no evidence that these animals showed any signs of precancerous or cancerous changes.

Here the author clearly states that cigarette smoke is highly likely to be carcinogenic in human lungs.

(2) One of the striking features of the Auerbach experiment was that practically every dog which smoked suffered significantly from the effects of the smoke, either in terms of severe irritation and bronchitis, precancerous changes or cancer. This, of course, is a much more extreme situation than in human beings where only one in ten heavy smokers get lung cancer and one in five suffer from some form of respiratory infection, often described as mild bronchitis. We can, therefore, question whether the beagle is in some way untypical of human behavior and the only reasonable argument against this is that the dogs were given a much more massive dose compared with the human dose and in the case of Auerbach's work, since the smoke bypassed the mouth, which sets as a good trap for certain constituents of the smoke, the dog lung was subjected to a much greater effect from the smoke.

(3) However, in spite of the qualifications in one and two, we believe that the Auerbach work proves beyond reasonable doubt that fresh whole cigarette smoke is carcinogenic to dog lungs and therefore it is highly likely that it is carcinogenic to human lungs. It is obviously impossible to be certain of the extrapolation from an animal lung to a human lung, but we have to bear in mind that the anatomy of the dog is relatively close to human anatomy and the type of tumor found in the dog was the same type as found in heavy smokers.

Here the author clearly states that smoke causes lung cancer:

To sum up, we are of the opinion that Auerbach's work proves beyond all reasonable doubt the causation of lung cancer by smoke, even though in an ideal situation it would have been preferable to avoid a surgical technique, and to allow the animals to live out their life span. Nevertheless, there are certain shortcomings of the experiment and it is easier to see these in hindsight.

23. YOUTH SMOKING DOCUMENTS:

This Philip Morris document from 1981 clearly shows that Philip Morris knew that teenagers used their product, studied it extensively and were worried about any decrease in youth smoking, since it would affect their future customers. When these documents were shown to Philip Morris CEO Geoffrey Bible at the Minnesota Medicaid trial, he said he was "shocked" by them.

The introduction shows that Philip Morris was worried about demographic trends showing decreases in youth smoking:

PHILIP MORRIS U.S.A.
INTER-OFFICE CORRESPONDENCE
RICHMOND, VIRGINIA
To: Dr. Robert B. Seligman   Date: March 31, 1981
From: Myron Johnston
Subject: *Young Smoker—Prevalence, Trends, Implications, and Related Demographic Trends*

For over fifteen years certain demographic and social trends have been moving in directions favorable to industry growth. Now, one by one, these powerful social and demographic factors are turning against us, and by 1985 all will be operating against us.

The trends are:

1. After increasing for over a decade, the prevalence of teenage smoking is now decling [*sic*] sharply.

2. After increasing for over a decade, the average daily consumption of teenage smokers is declining.

3. After increasing 18 percent from 1967 to 1976, the absolute number of 15–19-year-olds will decline 19 percent during the 1980s, with the period of sharpest decline beginning in 1981.

4. Beginning in 1981 the absolute number of 20–24-year-olds (the ages during which average daily cigarette consumption increases most rapidly) will begin to decline, after increasing for the past 20 years.

5. For the first time in a decade of polling, average daily cigarette consumption as reported on the National Panel has declined.

6. In 1985, after declining for nearly a decade, the number of people in the age group most disposed to quit smoking (ages 45–54) will begin to increase dramatically.

The inevitable outcome of these studies is that industry sales will decline. This is important, because tobacco executives have repeatedly testified to Congress that they do not market to children and that they do not need young people to start smoking. This document clearly contradicts that claim. These lies to Congress and the American people form the basis of the criminal investigation.

It is inevitable therefore, that industry sales will begin to decline within the next few years. Thus, Philip Morris USA can sustain its past rate of growth only by an acceleration of the rate of increase in market share. While this news is not good for the industry, I believe we can use these data and other data I plan to report on to good advantage in order to minimize the adverse effect on Philip Morris. This report deals with only one of these trends—teenage smoking and attitudes toward smoking, together with related demographics. Subsequent reports will cover the social, economic and psychographic characteristics of teenage smokers and the demographics of other significant age groups. Because the major data sources have just become available, and because of the importance of these data to the company, I have elected to report the data in a series of memoranda rather than wait and issue all of the material at once.

MEJ:yl
Attachments
CC: Mr. R. Thomson   Mr. J. Zoler (HYO)
    Mr. R. Daniel   Mr. T. Goodale (NYO)
    Dr. C. Levy
    Mr. L. Heyer

24. And, this earlier March 1979 memo regarding youth smoking, outlines plans to start a special resort program to represent a continuing brand presence among young adults. It then goes on to describe programs to give away Marlboro products at the beach and at other hangouts.

1979 Special Programs

1. *Resort coverage-in existence for eight years,* this program represents a continuing brand presence among young adults. For two to three weeks during the spring and summer breaks the Sales Force promotes the brand heavily at POS. Marlboro T-shirts, visors, etc. are given away at the beach, bars, and other hang outs. No publicity nor outside visibility is desired. The program is expanding and in '79 will cover the New England Shore, Myrtle Beach, Texas, Padre Island, the Ozarks, Wisconsin and the Jersey Shore.

2. *Summer Sampling.* Approximately 150 samplers are dispatched to beaches, shopping centers, and other markets of opportunity. This program maintains a pressure on the marketplace.

3. *Marlboro Chili Promotion.* Would be conducted in April. This promotion is a joint POS and media event.

4. *The Marlboro Cup.* September 8th, will mark the 7th running of the Cup.

5. *Marlboro Country Store.* This is an ad which has run previously in 1972 and 1975. It is a spread , which offers 12-14 Western cowboy type items. It is a self-liquidator and is scheduled to run in October weeklies and November monthlies.

25. The Committee of Counsel:

According to *Frontline*'s interview with Philip Morris executive Steve Parrish, the Committee of Counsel was a group of tobacco industry lawyers that met regularly to discuss legal issues of interest to the tobacco industry. And, according to *Frontline*'s interview with former federal prosecutor G. Robert Blakey, the Committee of Counsel was the organization that controlled all industry scientific research and, according to Blakey, managed the fraud committed by the industry on the American people.

This document is the notes from a 1981 meeting of the Committee of Counsel. It clearly shows that they discussed scientific projects ("Special Projects") which were designed to promote the idea that smoking does not cause disease.

Here it is clearly stated that they were discussing the science projects managed by the lawyers, which were called 'Special Projects.':

September 18, 1981

VIA FEDERAL EXPRESS
Joseph H. Greer, Esq.
Vice President and General Counsel
Liggett & Myers Tobacco Company, Inc.
West Main and Fuller Streets
Durham, North Carolina 27702

Dear Joe:

I am enclosing a copy of my notes taken at the meeting of the Committee of General Counsel which was held on September 10, 1981, at Charbourne, Parke.

You will see that the meeting covered five subjects as follows: (1) Special Projects, (2) Status of Cases, (3) NCI workshops on the side-stream smoke, (4) Literature Retrieval Division, and (5) the 20 Asbestos witnesses. I decided to send you a transcription of my notes because that seemed to be the most effective way to give you an accurate sense of how the meeting went. I hope the transcript accomplishes this purpose.

[The following] paragraph shows that the research done under the name "Special Projects" were [sic] designed to help lawyers in litigation by creating witnesses favorable to the tobacco industry. They were also designed to 'develop information regarding gaps in knowledge,' in other words, to create research which casts doubt on the smoking and health issue:

1. Special Projects—
Jacob Crohn called, said he had received a communication from Arthur Stevens who wanted a thorough-going understanding of what was happening and that there ought to be a meeting on the subject. Jacob then defined the special projects and their origin in litigating lawyer needs.
    Purposes:
1-develop witness-stimulate the interest of doctors.
2-develop information re gaps in the knowledge.

Here the speaker is worried about attacks on the "Special Projects." He expresses concerns over the fact that these projects are advocacy oriented, in other words, they are not for scientific purposes, but for public relations purposes.

Stevens It is timely to re-examine the special projects. Want to make it invulnerable to attack. He is concerned with degree to which we make advocacy primary and science becomes secondary. He knows it is difficult to find witnesses. He is concerned over the fact that some names appear on the list time and again; such as Sterling, Furst, Aviado, who will start to lose credibility for themselves and for us. He is concerned about the quality of the science to cultivate witnesses.

Here the speaker suggests that the projects should be advocacy oriented.

Jacob If you have a doctor, you have to keep him busy or he will lose interest. Sterling has been enormously helpful. Berkson receives a small check and he has been helpful.

Witt Maybe the approach ought to be advocacy first and science second.

Here the speaker is making an important clarification between the Council on Tobacco Research and the "Special Projects." The CTR was supposed to be an independent organization, so when the director did not like a project, but the industry wanted to continue it for advocacy purposes, it would become a lawyer's special project. This means, in layman's terms, that they would go ahead and fund the project through CTR, but it would be directly controlled by the lawyers. Generally, these projects were designed to help the lawyers disprove the links between smoking and diseases:

Stevens Two other factors that concern me:
    1. I need to know what the historical reasons were for the difference between the criteria for lawyers' special projects and CTR special projects.
    2. I understand that there will be times when we need to get money into the hands of a researcher like Janus, but I would rather not create a project that does not make any sense ("pseudo science").

Jacob When we started the CTR Special Projects, the idea was that the scientific director of CTR would review a project. If he liked it, it was a CTR Special Project. If he did not like it, then it became a lawyer's special project.

Stevens He took offense re scientific embarrassment to us, but not to CTR.

Here, they explain they were "afraid of discovery":

Jacob With Spielberger, we were afraid of discovery for FTC and with Aviado, we wanted to protect it under the lawyers. We did not want it out in the open.

26. Criminal Probe Timeline:

1954 The Tobacco Industry Research Committee (later becomes Council on Tobacco Research) issues a "Frank Statement" to the public, a nationwide two-page ad that states cigarette makers don't believe their products are injurious to a person's health.

1963 Brown & Williamson general counsel Addison Yeaman notes in a memo, "Nicotine is addictive. We are, then, in the business of selling nicotine, an addictive drug."

1964 U.S. Surgeon General Luther Terry issues the first surgeon general report citing health risks associated with smoking.

1965 U.S. Congress passes the Federal Cigarette Labeling and Advertising Act, requiring a surgeon general's warning on cigarette packs.

1971 All broadcast advertising for cigarettes is banned.

1982 U.S. Surgeon General C. Everett Koop finds that secondhand smoke may cause lung cancer.

1988 Judge Lee Sarokin rules that he has found evidence of tobacco industry conspiracy in the Cipollone case; Liggett is ordered to pay Cipollone $400,000 in compensatory damages.

1992 Matthew Fishbein and other U.S. Attorneys from the Eastern District of New York open a federal probe into criminal wrongdoing by the tobacco industry, focusing on Judge Sarokin's ruling in the Haines case; Sarokin called the industry the "king of concealment."

4/14/94 Seven tobacco company executives testify during Rep. Henry Waxman's congressional hearings that they believe "nicotine is not addictive."

May 1994 Scruggs hand carries Brown & Williamson internal documents to Rep. Waxman in Washington.

5/7/94 *New York Times* publishes Brown & Williamson internal documents, saying they were received by a government official.

5/12/94 Stan Glantz at the University of California receives Brown & Williamson internal documents from "Mr. Butts."

July 1994 Justice Department opens criminal investigation into possible perjury by top tobacco company executives in their testimony before the Congress during the Waxman hearings.

12/14/94 Congressman Marty Meehan sends an 111-page prosecution memo to the Justice Department, requesting that Janet Reno open a formal criminal investigation against the tobacco industry and several of their law firms and industry organizations.

Dec 1995 Jeffrey Wigand is questioned by U.S. Justice Department officials (grand jury testimony) in the criminal investigation of the tobacco Industry.

6/20/97 The tobacco companies and state attorneys general announce a landmark $368.5 billion settlement agreement.

1/7/98 Justice Department brings charges against the DNA Plant Technology Corporation for their cooperation in developing Y-1 Tobacco, with high levels of nicotine and illegally exporting seeds to Brazil. DNA Plant Technology settles the case in exchange for testimony against Brown & Williamson Tobacco Company.

1/29/98 Tobacco executives testify before Congress that nicotine is addictive under current definitions of the word and smoking may cause cancer.

9

Tobacco Litigation as Cancer Prevention: Dealing with the Devil

George J. Annas

Tobacco companies have come to personify the devil, and strategies to exorcise tobacco smoking from the United States proliferate. Tobacco's demonic status is even reflected in popular fiction. John Grisham's latest bestseller, *The Runaway Jury,* for example, is a broadside attack on tobacco companies. He opens the book by noting that tobacco companies "had been thoroughly isolated and vilified by consumer groups, doctors, even politicians."[1] This was bad, but it was getting even worse: "Now the lawyers were after them."[2]

Physicians often see trial lawyers as predators, but choosing sides between lawyers and big tobacco has, at least recently, seemed easy. The American Medical Association (AMA), for example, now endorses "all avenues" of litigation against the tobacco companies as a public health strategy.[3] As *New York Times* reporter Philip J. Hilts puts it in a recently published book, "The natural end for a tangle like the tobacco wars is in court."[4]

Lawsuits against tobacco companies are not a new phenomenon, but until 1996 they seemed singularly impotent. Chroniclers of tobacco litigation identify three waves of litigation.[5] The first dates from the time medical research first demonstrated the risks of cancer from smoking and continued until the early 1970s (1954 to 1973). The second wave (1983 to 1992) began in the early 1980s and ended with the dropping of the Cipollone case.[6] Tobacco companies paid nothing to claimants in any of these lawsuits, ultimately winning them all by relying on three arguments: smoking is the result of a free choice, there is no conclusive proof that tobacco causes disease, and the industry supports research on the effects of smoking on health.[7] The third wave, which dates from 1994, is seen as much more likely to succeed, because of the discovery of a vast array of previously secret documents that undercut the industry's own arguments, including documents indicating that the industry knew nicotine was addictive and used this knowledge to hook users.[8] A new study that shows how a tar ingredient, benzo(a)pyrene, causes cancer by affecting the *P53* gene is prompting tobacco companies to rethink their position on causation.[9] Moreover, while plaintiff lawyers had previously been totally outgunned financially by tobacco companies willing to pay virtually any price not to lose a case, third-wave cases have been brought by teams of law firms and by state attorneys general with the help of private lawyers.[10] The playing field has been leveled to such an extent that discussions have begun on how Congress might act to settle all tobacco lawsuits in a fair manner.

THIRD-WAVE CLASS-ACTION SUITS

The class action that can be said to have marked the beginning of the third wave is *Castano* v. *American Tobacco Co.,* filed on March 29, 1994, in federal district court in Louisiana.[11] Represented by more than sixty law firms, the class seeks damages from the tobacco companies only for the somewhat ambiguous "injury of nicotine addiction." The trial court defined the class broadly to include

> (a) All nicotine-dependent persons in the United States . . . who have purchased and smoked cigarettes manufactured by the tobacco companies;
> (b) the estates, representatives, and administrators of these nicotine-dependent cigarette smokers; and
> (c) the spouses, children, relatives, and "significant others" of those nicotine-dependent cigarette smokers and their heirs or survivors.[12]

A "nicotine-dependent" person was defined as any smoker "who has been diagnosed by a medical practitioner as nicotine-dependent" or as any "regular cigarette smoker" who has been "advised by a medical practitioner that smoking has had or will have adverse health consequences" and who thereafter did not quit smoking.[13] This is, of course, a potentially giant class, comprising millions of people. For any group to be certified as a class under the *Federal Rules of Civil Procedure*, the court must find, among other things, that "the questions of law or fact common to the members of the class predominate over any questions affecting only individual members, and that a class action is superior to other available methods for the fair and efficient adjudication of the controversy."[14] The trial court so found, but the case was reversed on appeal and the class decertified.[15]

As described by the appeals court, the key to the plaintiffs' complaint was the "wholly untested theory" that the tobacco companies "fraudulently failed to inform consumers that nicotine is addictive and manipulated the level of nicotine in cigarettes to sustain their addictive nature."[16] Specific allegations included fraud and deceit, the intentional infliction of emotional distress, violation of state consumer-protection statutes, breach of warranty, and strict product liability.[17] The remedy sought was compensatory and punitive damages, attorneys' fees, an admission of wrongdoing, and the use of profits for restitution and to establish a fund for medical monitoring. The appeals court refused to certify this as a class action, primarily because it believed that the trial court had considered neither how variations in the state laws would affect the outcome of individual cases nor how a trial on the merits of the cases would actually be conducted.[18]

Concerning the issues of state law, the appeals court noted that "in a multi-state class action, variations in state law may swamp any common issues" because states have different legal rules, "including matters of causation, comparative fault, and the types of damages available. . . ."[19] Specifically, the court noted that the members of the class had used "different tobacco products for different amounts of time and over different periods."[20] Knowledge of the dangers of smoking differed from person to person, as did the reason for the use of the product in the first place. The appeals court found the idea of millions of individual cases formidable, but concluded, "Absent considered judgment on the manageability of the class, a comparison to millions of individual trials is meaningless."[21] The court stated, "The collective wisdom of individual juries is necessary before this court commits the fate of an entire industry or indeed, the fate of a class of millions, to a single jury."[22] This May 1996 decision was a serious blow to all tobacco-related class-action lawsuits. Nonetheless, the plaintiffs almost immediately set about filing separate state class actions regarding addiction, and have already done so in about a dozen states.[23]

STATE REIMBURSEMENT SUITS

Potentially more important than class-action suits are suits to reimburse states for medical costs; nineteen states and more than a dozen cities, including New York City, have sued the tobacco companies on behalf of taxpayers to recover the share of Medicaid costs and payments for the uninsured that are attributable to tobacco-induced disease. The states are being aided by outside private counsel working on the basis of contingency fees. All of the state lawsuits include allegations of fraud and causing addiction, but the claims themselves vary.[24] The first case, for example, was filed in May 1994 by the attorney general of Mississippi, Mike Moore. The Mississippi lawsuit, which is set for trial in March 1997, rests on theories of unjust enrichment and restitution that are based on the claim that the state's taxpayers have been injured directly by the tobacco industry by having to pay the medical costs of the illnesses induced by tobacco products.[25]

The second suit, filed by Attorney General Hubert H. Humphrey III, of Minnesota, alleges that tobacco companies committed both antitrust conspiracy and consumer fraud in engaging in a "unified campaign of deceit and misrepresentation" to conceal information about addictiveness from the public.[26] In early October 1996, Humphrey filed a newly discovered 1980 internal memorandum from the British-American Tobacco Company, which he characterized as "an astounding disclosure" of the time when the tobacco companies decided to continue their "deadly cover-up" instead of admitting the truth for the sake of their "integrity."[27] The memo argued that acknowledging that cigarettes cause cancer would put the tobacco companies in a more credible position, positioning them "alongside the liquor industry as being socially responsible, in that we acknowledge our products can be harmful in excess."[28] The memo also contained a warning, "If the predictions of the U.S. lawyers are correct, we could lose a cancer suit, and this could lead to a new 'industry' in America and elsewhere, that of suing tobacco companies, costing a lot of money."[29] Such evidence also strengthens racketeering allegations under the Racketeer Influence and Corrupt Organizations Act (RICO), recently permitted to proceed in Florida, which could result in triple damages against the tobacco companies.[30]

These cases mark the first time states have sued anyone for having injured people for whom the state was in turn obligated to pay medical bills.[11] Robert I. Rabin of Stanford Law School has said that given the novelty of the cases, it is impossible to predict how they will fare, noting, "It is possible that with all the revelations [of company wrongdoing] there will be a much greater likelihood of overcoming the freedom of choice argument."[31] Assuming that one or more of these state-sponsored reimbursement lawsuits is successful, the question of measuring damages may be difficult. Of the smokers who die of smoking-related illnesses, most do not die until after they become eligible for Medicare. Thus, the cost of their final illness (other than long-term care expenses) is likely to be borne not by the city or the state, but by the federal government. Moreover, to the extent that the individual smoker dies earlier than he or she would otherwise have died, the federal government may even get a net savings from Social Security and Medicare— and also from Medicaid, which pays for nursing home care for nonsmokers who live longer than smokers. The extent to which federal financial burdens and benefits should be factored into state-level judgments, or whether the federal government should itself be a party to these cases, remains to be determined.

INDIVIDUAL-SMOKER LAWSUITS

Although class actions and state-sponsored lawsuits are the main characteristics of the third wave of tobacco litigation, individual lawsuits have been
given new life by the discovery of industry documents—such as that uncovered by Humphrey—concerning addiction, the concealment of research, and
obfuscation.[32] For the first time, a jury awarded damages ($750,000) to a
smoker, Grady Carter, of Jacksonville, Florida, in August 1996 (in *Cipollone*,
the damages were awarded to the smoker's spouse).[33] Lung cancer developed
in the 65-year-old Mr. Carter after he had been smoking for forty-three years.
The jury found that Brown and Williamson, the makers of Lucky Strike cigarettes, had failed to properly warn Carter of the risks of smoking before the
time that warning labels were required by federal law. The case was the first
in which internal Brown and William son documents were admitted into evidence, and the jury seems to have been convinced that the company should
have informed the public about the addictiveness of nicotine. Interviews with
three of the six jurors revealed that two of them were angry at what they saw
as the company's hypocritical defense: the company had accumulated "reams
of evidence that smoking was harmful but continued to tell the public that the
hazards of smoking were not proved.[34] The jury also seems to have been
impressed that Mr. Carter admitted some responsibility for continuing to
smoke (he picked a physician who smoked so he would not be pressured by
his doctor to quit), sought a relatively small amount of money ($1.5 million),
and did not ask for punitive damages.[35]

In reaction to the *Carter* case, the stock prices of Philip Morris and RJR
Nabisco dropped 14 percent and 13 percent, respectively, in one day, even
though these tobacco companies were not directly involved in the litigation.[36]
Their stock prices later recovered, however, and the entire industry breathed
easier (and its stock prices rose) when a jury returned a verdict for the
defense in a later case, in Indiana, in which the company's internal documents were not admitted into evidence.[37] The Florida verdict has rekindled
interest in pursuing individual lawsuits, and a string of even relatively small
victories could go a long way toward putting the tobacco companies out of
business, as their shareholders seem to realize. Carter's attorney, Norwood
Winer, has another two hundred cases filed and plans to bring one case a
month to trial.

POSSIBLE GLOBAL SETTLEMENTS

In March 1996 the Liggett Group, the smallest of the major U.S. tobacco companies, offered to settle four of the five state suits then pending and the *Castano* class action. Liggett offered to pay each state (Florida, Massachusetts, Mississippi, and West Virginia) $4 million over a period of ten years and between 2 and 7 percent of its pretax income over twenty-four years and to settle *Castano* by paying another 5 percent of pretax income for twenty-five years for programs to help people stop smoking.[38] The company also agreed not to give out free samples or use cartoon characters in its ads.[39] The deal was originally proposed by Liggett's majority shareholder, Bennett S. LeBow, and included the right of any company Liggett merged with to make the same deal. LeBow's goal was to influence RJR Nabisco's shareholders to vote for a merger with his company. Liggett retained the right to withdraw from the agreement if the other tobacco companies won their suits on the merits, and the company could terminate the *Castano* portion if the class certification was reversed on appeal (as it was). The deal would have cost Liggett approximately $31 million over twenty-five years, far less than it would be likely to spend on legal fees.[40]

Liggett did settle with five states, has agreed to pay each $1 million, and intends to pursue settlement with the other states. But the merger did not succeed, no other company joined Liggett, and the proposal may still unravel.[41] LeBow had indicated that his company "just can't afford a scorched-earth litigation policy. . . . One major judgment against Liggett would put us out of business."[42] He continues to encourage the larger tobacco companies to pursue a global settlement.[43]

One such global-settlement proposal was floated in August 1996 by attorney Richard Scruggs, who is working with Mississippi's attorney general and apparently has the backing of Scruggs's brother-in-law, Senate Majority Leader Trent Lott. Under the proposal, the tobacco companies would pay about $6 billion in the form of grants to the fifty states in 1997, with the cost for each company based on the number of cigarettes it sells in the United States.*[44] Thereafter, the manufacturers would contribute about $100 billion over a period of fifteen years—or between 30 and 40 cents for every pack sold. In addition to dismissing all the state suits, Congress would take jurisdiction over tobacco and adopt the regulations of the Food and Drug Administration (FDA) on advertising directed at young people as law.[45] Jurisdiction would, however, return to the FDA if smoking rates among young people failed to decline within a specific period (the industry was said to see this as a "deal breaker").[46] Lawsuits would be drastically curtailed for the

---

*The deal subsequently fell through. (Eds.)

next fifteen years, although specific details were not made public. Damages for pending lawsuits would be capped.[47] The mere fact that this proposal was seriously discussed for a couple of weeks is noteworthy; it may be the basis of further discussions in the next Congress, which is the body that would have to enact any such global arrangement for it to be effective.[48]

Richard Kluger, the author of *Ashes to Ashes*, had earlier suggested an alternative global settlement:

> 1. Congress would [grant blanket] . . . immunity to the tobacco companies against all pending and future product liability claims.
> 2. The FDA would be given regulatory oversight of the manufacture and packaging of cigarettes, including the power to set maximum levels for their hazardous ingredients.
> 3. Health warning labels would be enlarged to occupy the entire back of all cigarette packs and would carry far more informative language.
> 4. . . . OSHA [Occupational Safety and Health Administration] regulations restricting smoking at most workplaces . . . and FDA [regulations regarding advertising would be promptly implemented]. . . .
> 5. The federal cigarette tax would be doubled to 48 cents to pay for enforcing these new regulations. An additional 2-cents-a-pack levy would pay for an anti-smoking advertising campaign. . . .[49]

It is hard to imagine that more specific or larger warning labels would have much of an effect on smokers, and although raising the tax on cigarettes may discourage young smokers, it strikes hardest at addicted low-income smokers.[50] Moreover, there seems to be no rationale for granting the tobacco companies blanket immunity for past wrongdoings—at least for lawsuits in which fraud can be proved. On the other hand, limited immunity may be a price worth paying for FDA regulatory authority over tobacco that would have a real chance to lead to cigarettes that are safer and contain progressively lower levels of nicotine. Both of these settlement proposals have serious shortcomings, but their existence is itself novel, and the search for some global settlement is gaining ground as litigation intensifies and the public's disgust with the tobacco industry grows.

The AMA recently indicated its distaste for the tobacco industry's projected (and probably protracted) litigation against the FDA's proposed regulations governing the access of children to tobacco products and advertising aimed at children.[51] The organization has advised physicians to focus their antitobacco efforts on persuading their patients not to smoke (and helping them quit) and on working at the state and local level for anti-smoking legislation.[52] This is reasonable advice. The new chief executive officer of RJR Nabisco, attorney Steven E Goldstone, gave up cigarette smoking at his physician's insistence seventeen years ago.[53] Goldstone is happy, however, to have his customers risk their health with his tobacco products. In his words,

"Not to be too red-white-and-blue about it, but taking risks is what this country is about."[54] And preventing unnecessary illness and injury is what public health is all about.

One risk Goldstone does not seem willing to take, however, is that society's increasing disgust with the tobacco companies will hold down the price of his company's stock. Thus, in an October 21, 1996, interview concerning third-quarter earnings, he said he was looking for a negotiated settlement to the legal war on tobacco, declaring: "I have to believe that both the industry and Congress—no matter who's in Congress—will be willing to talk about it. I'm confident President Clinton will as well."[55]

The acceptability of any global settlement will, of course, depend on one's goals in the tobacco wars. Protecting individual choice while minimizing health hazards seems reasonable, as does putting tobacco under the jurisdiction of the Consumer Protection Agency. The 1980 internal tobacco-company memorandums had it right: cigarettes are a hazardous product that, like alcohol, should be recognized and regulated as such. Prohibition has not worked and will not work, and to the extent that the proposed OSHA workplace rules would amount to a total prohibition on smoking in all workplaces, they would not work either. The twin goals of reducing smoking and making smoking itself less addictive and safer are laudable. The percentage of adult tobacco smokers in the United States seems unlikely to grow larger than its current 25 percent and will most likely continue to decrease as the habit becomes even more socially unacceptable. It is also perfectly reasonable to restrict the access of children to cigarettes and ban advertising aimed at them—something the tobacco companies can (and should) do voluntarily. Increasing taxes on cigarettes to fund anti-smoking advertising and smoking-cessation programs also seems reasonable, although using this regressive tax for other social programs (such as Medicaid) is unfair to addicted smokers.

The key to public health action on the tobacco front seems to lie in combining strategies to discourage children from smoking and in producing a safer and less addictive cigarette for those who cannot, or will not, resist the temptation to smoke. A truly global settlement must transcend U.S. boundaries, and a U.S. settlement should help set worldwide standards for tar and nicotine.[56] Litigation has many problems, but to the extent that litigation has made a global settlement at least possible, it is time to work out reasonable terms.

NOTES

1. J. Grisham, *The Runaway Jury* (New York: Doubleday, 1996).
2. Ibid.

3. J. S. Todd, D, Rennie, R. E. McAfee, et al., "The Brown and Williamson Documents: Where Do We Go from Here?" *JAMA* 274 (1995): 256–58.

4. P. J. Hilts, *Smoke Screen: The Truth behind the Tobacco Industry Coverup* (Reading, Mass.: Addison-Wesley, 1996), p. 195.

5. Ibid.; R. A. Daynard and G. E. Kelder, "Waiting to Exhale," *Boston Globe,* February 11, 1996, p. 81.

6. G. J. Annas, "Health Warnings, Smoking, and Cancer—the *Cipollone* Case," *New England Journal of Medicine* 327 (1992): 1604–1607.

7. Hilts, *Smoke Screen,* p. 195; R. Kluger, *Ashes to Ashes: America's Hundred-Year Cigarette War, the Public Health, and the Unabashed Triumph of Philip Morris* (New York: Alfred E. Knopf, 1996).

8. G. E. Kelder and R. A. Daynard, "Tobacco Litigation as a Public Health and Cancer Control Strategy," *JAMA* 51 (1996): 57–62; S. A. Glantz, J. Slade, L. A. Bero, P. Hanaher, and D. E. Barnes, *The Cigarette Papers* (Berkeley and Los Angeles: University of California Press, 1996).

9. S. L. Hwang, "Tobacco Firms May Shift Tack on Cancer Link," *Wall Street Journal,* October 21, 1996, p. B1; M. F. Denissenko, A. Pao, M-s. Tang, and G. R. Pfeifer, "Preferential Formation of Benzo[a]pyrene Adducts at Lung Cancer Mutational Hotspots in *PS53*," *Science* 274 (1996): 430–32.

10. Kelder and Daynard, "Tobacco Litigation," pp. 57–62.

11. *Castano v. American Tobacco Co.,* 160 F.R.D. 544 (1995).

12. Ibid.

13. Ibid.

14. *Castano v. American Tobacco Co.,* 84 F.3d 734 (1996).

15. Ibid.

16. Ibid.

17. Ibid.

18. Ibid.

19. Ibid.

20. Ibid.

21. Ibid.

22. Ibid.

23. C. MacLachlan, "More RICO Counts for Tobacco," *National Law Journal,* January 6, 1997, p. A7.

24. C. MacLachlan, "Now Spotlight Is on States in Tobacco War," *National Law Journal,* June 3, 1996, p. Al.

25. Kelder et al., "Tobacco Litigation," pp. 57–62.

26. Ibid.

27. "A.G.: Tobacco Papers Are 'Astounding,' " *National Law Journal,* October 21, 1996, p. A5.

28. Ibid.

29. Ibid.

30. MacLachlan, "More RICO Counts for Tobacco," p. A7.

31. MacLachlan, "Now Spotlight Is on States in Tobacco War," p. Al.

32. Hilts, *Smoke Screen,* p. 195; Glantz et al., *The Cigarette Papers.*

33. S. L. Hwang, M. Geyelin, and A. M. Freedman, "Jury's Tobacco Verdict Suggests Rough Times Ahead for the Industry," *Wall Street Journal,* August 12, 1996, p. Al.

34. Ibid.

35. Ibid.

36. Ibid.

37. M. Geyelin, "Is Tobacco Trial a 'Must Win' for Industry?" *Wall Street Journal,* August 21, 1996, p. B1.

38. A. M. Freeman, S. L. Hwang, S. Lipin, M. Geyelin, "Breaking Away: Liggett Group Offers First-Ever Settlement of Cigarette Lawsuits," *Wall Street Journal,* March 13, 1996, p. A1.

39. Ibid.

40. Ibid.

41. B. J. Feder, "Liggett's Tobacco Settlement in Danger of Coming Undone," *New York Times,* September 7, 1996, p. 38.

42. Ibid.

43. Ibid.

44. M. Geyelin, "States Greet Plan to Settle Tobacco Suits with Skepticism, But Leave Door Open," *Wall Street Journal,* August 29, 1996, p. B14; M. Geyelin, "Plan to Settle Tobacco Cases Draws Fire," *Wall Street Journal,* August 27, 1996, p. A3.

45. Geyelin, "States Greet Plan to Settle Tobacco Suits with Skepticism," p. B14; G. J. Annas, "Cowboys, Camels, and the First Amendment—the FDA's Restrictions on Tobacco Advertising," *New England Journal of Medicine* 335 (1996): 1779–83.

46. Geyelin, "Plan to Settle Tobacco Cases Draws Fire," p. A3.

47. B. Weiser, "SmokeEnders," *Washington Post Magazine,* December 8, 1996, pp. 15–19, 28–35.

48. Ibid.

49. R. Kluger, "A Peace Plan for the Cigarette Wars: Dance with the Devil," *New York Times Magazine,* April 7, 1996, pp. 28–54.

50. S. D. Sugarman, "Smoking Guns," *Science* 273 (1996): 744–75.

51. Annas, "Cowboys, Camels, and the First Amendment," pp. 1779–83.

52. "The Smoke Hasn't Cleared," *American Medical News,* October 14, 1996, p. 17.

53. B. J. Feder, "Keeping Cool in a Roomful of Smoke at RJR Nabisco," *New York Times,* July 28, 1996, p. Fl.

54. Ibid.

55. S. L. Hwang, "RJR's Profit Rose 4 Percent in Third Period; Stock Price Frustrates Chief Executive," *Wall Street Journal,* October 22, 1996, p. B12.

56. N. Gray, "The Global Cigarette," *BMJ* 313 (1996): 1348.

10

Tobacco Industry Tactics*

Edward L. Sweda Jr. and Richard A. Daynard

In the field of public policy, the tobacco industry has a long and usually successful track record in influencing legislators and other decision makers. This is especially true at the national or state level; while the industry has engaged in battles in cities and towns, its rate of success is notably poorer as they go closest to the people. Thus, the tobacco industry turns to one of its favorite strategies—preemption. In effect, the lesson to be learned is this: if you can't win at a particular level of government, then make that level of government irrelevant by taking away its power to act.

So, in 1994, after years of watching California communities pass and implement tough local laws requiring smoke-free public places, including restaurants, the tobacco industry poured over $18 million into a campaign to sponsor its preemption proposal and to collect the necessary signatures to put the proposal on the November ballot as a binding referendum. And in its efforts to obtain signatures for its effort to preempt local laws, Philip Morris falsely persuaded potential signers that its goal was to achieve a law to restrict smoking in public. California's secretary of state, Anthony Miller, accused Philip Morris's front group—called Californians for Uniform Statewide Restrictions (CUSR)—of outright deception. CUSR made no mention of its tobacco connections. "A great many signers have been duped, and they are furious and I don't blame them. Don't be fooled by petitions sponsored by the tobacco industry," said Miller.[1]

Once made aware of the tobacco industry's backing of Proposition 188,

Reprinted from *British Medical Bulletin* 52, no. 1, Edward L. Sweda Jr. and Richard A. Daynard, "Tobacco Industry Tactics," pp. 183–92, copyright © 1996, by permission of the publisher Churchill Livingstone.

*The authors wish to thank Ann. B. Toback for her assistance in preparing this article.

California voters repudiated it at the polls in November 1994, 70.5 percent to 29.5 percent.

Where they have been unsuccessful at preempting local authority to act, the tobacco lobby is not above acting directly to try to sway the balance on an upcoming vote by a city council. A recent example of this activity occurred in Cambridge, Massachusetts, where the city council was considering amending its existing ordinance (passed in 1987, requiring "no-smoking" areas of at least 25 percent of the seating capacity in restaurants over twenty-five seats) to shrink any permissible smoking section to 15 percent of the seats. Less than a week before the scheduled vote, Philip Morris launched what the *Boston Globe* described as "an aggressive last-minute phone bank operation" which was trying to stir up voter opposition to the ordinance.[2]

Alliances with restaurant associations are nothing new for the tobacco industry. One example occurred in 1993 and 1994 in Massachusetts when Roger Donoghue worked simultaneously as a registered lobbyist at the State House for both the Massachusetts Restaurant Association and the R. J. Reynolds Tobacco Company. . . .

Tobacco companies have long espoused the public position that smoking is "an adult custom." Thus, children should simply be patient and wait until they become eighteen years of age, at which time they will be sufficiently "mature" to make a personal "choice" as to whether or not to smoke. No mention is made of disease or addiction or anything negative about tobacco products. Rather, cigarettes are portrayed as the "forbidden fruit" which remains ubiquitous throughout society.

The nicotine cartel has also been alarmed by the bad publicity that retailers around the United States have received when they were caught illegally selling tobacco products to minors. R. J. Reynolds has launched a campaign with the national Jaycees—national junior Chambers of Commerce—purportedly designed to discourage sales to children. In December 1990, the Tobacco Institute initiated the "It's the Law" campaign, which featured orange and blue signs posted in stores warning that "it's the law" that tobacco sales are prohibited to those under the age of eighteen. Of course, no mention is made as to why tobacco sales to minors should not occur. Never are any health issues raised in the industry's promotional material.

The tobacco industry has repeatedly refused to provide the public—or even its own shareholders—with evidence that would show the effectiveness or noneffectiveness of the industry-created and industry-financed campaigns against sales to minors. A glimpse of the industry's true position on this important issue can be seen in some promotional material for retailers that was disseminated by R. J. Reynolds, which designated June 1995 as "National Awareness Month" about the problem of illegal tobacco sales to children. The R. J. Reynolds' "Dear Retailer" letter states that "while accessibility at retail is not the reason kids start using tobacco products, it does provide them with the opportunity to continue." It goes on to allege: "we also recognize the efforts of organized sting operations across the country that may have serious ramifications for retailers. These sting operations do not focus on education. The objective of these operations seems to be to make the retailer look bad rather than to work with the retailer to solve the problem." Again, there is no mention of addiction, disease, or health in this letter to retailers. . . .

If there is not an appropriate group or entity to make an alliance with on a particular subject, the tobacco industry does the next best thing—it creates them! A prime example in the United States is the National Smokers Alliance (NSA). Maintaining the guise of a spontaneous grass-roots uprising of millions of smokers outraged at the steady infringement of their God-given rights as Americans, the NSA is in reality an "astro-turf" organization, designed to give the appearance of a legitimate expression of genuine anger at the grass roots, but created and financed by powerful outside interests. So, the NSA came into existence with the benefit of seed money from Philip Morris's public relations firm, Burson-Marsteler. It quickly claimed over a million members. The term "member" was defined simply as someone signing his name to a form provided by signature gatherers who were paid per signature and who gave prospective "members" free gifts, such as a key chain or lighter.

Another example of tobacco industry fabrication of allies is the United Restaurant, Hotel and Tavern Association (URHTA) of New York State which placed full-page advertisements in the *New York Times* in September 1994 to oppose the smoke-free ordinance proposed by the New York City Council. Joe Cherner of Smoke-Free Educational Services not only discovered that URHTA did not even have a telephone listing in New York City and that its supposed chapters in Queens, Brooklyn, the Bronx, and Staten Island were all defunct, but also that the URHTA representative at a City Council hearing admitted that the advertisements were, in fact, paid for by tobacco interests.[3] Similarly, in California, a group called Restaurateurs for a Sensible, Voluntary Policy (RSVP) was created by tobacco interests.[4]

Not surprisingly, the "rights" of smokers, according to the NSA, are fully consonant with the financial interests of the tobacco industry. For example, the "right" of smokers to learn about the various ingredients in tobacco products or to bring a product liability suit against tobacco companies is not what the NSA advocates. This point was crystallized on October 28, 1994, when attorney Ronald Motley of Ness, Motley, Loadholt, Richardson & Poole cross-examined William J. Althaus, NSA chairman, at Occupational Safety and Health Administration's (OSHA) hearings on workplace smoking rules. Asked by Motley if smokers have a right to be informed about what substances are in tobacco and the impact they may have on their health, Althaus replied, "I have no opinion on that." When asked if he believed smoking is addictive, he replied, "I have no idea." While Althaus earlier had blasted the proposed OSHA regulation of smoking in the workplace as an unfair burden on NSA's members, he offered no opinion regarding the health risks of a product that will bring about the premature deaths of thousands of NSA's members.[5]

An example of an NSA attempt at public education was its hiring of an airplane to tow a banner reading "Mall St. Matthews Discriminates Against Smokers," referring to a mall in Louisville, Kentucky. One might expect that a mall that truly "discriminates" against smokers would bar them from entering the mall to shop. Instead, what got the folks at NSA agitated was that a mall in a major tobacco-growing state had the audacity to make a voluntary business decision to adopt a smoke-free policy. If one were to logically follow the reasoning behind the NSA's banner, St. Matthew's Church equally "discriminates" against smokers when it prohibits congregants from smoking during Sunday Mass.

Extremism is one of NSA's traits. The April 1995 issue of its newsletter, *NSA Voice,* quotes syndicated newspaper columnist Walter Williams, complaining about the plans of eight major airlines to ban smoking on international flights. "Many Americans think it's good to restrict smoking and applaud the intimidation tactics by the anti-smoking lobby. We should remember that it was decent, well-meaning Germans who helped create an all-powerful government to do good things but didn't figure they were building the Trojan Horse for Adolf Hitler. Similarly, Americans are making it easy for a future tyrant." This is NSA's response to an effort to remove a toxic pollutant from airline cabins. . . .

Laden with money and often dissatisfied with the editorial content of newspapers and magazines, the tobacco companies have bought full-page ads, some of which appear as thinly disguised legitimate articles, in major publications across the country to send out their message on a wide variety of public policy issues affecting tobacco. A major round of such advertisements occurred shortly after a spate of negative publicity that the industry received after the congressional hearings in the spring of 1994. R. J. Reynolds's series of ads included headlines such as "Today It's Cigarettes. Tomorrow?," "Smoking in a Free Society," "Secondhand Smoke: How Much Are Nonsmokers Exposed To?" and "Is the Government Going Too Far?" The three prongs of tobacco's propaganda are: (i) dismissing health concerns; (ii) emphasizing people's "rights"; and (iii) bashing government (in R. J. Reynolds's ads, the 'G' in government is always capitalized, thus making it bigger and more menacing). . . .

The tobacco industry can influence public opinion in ways that are not readily apparent to the general public. For example, an editorial in the *New York Post* entitled "No-Smoking's Victims" berated the purported negative effects on the restaurant business inflicted by New York's smoke-free ordinance. "This time the butt-inski brigade seems to have gone too far. The health fascists, as predicted, have actually injured a vital New York City industry," began the editorial. What was the source of the assurance that no-smoking laws are bad for restaurant business? "Surveys conducted independently—one by a tobacco-rights group, one by the New York Tavern and Restaurant Association—concluded that folks are staying out of eateries in large numbers."[6]

Rupert Murdoch, the editor-in-chief of the *New York Post,* has been a member of the board of directors of Philip Morris since 1989. Those who read the *Post*'s vitriolic editorial that day were not apprised of that fact.

Money is in plentiful supply at tobacco industry headquarters. An article in *Business Week* details how the tobacco lobby successfully persuaded the Florida legislature to repeal a 1994 statute that makes it easier for the state of Florida to bring litigation against tobacco companies for reimbursement of Medicaid and other health benefits payments. The article, entitled "Full-Flavored, Unfiltered Statehouse Shenanigans," described the "Tobacco Team"—the two dozen lobbyists who descended on the Florida legislature in Tallahassee. "The industry relied on its traditional strengths: money, power, and influence. The combination worked once again—proof that tobacco makers are far from vanquished by negative public opinion and anti-smoking legislation." Governor Lawton Chiles has promised to veto the repeal of the statute. The article concludes: "polls indicate two-thirds of Floridians favor his law, and he'll work to lure enough Democratic legislators to avoid an override. But Team Tobacco has staying power. Public opinion is against it. Yet money, and legal acumen, often talk louder than voters."[7]

An example of the tobacco industry's proclivity to bully small municipalities occurred in late 1994 in the town of Puyallup, Washington. The Puyallup City Council passed an ordinance on August 1 to require all restaurants in that city of 27,000 to be smoke-free as of January 1, 1995. However, on December 19, less than two weeks before the new law was to take effect, the council voted 6 to 1 to reverse itself and repeal the ordinance. What had happened in the intervening months that had such a profound effect on the city councillors?

On November 29, nine restaurants in Puyallup filed a civil rights suit to challenge the ordinance. Among the allegations contained in the complaint filed by the plaintiffs was the assertion that the ordinance was preempted by state law because the Washington Clean Indoor Air Act, set forth at RCW 70.160, permitted smoking sections in restaurants. The plaintiffs also imaginatively alleged that the city had unlawfully and substantially deprived plaintiffs' rights guaranteed by the U.S. Constitution including, but not limited to, violating the "takings" clause (which requires the government to pay compensation for private property which it seizes) of the Fifth Amendment.

The lawsuit was financed by the R. J. Reynolds Tobacco Co. Rather than expend the funds necessary to fight the lawsuit in court, the City Council backed down and decided to repeal the ordinance before the public had any opportunity to benefit from it. Tobacco money had once again prevailed over the public health.

According to *Can't Kick the Habit... The Tobacco Industry Washington*, a lengthy study unveiled in March 1995 by Common Cause, a citizens' lobbying group, "twelve tobacco industry companies and lobbying groups, along with their executives, gave a total of $16,738,872 in political action committee (PAC) and soft money contributions during the past decade—a decade in which increasing public scrutiny of the health effects of smoking and tobacco use resulted in relatively little congressional action on anti-tobacco legislation." Common Cause president, Ann McBride, said that the "tobacco lobby's use of political contributions is a classic example of the influence-money scandal at work in Washington. Members of Congress are as addicted to large campaign contributions as smokers are to nicotine." The breakdown was as follows: Philip Morris $5,083,557; R. J. Reynolds $4,879,975; US Tobacco $2,882,438; and Tobacco Institute $1,618,979.

The recipients of the campaign contribution money were not chosen at random. For example, in the spring of 1994, legislation to ban smoking in most public buildings was approved by the House Subcommittee on Health and the Environment and sent along to the full Energy and Commerce Committee. The full committee postponed scheduled mark-ups on that bill (H.R. 3434) and never took final action on it. Members of the 103rd Congress who served on the Energy and Commerce Committee received $860,658 from tobacco industry PACs during the decade 1985–1994 (an average of $19,560 each). The average member of Congress over that same time span received $9,409 from tobacco PACs, less than half of the amount received by committee members.[8]

Glantz and Begay have documented the significant influence of tobacco industry campaign contributions on state lawmakers in California, independent of their constituents' support for tobacco control.[9]

Tobacco companies are equally virulent in their use of the judicial system to intimidate those who would criticize or regulate them. While the combined resources of scientists, NGOS, the media, and local and national governments obviously far exceed the wealth of even the tobacco industry, the industry is able to threaten and deter (though only rarely to defeat) individuals and entities in each of these categories through a "divide and conquer" strategy.

Beginning in 1953, the industry adopted "a holding strategy,"[10] consisting of:

- creating doubt about the health charge without actually denying it.
- advocating the public's right to smoke, without actually urging them to take up the practice.

- encouraging objective scientific research as the only way to resolve the question of health hazard.

As for individual scientists who had reached troublesome findings, Philip Morris in 1981 proposed "attacking researchers themselves, where vulnerable."[11] Current and former employees and contractors are held on a tight leash: thus, R. J. Reynolds Tobacco Co. obtained an injunction to keep a former scientist from discussing work done for the company to determine how smoking causes emphysema,[12] while Council for Tobacco Research agents threatened a major recipient of research funds that publishing his result—that inhaling smoke does cause cancer in laboratory animals—would end their relationship. When he published anyway, his funding was indeed cut off, and his efforts to publicize his results were surreptitiously undermined.[13]

Avoiding Faustian bargains with the tobacco industry does not protect scientists from harassment and intimidation, however. Dr Irving Selikoff's data for his pathbreaking studies on the relationship between asbestos exposure, smoking, and lung cancer were subpoenaed by the tobacco industry,[14] as were the records of the process leading up to the various surgeon general's reports on smoking and health,[15] as were the data and other records of the researchers who concluded that the "Joe Camel" advertising campaign appealed to children and teenagers.[16]

Even reporting studies done by others can be hazardous, if the tobacco industry is displeased. In 1987 the Dutch Foundation on Smoking and Health (StiVoRo) dared to state, as part of a public education campaign, that passive smoking badly affects one's health. The joint tobacco quickly sued, accusing StiVoRo of "misleading the public." The court sided with StiVoRo, and the tobacco companies finally withdrew their claims and agreed to pay legal costs.[17] But, for forty-two months, StiVoRo was distracted from its tobacco control efforts by having to fight this rearguard action. News media have had the same experience: Philip Morris filed a $10 billion lawsuit against the American Broadcasting Company and two of its journalists for daring to suggest that the industry "spiked" cigarettes with nicotine.[18]

It is perhaps not surprising that the industry feels free to sue local governments like Puyallup, Washington (discussed above), Provincetown, Massachusetts (unsuccessful industry effort to overturn ban on cigarette vending machines), or even New York City (successful "preemption" attack on ban on taxicab-top cigarette advertising).[19] But the industry has also taken on the US Environmental Protection Agency (for daring to conclude that environmental tobacco smoke causes lung cancer) and the Canadian government (for presuming to have the constitutional power to ban cigarette advertising).[20] Presently, it is threatening governments throughout the world with the preposterous legal claim that label regulations infringe the companies' trademark rights, in violation of international conventions.

The point of these tactics—whether political, public relations, or legal— is not to win. The tobacco executives know that, at least in developed countries, they are fighting a losing battle. But the tactics do succeed in distracting and intimidating tobacco control forces, and delaying (and occasionally reversing) tobacco control gains. And every year of delay means billions of dollars in profits, albeit at the cost of millions of lives.

NOTES

1. *San Francisco Chronicle,* April 18, 1994.

2. F. Philips, "Tobacco Firms Court Cambridge Smokers," *Boston Globe,* May 6, 1995, pp. 13, 20; and C. Paige, "Tobacco Giant's Campaign Calls on Cambridge Residents," *Boston Herald,* May 6, 1995, p. 7

3. L. Smith, "Big Apple Breathes Easy," *Tobacco Control* 4 (1995): 15–17.

4. S. A. Glantz and L. R. A. Smith, "The Effect of Ordinances Requiring Smoke-Free Restaurants on Restaurant Sales," *American Journal of Public Health* 84 (1994): 1081–85.

5. "National Smokers Alliance Chairman Cross-Examined by Castano Litigator at OSHA Indoor Air Quality Hearing," *Tobacco Products Litigation Reporter* 9, no. 5 (1994): 1.88, 1.89.

6. "No-Smoking's Victims," *New York Post,* May 18, 1995, p. 22.

7. M. Mallory, "Full-flavored, Unfiltered Statehouse Shenanigans," *Business Week,* May 22, 1995, p. 52.

8. "Can't Kick the Habit," *Common Cause* media release. March 24, 1995. This study does not address the tobacco industry's contributions to officials at the state or local level.

9. S. A. Glantz and N. E. Begay, "Tobacco Industry Campaign Contributions Are Affecting Tobacco Control Policymaking in California," *JAMA* 272 (1994): 1176–82.

10. Memorandum to Horace R. Kornegay from Fred Panzer, May 1, 1972. Exh. P–1105, *Cipollone* v. *Liggett Group, Inc.,* reprinted in *Tobacco Products Litigation Reporter* 3, no. 4 (1988): 3.368–3.370

11. Memorandum to H. Cullman/J.C. Bowling from J. J. Morgan, March 24. 1981, Exh. P–2745, *Cipollone* v. *Liggett Group, Inc.,* reprinted in *Tobacco Products Litigation Reporter* &B3, no. 5 (1988): 3.423.

12. *R. J. Reynolds Tobacco Co.* v. *Colluci,* 8.2 TPLR 2.225 (N.C. Super. Ct. 1993).

13. Confidential memorandum to 'Henry-Tom' from Leonard Zahn, April 22,1974, Exh. P–1205A, *Cipollone* v. *Liggett Group, Inc.,* reprinted in *Tobacco Products Litigation Reporter* 3, no. 5 (1988): 3.416–3.417.

14. *Mt. Sinai School of Medicine* v. *American Tobacco Co.,* 866 F.2d 552 (2d Cir. 1989).

15. *Cipollone* v. *Liggett Group, Inc.,* 2.7 TPLR 2.119 (US Ct. App., 4th Cir. 1987).

16. J. R. DiFranza, "If the Science Is Irrefutable, Attack the Scientist," *Tobacco Control* 1 (1992): 237–38.

17. R. DeJong, "A Defeat for the Tobacco Industry," *World Smoking Health* 17 (1992): 23.

18. A. A. Skolnick, "Burning Mad Tobacco Firms Turn Up Heat on Major News Media. *Newsletter of the National Association of Screenwriters* 42 (1994): 1–5.

19. *Take Five Vending Co.* v. *Provincetown,* 415 Mass. 741, 615 NE 2d 576 (1993); *Vango Media* v. *City of New York,* 829 F. Supp. 572 (SDNY 1993).

20. *Flue-Cured Tobacco Cooperative Stabilization Corp.* v. *EPA,* 857 F. Supp. 1137 (MDNC 1994); J. Ronson and R. Cunningham, "Fighting for Health: The Canadian Tobacco Advertising Case," *World Smoking Health* 17 (1992): 24–25.

11

Smoking, Stigma, and the Purification of Public Space

Blake D. Poland

Increasingly, governments in Canada (as elsewhere in the Western world) are turning to public policy legislation to assist in the reduction of cigarette smoking. In addition to the taxation of tobacco products, controls on tobacco advertising, and raising the legal age at which cigarettes can be purchased, governments at all levels (federal, provincial, municipal) are enacting more restrictive legislation regarding where smoking can occur in indoor environments outside the home. These areas I loosely refer to as *public space*. They are often publicly used but privately owned as in restaurants, shopping mall, and the workplace. My intention is not to describe the evolution of these policies nor to account for them with reference, for example, to the emerging interest in "healthy public policy" within health promotion, which has been well described by others (see, e.g., Leichter, 1991; Goodin, 1989).

Rather, this chapter represents an analysis of the interpersonal mechanisms by which institutional initiatives (specifically, tobacco policy interventions to restrict smoking in public places) attempt to produce social change. The arena of tobacco control is a particularly interesting one in which to examine these issues because smoking has become a politically charged issue that involves considerable financial and other vested interests on both sides of the debate and because the political correctness of the tobacco control agenda in Canada may obscure the essentially socially constructed and political nature of the "problem" and its "solutions" (Eakin et al., 1994). In this examination of the social geography of tobacco control my interest, in particular, is on the ways in watch the social construction of

Reprinted from Robin Kearns and Wil Gester, eds., *Putting Health into Place: Landscape, Identity & Well-Being* (1998) with the permission of Syracuse University Press.

smoking as a moral social problem is partly predicated on (although also facilitative of) the legal control of space. This control involves the exercise of power, which is directed at the manipulation of individual behavior through the selective criminalization of smoking on a territorial basis and which is experienced interpersonally as the stigmatization of smoking behavior.

In this chapter I account for some of the complexities and contradictions arising from my interviews with smokers, tobacco control advocates, and others, which formed part of a qualitative evaluation of a large community-based smoking cessation intervention in Brantford: the community intervention trial for smoking cessation (COMMIT).[1] Although I draw on the testimony of those interviewed, my hypotheses extend well beyond the data and are only loosely grounded in it because (1) many of the ideas for this chapter developed after the interviews and focus groups were complete and (2) the regulation of public and private space was only one of many topics explored in the interviews (whose focus was primarily on the nature of the assistance the Brantford COMMIT intervention provided to smokers interested in quitting). The ideas in this chapter are, therefore, presented as a set of propositions in need of further investigation and are intended to stimulate debate about the spatial dynamics of tobacco control in North America.

The remainder of this chapter comprises two principal sections. In the first I address the lived experience of tobacco control at the interpersonal level, drawing on symbolic interactionist perspectives, particularly Goffman's work on stigma. In the second section more formal (legislative) restrictions on where people can smoke are explored as an illustration of class-based conflicts over the purification of public space.

SMOKING AS STIGMA: SOCIAL NORMS AND BEHAVIOR IN PUBLIC

Federal, provincial, and municipal legislation in Canada has made a growing number of public shopping malls, restaurants, aircraft, buses, trains, and other public environments smoke-free or has limited smoking to designated areas. In the absence of formal enforcement, sanctions are maintained primarily through interpersonal social relations and social norms. Indeed, one focus of intervention has been the use of social marketing and community mobilization strategies to attempt to engineer changes in community social norms (e.g., the aforementioned COMMIT trial). Survey research now indicates that a majority of smokers are supportive of restrictions on smoking in public, viewing it as a reasonable courtesy to nonsmokers (e.g., Pederson et al., 1989; Ashley, Bull, and Pederson, 1994). In addition to the collective social recognition of the right of nonsmokers to smoke-free air the tendencies in Canadian culture toward politeness, to do what is expected, and to obey the law, would appear to contribute to the success of anti-smoking regulations. These observations are consistent with Foucault's claim that many so-called advanced societies arc characterized by social control based on self-censorship (internalization of the panoptic gaze) rather than by displays of brute force (Foucault, 1980). It is, therefore, possible that many of the legislative reforms such as restrictions on smoking in public succeed in the main because of this tendency toward self-censorship coupled with subtle cues from nonsmokers signaling inappropriate behavior.

Erving Goffman (1959, 1963a, 1963b, 1971) has written extensively on the nature and social regulation of behavior in public places. Goffman turned his attention not to the perpetrators of inappropriate behavior, but to the rules and social circles that are offended by such transgressions. As his contemporary Howard Becker wrote in the seminal book *Outsiders: Studies in the Sociology of Deviance,* "Social groups create deviants by making the rules whose infraction constitutes deviance, and by applying those rules to particular people and labeling them as outsiders" (1963, 8). Goffman explicated a complex and implicit social order of moral norms regulating human behavior of which public order was a subset concerned with conduct in public. The public realm can be defined as "those nonprivate sectors or areas of urban settlements in which individuals in copresence tend to be personally unknown or only categorically known to one another" (Lofland, 1989, 453). One class of interactional principles governing public behavior pertains to the social etiquette of movement, such as how to negotiate crowded streets or to find a seat on a bus, relating to physical contact and personal space between strangers. Another class of unwritten rules of social conduct more directly concerns interpersonal exchange, three of which Lofland (1989) identifies as predominant. The first interaction rule is civil inattention: that is, acknowledging the presence of others but not routinely engaging them in conversation (neither staring at nor completely ignoring others). Second, people function as audiences for each other and for activities that surround them in public settings. The third interactional principle identified by Lofland is being civil toward what one would usually find offensive by not drawing undue attention to it or approaching the person directly.

These so-called rules are more than mere conventions in that social competence is demonstrated by abiding by them; they are fundamental to social and cultural identity. Because the meaning of acts varies according the context in which they occur, the apparent "freedom of choice" within a class of possible accepted behavior obscures from view the constraints regarding the nature of the choice set in the first place (Goffman, 1963a). In terms of smoking it is crucial to understand that these three interactional principles create a situation in which people are generally reluctant to "make a scene" or to draw attention to themselves by raising objections to someone else's inappropriate smoking.

Generally speaking, in Canada it is not usual to approach strangers about their behavior; in fact, one has to "get up the courage" to do so. Instead, often somewhat subtler means are used to the same effect. Goffman (1963a, 1963b) has outlined a number of (primarily nonverbal) ways in which people act to enforce social behavioral codes that operate precisely *because* of the principle of civil inattention. For example, staring is impolite and causes discomfort to the recipient. It is, therefore, often an effective tool to bring others "into line" by indicating that their behavior is the object of unusual attention. Likewise, sideways glances, body language, throat clearing, moving away, and other actions can be cues that someone's smoking is not appreciated. These are not direct verbal communications, however, and the targets of such disapproval can, in pretending not to notice these cues, succeed in getting the offended parties to desist because they would have to "up the ante" and make a more public (and potentially uncomfortable) objection to the smoker's behavior, thereby drawing attention to themselves and risking public rejection or confrontation. These observations seem straightforward, but they draw attention to the highly developed symbolic cultural bases of public behavior and, therefore, their relevance to how legislative reform is experienced and translated into everyday life and the geographic and temporal specificity of their effects (what Kleinman, 1991, has called "local moral cultures") in terms of the microsocial contexts in which smoking (and publicly objecting to the smoking of others) is deemed appropriate.

It has been suggested that "threats of shame (self-imposed punishment) and threats of embarrassment (socially imposed punishment) function much as threats of state-imposed legal sanctions to reduce the expected utility of illegal behavior and, thus, to increase the likelihood of compliance with the law" (Grasnick, Bursik, and Kinsey, 1991, 233). It has also been suggested that anti-littering campaigns such as "Keep America Clean" or anti-smoking educational programming can bolster social sanctions, increasing threats of shame or embarrassment. The assumption is that the potential for shame, rather than just the belief in the merits of the behavior or its regulation, will be what motivates people to comply. Supporting this hypothesis are public opinion surveys that suggest that 76 percent of smokers in Ontario would comply with more stringent regulations on smoking even though many were not in favor of them (Pederson et al., 1986) although other explanations may also account for these results (e.g., feeling powerless to resist or hoping the new rules would help them kick the habit).

I now return to the primary data collected as narratives during the Brantford study. Despite the stigmatizing effects of tobacco control legislation combined with the inconvenience of restrictions on smoking in public places and in the workplace, almost all of the smokers interviewed were supportive in principle of the existence of restrictions (twenty-nine in favor out of the thirty-one cases in which it was discussed), and nineteen out of twenty-six felt that restrictions help smokers cut down or quit (Poland, 1993a). Jessica described how restrictions in her workplace made a difference for her.

> When I could smoke at my desk, especially if it was pressured, or a lot of people would stop and drop in and a lot of those people were smokers—then, yes I smoked a lot more. . . . So . . . although sometimes it annoys me, I think that restricting areas . . . is helpful. You know, it allows you to know that, yes, you can do it. You can go without a cigarette and you'll survive and the world won't fall apart; you'll be okay.

Emily said that restrictions preventing her from smoking in certain places really did not bother her much, but added: "What does bother me is if you do smoke and if you're out in a public place like a dance or whatever, people just look at you and, you know, turn up their noses and you know, whatever. That . . . kind of bothers me. If I'm some place and that does happen, I won't smoke after that." Likewise, in discussing the impact of restrictions on smoking Marilyn felt that it had encouraged people to cut down or quit, but added: "I think also though you'll find a lot more closet smokers out there because you do feel shame when you light up a cigarette, so you tend to hide. It may not make everyone quit; it just makes you more self-conscious, so you hide out with the rest of the lepers [laughs] and have your cigarette, you know?" Among those who acknowledged some impact of workplace restrictions on their own smoking behavior, several indicated that although they resented the restrictions, they felt they were, perhaps, being done a favor. Several indicated they would welcome even more stringent regulations, and some of them had devised rules for themselves to limit their smoking at work as part of their own cessation strategies. Bob summarized perhaps better than most what many of the other smokers were thinking in this regard, not just about workplace restrictions but about restrictions in general:

> Oh, yeah, it has to help people cut down. I mean, . . . they're going to resent the hell out of it, but yeah, it'll help people cut down, I think, it's a double-edged sword. As much as I hate the fact that it's being regulated to the point where it's . . . the big brother syndrome. . . . Then again, I like the fact that people can take their children out and not expose them to second-hand smoke. I like the fact that you can go into a restaurant and enjoy your meal without smoke wafting from— because . . . I know when I'm eating I don't like second-hand smoke. But, yeah, the medical costs, the health care costs of people smoking . . . I respect why it's happening. I just resent the way it's being done sometimes. I mean, the end result is good. Anytime you can stop a person from lighting up a cigarette, whether they resent the fact or not, you're doing them a favor and the people around them a favor.

As Bob's testimony illustrated, though, support in principle does not always translate into support in practice for how restrictions are devised, phrased, and enforced.

Their predicament is an uncomfortable one for many smokers. Although several admitted that the rising "nuisance factor" was accelerating their readiness to quit, others wondered what good it would do for those who were still too addicted to be able to quit. According to Anne, "[The increasingly negative social evaluation of smoking] makes you feel bad, it makes you feel that you're doing something that's dirty . . . but what good is that? . . . It does get the message across, there's no doubt about it, but then where do you go from there? You carry on smoking and feel bad because you're smoking." In some cases the feelings of diminished worth and stigmatization were voiced very poignantly.

> I mean, everyone makes a smoker feel guilty. I know I felt terribly guilty. When I smoked, I felt like I had the plague. You know, like I'm an unclean, unfit person because I smoked, and that's a terrible feeling. Do you know what that does to you, really? That really makes you feel like hell . . . you know, that you're a bad person because you smoke.

Testimonies such as these forced me to remember some of the taken-for-granted assumptions I had about the uniquely benevolent nature of tobacco control, including interventions designed to reduce the social acceptability of smoking, whatever my convictions about the physical harms associated with smoking.

Clearly, part of this contextuality relates to the smoker's sense of place and experience of place not just as private and public space but as a series of contingent behavior settings. Several of the quotes above suggest how the regulation of space is experienced by smokers. It appears from this research that one (but not the only) experience of the purification of public space at the level of social interaction is that of stigmatization.

The smokers interviewed in the Brantford study clearly varied in the degree to which they appear to have internalized feelings of guilt and shame associated with the stigmatization of smoking. In fact, several expressed opinions more resembling indignation and resistance although the majority appeared to classify themselves, as might be expected, as "considerate" smokers. Many saw this as the new (and appropriate) norm among smokers: reasonable accommodation of the rights of nonsmokers to smoke-free air. But in many cases deference was more than a sign of courtesy: smokers simply did not feel *comfortable* about lighting up around those who did not smoke. There came a point at which it simply detracted from the enjoyment of smoking. As Jessica put it, "I guess it depends on how comfortable I am with the person that I'm with. . . . It's like smoking in front of my father. No way. I'll just, I'll die with every puff. So . . . if you know the person is accepting of it, and it's not offending them, then you're comfortable to do it. I guess that's true with a lot of the social things." For several respondents the perceived declining social acceptability of smoking has meant an increasing sense of "dis-ease" about their own smoking among strangers or in public. Shauna, for example, indicated that "I try not to smoke as much any more when I am in other company because it is so unacceptable these days, and they want to make you feel so —, so when I am out in a social situations, I don't smoke nearly as much as I used to, especially at parties and people's homes or meetings." The above quotations indicate that changes in the perceived social acceptability of smoking contribute to the maintenance and enforcement of regulations through self-censorship of public behavior, perhaps because a common experience of the purification of public space at the level of social interaction is that of stigmatization.

To "moral entrepreneurs" (Pfuhl and Henry, 1993) and health professionals, the shift in social norms that led smoking to be seen in many quarters as socially inappropriate behavior has been celebrated as a public health victory (Allen and Adler, 1989). Yet it is through the sort of interpersonal mechanisms described above (in addition to messages in the print and electronic media) that, in the context of daily lived experience, not just smoking as a behavior but smokers as people have become stigmatized. According to Goffman, stigma is defined as the "deeply discrediting" (1963b, 3) stereotypes about the meaning of a particular social, physical, or behavioral attribute (such as smoking) that reinforce negative judgments about the moral status of persons with those (stigmatizing) attributes (e.g., smokers being stereotyped as weak-willed, dirty, or uncouth). For the socially and economically disadvantaged (former psychiatric patients, the homeless and the unemployed, unskilled manual laborers, welfare recipients, aboriginal peoples, or single mothers) who disproportionately rely on smoking as one of very few coping mechanisms available to them in dealing with the stresses of everyday life, the stigma of being a smoker can be seen as yet another form of social disapproval that may diminish their dignity as worthy human beings struggling to achieve the same basic human goals as the rest of us regarding physical comfort, happiness, and personal growth.

Complicating matters for smokers is the fact that some interactional principles pertaining to behavior in the public realm appear to be in conflict with others and that smoking can be either a social lubricant or stigmatizing, depending on the circumstances. For example, a cigarette or a light offered from, or accepted by, a stranger serves to break the ice and establish reciprocity and friendship by exchange (an extension of hospitality). Smoking has long been a symbol of identification in and of itself (symbolizing status, rebelliousness, or risk taking) (Robbins and Kline, 1991). Smoking also contributes to social competence by helping one be more composed through the management of negative emotions, notably anger (Fergusson, 1987; Ashton and Stepney, 1982), particularly among women, whose gendered socialization prescribes anger management (Jacobsen, 1986), and improving vigilance on the job when stress or boredom are high (which can be seen as a form of occupational role adaptation) (Krogh, 1991). It also performs an important function in legitimating, social disengagement for the purposes of relaxation and regaining one's composure (McCracken, 1992). As the title of a recent book by Richard Klein (1993) suggests, cigarettes are sublime for many users as surely as they are addictive and harmful and, therefore, are the source of considerable ambivalence for many smokers.

Furthermore, a state of flux in what rules of public conduct apply to smokers and under what circumstances appears to have created confusion and uncertainty for some smokers about "coming out" in public about their habit. People who smoke, therefore, must often seek supportive environments to engage in the act of smoking. As smokers negotiate the various corridors of public and private space during everyday life, they must continually and reflexively monitor which spaces are permissive and which are spaces of denial vis-à-vis smoking. In many cases, it would appear that the uncertainty about where and when it is permissible to smoke eventually becomes normalized as "par for the course" of living with social restrictions on one's behavior. In the words of one smoker,

> I've found that I've become more and more aware of nonsmoking places now because I'm looking for a place to smoke. You know, you walk into a place and of course, where's the sign? Here or not? So, yeah, I've become more aware of that, whereas maybe three or four years ago it was not a big deal. Now, I look all the time. I have to know where I can smoke, where I'm going to sit, that type of thing. It becomes second nature.

There is uncertainty in the new moral order; public health discourse is not all-encompassing and may be resisted. Not only the legal status of smoking but the social acceptability of it is highly situational not only across but even within particular behavior settings.

In *Stigma* Goffman (1963b) observes that the stigmatized often seek each other out and congregate in the same places and may become represented by their own organizations that challenge the cultural construction of their stigma (itself the basis for many social movements, e.g., the gay rights movement). The (re)emergence of smoking parlors in parts of the United States and a number of smokers rights groups (such as the Smokers' Freedom Society in Canada) bear witness to similar trends in the realm of smoking.

The social construction of deviance and the politics of social control have resulted in the creation of stigmatizing spaces in which smokers literally feel out of place and designated or informal spaces where smokers congregate to smoke. Given the spaces occupied by the different players, it seems reasonable to conclude that meanings penetrate into these settings to different degrees, depending to some extent on where smokers congregate. This conclusion appears to be consistent with literature on deviance insofar as all forms of deviance have distinctive geographies (Sacco, 1988). Several respondents in the Brantford study, including those quoted above, reported feeling uneasy in open public places. When asked where they felt comfortable smoking, many respondents mentioned their own homes, cars, or behavioral settings permissive of smoking (e.g., parties of smoking friends, bars, or some restaurants). It is noteworthy that class divisions in the prevalence of smoking may be reflected in the spatial ordering (and segregation) of spaces in which smoking is most prevalent and socially acceptable, just as class divisions in society are reproduced in—and fundamentally structure—the nature of tobacco control efforts across space and time fueled in part by the dialectic relationship between spatial and social segregation, which is discussed more fully later in the chapter.

The concept of *behavior settings* (Fuhrer, 1990) seems particularly appropriate here. Behavior settings are culturally constructed but individually mediated interactional and activity microenvironments with (1) their own cultural codes of conduct (e.g., one behaves differently in a library than in a bar), (2) situational characteristics (e.g., being in a restaurant with a work acquaintance versus with a lover), and (3) temporal variations (organization of the twenty-four hour day, changes in the nature of a setting over time). This allows one, firstly, to close the gap between psychology, geography, and sociology through careful specification of the parameters and roles of behavior settings in terms of individually apprehended reality and the denotative geography and topography of the setting (Fuhrer, 1990) and, thus, secondly, to identify and account for behavior settings in which smoking is socially constructed as more or less permissible (e.g., bars versus maternity wards). One might also investigate how individual biographies (life paths) intersect with particular institutional projects (such as tobacco control) in historically and spatially contingent ways in specific places or locales (cf. Pred, 1986; Giddens, 1984). It should also be possible to chronicle and account for changes and spatial/temporal differentiations in the rule structures guiding behavior in public space to which participants must adapt, which signal the contextual embeddedness of lay knowledgeability.

Given the "reasonable" claims of nonsmokers to smoke-free air, many smokers may feel themselves faced with two alternatives. One alternative is to adopt the etiquette of the "considerate" smoker to minimize the effects on others. In much the same way as etiquette books once formalized rules of appropriate public conduct for "women of sophistication" decades ago, smokers themselves have drafted similar "guidelines for the courteous smoker" (Smokers' Freedom Society, 1992). Another option open to smokers is to gradually retreat from the public realm altogether. In the Brantford research it was evident that many respondents felt a retreat from the public realm was increasingly being required of them whether they liked it or not. Some foresaw the day when smoking, like sex, would be something that was done in private among consenting adults.

While anticipating further encroachments on their "rights" as smokers, many respondents appeared to "draw the line" at the threshold of private space and the public domain, asserting that what they did in their own home or car was their own business. Given the history of private property rights, individualism, and public responsibilities of citizenship enshrined in North American culture, it is to be expected that one of the primary distinctions governing the categorization of space for smokers is that of public versus private space. There is an unfortunate irony, however, in the fact that those most heavily exposed to sidestream smoke are the family members of heavy smokers and, perhaps, more so as some smokers who retreat from the public realm compensate by increasing their smoking during off-work hours and in private spaces such as the family car and home. Smoking at home is, therefore not just "their own business" but also that of their families, who, it is often expected, voluntarily tolerate greater risks than strangers would be willing to put up with.

Of course, this says little about the organization of space within the home (including the power relations implicated therein) and its relationship to substance abuse (see Lowe, Foxcroft, and Sibley, 1993). A recent analysis of 1993 survey data for the province of Ontario indicates that the majority of smokers feel that parents with young children should either limit their smoking to "another part of the house" or not smoke at all (Bondy and Ferrence, 1995). Recent small-scale interview and focus group studies with smokers in Ontario suggest that many parents have developed compensatory rules governing where they smoke in the home (e.g., not in the children's room, not in their presence, or not in the house at all) in an attempt to reduce the exposure of their children to second-hand smoke (Bondy et al., 1995, Rhyne, 1994) despite research that indicates most of the airborne chemicals other than nicotine associated with smoking are spread relatively evenly throughout the average home even when smoking is restricted to certain rooms (Lofroth, 1993).

Another paradox in smokers' claims to personal autonomy in the home and control over private space is that several respondents in the Brantford study also acknowledged not always feeling able to control the smoking of others in their own home. This was particularly true for those who had recently quit and who, as much as they wanted to, were reluctant to ask visiting friends not to smoke for fear of jeopardizing their relationship. A number of respondents in the Brantford study expressed concern that their quitting might come between them and their friends. Interviews conducted with current and former smokers suggested that this could occur in at least three ways: (1) being more edgy as a result of withdrawal symptoms associated with quitting; (2) feeling it is risky to ask friends who visit not to smoke; and (3) reluctance to encourage friends to quit for fear of appearing to "evangelize" to them. The reluctance to alienate smoking friends may create a dilemma for some smokers because the fact that the social network patterns of former smokers more closely approximates that of nonsmokers than of smokers (Ferguson, 1987) suggests that former smokers must surround themselves with nonsmokers if they are to maintain abstinence successfully.

If rules and social norms guiding behavior in public and private space seem convoluted, in a state of flux, and even contradictory, then those pertaining to the contested territory of privately owned but publicly used spaces are potentially even more problematic. The law currently gives the private owners of publicly used areas such as shopping malls sweeping legal powers to detain and deport people (such as loitering teenagers, panhandlers, and the homeless) who are perceived to be threatening to the sanitized middle-class atmosphere the owners deem most conducive to profitable business (Hopkins, 1993). Assumptions about the inherent rights that should be accorded to the economically advantaged (property owners) are deeply embedded in the collective Western psyche. Survey research suggests that a majority (smokers and nonsmokers) consider the responsibility of designating nonsmoking floor space in restaurants (and stores) to be the appropriate purview of owners/managers and their clientele rather than government (Pederson et al., 1986, 1987). The same polls show that if the impetus were to come from government, respondents preferred that it come from local government rather than from provincial or federal authorities. Although no explanation for this was provided, it is noteworthy that the role of *local* government has been increasing as both an object and an agent of regulation in many areas of public policy, which may have contributed to uneven public policy development between municipalities (Goodwin, Duncan, and Halford, 1993) in tobacco control as in other issues.

In light of these considerations I focus in the next section on the more *formal* regulation of public behavior in the form of legislation and examine the nature of restrictions concerning where people can smoke as an extension of class-based conflicts over the purification of public space.

THE REGULATION OF PUBLIC BEHAVIOR: SOCIAL CLASS AND THE APPROPRIATION OF PUBLIC SPACE

Restrictions on smoking are consistent with—and an outgrowth of—a long history of the regulation of public behavior and of the regulation of the body (cf. Turner, 1987), defining and controlling that which is normal or socially acceptable. Legal (and social) sanctions prohibiting such acts as public nudity, loud noise, and the use of skateboards apply to public parks and other spaces. Insofar as public spaces are created and maintained in the interest of public welfare, then restrictions on noxious behavior that might impede other people's enjoyment of those areas seem logical and consistent with an interest in the public good. Further, insofar as environmental tobacco smoke (ETS) can be shown to be deleterious to the health of nonsmokers (Chilmonczyk et al., 1993; Dayal et al., 1994), such restrictions are consistent with a history of public health legislation governing restaurant food quality and other aspects of commercial and private activity that might compromise public health. At the same time one paradoxical outcome of such legislation is frequently the systematic (if unintentional) exclusion of certain "less socially desirable" groups (groups of teenagers, vagrants, informal retailers, alcoholics, the elderly) from many public spaces, in part because legislation tends to enshrine white adult middle-class etiquette as the yardstick of socially acceptable behavior.

Sibley describes the purification of space as involving the "rejection of difference and securing of boundaries to maintain homogeneity" (1988, 409). He argues that the tendency toward social, economic, and geographic segregation of social groups from one another (particularly acute in large urban centers in North America today) feeds on itself in that "distancing and a narrow range of encounters contribute to the stereotyping of 'others.' " Further, "nonconformity is more likely to be recognized in a purified (relatively homogeneous) than in a heterogeneous community" (Sibley, 1988, 418–19). Generally, the middle-class and economic/political elites also live in a healthier set of environments in which second-hand smoke becomes an issue of relative importance compared to those who live and work in generally unhealthy or oppressive conditions. Moreover, fewer of the middle and upper classes smoke so that by virtue of being less common, smoking appears less socially acceptable to them and even becomes, in the minds of many, a marker of low social standing (for them, stigmatizing). Each of these factors contributes to the accentuation of "difference" based on class and to efforts to secure this difference in territorial terms as a distancing from the 'other.' A dialectical relationship between spatial and social segregation develops that contributes to the purification of public space.

Although these factors may contribute to the declining social acceptability of smoking and, hence are applauded by public health advocates, they also raise fundamental questions about who controls public space and to what ends and, therefore, who controls the power relations implicated in (and social control overtones behind) the anti-smoking movement. Social groups have different degrees of access to power to shape the nature of legal controls over the use of public space. Control in this context may be defined as "the ability of an individual or group to gain access to, utilize, influence, gain ownership over, and attach meaning to a public space" (Francis, 1990, 168). The gender and class dimensions of the purification of public space may be profound and should be investigated more thoroughly. What follows are speculations about what may be occurring that require empirical validation. It seems safe to assume that groups of lower socioecononomic status (SES) generally have less access to recreational space than do their higher SES counterparts, are more likely to rent than to own accommodations, and, therefore, rely (perhaps disproportionately) on public space for a variety of functions, including much of their social interaction. For example, they may not have comfortable suburban homes with separate living rooms or private yards in which to entertain friends and instead rely on local coffee shops, malls, and parks as social meeting places. Consider former psychiatric patients (the majority of whom smoke), some of whom must vacate lodging homes during daytime hours and, hence, in winter rely on indoor publicly used spaces available to them. The poor elderly, rooming house occupants, many youths, and others with limited access to private space may be other examples of groups who may rely disproportionately on public space for social interaction. Some of those most in "need' of indoor public space may be among those hardest hit by the restrictions. In these cases restrictions on smoking may *in effect,* although probably not by intent, discriminate by socioeconomic status.

Some other (very smokey) indoor areas that have hitherto escaped regulation (with respect to smoking), however, such as bars and bingo halls are less frequented by middle-class families and are the behavior settings in which smoking is the most permissible socially. In addition, many people in nonprofessional and trade occupations (e.g., painters, construction workers) work in environments that are not regulated or easily regulatable because, in at least some of these cases, they do nor occupy on an ongoing basis a shared (indoor) space that can be regulated formally through the legal system.

These discrepancies and variations in the spatial coverage of formal tobacco control legislation, exemplary as they are of the contingent nature of social control pointed to by critical legal geographers (e.g., Clark, 1989a; Blomley, 1994), may, to an extent, be the result of political expediency. Regulations are predictably created first where one has the most support, in other words, where the majority are nonsmokers in spaces occupied by middle-class professionals (such as office buildings), and so on. It may prove to have been much easier to create nonsmoking environments for nonsmokers than to do so for smokers, many of whom encounter smoking in the home, with peers, and among relatives in ways that nonsmokers typically do not.

It is noteworthy in this regard that different social groups may vary considerably in their norms and expectations about the control of public space. According to research conducted by Lee (1972), the middle class tends to view public space as not for the appropriation of any one group and prefers to rely on formal modes of social control based upon notions of public morality and bolstered by the law and its enforcers. Lower-income groups, however, were reported to view public space as regulated informally rather than through external agents such as the police; in other words it was expected that people would watch out for themselves. Furthermore, in order to be comfortable, it was seen as entirely appropriate (perhaps necessary) that each group have its own space.

Whenever power is exercised by one group over another, the possibility of resistance is created (Eakin et al., 1994; Clark, 1994). One might well ask what spaces are appropriated by smokers in light of their retreat from the workplace and many public places. To quote from Warf (1991, 568), "space is pregnant with conflict." Cast out of these spaces, some feel like outcasts, Yet camaraderie develops among some "deviants" thrown together in this process that is described by Goffman (1963b) and by a number of smokers in the Brantford study (e.g., the quote earlier in the chapter about "hanging out with the other lepers"). In fact, recent tobacco industry advertising has begun to use ads that not only empathize with the plight of the "banned" smoker but appear also to portray the camaraderie of "outsidership" as the new "cool" rebellious identity (Mahood, 1994).

Given intergroup conflicts over the control of public space, tobacco control may be one example of a wider issue of *territoriality*, which can be defined as "the attempt by an individual or group to affect, influence, or control people, phenomena, and relationships by delimiting and asserting control over a geographic area" (Sack, 1986, 19). Territoriality involves specification of an area, communication of the restrictions (e.g., sign), and enforcement (or threat thereof). Johnston (1990) has argued that the ability of the state (and its agencies) to control the behaviors of its citizenry resides largely in its sovereign power within bounded territories to enact and enforce legal rules of conduct. Thus, the power of the state is inextricably linked to place. Territorial approaches to social control are relatively ubiquitous in capitalist society as the institutionalization of human relations in space (Sack, 1986). In fact, it has been argued that as urban societies become more complex and impersonal, formalized regulations gradually replace informal social sanctions on public behavior and become enshrined in law (Black, 1989). Furthermore, it has been suggested that territorial approaches to social control focus attention away from the exercise of power to the (spatial) objects of its control (Sack, 1986), obscuring the interests vested in social control. The relationship between controller and controlled is depersonalized when territories appear to be doing the controlling ("this is not allowed here," rather than "I say that you cannot") (Johnston, 1990).

Of course, this approach to social control via legal control of spaces arises as a strategy to "manage" issues that have been defined as "public problems," which themselves share a number of characteristics (Smith, 1988): (1) they are problems that are no longer considered only "private," and are, therefore, the subject of state intervention; (2) they involve some degree of stigma; (3) their definition and interpretation is relative and contextual; (4) they are often persistent over time (despite often massive intervention), wherein the management of public problems has become "a major growth industry"; (5) etiological explanations traditionally locate causal factors within the individual, and (6) they are often highly interrelated (concentrated in a few urban locations and population subgroups). Smoking has clearly become one such "public problem."

It is noteworthy that not only are smoking restrictions highly selective, but their implementation (interpretation and enforcement) is variable between and within municipalities and across provincial jurisdictions within Canada as well. This variability is not just in terms of "local legal cultures" but also at a microsocial level, dependent on the interactional context and behavioral setting, as discussed above. It is, therefore, crucial that one understand space as a medium of social interaction and not just as a passive container (cf. Sayer, 1984; Thrift, 1983). One is led to concur with Kearns (1993) that what is required is a reconstituted geography of health that inserts place back into the experience (and production) of health and illness and the time-space "distanciation" (Giddens, 1984) of the activities of public health professionals as "moral entrepreneurs" (Becker, 1973; Pfuhl and Henry, 1993).

CONCLUSION

It appears that in an attempt to control smoking behavior public space is manipulated by those with the power selectively to regulate tobacco use in certain places, but that despite their apparent success in reducing unwanted exposure to ETS or in reducing smoking itself, (1) these measures may not be evenly or consistently distributed with respect to social class, and (2) they may contribute to the stigmatization of smoking (and, by extension, of smokers) as a form of social control over tobacco use. It is, therefore, possible that the nature and implementation of tobacco control activities in space and time has contributed, albeit inadvertently, to the intensification of existing inequalities at several levels. These inequalities may also be gendered and ethnically concentrated and pertain, in part, to the clustering of smokers (and of microsocial environments conducive to smoking) in economically and educationally disadvantaged groups. This concentration, in turn, is capitalized upon by the tobacco industry, which plays up the countercultural (somewhat outside the mainstream, but still "hip") connotations of smoking. Furthermore, geosocial irregularities in the application of healthy public policy (not only between but within municipalities and between different types of behavior settings) also contribute to social class differences in the impacts of tobacco control. Goffman's work on stigma can also be employed to consider the nature of the lived experience of tobacco control by smokers in daily life as the production and management of stigma.

My purpose in this chapter has been to explore some of the spatial dimensions of tobacco control in Canada. To determine whether these conclusions can be substantiated it will be necessary to conduct further empirical research (1) to explore in greater detail, from a phenomenological perspective, the daily lived experiences of smokers vis-à-vis tobacco control and (2) to investigate potential class biases in the sociogeographic distribution of restrictions (and their impacts) within and between municipalities, work sites, and other behavior settings.

NOTE

1. The Community Intervention Trial (COMMIT) for smoking cessation, sponsored by the U.S, National Cancer Institute, concluded four years of intervention in the fall of 1993 and was the largest randomized control trial of a community-based approach to smoking cessation ever mounted. In Brantford, the extensive standardized (and largely quantitative) evaluation protocol was supplemented by an ancillary qualitative evaluation study to attempt to understand better the impacts of the trial locally as part of the author's doctoral research. A range of qualitative methods was used, which included individual depth interviews and focus groups with intervention staff, project volunteers, and other key informants and with a cross section of members of a smokers' network established by COMMIT for smokers interested in quitting, the analysis of program documentation, and direct observation. For a fuller description see Poland, 1993a, and Poland et al., 1996.

REFERENCES

Allen, S., and B. Adler. (1989). *The Passionate Nonsmoker's Bill of Rights: The First Guide to Enacting Nonsmoking Legislation.* New York: William Morrow & Co.

Anonymous. (1986). "Americans Support Smoking Controls in Workplace, Agree That Smokers Should Refrain from Smoking Near Nonsmokers." *Smoking and Health Reporter* 3:4.

Ashley, M. J., S. Bull, L. L. Pederson. (1994). *Restrictive Measures on Smoking in Canada* (Otru Working Papers Series, No. 1). Toronto: Ontario Tobacco Research Unit.

Ashton, H., and R. Stepney. (1982). *Smoking: Psychology and Pharmacology.* London: Tavistock.

Becker, H. (1973). *Outsiders: Studies in the Sociology of Deviance* (rev. ed.). New York: Free Press.

Bernstein, R. J. (1976). *The Restructuring of Social and Political Theory.* Philadelphia: University of Pennsylvania Press.

Black, D. (1989). *Sociological Justice.* New York: Oxford University Press.

Blacksell, M., C. Watkins, and K. Economides. (1986). Human Geography and Law: A Case of Separate Development in Social Science." *Progress in Human Geography* 10: 371–96.

Blomley, N. K. (1989). "Text and Context: Rethinking the Law-Space Nexus." *Progress in Human Geography* 13, no. 4: 512–34.

———. (1992). "Spacing Out: Towards a Critical Geography of Law." *Osgoode Hall Law Review* 30, no. 3: 661–90.

———. (1994). *Law, Space, and the Geographies of Power.* New York: Guilford Press.

Blomley, N. K., and G. L. Clark. (1990. "Law, Theory, and Geography." *Urban Geography* 11, no. 5: 433–46.

Bondy, S., et al. (1995). *Promoting Smoke-Free Families.* Toronto: Ontario Tobacco Research Unit.

Bondy, S., and R. Ferrence. (1995). *Smoking Behaviour and Attitudes in Ontario, 1993* (Otru Working Paper Series, No. 2). Toronto: Ontario Tobacco Research Unit.

Chaney, D. (1994). *The Cultural Turn: Scene-Setting Essays on Contemporary Cultural History.* New York: Routledge.

Chilmonczyk, B. et al. (1993). "Association Between Exposure to Environmental Tobacco Smoke and Exacerbations of Asthma in Children." *New England Journal of Medicine* 328, no. 23: 1665–69.

Clark, C. (1994). "Managing Righteousness: Smokers' Strategies In Problematic Public Encounters" (Unpublished Manuscript). Indianapolis: Indiana University.

———. (1989b). "The Geography of Law." In *New Models in Geography: The Political Economy Perspective,* eds. R. Peet and N. Thrift. London: Unwin Hyman.

———. (1989a). "Law and the Interpretive Turn in the Social Sciences." *Urban Geography* 10, no. 3: 209–28.

Cohen, I. J. (1989). *Structuration Theory: Anthony Giddens and the Constitution of Social Life.* London: Macmillan.

Dayal, H. H. et al. (1994). "Passive Smoking in Obstructive Respiratory Diseases in an Industrialized Urban Population." *Environmental Research* 65: 161–71.

Eakin, J., A. Robertson, B. Poland, D. Coburn, and R. Edwards. (1996). "Towards a Critical Social Science Perspective on Health Promotion Research." *Health Promotion International* 11, no. 2: 157–65.

Erickson, P. G. (1993). "The Law, Social Control, and Drug Policy: Models, Factors, and Processes." *The International Journal of Addictions* 28: 1155–76.

Erickson, P. G., and C. A. Ottaway. (1993). "Policy: Alcohol and Other Drugs." *Annual Review of Addictions Research and Treatment* 3: 331–41.

Ferguson, T. (1987). *The No-Nag, No-Guilt, Do-It-Your-Own-Way Guide to Quitting Smoking.* New York: Ballantine.

Ferrence, R. (1990). *Deadly Fashion: The Rise and Fall of Cigarette Smoking in North America.* New York: Garland.

Fiske, J. (1989). *Reading the Popular.* Boston: Unwin Hyman.

Foucault, M. (1980). *Power/Knowledge.* New York: Pantheon.

Francis, M. (1990). "Control as a Dimension of Public-Space Quality." In *Public Places and Spaces,* R. Altman and E. Zube. New York: Plenum Press.

Fuhrer, U. (1990). "Bridging the Ecological-Psychological Gap: Behavior Settings as Interfaces." *Environment and Behavior* 22, no. 4: 518–37.

Giddens, A. (1979). *Central Problems In Social Theory: Action, Structure and Contradiction in Social Analysis.* London: Macmillan.

———. (1984). *The Constitution of Society.* Berkeley and Los Angeles: University of California Press.

Giroux, H. A. (1994). *Disturbing Pleasures: Learning Popular Culture.* New York: Routledge.

Goffman, E. (1959). *The Presentation of Self In Everyday Life.* Penguin.
— — —. (1963a). *Behavior in Public Places.* New York: Macmillan.
— — —. (1963b). *Stigma: Notes on the Management of Spoiled Identity.* Englewood Cliffs, N.J.: Prentice-Hall.
— — —. (1971). *Relations in Public: Microstudies of the Public Order.* New York: Basic Books.
Goodin, R. E. (1989). *No Smoking: The Ethical Issues.* University of Chicago Press.
Goodwin, M., Duncan, S., and Halford, S. (1993). "Regulation Theory, the Local State, and the Transition of Urban Politics. Environment and Planning." *D: Society and Space* 11: 67–88.
Grasmick, H. G., R. J. Bursik, and K. A. Kinsey. (1991). "Shame and Embarrassment as Deterrents to Noncompliance with the Law: The Case of an Anti-littering Campaign." *Environment and Behavior* 23, no. 2: 233–51.
Gusfield, J. R. (1989). "Constructing the Ownership of Social Problems: Fun and Profit in the Welfare State." *Social Problems* 36: 431–41.
Healey, P. (1986). "Interpretive Policy Inquiry: A Response to the Limitations of the Received View." *Policy Sciences* 19: 381–96.
Herbert, D. T. (1983). "Crime and Delinquency." In *Progress in Urban Geography,* ed. M. Pacione. London: Croom Helm.
Holstein, J. A., G. Miller, eds. (1993). *Reconsidering Social Constructionism: Debates in Social Problems Theory.* New York: Aldine De Gruyter.
Hopkins, J. (1993). A Balancing Act? Trespass Amendments For Public/Private Places." *Urban Geography* 14, no. 2: 114–18.
Illich. (1977). "Disabling Professions." In *Disabling Professions,* eds. I. Illich, I. K. Zola, J. Mcknight et al. London: Marion Boyers Publishing Ltd.
Jacobsen, B. (1986). *Beating the Ladykillers: Women and Smoking.* London: Pluto Press.
Jennings, B. (1983). "Interpretive Social Science and Policy Analysis." In *Ethics, the Social Sciences, and Policy Analysis,* eds. D. Callahan and B. Jennings. New York: Plenum.
Johnston, R. J. (1990). "The Territoriality of Law: An Exploration." *Urban Geography* 11, no. 6: 548–65.
Kearns, R. A. (1993). "Place and Health: Toward a Reformed Medical Geography." *The Professional Geographer* 45, no. 2: 139–48.
Klein, R. (1993). *Cigarettes Are Sublime.* Durham, N.C.: Duke University Press.
Kleinman, I. (1991). "Towards An Ethnography of Suffering: A Qualitative Approach to the Study of the Illness Experience." Paper Presented at the Qualitative Health Research Conference, Edmonton, Alberta (Canada), February 22–23.
Krogh, D. (1991). *Smoking: The Artificial Passion.* New York: W. H. Freeman.
Lee, R. G. (1972). "The Social Definition of Outdoor Recreation Places." In *Social Behavior, Natural Resources and the Environment,* W. Burch. New York: Harper and Row.
Leichter, H. M. (1991). *Free to Be Foolish: Politics and Health Promotion in the United States and Great Britain.* Princeton, N.J.: Princeton University Press.
Lofland, L. H. (1989). "Social Life in the Public Realm: A Review." *Journal of Contemporary Ethnography* 17, no. 4: 453–82.
Lofroth, G. (1993). "Environmental Tobacco Smoke: Multicomponent Analysis and Room-to-Room Distribution in Homes." *Tobacco Control* 2: 222–25.
Lowe, G., D. Foxcroft, and D. Sibley. (1993). *Adolescent Drinking and Family Life.* Chur, Switzerland: Harwood Academic Press.
Mahood, G. (1994). "The Empathy Advertising Campaign—Preparing Smokers for the Inevitable Social Isolation." *Tobacco Control* 3: 270–72.
Markle, G. E., and R. J. Troyer. (1979). "Smoke Gets in Your Eyes: Cigarette Smoking as Deviant Behavior." *Social Problems* 21: 611–25.
Maynard, D. (1989). "On the Ethnography and Analysis of Discourse in Institutional Settings." *Social Problems* 1:127–46.

McCracken, C. (1992). *"Got a Smoke?"*. *A Cultural Account of Tobacco in the Lives of Contemporary Teens.* Research Report for the Ontario Ministry of Health Tobacco Strategy. Toronto: Ontario Ministry of Health.

McKnight, J. (1977). "Professionalized Service and Disabling Help." In *Disabling Professions,* eds. I. Illich, I. K. Zola, J. Mcknight et al. London: Marion Boyers Publishing Ltd.

Ong, A. (1994). "Making the Biopolitical Subject: Cambodian Immigrants, Refugee Medicine and Cultural Citizenship in California." *Social Science and Medicine* (Forthcoming).

Pederson, L., et al. (1989). "A Population Survey on Legislative Measures to Restrict Smoking in Ontario: 3. Variables Related to Attitudes of Smokers and Nonsmokers." *American Journal of Preventive Medicine* 5: 313–22.

— — —. (1986). "A Population Survey on Legislative Measures to Restrict Smoking in Ontario: 2. Knowledge, Attitudes, and Predicted Behaviour." *American Journal of Preventive Medicine* 2, no. 6: 316–23.

— — —. (1987). "A Population Survey in Ontario Regarding Restrictive Measures on Smoking: Relationship of Smoking Status to Knowledge, Attitudes and Predicted Behaviour." *International Journal of Epidemiology* 16, no. 3: 383–91.

Pfuhl, E. H., and S. Henry. (1993). *The Deviance Process* (3rd ed.). New York: Aldine De Gruyter.

Poland, B. (1993). "From Concept to Practice in Community Mobilization for Health: A Qualitative Evaluation of the Brantford Commit Intervention for Smoking Cessation." McMaster University, Hamilton On: Doctoral Dissertation.

— — —. (1992). "Learning to 'Walk Our Talk': The Implications of Sociological Theory for Research Methodologies in Health Promotion." *Canadian Journal of Public Health* 23: S31–S46.

— — —. (1993). "Some Promises and Pitfalls of Lay Perception Research in the Social and Health Sciences." *The Operational Geographer* 11: 23–27.

Poland, B., S. M. Taylor, J. Eyles, and N. F. White. (1995). "Qualitative Evaluation of the Brantford Commit Intervention Trial: The Smokers' Perspective." *Health and Canadian Society* (Forthcoming).

Pred, A. (1986). Place, Practice and Structure. Cambridge: Polity Press.

Pue, W. W. (1990). "Wrestling with Law: (Geographical) Specificity vs. (Legal) Abstraction." *Urban Geography* 11, no. 6: 566–85.

Rhyne, I. (1994). ETS *In the Home: A Study of Knowledge, Attitudes, and Receptiveness to Change among Parents Who Smoke.* North York, On: Institute for Social Research.

Robbins, M. C., and A. Kline. (1991). "To Smoke or Not to Smoke: A Decision Theory Perspective." *Social Science and Medicine* 33, no. 12: 1343–47.

Rubington, E., and M. S. Weinberg. (1961). *Deviance: The Interactionist Perspective* (4th Ed). New York: Macmillan.

Sacco, V.F. (1988). *Deviance: Conformity and Control in Canadian Society.* Scarborough, On: Prentice-Hall.

Sack, R. D. (1986). *Human Territoriality: Its Theory and History.* Cambridge University Press.

Sayer, A. (1984). *Method in Social Science: A Realist Approach.* London: Hutchinson.

Scott, C. J., and S. G. Gerberich. (1989). "Analysis of A Smoking Policy in the Workplace." *AAOHN Journal* 37: 265–73.

Shutz, A. (1962). *Collected Papers,* Volume 1.

Sibley, D. (1988). Survey 13: Purification of Space. Environment and Planning D: Society and Space. 6: 409–21.

Smith, C. J. (1988). *Public Problems: The Management of Urban Distress.* New York: Guilford Press.

Smokers' Freedom Society. (1992). "Guidelines for the Courteous Smoker." *Today's Smoker,* Spring-Summer: 5.

Spector, M., and J. I. Kitsuse. (1977). *Constructing Social Problems*. Benjamin/Cummings Publishing.

Stave, G. M., and G. W. Jackson. (1991). "Effect of a Total Work-Site Smoking Ban on Employee Smoking and Attitudes." *Journal of Occupational Medicine* 33: 884–90.

Stones, R. (1991). Strategic Context Analysis: A New Research Strategy for Structuration Theory." *Sociology* 25, no. 4: 673–95.

Thrift, N. (1983). On the Determination of Social Action in Space and Time. Environment and Planning D: Society and Space, 1: 23–57.

Tonnies, F. (1887, 1963). *Community and Society* (translation edited by C. P. Loomis). New York: Harper & Row.

Torgerson, D. (1986). "Interpretive Policy Inquiry: A Response to Its Limitations." *Policy Sciences* 19: 397–405.

Turner, B. S. (1987). *Medical Power and Social Knowledge*. Newbury Park, Calif.: Sage.

Warf, B. (1991). "Power, Politics, and Locality." *Urban Geography* 12, no. 6: 563–69.

White, P. (1991). "Enemies of the People: The Tobacco Pushers." In P. Draper, *Health through Public Policy*. London: Merlin Press.

Wrong, D. (1979). *Power: Its Form, Bases and Uses*. New York: Harper and Row.

12

Judicial Approaches to Tobacco Control: The Third Wave of Tobacco Litigation as a Tobacco Control Mechanism*

Graham E. Kelder Jr. and Richard A. Daynard

Tobacco products liability litigation provides one of the most promising means of controlling the sale and use of tobacco. Recent factual developments—concerning: (1) the addictiveness of nicotine; (2) tobacco industry knowledge of this addictiveness; and (3) the industry's efforts to conceal its knowledge from the public while making its products more addictive—and innovative legal devices, strategies, and tactics being employed by plaintiffs' attorneys make it unlikely that the tactics used by the tobacco industry to defeat plaintiffs in the first (1954 to 1973) and second (1983 to 1992) waves of tobacco litigation will succeed in the third wave of tobacco litigation. For, unlike the earlier cases, the class actions and medical cost reimbursement suits of the third wave are characterized by a number of factors that enable plaintiffs to overcome the previously impenetrable defenses of the tobacco industry. These include a number of factors that make it easier for plaintiffs' attorneys to present enough evidence to the jury of the tobacco industry's decades-long conspiracy of misinformation and deceit around the issues of the addictiveness of nicotine and the harmfulness of tobacco. This evidence includes: (1) new information garnered from internal industry documents and former tobacco industry researchers and executives concerning tobacco industry knowledge of the addictive and pharmacologic properties of nicotine, industry attempts to hide this knowledge, and industry efforts to manipulate nicotine levels so as to addict smokers; (2) the absence of blameworthy

Reprinted from the *Journal of Social Issues*, vol. 53, no. 1 (1997), with the permission of Blackwell Publishers.

*The authors would like to thank Raymond C. Porfiri and Karen J. Bacon for their assistance with this article.

plaintiffs in both classes of cases; and (3) the likely unavailability to the industry of its two favorite affirmative defenses—assumption of the risk and contributory negligence—in the state medical cost reimbursement actions. These new factors also include a number of legal devices, strategies, or tactics designed to circumvent the tobacco industry's abusive discovery practices and to overcome the tremendous resource advantages enjoyed by the industry in previous litigation: (1) the expenditure of time, money, and resources on behalf of thousands or millions of plaintiffs (as opposed to a single plaintiff) in the class action lawsuits; (2) an array of well-financed and well-organized plaintiffs' attorneys sharing resources and information in both classes of cases; and (3) the securing of case management orders in cases brought on behalf of individual plaintiffs. These factors have contributed to some recent successes in getting juries to blame the manufacturer of the instrument of harm—the cigarette—for the injuries caused by it.

Victory in any of the class actions would result in a partial transfer of costs from injured smokers to the tobacco industry. Victory in any of the medical cost reimbursement suits would result in a transfer of costs from injured states forced to shoulder the economic burden of tobacco-induced illnesses to the tobacco industry. Such a transfer of costs would likely have the immediate impact of raising cigarette prices, thereby lowering cigarette consumption.

The amount of exposure faced by the tobacco industry is quite substantial. The annual cigarette-caused medical costs and productivity losses, divided by annual cigarette sales, have been conservatively estimated at $2.17/pack in 1985 dollars (Levoy, 1996). Of course, every affected smoker will not sue, and every meritorious suit will not succeed. On the other hand, the manufacturers have to cover their defense costs as well, and punitive judgements well above the amounts needed for compensation. Furthermore, even a very small increase—such as $.25/pack—will have very significant consumption effects. Price increases of 10 percent have been shown to produce overall consumption decreases of 4 percent, with 14 percent decreases among males twelve to seventeen years old (Levoy, 1996). Because 50 percent of smokers begin by age fourteen and the great majority by age eighteen (Levoy, 1996), the reductions in smoking by children and teenagers may be the most relevant for cancer control purposes. In any event, the hypothesized $.25/pack, 20 percent price increase would produce long-term reductions of at least 10,000 cigarette-caused cancer deaths annually, and possibly many more (Daynard, 1988).

The longterm effects of victories in the class actions and medical cost reimbursement suits of the third wave would probably be much more devastating to the industry. Third-wave victories may drive home the point about the dangers of smoking, while forcing the industry to stop its deceptive advertising, promotion, and public relations. Finally, materials documenting the industry's disinformation campaign, discovered by plaintiffs' attorneys, may hinder industry lobbying efforts against other anti-smoking strategies. Products liability suits have achieved similar effects with respect to asbestos and other dangerous products (Daynard, 1988).

THE FIRST AND SECOND WAVES OF TOBACCO LITIGATION

Throughout the first (1954–1973) and second (1983–1992) waves of tobacco litigation, the tobacco industry steadfastly maintained that its products were not harmful. Plaintiffs in the first wave of tobacco litigation were, in fact, hampered by the paucity of medical studies establishing the link between smoking and disease (Edell, 1986). This led to difficulties in establishing proximate cause. But even in the second wave of tobacco litigation, when medical studies had firmly established the direct connection between smoking and disease (Edell, 1986), the tobacco industry paradoxically argued with great success that smokers had freely chosen to smoke and had thereby assumed the risks of smoking and negligently contributed to their own harm. The defenses of assumption of the risk and contributory negligence were greatly strengthened by the Federal Cigarette Labeling and Advertising Act's imposition of a warning label on all cigarette packaging and advertising (Federal Cigarette Labeling and Advertising Act, 1994). The result was that, rather than identifying the tobacco industry as the cause of the myriad tobacco-induced illnesses, jurors instead tended to blame plaintiffs who had continued to smoke despite health warnings about the link between tobacco use and disease (Daynard, 1994).

In the first and second waves of tobacco litigation, the tobacco industry also successfully pursued a "king of the mountain" strategy (Daynard, 1994) by taking deposition after deposition, and filing and arguing absolutely every motion it could possibly argue, thus threatening to bankrupt and bloody any plaintiff's attorney. This strategy was succinctly described by J. Michael Jordan, an attorney who successfully defended R. J. Reynolds in the 1980s, in an internal memo to his colleagues:

> The aggressive posture we have taken regarding depositions and discovery in general continues to make these cases extremely burdensome and expensive for plaintiffs' lawyers. . . . To paraphrase General Patton, the way we won these cases was not by spending all of [RJR's] money, but by making the other son of a bitch spend all his. (*Haines* v. *Liggett Group,* 1993)

The experience of the law firms that pursued the landmark *Cipollone* case is illustrative of what happened in many of the individual lawsuits in the first and second waves of tobacco litigation. Over one hundred motions were filed, and most of the motions were argued. There were also four interlocutory applications, one resulting in the grant of an appeal and the Third Circuit's initial decision on preemption (*Cipollone* v. *Liggett Group*, 1986), an appeal from the final judgment to the Court of Appeals following a trial of about four months (*Cipollone* v. *Liggett Group*, 1990), and two petitions for certiorari to the Supreme Court of the United States, one of which was granted resulting in an argument, and then a reargument, before that Court (*Cipollone* v. *Liggett Group*, 1992). The firms advanced over $500,000 in out-of-pocket expenses and approximately $2,000,000 in lawyer and paralegal time in connection with the *Cipollone* trial, and over $150,000 in out-of-pocket expenses and over $900,000 in attorney and paralegal time in post-trial proceedings (*Smith* v. *R. J. Reynolds*, 1994).

The *Cipollone* trial had eventually resulted in a $400,000 verdict which was overturned by the Third Circuit on various technical grounds (*Cipollone* v. *Liggett Group*, 1986), and the case was remanded for trial (*Cipollone* v. *Liggett Group*, 1990). A trip to the United States Supreme Court strengthened the plaintiff's case (*Cipollone* v. *Liggett Group*, 1992), but the law firms representing the estate of Rose Cipollone—faced with the loss of hundreds of thousands of dollars—withdrew from the case before it went to trial (*Smith* v. *R. J. Reynolds*, 1994).

OVERVIEW OF THE CLASS ACTIONS AND MEDICAL COST REIMBURSEMENT LAWSUITS OF THE THIRD WAVE

Any discussion of the third wave of tobacco litigation must begin with an overview of the class actions and medical cost reimbursement lawsuits that comprise it. The third wave of tobacco litigation began in March 1994 with the decision of a Florida appellate court in *Broin* v. *Philip Morris Companies, Inc.* (*Broin* v. *Philip Morris*, 1994) and the filing of *Castano* v. *The American Tobacco Company* in federal court in Louisiana (*Castano* v. *American Tobacco*, 1994). The class members in *Broin*, which was filed on October 31, 1991, are nonsmoking flight attendants who assert that they are suffering from diseases and disorders caused by their exposure to second-hand smoke emitted from passengers' cigarettes (*Broin* v. *Philip Morris*, 1991). *Castano* v. *The American Tobacco Company* was filed on March 29, 1994, in federal court in Louisiana (*Castano* v. *American Tobacco*, 1994). Like Engle, the plaintiffs' claims in *Castano* focus on defendants' intentional manipulation of the levels of nicotine, known to them to be a hazardous and addictive substance.

On May 23, 1996, a three-judge panel of the United States Court of

Appeal for the Fifth Circuit ("the Fifth Circuit") concluded that the United States District Court for the Eastern District of Louisiana ("the District Court") erred in certifying *Castano* v. *American Tobacco Company* as a class action. Had it been allowed to proceed, *Castano* probably would have been the largest class action in this nation's history. The Fifth Circuit decided, however, that the District Court ignored "variations in state law and how a trial on the alleged causes of action would be tried" when it certified *Castano*. The Fifth Circuit also stated in its opinion that it did not want a single jury to decide the fate of the entire tobacco industry. Deciding that the errors could not be corrected on remand "because of the novelty of plaintiffs' claims," the Fifth Circuit panel vacated the District Court's certification order and remanded the case with instructions that the District Court dismiss the class complaint (*Castano* v. *American Tobacco*, 1996).

Plaintiffs' lawyers will now pursue Plan B and file statewide class actions in state courts around the nation. The fate of the tobacco industry will now be decided by scores of juries all across the nation (Kelder, 1996c). Four of the statewide class actions that have been filed in the wake of the decertification of *Castano* are modeled after the *Castano* case (see, e.g., *Scott* v. *American Tobacco*, 1996) and are being pursued by attorneys who were involved in the *Castano* lawsuit.

The plaintiffs in *Engle* v. *R. J. Reynolds Tobacco Company*, filed on May 5, 1994, base their eight-count complaint on the assertion that the defendant tobacco companies and their agents knew that nicotine was addictive, claimed unceasingly that it was not, and made every effort to suppress scientific and medical evidence of nicotine's addictiveness (*Engle* v. *R. J. Reynolds*, 1994). The plaintiffs' claims focus on the defendant's intentional manipulation of the levels of nicotine in their tobacco products so as to make them addictive, while concealing information about the addictive nature of nicotine (*Engle* v. *R. J. Reynolds*, 1994).

The wave of state reimbursement suits was initiated on May 23, 1994, when Mississippi Attorney General Mike Moore filed an unprecedented lawsuit against the tobacco industry on behalf of the state's taxpayers to recoup Mississippi's share of the Medicaid costs necessitated by tobacco-induced diseases. Rather than proceeding in a trial court on a theory of subrogation (whereby the State would have stood in the shoes of injured smokers), Moore chose to proceed in equity (i.e., before a single judge in a nonjury proceeding) on theories of unjust enrichment and restitution. Moore's equity claims were grounded in the notion that the State of Mississippi had been injured directly by the behavior of the tobacco industry because Mississippi's taxpayers had been forced to pay the state's Medicaid costs due to tobacco-related illnesses (*Moore* v. *American Tobacco*, 1994).

As of September 11, 1996, fourteen other states had filed medical cost reimbursement suits: Minnesota, West Virginia, Florida, Massachusetts,

Louisiana, Texas, Maryland, Washington, Connecticut, Kansas, Arizona, Michigan, Oklahoma, and New Jersey (Kelder, 1996a). The premise upon which all of the other medical cost reimbursement lawsuits are based is the one initially put forward in the Mississippi suit: that the tobacco industry should pay for the staggering health care costs caused by its tortious conduct. Several of these other lawsuits have unique and significant characteristics or marked "firsts" in this wave of litigation; however, all share the goal of recovering costs to the states incurred by tobacco-related diseases. Other states are likely to file medical cost reimbursement lawsuits in the near future. More than thirty states were represented at a Tobacco Products Liability Project conference sponsored by the Robert Wood Johnson Foundation in November 1995. A similar number appeared at a followup meeting in Chicago on May 3, 1996.

FACTORS CONTRIBUTING TO THE SUCCESS OF THIRD-WAVE TOBACCO LIABILITY LAWSUITS

New Evidence

A series of revelations of tobacco industry knowledge of the addictive and pharmacologic properties of nicotine and of tobacco industry efforts to manipulate nicotine levels to addict smokers has uncovered facts that tend to absolve users of tobacco products of responsibility for their addiction and place the onus squarely on the industry. The third wave of tobacco litigation was sparked by an FDA letter and a television investigative report. On February 25, 1995, FDA Commissioner David Kessler, M.D., J.D., relying primarily on a document discovered in the *Cipollone* case, sent a letter to the Coalition on Smoking Or Health reporting that the FDA had received "mounting evidence" that "the nicotine ingredient in cigarettes is a powerfully addictive agent" and that "cigarette vendors control the levels of nicotine to satisfy this addiction" (Kessler, 1994). He suggested that these conclusions, if established in an administrative or judicial proceeding, would justify regulating cigarettes as a drug and ultimately banning tobacco products "containing nicotine at levels that cause or sustain addiction" (Kessler, 1994).

On February 28, 1994, the ABC broadcast news magazine *Day One* ran an exposé on tobacco industry manipulation of nicotine levels in tobacco products to addict smokers. A second *Day One* story about the secret list of cigarette ingredients ran on March 7, 1994. Philip Morris responded by suing ABC in state court in Richmond, Virginia (giving Philip Morris the "home court" advantage) for libel, claiming that the program cost the company $5 billion in lost revenue.

The ABC reports and Dr. Kessler's public statements prompted Representative Henry Waxman (Dem.-CA), then-chairman of the Health and Environment Subcommittee of the House Energy and Commerce Committee, to hold a series of nationally televised hearings on nicotine manipulation and other tobacco industry practices. At the March 25, 1994, subcommittee hearing on nicotine manipulation, FDA Commissioner Kessler testified that many modern cigarettes are "high-technology nicotine delivery systems" (Regulation of Nicotine-containing Tobacco Products, 1994). During the course of this and subsequent appearances before the subcommittee, Dr. Kessler testified about the use of genetically engineered, nicotine-enhanced tobacco in U.S. cigarettes, tobacco industry patenting of techniques for nicotine manipulation, and secret industry research on the pharmacological effects of nicotine (Regulation of Nicotine-containing Tobacco Products, 1994). At the April 14, 1994, subcommittee hearing on nicotine manipulation, seven tobacco CEOs testified under oath that they believed nicotine is not addictive and that smoking has not been shown to cause cancer (Daynard, 1994). The subcommittee's hearings resulted in the release of damaging internal industry documents (Barnes et al., 1995b).

The pursuit of the tobacco industry continued on into the spring of 1994 when, due to the continuing efforts of investigative journalists and others, internal Brown & Williamson Tobacco Company (B&W) documents were leaked to the press. On May 7, 1994, the *New York Times* ran a front-page story on the leaked documents, and this was followed by stories in the *Wall Street Journal, USA Today, the Washington Post,* and a host of other newspapers (Gottlieb, 1994). The documents indicate that B&W had studied nicotine for years; that its internal stance on several issues related to smoking and health differed from what it was telling the public, that it had, but withheld, findings about the addictiveness of nicotine and the health dangers of both smoking and environmental tobacco smoke, and that B&W attorneys were involved in the management of research projects (Gottlieb, 1994).

Since the genesis of the third wave of tobacco litigation in the spring of 1994, revelations about the tobacco industry's knowledge of the harmfulness of smoking and the addictiveness of nicotine continued to surface in the form of: (1) Philip Morris documents indicating that the company's researchers had studied and written about the pharmacological effects of nicotine on smokers (Collins and Hilts, 1995); (2) an analysis of the documents obtained by B&W and B&W's parent, British American Tobacco Company (BATCO) (Barnes et al., 1995b); (3) R. J. Reynolds Tobacco Company documents obtained by investigative journalists (Levy, 1995); (4) the November 1995 deposition testimony of Dr. Jeffrey Wigand, B&W's former vice president for research (*Moore* v. *American Tobacco,* 1996); and (5) sworn statements given to the Food and Drug Administration (that were first made public on March 18, 1996) in which three former Philip Morris employees said that

Philip Morris not only believes it is in the nicotine-delivery business but controls nicotine levels in its brands (Uydess Statement, 1996; Rivers Statement, 1996; Farone Statement, 1996). Dr. Uydess's statement includes the following comment:

> Tobacco companies like Philip Morris learned a long time ago, that it was hard to get people to stay with a good tasting product if the nicotine level was too low. . . . Philip Morris clearly understood . . . that they could develop a market for a medium- to high-nicotine product that had marginal taste, but that they would have trouble sustaining the sales of a good-tasting product that was too low in nicotine. (Uydess Statement, 1996)

Similar statements were made by Dr. William A. Farone, former director of applied research at Philip Morris, and Dr. Jeffrey Wigand, former Brown and Williamson vice president for research. In addition, the contents of internal R. J. Reynolds Tobacco Company documents leave no doubt that R. J. Reynolds knew of the addictiveness of nicotine (Levy, 1995).

The series of revelations described above has generated a new set of facts that can be used by plaintiffs pursuing the cases of the third wave of tobacco litigation. Over the course of the last three decades, the tobacco industry repeatedly had made representations that (1) nicotine is not pharmacologically active, addictive or harmful, and (2) the industry does not manipulate nicotine levels in its products so as to addict or maintain the addiction of consumers. The recent evidence makes clear, however, that the industry was well aware of the pharmacologically active, addictive, and harmful nature of its products, and that it took active steps to hide this information from its customers and the public at large. These revelations indicate that the tobacco industry does manipulate nicotine levels in its products so as to addict or maintain the addiction of consumers (cf. Barnes et al., 1995b).

The FDA concluded in the findings it published in the *Federal Register* on August 11, 1995, that the Council for Tobacco Research (CTR) does substantial research on nicotine's pharmacological effects on the brain (Nicotine in Cigarettes, 1995) and that CTR personnel have revealed their knowledge that nicotine is a psychoactive drug (Nicotine in Cigarettes, 1995). CTR was, in fact, looked upon by the industry as a source of information about the industry's knowledge of nicotine's addictiveness and techniques for manipulation of nicotine levels (Nicotine in Cigarettes, 1995). The FDA's findings also indicate that at least some of the industry's nicotine research was shared among tobacco companies (Nicotine in Cigarettes, 1995).

The industry has also claimed that there is no definitive proof that smoking causes diseases such as cancer and heart disease. Yet, the documents show that, by the 1960s, B&W and BATCO had proven in their own laboratories that cigarette tar causes cancer in laboratory animals (Barnes et al., 1995b). Finally, the industry has claimed that it is committed to determining the scientific truth about the health effects of tobacco both by conducting internal and by funding external research. The B&W-BATCO documents indicate that, rather than conducting objective scientific research, B&W attorneys have been involved in the selection and dissemination of information from internal as well as external scientific projects for decades (Barnes et al., 1995a). The industry misrepresented the work of the CTR as objective scientific research on smoking and health, while funneling research through attorneys to gain the protection of attorney-client privilege. The documents also include descriptions of how to dispose of damaging documents held by the company's research department (Barnes et al., 1995a).

Dr. Jeffrey Wigand also charged that B&W in-house lawyers repeatedly hid potentially damaging scientific research and altered minutes of scientific meetings. Dr. Wigand testified that J. Kendrick Wells, Brown & Williamson's assistant general counsel, routinely stamped sensitive scientific research "confidential" or "attorney/client work product," even though it had not specifically been created for preparation or use in litigation. Dr. Wigand also testified that, following a meeting of top scientists from B&W and its affiliates in Vancouver, British Columbia, in 1989, Mr. Wells eliminated roughly twelve pages of the meeting's minutes. Wigand said that the missing pages detailed "the company's research on a safer cigarette and on nonaddictive nicotine alternatives" (Freedman, 1996; *Moore* v. *American Tobacco,* 1996).

Shortly after the 1989 Vancouver meeting, Wigand testified that he was summoned to Mr. Sandefur's office and told "there would be no further discussion or efforts on any issues related to a safer cigarette." Wigand also testified that Mr. Sandefur told him "that there can be no research on a safer cigarette. Any research on a safer cigarette would clearly expose every other product as unsafe and, therefore, present a liability issue in terms of any type of litigation." Wigand also asserted that top company officials insisted that coumarin, a compound found in rat poison, remain as an additive in pipe tobacco, even though Wigand told them he was concerned about its safety (Freedman, 1996; *Moore* v. *American Tobacco,* 1996).

THE ABSENCE OF BLAMEWORTHY PLAINTIFFS AND SUBSEQUENT LOSS OF THE "ASSUMPTION OF RISK" DEFENSE

What all of the cases of the third wave of tobacco litigation have in common, and what will distinguish them in the minds of jurors from the previous two waves of litigation, is the absence of a blameworthy plaintiff. Although addiction had been argued previously, what is new about *Engle* and the statewide successors to *Castano* is the argument that the secret manipulation of nicotine levels by the tobacco industry so as to better addict smokers removes any blame from the plaintiffs and places it squarely on the defendants. It is also unlikely that jurors will blame the nonsmoking flight attendants in *Broin* for having continued to work in smoky airplanes.

The most obvious and undeniable absence of blameworthy plaintiffs occurs in the state medical cost reimbursement actions. The tobacco companies won many of the first- and second-wave cases by asserting the defenses of assumption of risk and contributory negligence, or by asserting that the smoker's willfulness, not the industry's misbehavior, was the proximate cause of the smoker's smoking and consequent illness. Proving assumption of risk in a lawsuit against the tobacco industry generally consists of showing that the injured smoker, knowing the dangers and risks involved in smoking, chose to smoke anyway, and proving contributory negligence generally consists of showing that, by smoking, the injured smoker breached his or her duty to protect him- or herself from injury, and thereby contributed to the harm suffered. These defenses should not be available to the tobacco industry in medical cost reimbursement suits, because these suits are not brought on behalf of injured smokers. They are brought, instead, on behalf of the states themselves to recover the medical costs they have been forced to pay to care for indigent smokers. The tobacco industry cannot plausibly argue that the states chose to smoke or that they contributed to the harm caused them by tobacco products.

THE EXPENDITURE OF TIME, MONEY, AND RESOURCES ON BEHALF OF THOUSANDS OR MILLIONS IN THE CLASS ACTION LAWSUITS

The great advantage of the class actions being pursued in the third wave of tobacco litigation is that resources are expended on behalf of thousands or millions of class members rather than on behalf of a single individual. This provides more of a level playing field and means that the tobacco companies will not be able to successfully pursue their usual first- and second-wave strategy of forcing opponents to spend exorbitant sums of money until, nearly bankrupted, they are forced to withdraw. In its unanimous decision, the appellate court in *Broin*, after considering and rejecting defense objections to plaintiffs' request for class certification, alluded to the great promise that the class action strategy holds for plaintiffs challenging the tobacco industry:

> if we were to construe the rule to require each person to file a separate lawsuit, the result would be overwhelming and financially prohibitive. Although defendants would not lack the financial resources to defend each separate lawsuit, the

vast majority of class members, in less advantageous financial positions, would be deprived of a remedy. We decline to promote such a result. (*Bevin* v. *Philip Morris*, 1994)

Whereas a national class action whose class contains many members from many different states may be unjustly criticized as being unmanageable because of its vast size, and because it may involve conflicts over which states' legal standards should be used to decide the case, statewide class actions, such as *Engle* and the cases filed thus far in the wake of the demise of *Castano*, are immune from such criticisms. Statewide class actions will be more manageable, and state courts won't have to reconcile the laws of different states.

The class action strategy is alive and well. What's changed post-*Castano* is that the tobacco industry will not have to face a single class action of gigantic proportions. The industry will instead face scores of huge statewide class actions. Plaintiffs now have more forums in which they might win. Time, money, and resources will now be expended, not on behalf of a national class action composed of some 50 million plaintiffs, but on behalf of statewide classes composed of thousands or hundreds of thousands of plaintiffs. In large states like California and New York, the classes may be composed of millions of plaintiffs. Like *Castano*, all of these statewide cases will be more cost-effective and, thus, easier to pursue than the individual cases in the first and second waves were. The tobacco companies will not be able to win these statewide classes by attempting to bloody and bankrupt the plaintiffs' attorneys who dare to challenge them as they did in the first and second waves of tobacco litigation.

This is, in part, due to an array of well-financed and well-organized plaintiffs' attorneys sharing resources and information. Chief among the cases being prosecuted by extremely well-organized and well-financed attorneys was the *Castano* case (*Castano* v. *American Tobacco*, 1994). The class was represented by a consortium of more than sixty law firms from across the United States, most of which had pledged $100,000 per year in support of the litigation. Although the *Castano* case was decertified, the attorneys in the *Castano* consortium have $2.2 million on hand, and $1.5 million comes into the consortium every three months as each of the sixty firms involved antes up. These are the attorneys who will be leading the charge in the statewide class actions in state courts (Kelder, 1996c).

The states that have thus far filed medical cost reimbursement suits have at their disposal the financial resources of their respective states. In several states, outside counsel has advanced the costs of attorney time and expenses on a contingent fee basis. In Minnesota, Blue Cross-Blue Shield has joined the state as a co-plaintiff and is covering out-of-pocket expenses plus a contribution to attorney time. In Massachusetts, Blue Cross and Blue Shield is contributing generously to out-of-pocket expenses (Kelder, 1995).

The attorneys involved in all of these suits are also sharing information with one another on an unprecedented scale. On May 28, 1996, the United States Supreme Court, without comment, left intact a Minnesota Supreme Court ruling that the tobacco industry must turn over to the plaintiffs in Minnesota's medical cost reimbursement suit the computer databases that comprise an index to millions of internal industry documents obtained in the suit. The databases could provide to the plaintiffs' attorneys pursuing the myriad cases of the third wave of tobacco litigation the precise tool they require to proceed quickly and efficiently with discovery and information-gathering in their respective lawsuits (*Philip Morris* v. *CIR,* 1996).

The databases' index could save plaintiffs' lawyers research time and speed, thus making it easier and more economical for plaintiffs to develop and prove their cases. The databases, which provide a guided tour to the documents, will make it easier for plaintiffs' attorneys to find the proverbial needle in the haystack because the databases allow plaintiffs to have a list of needles. Estimates are that, without the databases, it would take nine years for five attorneys working twelve hours a day, five days a week, to sort through the documents.

THE SECURING OF CASE MANAGEMENT ORDERS IN CASES BROUGHT ON BEHALF OF INDIVIDUALS

As discussed more fully above, one way to circumvent the tobacco industry's "king of the mountain" strategy is to pursue class actions which are more cost-effective because money is expended in these cases on behalf of thousands or millions of plaintiffs as opposed to a single plaintiff. A second legal device that can be used to circumvent the tobacco industry's "king of the mountain" strategy is a case management order that places limits on discovery and sets time standards for the conduct of cigarette cases.

On January 23, 1996, the Circuit Court for Duval County, Florida, issued a case management order that "applies to all cigarette injury cases presently filed and filed in the future by the law firm of Spohrer, Wilner, Maxwell, Maciejewski, & Stanford, P.A. in Duval County Circuit Court, Duval County, Florida" (*In re: Cigarette Cases,* 1996). The case management order sets time standards, places limits on discovery and allows for the expedited elevation of backup cases to primary status when a case scheduled for trial is dismissed (*In re: Cigarette Cases,* 1996). The case management order dictates that cases are identified as cigarette injury cases as soon as they are filed. They are then assigned sequentially to one of the circuit court's eight divisions so as to evenly distribute the number of cases pending in each of these divisions. The eight divisions then rotate so that each month one of them will provide a trial setting for cigarette cases. In the division whose turn it is for that month, there will be one cigarette injury case identified as the primary trial case for that month. A cigarette trial list will then provide for a sequenced list of backup cases that are ready for trial (*In re: Cigarette Cases,* 1996). That means that if the primary case is dismissed, continued, or for other reasons cannot be tried, the first backup case will be tried. The short of it is that if the tobacco industry's "king of the mountain" strategy succeeds in knocking out the primary case, a backup case will be tried.

The case management order also calls upon the parties to prepare a uniform discovery and pretrial order providing for consistent standards in discovery practice, including timely disclosure of witnesses and exhibits (*In re: Cigarette Cases,* 1996). This means that the tobacco industry will not be able to abuse the discovery process—filing any and every motion and burying its opponents in paper—as it has often been accused of doing in cases filed against it in the past.

The Carter Case as Emblematic of a New Paradigm in Tobacco Litigation

The factors discussed above form a new paradigm through which the tobacco industry and smoking will be seen by jurors, judges, the public, and government in the third wave of tobacco litigation (Daynard & Kelder, 1995). The tobacco companies will no longer be seen as honest purveyors of a legal and perhaps harmless recreational substance that some individuals develop the habit of using. They will be seen, rather, as the dishonest pushers of a drug called nicotine, a substance that they recognized as harmful and addictive over thirty years ago. They will be seen as shameless frauds who deliberately deceived the public into believing that their product was safe and nonaddictive, while conspiring to keep the industry's knowledge to the contrary secret, manipulating the levels of nicotine in its products so as to better addict the users of nicotine, and targeting young women, children and minorities in its advertising campaigns in order to addict a new generation of nicotine users to replace those who died from the consequences of their addiction. This new paradigm should result in jurors blaming the tobacco industry, rather than smokers, for the harm smokers have suffered at the hands of cigarettes.

A recent Florida case is emblematic of this new paradigm and the results it is likely to produce. On August 9, 1996, a six-person jury in Jacksonville, Florida, awarded a verdict of $750,000 to Grady Carter, a former air traffic controller who smoked from age seventeen in 1947 until he was diagnosed with lung cancer in 1991, and his wife, Mildred Carter, who sued Brown & Williamson Tobacco Co. in 1995 on the grounds of negligence and strict liability. This was the first jury to decide a case in the third wave of tobacco litigation, and the first jury in a tobacco products liability case to have presented to it the damning information contained in the Brown & Williamson internal documents. In so ruling, the jury found that the Lucky Strike cigarettes manufactured by Defendant Brown & Williamson Tobacco Corporation, as successor by merger to the American Tobacco Company, were "unreasonably dangerous and defective." In contrast, on August 23, 1996, an Indiana jury found four cigarette makers were not responsible for a long-time smoker's cancer death. After sixteen hours of deliberation, a Superior Court jury rejected the claims by Yvonne Rogers that four tobacco companies sold products that were defective to her husband, Richard (Daynard et al., 1996).

Although the tobacco industry would like the press and the public to view the plaintiffs' victory in *Carter* v. *American Tobacco* as an "aberration" and the plaintiff's loss in *Rogers* as confirmation of that view, comparing *Carter* to *Rogers* is like comparing the proverbial apples to oranges. *Rogers*—a case filed back in the second wave of tobacco litigation—is typical of the individual cases of the second wave, in that no internal industry documents were admitted into evidence and no special techniques were used to overcome the abusive discovery tactics of the tobacco industry. Despite these facts, the real truth of the matter is that the tobacco industry would have lost the *Rogers* case, too, had it not been for a peculiarity of Indiana law that prevents juries from ruling for plaintiffs if plaintiffs bear more than 50 percent of the blame for their injuries. This is not the law in most states. *Carter* is typical of the new breed of cases of the third wave of tobacco litigation. The *Carter* jury was exposed to the damaging facts contained in the Brown & Williamson documents, and the lawyers prosecuting the *Carter* case on behalf of the plaintiffs used the previously described technique of securing a case management order to short-circuit the abusive discovery tactics of the tobacco industry (Daynard et al., 1996).

The *Carter* victory—only the third instance in which an American jury has ever awarded damages to a plaintiff in a cigarette products liability case—should, in fact, be seen as ushering in a new era in tobacco litigation in which the tobacco industry will be held accountable for its misdeeds. The first ever damages award—$400,000 to the family of Rose *Cipollone*—was overturned by the Third Circuit on various technical grounds. The second damages award came on August 31, 1995, when a California state court jury awarded $2 million—$1.3 million in compensatory damages and $700,000 in punitive damages—to Milton J. Horowitz, a 72-year-old university professor, clinical psychologist and former smoker, who claimed his mesothelioma was caused by the asbestos contained in the Micronite filter in the Kent cigarettes he used to smoke. Lorillard was held liable for a $1.21 million share of the damages and Hollingsworth & Vose, the manufacturer of Kent's Micronite filter, was assigned a share of $790,000 (Daynard et al., 1996).

The true significance of the *Carter* verdict lies in the fact that Norwood "Woody" Wilner and his colleagues at Spohrer, Wilner, Maxwell,

Maciejewski & Stanford, P.A. have shown attorneys all across the nation the way to win an individual cigarette products liability action against the tobacco industry. The keys are: (1) the use of some sort of legal device, strategy, or tactic to circumvent the tobacco industry's abusive discovery practices; and (2) to present enough evidence to the jury of the tobacco industry's decades-long conspiracy of misinformation and deceit around the issues of the addictiveness of nicotine and the harmfulness of tobacco, so that the jury blames the tobacco company rather than the smoker for the injuries caused.

The admission of the Brown & Williamson documents into evidence in the *Carter* trial played a key role in Woody Wilner's victory. According to an article published by the *Wall Street Journal* on August 12, 1996, the first jury to see the Brown & Williamson documents assigned those documents a key role in their decision:

> In interviews over the weekend with three of the six jurors, two expressed anger over the internal documents and all three complained about a key contradiction in the company's defense. Brown & Williamson produced reams of evidence suggesting Mr. Carter was aware smoking was harmful but, at the same time, the company vehemently insisted the perils of smoking aren't proved. "To me, it boiled down to two words, crass hypocrisy," says Samuel Gaskins, sixty, a retired postal-service supervisor, who served as jury foreman. "They can't have it both ways." (Hwang et al., 1996)

The impact that internal industry documents such as the Brown & Williamson documents can have on juries is underscored by the fact that in *Cipollone,* the only other case to make substantial use of industry documents, the jury awarded the plaintiff $400,000. The documents in *Cipollone* included evidence that: Liggett & Myers (L&M) knew by the early 1970s how to make a safer cigarette, but suppressed it, for fear that implicit in marketing it would be the admission that L&M's other cigarettes were unsafe; Philip Morris had identified a wide variety of carcinogens and co-carcinogens in cigarette smoke by the early 1960s, but kept mum; and Lorillard had concluded in 1964 that the published evidence justified a "presumption" that smoking causes lung cancer, but did nothing to inform or protect its customers (Daynard et al., 1996). The jury in *Rogers* did not get to see the kind of damning evidence to which the *Cipollone* and *Carter* juries were exposed.

Future plaintiffs' attorneys can avail themselves of the Brown & Williamson documents, the Philip Morris documents, the R. J. Reynolds documents, and the testimony of whistle blowers like Jeffrey Wigand and Ian Uydess. They can also copy the innovative tactics of Woody Wilner and secure a case management order like the one in *Carter*. In the end, the verdicts in *Carter* and *Rogers* demonstrate that the tide is turning against the tobacco industry.

CONCLUSION

The new paradigm discussed at length above may lead to the "catastrophe" that proves to be the undoing of the tobacco industry. As happened with asbestos, litigation against the tobacco industry may come to consist of tens of thousands of cases. The major tobacco companies would then have to retain counsel in every large city in the United States, fresh liability insurance would probably become unavailable to them, and their financial statements would reflect the kind of contingent liabilities that frighten most prudent investors (Daynard, 1988).

In fact, the third wave of tobacco litigation has already resulted in one landmark settlement. On March 15, 1996, the State of West Virginia, the State of Florida, the State of Mississippi, the Commonwealth of Massachusetts, and the State of Louisiana (collectively, "Plaintiffs" or "the Settling States") entered into an agreement with Brooke Group Ltd. ("Brooke Group"), a Delaware corporation, and Liggett Group, Inc. ("Ligett"), a Delaware corporation, to settle the Brooke Group/Liggett portion of these states' medical cost reimbursement actions (Shao, 1996). This settlement represents a breach in the tobacco industry's previously impenetrable defenses. The tobacco industry is no longer presenting a united front in the face of the third wave of tobacco litigation. This is also an extraordinary development because the industry is very proud of its unbroken record of the last forty years of never settling or never paying out a penny in damages to plaintiffs. This means that the multiparty strategy of the third wave of tobacco litigation has achieved its first victory. If Liggett is the fault line, the third wave's multiparty strategy is the geological pressure that caused the earthquake that this settlement represents.

The August 9, 1996, defeat of the tobacco industry in *Carter* v. *American Tobacco* and the promulgation of the FDA's recent final rule on tobacco have led to discussion of a global legislative settlement of all tobacco litigation. The *Wall Street Journal* reported on August 26, 1996, that Trent Lott, the man who succeeded Bob Dole as Senate Majority Leader, has agreed to broker a global legislative proposal that would allow the tobacco industry to avoid FDA regulation and grant cigarette manufacturers sweeping immunity from products liability suits for the next decade and a half (Freedman & Hwang, 1996). According to the *Journal,*

> Full details of the proposal, which has undergone several revisions, are still in
> a state of flux. But the latest draft calls for the tobacco industry to pay $6 bil-
> lion in 1997, with the sum escalating to about $10 billion in the fourth year and
> continuing over the next eleven years. About 95 percent of the money, which
> would be administered by a presidential-appointed administrator, would be paid

out in grants to the nation's fifty states. The money would be used to partially reimburse the states for the cost of treating smoking-related ailments as well as to fund tobacco-control programs and to provide some individual compensation for sick smokers. (Freedman & Hwang, 1996, p. A2)

The plan also requires the industry to drop any lawsuits it has brought against industry defectors and whistle blowers (Freedman & Hwang, 1996).

In exchange for this, the industry would gain immunity from virtually all liability suits for the next fifteen years. The exception would be class-action or individual suits already under way, but they would have a damages cap imposed upon them. The tobacco industry would also escape FDA regulation of nicotine as a drug and cigarettes as drug delivery devices, but the FDA's current recommendations would be enacted into law (presumably by Congress). The *Journal* also reported that "if youth smoking rates fail to decline by 50 percent within a certain period of time, jurisdiction would revert back to the [FDA]" (Freedman & Hwang, 1996, p. A2).

The proposal raises serious questions for the public health. Does it represent the successful realization of the tobacco control goals of tobacco litigation or does it fall short of these goals?

REFERENCES

Barnes, D. E., L. Bero, S. A. Glantz, P. Hanauer, & J. Slade. (1995a). "Lawyer Control of Internal Scientific Research to Protect against Products Liability Lawsuits: The Brown and Williamson Documents." *Journal of the American Medical Association* 274: 234–40.

Barnes, D. E., L. Bero, S. A. Glantz, P. Hanauer, & J. Slade. (1995b). "Looking Through a Keyhole at the Tobacco Industry: The Brown & Williamson Documents." *Journal of the American Medical Association* 274: 219–58.

Complaint, *Broin* v. *Philip Morris,* 6.4 Tobacco Prods. Litig. Rep. 3.465 (1991).

Broin v. *Philip Morris,* 641 So.2d 888 (Fla. 1994).

First Amended Complaint, *Castano* v. *American Tobacco,* 9.2 Tobacco Prods. Litig. Rep. 3.49 (1994).

Castano v. *American Tobacco,* 10.1 Tobacco Prods. Litig. Rep. 2.1 (1995).

Castano v. *American Tobacco,* 11.3 Tobacco Prods. Litig. Rep. 2.99 (1996).

Cipollone v. *Liggett Group,* 112 S. Ct. 2608 (1992).

Cipollone v. *Liggett Group,* 893 F.2d 541 (3d Cir.1990).

Cipollone v. *Liggett Group,* 789 F.2d 181 (3d Cir.1986).

Collins, J. & Hilts. P. J. (1995, June 8). "Records Show Philip Morris Studied Influence of Nicotine." *The New York Times,* p. 1.

Daynard, R. A. (1994, November). "The Third Wave of Tobacco Products Liability Cases." *Trial* 30: 34–40.

Daynard, R. A. (1988). "Tobacco Litigation as a Cancer Control Strategy." *Journal of the National Cancer Institute* 80: 9.

Daynard, R. A., & G. E. Kelder. (1995, November). "The Tobacco Industry Under Fire." *Trial* 31: 20–25.

Edell, M., (1986, Fall) "Cigarette Litigation: The Second Wave." *Tort & Insurance Law Journal* 22: 90.

Amended Complaint, *Engle* v. *R. J. Reynolds,* 9.3 Tobacco Prods. Litig. Rep. 3.293 (1994).

Federal Cigarette Advertising and Labeling Act, 15 U.S.C. §§ 1331–41, (1994).

Federal Racketeer Influenced and Corrupt Organizations Act, 18 U.S.C. §§ 1960–1968, (1994).

Freedman, A. (1996, January 26). "The Deposition: Cigarette Defector Says CEO Lied to Congress about View of Nicotine." *The Wall Street Journal*, p. Al.

Freedman, A., & S. Hwang. (1996, August 26). "Legislation Plan on Tobacco Advances." *The Wall Street Journal*, p. A2.

Gottlieb, M. (1994, May). "Pandora's Box of Documents Explodes." *Tobacco on Trial,* 1994 no. 4: 1.

Haines v. *Liggett Group,* 814 F Supp. 414 (D.N.J. 1993).

Hwang, S., M. Geyelin, & A. Freedman. (1996, August 12). "Jury's Tobacco Verdict Suggests Tough Times Ahead for the Industry." *The Wall Street Journal*, p. Al.

Case Management Order, *In re: Cigarette Cases,* 11.1 Tobacco Prods. Litig. Rep. 2.3 (1996).

Kelder, G. (1995, March). "Filing of Florida Lawsuit and Ruling in Mississippi Strip Tobacco Industry of Its Favorite Legal Defenses." *Tobacco On Trial,* 1995, no. 2: 1.

———. (1996a, September). "Hurricane Season Begins with a Storm of Suits by Attorneys General." *Tobacco On Trial,* 6: 15.

———. (1996b, January). "Once More Unto the Breach." *Tobacco On Trial,* 1: 1.

———. (1996c, June). "The Sorcerer's Apprentice." *Tobacco On Trial,* 4: 1.

Kessler, D. (1994, February 25). Letter to the Coalition on Smoking Or Health re: FDA regulation of cigarettes as drugs.

Levoy, J. (1996, January 27). "Discount Cigarette Stores on the Rise." *Los Angeles Times,* p. A1.

Levy, D. (1995, October 6). "RJR Memo Targeted Teen Market." *USA Today,* p. 1D.

Complaint, *Moore* v. *American Tobacco,* 9.2 Tobacco Prods. Litig. Rep. 3.35 (1994).

Deposition of Jeffrey Wigand, *Moore* v. *American Tobacco,* 11.1 Tobacco Prods. Litig. Rep. 3.1 (1996).

U.S. Food and Drug Administration. (August, 1995). Nicotine in Cigarettes and Smokeless Tobacco Products is a Drug and These Products are Nicotine Delivery Devices Under the Food, Drug and Cosmetic Act. published at 60 Fed. Reg. 41, 454–41, 787 (Aug. 11, 1995).

Statement of Dr. William Farone, Nicotine in Cigarettes and Smokeless Tobacco Products is a Drug and These Products are Nicotine Delivery Devices Under the Food, Drug and Cosmetic Act, published at 11.2 Tobacco Prods. Litig. Rep. 8.13 (1996).

Statement of Jerome Rivers, Nicotine in Cigarettes and Smokeless Tobacco Products is a Drug and These Products are Nicotine Delivery Devices Under the Food, Drug and Cosmetic Act, published at 11.2 Tobacco Prods. Litig. Rep. 8.11 (1996).

Statement of Dr. Ian Uydess, Nicotine in Cigarettes and Smokeless Tobacco Products is a Drug and These Products are Nicotine Delivery Devices Under the Food, Drug and Cosmetic Act, published at 11.2 Tobacco Prods. Litig. Rep. 8.1 (1996).

Philip Morris v. *CIR,* 116 S. Ct. 1849 (1996).

Regulation of Nicotine-containing Products under the Federal Food, Drug and Cosmetic Act, 1994: Hearings Before the Subcomm. On Health & the Environment of the House Comm. on Energy & Commerce. 103d. Cong., 2d Sess. (statement of Dr. David Kessler, Commissioner, FDA).

R. J. Reynolds v. *Engle,* 11.1 Tobacco Prods. Litig. Rep. 2.1 (1996).

Complaint, *Scott* v. *American Tobacco,* 11.4 Tobacco Prods. Litig. Rep. 3.514 (1996).

Shao, M. (1996, March 14). "Tobacco Firm Agrees to Settle Suit; Move Is Called a Milestone in Cigarette Wars." *The Boston Globe*, p. 1.

Smith v. *R. J. Reynolds.* 9.4 Tobacco Prods. Litig. Rep. 2.105 (1994).

Suggestions for Further Reading

Annas, G. J. (1996). "Cowboys, Camels, and the First Amendment—The FDA's Restrictions on Tobacco Advertising." *New England Journal of Medicine* 335, no. 23: 1779–83.

Arno, P., A. Brandt, L. Gostin, and J. Morgan. (1996). "Tobacco Industry Strategies to Oppose Federal Regulation." *Journal of the American Medical Association* 275, no. 6: 1258–62.

Best, J. A., and M. Bloch. (1979). "Compliance in the Control of Cigarette Smoking." In *Compliance in Health Care*, eds. R. E. Haynes, D. W. Taylor, and D. L. Sackett. Baltimore: Johns Hopkins University Press.

Brecher, E. M., and the Editors of *Consumer Reports*. (1972). "Tobacco" and "Nicotine as an Addicting Drug" (chapters 23 & 25). In *Licit & Illicit Drugs*. Boston: Little, Brown and Company.

Clarke, P. B. S. (1987). "Nicotine and Smoking: A Perspective from Animal Studies." *Psychopharmacology* 92: 135–43.

Council on Scientific Affairs. (1990). "The Worldwide Smoking Epidemic: Tobacco Trade, Use, and Control." *Journal of the American Medical Association* 263, no. 24: 3312–18.

DiFranza, J. R., and J. B. Tye. (1990). "Who Profits from Tobacco Sales to Children?" *Journal of the American Medical Association* 263: 2784–87.

Editorial. (1996). "The Ledger of Tobacco Control: Is the Cup Half Empty or Half Full?" *Journal of the American Medical Association* 275: 1281–84.

Fiore, M. C., et al. (1990). "Methods Used to Quit Smoking in the United States: Do Cessation Programs Help?" *Journal of the American Medical Association* 263: 2760–65.

Frolich, E. (1995). "Statutes Aiding States, Recovery of Medicaid Costs from Tobacco Companies: A Better Strategy for Redressing an Identifiable Harm?" *American Journal of Law and Medicine* 21: 445–72.

Glantz, S. (1996). *The Cigarette Papers*. Los Angeles: UCLA Press.

Glynn, T. J. (1990). "Methods of Smoking Cessation—Finally, Some Answers." (Editorial). *Journal of the American Medical Association* 263: 2795–96.

Goldstein, A. O., and Bearman, N. S. (1996). "State Tobacco Lobbyists and Organizations in the United States: Crossed Lines." *American Journal of Public Health* 86: 117–42.

Gostin, L. O., Arno, P. S., and Brandt, A. M. (1997). "FDA Regulation of Tobacco Advertising and Youth Smoking: Historical, Social, and Constitutional Perspectives." *Journal of the American Medical Association* 277, no. 5: 410–18.

219

Hansen, M. (1997). "Capitol Offensives." *American Bar Association Journal,* January, 50–56.

Jaffe, J. H., and Kanzler, M. (1980). "Tobacco Use as Drug Abuse." In *The Yearbook of Substance Use and Abuse,* volume 2, eds. L. Brill and C. Winnick, 325–49. New York: Human Sciences Press. (1990). *Journal of the American Medical Association* 264, no. 12.

Kessler, D. A., A. M. Witt, P. S. Barnett, M. R. Zeller, S. L. Natanblut, J. P. Wilkenfeld, C. C. Lorraine, L. J. Thompson, and W. B. Schultz. (1996). "Food and Drug Administration's Regulation of Tobacco Products." *New England Journal of Medicine,* 335(13), 988–994.

Kozlowski, L. T., D. A. Wilkinson, W. Skinner, C. Kent, T. Franklin, and M. Pope. (1989). "Comparing Tobacco Cigarette Dependence with Other Drug Dependencies: Greater or Equal 'Difficulty Quitting' and 'Urges to Use,' but Less 'Pleasure' from Cigarettes." *Journal of the American Medical Association* 261: 898–901.

Krasnego, N. A. (Ed.) (1979). "Cigarette Smoking as a Dependence Process." *Research Monograph* 23. Rockville, Md.: National Institute on Drug Abuse.

Novotny, T., and M. Siegel. (1996). "California's Tobacco Control Saga." *Health Affairs* 15: 58–72.

Pertschuk, M. (1997). "Making Deals with the Devil." *The Washington Post,* May 11, Cl.

Pierce, J. P., M. C. Fiore, T. E. Novotny, E. J. Hatziandreu, and R. M. Davis. (1989). "Trends in Cigarette Smoking in the United States: Educational Differences Are Increasing." *Journal of the American Medical Association* 261: 56–60.

Samuels, B., and S. Glantz. (1991). "The Politics of Local Tobacco Control." *Journal of the American Medical Association* 266: 2110–17.

Schacter, S. (1977). "Nicotine Regulation in Heavy and Light Smokers." *Journal of Experimental Psychology:* General 106: 13–19.

———. (1978). "Pharmacological and Psychological Determinants of Smoking." *Annals of Internal Medicine* 88: 104–14.

Siegel, M., and L. Biener. (1997). "Evaluating the Impact of Statewide Anti–Tobacco Campaigns." *Journal of Social Issues* 53, no. l: 147–68.

Slade, J., L. A. Bero, P. Hanauer, D. E. Barnes, and S. A. Glantz. (1995). "Nicotine and Addiction: The Brown and Williamson Documents." *Journal of the American Medical Association* 274, no. 3: 225–33.

Meade, K. E. (1996). "Breaking Through the Tobacco Industry's Smoke Screen: State Lawsuits for Reimbursement of Medical Expenses." *The Journal of Legal Medicine* 17, 113–141.

Moore, S., S. M. Wolfe, D. Lindes, and C. E. Douglas. (1994). "Epidemiology of Failed Tobacco Control Legislation." *Journal of the American Medical Association* 272: 1171–75.

New York City Department of Health. (1995). Smoke–free Air Act (sl7–501–17–514).

———. (1994). *Survey of Restaurant Smoking.*

Skolnick, A. (1995). "Spate of Lawsuits May Finally Find Chink in Tobacco Industry's "Impenetrable Armor." *Journal of the American Medical Association* 273: 1080–81.

Smart, D. C. (1994). "Interposition in the U.S. Tobacco Market." *Social Science and Medicine* 39, no. 12: 1681–82.

The Smoking Cessation Clinical Practice Guideline Panel and Staff. (1995). "The Agency for Health Care Policy and Research Smoking Cessation Clinical Practice Guideline." *Journal of the American Medical Association* 275: 1270–80.

Traynor, M., M. Begay, and S. Glantz. (1993). "New Tobacco Industry Strategy to Prevent Local Tobacco Control." *The Journal of the American Medical Association* 270: 479–86.

U.S. Department of Health and Human Services. (1993). *Major local tobacco control ordinances in the United States.* Bethesda, Md.: National Institutes of Health.

———. Healthy People 2000. *U.S. Department of Health and Human Services Publication No. (PHS) 91–50213.*

Part III

Liberty at Stake: Smoking as Choice, Regulation as Coercion

13

The Control of Conduct: Authority versus Autonomy

Thomas Szasz

There is only one political sin: independence; and only one political virtue: obedience. To put it differently, there is only one offense against authority: self-control; and only one obeisance to it: submission to control by authority.

Why is self-control, autonomy, such a threat to authority? Because the person who controls himself, who is his own master, has no need for an authority to be his master. This, then, renders authority unemployed. What is he to do if he cannot control others? To be sure, he could mind his own business. But this is a fatuous answer, for those who are satisfied to mind their own business do not aspire to become authorities. In short, authority needs subjects, persons not in command of themselves—just as parents need children and physicians need patients.

Autonomy is the death knell of authority, and authority knows it: hence the ceaseless warfare of authority against the exercise, both real and symbolic, of autonomy—that is, against suicide, against masturbation, against self-medication, against the proper use of language itself![1]

The parable of the Fall illustrates this fight to the death between control and self-control. Did Eve, tempted by the Serpent, seduce Adam, who then lost control of himself and succumbed to evil? Or did Adam, facing a choice between obedience to the authority of God and his own destiny, choose self-control?

How, then, shall we view the situation of the so-called drug abuser or drug addict? As a stupid, sick, and helpless child, who, tempted by pushers, peers, and the pleasures of drugs, succumbs to the lure and loses control of

Reprinted from T. S. Szasz, *Ceremonial Chemistry: The Ritual Persecution of Drugs, Addicts, and Pushers,* rev. ed. (1985), with the permission of Learning Publications, Inc.

himself? Or as a person in control of himself, who, like Adam, chooses the forbidden fruit as the elemental and elementary way of pitting himself against authority?

There is no empirical or scientific way of choosing between these two answers, of deciding which is right and which is wrong. The questions frame two different moral perspectives, and the answers define two different moral strategies: if we side with authority and wish to repress the individual, we shall treat him as if he were helpless, the innocent victim of overwhelming temptation; and we shall then "protect" him from further temptation by treating him as a child, slave, or madman. If we side with the individual and wish to refute the legitimacy and reject the power of authority to infantilize him, we shall treat him as if he were in command of himself, the executor of responsible decisions; and we shall then demand that he respect others as he respects himself by treating him as an adult, a free individual, or a "rational" person.

Either of these positions makes sense. What makes less sense—what is confusing in principle and chaotic practice—is to treat people as adults and children, as free and unfree, as sane and insane.

Nevertheless, this is just what social authorities throughout history have done: in ancient Greece, in medieval Europe, in the contemporary world, we find various mixtures in the attitudes of the authorities toward the people; in some societies, the individual is treated as more free than unfree, and we call these societies "free"; in others, he is treated as more determined than self-determining, and we call these societies "totalitarian." In none is the individual treated as completely free. Perhaps this would be impossible: many persons insist that no society could survive on such a premise consistently carried through. Perhaps this is something that lies in the future of mankind. In any case, we should take satisfaction in the evident impossibility of the opposite situation: no society has ever treated the individual, nor perhaps could it treat him, as completely determined. The apparent freedom of the authority, controlling both himself and subject, provides an irresistible model: if God can control, if pope and prince can control, if politician and psychiatrist can control—then perhaps the person can also control, at least himself.

The conflicts between those who have power and those who want to take it away from them fall into three distinct categories. In moral, political, and social affairs (and I of course include psychiatric affairs among these), these categories must be clearly distinguished; if we do not distinguish among them we are likely to mistake opposition to absolute or arbitrary power with what may, actually, be an attempt to gain such power for oneself or for the groups or leaders one admires.

First, there are those who want to take power away from the oppressor and give it to the oppressed, as a class—as exemplified by Marx, Lenin, and the Communists. Revealingly, they dream of the "dictatorship" of the proletariat or some other group.

Second, there are those who want to take power away from the oppressor and give it to themselves as the protectors of the oppressed—as exemplified by Robespierre in politics; Rush in medicine; and by their liberal, radical, and medical followers. Revealingly, they dream of the incorruptibly honest or incontrovertibly sane ruler leading his happy or healthy flock.

And third, there are those who want to take power away from the oppressor and give it to the oppressed as individuals, for each to do with as he pleases, but hopefully for his own self-control—as exemplified by Mill, von Mises, the free-market economists, and their libertarian followers. Revealingly, they dream of people so self-governing that their need for and tolerance of rulers is minimal or nil.

While countless men say they love liberty, clearly only those who, by virtue of their actions, fall into the third category, mean it.[2] The others merely want to replace a hated oppressor by a loved one—having usually themselves in mind for the job.

As we have seen, psychiatrists (and some other physicians, notably public health administrators) have traditionally opted for "reforms" of the second type; that is, their opposition to existing powers, ecclesiastic or secular, has had as its conscious and avowed aim the paternalistic care of the citizen-patient, and not the freedom of the autonomous individual. Hence, medical methods of social control tended not only to replace religious methods, but sometimes to exceed them in stringency and severity. In short, the usual response of medical authority to the controls exercised by nonmedical authority has been to try to take over and then escalate the controls, rather than to endorse the principle and promote the practice of removing the controls by which the oppressed are victimized.

As a result, until recently, most psychiatrists, psychologists, and other behavioral scientists had nothing but praise for the "behavioral controls" of medicine and psychiatry. We are now beginning to witness, however, a seeming backlash against this position, many behavioral scientists jumping on what they evidently consider to be the next "correct" and "liberal," position, namely, a criticism of behavioral controls. But since most of these "scientists" remain as hostile to individual freedom and responsibility, to choice and dignity, as they have always been, their criticism conforms to the pattern I have described above: they demand more "controls"—that is, professional and governmental controls—over "behavior controls." This is like first urging a person to drive over icy roads at breakneck speed to get over them as fast as possible, and then, when his car goes into a skid, advising him to apply his brakes. Whether because they are stupid or wicked or both, such persons invariably recommend fewer controls where more are needed, for example in relation to punishing offenders—and more controls where fewer are needed, for example in relation to contracts between consenting adults.

Truly, the supporters of the Therapeutic State* are countless and tireless—now proposing more therapeutic controls in the name of "controlling behavior controls."[3]

Clearly, the seeds of this fundamental human propensity—to react to the loss of control, or to the threat of such loss, with an intensification of control, thus generating a spiraling symbiosis of escalating controls and countercontrols—have fallen on fertile soil in contemporary medicine and psychiatry and have yielded a luxuriant harvest of "therapeutic" coercions. The alcoholic and Alcoholics Anonymous, the glutton and Weight Watchers, the drug abuser and the drug-abuseologist—each is an image at war with its mirror image, each creating and defining, dignifying and defaming the other, and each trying to negate his own reflection, which he can accomplish only by negating himself.

There is only one way to split apart and unlock such pairings, to resolve such dilemmas—namely, by trying to control the other less, not more, and by replacing control of the other with self-control.

The person who uses drugs—legal or illegal drugs, with or with or without a physician's prescription—may be submitting to authority, may be revolting against it, or may be exercising his own power of making a free decision. It is quite impossible to know—without knowing a great deal about such a person, his family and friends, and his whole cultural setting—just what such an individual is doing and why. But it is quite possible, indeed it is easy, to know what those persons who try to repress certain kinds of drug uses and drug users are doing and why.

As the war against heresy was in reality a war for "true" faith, so the war against drug abuse is in reality a war for "faithful," drug use: concealed behind the war against marijuana and heroin is the war for tobacco and alcohol; and, more generally, concealed behind the war against the use of politically and medically disapproved drugs, is the war for the use of politically and medically approved drugs.

Let us recall, again, one of the principles implicit in the psychiatric perspective on man, and some of the practices that follow from it: the madman is a person lacking adequate internal controls over his behavior; hence, he requires—for his own protection as well as for the protection of society—external restraints upon it. This, then, justifies the incarceration of "mental patients" in "mental hospitals"—and much else besides.

The drug abuser is a person lacking adequate internal controls over his drug use; hence, he requires—for his own protection as well as for the protection of society—external restraints upon it. This, then, justifies the prohibition of "dangerous drugs," the incarceration and involuntary treatment of "addicts," the eradication of "pushers"—and much else besides.

---

*The Therapeutic State refers to the polity uniting medicine and state, much as church and state formerly were united. (Eds.)

Confronted with the phenomena of "drug abuse," and "drug addiction," how else could psychiatry and a society imbued with it have reacted? They could respond only as they did—namely, by defining the moderate use of legal drugs as the result of the sane control of resistible impulses; and by defining the immoderate use of any drug, and any use of illegal drugs, as the insane surrender to irresistible impulses. Hence the circular psychiatric definitions of drug habits, such as the claim that illicit drug use (for example, smoking marijuana) causes mental illness and also constitutes a symptom of it; and the seemingly contradictory claim that the wholly similar use of licit drugs (for example, smoking tobacco) is neither a cause nor a symptom of mental illness.

Formerly, opium was a panacea; now it is the cause and symptom of countless maladies, medical and social, the world over. Formerly masturbation was the cause and symptom of mental illness; now it is the cure for social inhibition and the practice ground for training in heterosexual athleticism. It is clear, then, that if we want to understand and accept drug-taking behavior, we must take a larger view of the so-called drug problem. (Of course, if we want to persecute "pushers" and "treat addicts," then information inconvenient to our doing these things will only get in our way. Drug-abuseologists can no more be "educated" out of their coercive tactics than can drug addicts.)

What does this larger view show us? How can it help us? It shows us that our present attitudes toward the whole subject of drug use, drug abuse, and drug control are nothing but the reflections, in the mirror of "social reality," of our own expectations toward drugs and toward those who use them; and that our ideas about and interventions in drug-taking behavior have only the most tenuous connection with the actual pharmacological properties of "dangerous drugs." The "danger" of masturbation disappeared when we ceased to believe in it: we then ceased to attribute danger to the practice and to its practitioners, and ceased to call it "self-abuse."

Of course, some people still behave in disagreeable and even dangerous ways, but we no longer attribute their behavior to masturbation or self-abuse. We now attribute their behavior to self-medication or drug abuse. We thus play a game of musical chairs with medical alibis for human desire, determination, and depravity. Though this sort of intolerance is easy, it is also expensive: it seems clear that only in accepting human beings for what they are can we accept the chemical substances they use for what they are. In short, only insofar as we are able and willing to accept men, women, and children as neither angels nor devils, but as persons with certain inalienable rights and irrepudiable duties, shall we be able and willing to accept heroin, cocaine, and marijuana as neither panaceas nor panapathogens, but as drugs with certain chemical properties and ceremonial possibilities.

NOTES

1. T. Szasz, *The Second Sin* (Garden City, N.Y.: Doubleday, 1973).

2. L. von Mises, *Human Action: A Treatise on Economics* (New Haven: Yale University Press, 1949).

3. See, for example, S. Auerbach, " 'Behavior Control' Is Scored," *Miami Herald,* December 28, 1972, p. 15-A.

14

The Tyranny of Experts: Blowing the Whistle on the Cult of Expertise

Morris E. Chafetz

For most of my professional life, I have been involved in the study of an emotionally charged subject: people's relations with alcohol beverages. As a public servant and as a private citizen, I have seen what emotional investment in a subject can do to anyone's objectivity. I have seen alcohol researchers literally shout down each other with conflicting interpretations of the same data. I have seen the preliminary results of small, uncontrolled research studies blazoned across the front pages of newspapers as incontrovertible fact. I have seen impressive-looking but essentially meaningless statistical charts and graphs accompanying major articles in prestigious scientific journals.

When it comes to subjugating objectivity to the service of emotion, I've seen a lot of it done. From time to time, I've done it myself; but I didn't recognize the seduction when it was done to me.

If I, a physician, a psychiatrist, once head of a powerful government agency, with longtime ties to the academic and government worlds of science and statistics, can be so misled, what about people who have not had such rigorous training? How do they make sense of the cacophony of voices giving conflicting advice about every subject imaginable? Health. Nutrition. Child rearing. Alcohol. Drugs. Safe food. Pollution. Who has the answers?

I believe this question is the most important one of our day. Many people believe someone does, in fact, have answers that they do not possess. Because they want to believe in that magical "someone," they are defenseless against those who claim to have special knowledge. They are fair game

This article is excerpted and adapted, with the author's permission, from *The Tyranny of Experts: Blowing the Whistle on the Cult of Expertise* (New York: Madison Books, 1996).

for anyone who offers them comforting certainties, unambiguous rules of conduct, and ways to identify themselves within the complex, fast-moving society we live in. Awash in prescriptions and proscriptions but lacking a means of judging the validity of what they hear, they soon find themselves ruled by a tyranny of experts.

The people I call tyrants are people who overstep the limits of their technical expertise and who use their specialized knowledge to dictate how others should live. In our world of instant communication, we know who these experts are. Many are scientists, public interest advocates, researchers, lawyers, physicians, psychologists, social workers, government bureaucrats, and others who, through our mass media, parlay their credentials into power bases. From these power bases, they tell us what to eat, drink, and enjoy, how to relate to one another, and how to live.

The pronouncements of experts fill the moral and ethical vacuum left by the demise of the extended family and the waning of religious and political leadership. In many areas where basic values and personal views of the world once helped people make choices, they now turn to experts for what they believe is definitive information. In a world reeling from the dizzying pace of growth and change, being told what to eat, how much sleep to get, and how to rear children gives people a semblance of certainty that is difficult to come by anywhere else.

Because the experts fill a genuine need for order in the chaotic whirl of high-tech, high-speed living, some of us remain stunningly blind to their pervasive, massive encroachment on the prerogatives of our private lives, as well as to the possibility that something besides pure benevolence motivates their actions. Our innate self-protectiveness is disarmed but not broken. That characteristic American prickliness, for example, comes to the fore when we learn that the video store's computer keeps a record of all the videos we rent. The potential misuse of such information violates our privacy and conjures up images of Big Brother and the "thought police" of George Orwell's novel *1984*. To me, a far more chilling prospect is the surrender of our right to choose in return for promises of happiness and harmony, as in the fictional society described by Aldous Huxley in *Brave New World*. We are learning that the most powerful tyrant of all is one who possesses the consent of the tyrannized.

I believe we are in danger of surrendering our intellectual and emotional liberty to those who would warn, advise, and guide us, people who manipulate us with their specialized knowledge and increasingly determine the political, moral, and social climate of our country. I fear the brave new world their tactics threaten to bring upon us. I want us to regain our right to think for ourselves by withdrawing our consent to their ascendancy.

The irony of our surrender to the experts is that they don't even deliver the peace of mind they promise. Ask yourself a simple question: do you truly feel safer, saner, and more secure because of everything you've been told by the health experts, the environmental experts, the legal experts, the child development experts, the crime experts, the alcohol experts? Or are you becoming more fearful? More anxious about your health? Less secure about your abilities as a spouse, a child, a parent? Less confident about the future?

DEATH, FEAR, AND THE PROMISED LAND

Most of us become aware of death at an early age, when a relative or a pet dies. At first, the concept of death may not be fully understood; but in time, the realization that the person or pet no longer exists in the physical world becomes clear. At that point we begin to make a personal connection between death and ourselves. Once we make this connection, we devote much of our mental energy to strategies for avoiding death. These strategies manifest themselves in a variety of ways. Religion is a favored comforter. It tempers the fear of oblivion by promising the hope of an afterlife.

Unquestioning faith in doctors and the power of medicine has also been a favored balm for the fear of death. With the medical profession's seemingly intimate connection to the mysteries of life and death, doctors have long enjoyed a godlike aura.

From the earliest shaman to today's neurologist, doctors and their forebears have distracted us from the fear of death with prognostication and medication. Their job is often made easier when pain and illness produce regressive (childlike) behavior. When we regress we are more vulnerable to the magic of formulas and symbols. What makes us easy prey to regressive behavior is what Ernest Becker contends in his book *Denial of Death* (1973): that our greatest fear is the certainty of our own death.

When we are sick, most of us don't care to inquire how our physician reaches the conclusion that we have X disease and not Y disease. We simply want comfort and certainty. We want the doctor to tell us we will not die. We want to believe that the miracle of technology and the wisdom of the doctor are great enough to forecast the future and to control all the variables that can affect our health and well-being. But that can't be. No one is that omnipotent. Tragic examples abound of the unabashed trust people put in doctors' omnipotence.

The formulas we associate with good health do not always contain the essential ingredients. Just as we cannot foresee the future, doctors cannot measure or control hidden variables when they make their pronouncements. But recent technological advances have so intensified our fantasies about medical omnipotence that neither doctor nor patient has a clear idea of the limits of medical science.

A life without limits is a life dominated by obsession. The obsession with cheating death has turned our pursuit of health into a sickness. The impact of simple lifestyle changes on our overall health has increased, not diminished, our anxieties. Ironically, we have become more susceptible than ever to our fears.

WHAT DOES MEDICINE REALLY KNOW ABOUT RISK?

Risk is a concept central to the power of the medical experts. They want to reduce our "risk" of illness. But we have to ask, on what basis do they establish the risk associated with any behavior? Consider the concern over cancer risk.

Biochemist Bruce Ames, who developed the widely used Ames Test to determine whether particular environmental chemicals increase the risk of cancer, has repudiated the conclusions of much of his earlier research. Ames now believes that one of the standard ways of testing carcinogenicity—giving rats megadoses of the substance in question (called the maximum tolerated dose or MTD)—ignores the fact that the body's reaction to a substance depends on the dosage taken in.

The body is efficient at neutralizing small doses of carcinogens and other toxins, but it becomes overwhelmed when large quantities are introduced all at once. Megadoses may approximate the amount taken into the body over the course of a year or so, but ingesting a year's dose in an hour invalidates the test and overstates the risk of cancer.

Ames believes that MTD tests could label as lethal over half of all chemicals, whether natural or manufactured. The newly founded panel on risk at the National Academy of Sciences agrees in principle with his assessment. As an example of the excesses that can result when MTD testing is the primary method of determining risk, consider the case of dioxin, the chemical in Agent Orange.

Dioxin was once pronounced "the most dangerous substance on the face of the earth." Yet dioxin now appears to be less dangerous than was previously thought. Reinterpretation of the original animal studies shows that the danger was overestimated. And the only study to definitively link dioxin to excess cancer deaths found a slightly increased risk among 1,500 workers who had been exposed to five hundred times the federally designated acceptable level—the highest exposure level in history. No increased risk of cancer was found in the same study among 3,500 workers who received an average of ninety times the acceptable level of exposure.

Sometimes risk is merely an artifact of our methods of assessment. Consider the case of human papillomavirus, suspected as a cause of cervical cancer because the virus has been found in some women (11.5 percent) who develop the disease. Recently, a new, more sensitive screening procedure has found the human papillomavirus in 46 percent of women in routine gynecological testing.

Researchers may now have to rethink their ideas about risk involving the virus and cervical cancer, since far more women who do not get cancer carry the virus than women who do get cancer. It appears the risk of getting cervical cancer from human papillomavirus went down when better testing was developed. That's the tyranny!

MANUFACTURE OF VICTIMS

When tragedy strikes, being able to identify an "innocent victim" as someone who is subject to the whims of fate—dependent, unsuspecting, blameless—is a convenient label. A victim, therefore, presents no ambiguities and no confusing questions of responsibility to weigh and feel troubled about. The victim is innocent; therefore, someone or something else must be responsible.

When something bad happens to an innocent victim, especially one from those groups society views as vulnerable—children, women, and the elderly—our social guardians will feel justified in venting their most primitive emotions. I recall the pure anger of a store owner in New Hampshire, for example, when a four-year-old girl he didn't know was killed by a drunk driver. "Four years old," he kept saying, like a litany. He became angry with me when I asked whether it would have been different if the person killed had been an adult.

Victims also provide society with a simple way to think about complex social problems. When dealing with the problems of drugs, crime, poverty, traffic fatalities, and other social problems, our surrogate parents, the experts, seem to provide easy and fast solutions. Our social guardians focus their expertise on devising protective social policies for innocent victims, but neglect to deal with the underlying problems. They succeed in giving comfort in two ways.

First, their agenda allows other people to distance themselves from the plight of the victims. Second, by making the victim an emotional symbol, they can further their larger agenda: power and conformity. They define the situation as something that can be solved by simply finding and punishing the person or thing they view as responsible.

The manufacture of the label victim encourages a simplistic view of the world. It turns the world into good guys and bad guys, victims and victimizers, the innocent and the culpable. Life, however, is rarely that neat and simple. In seeing only black and white and ignoring the gray under the guise of protecting the innocent, great harm can be done.

THE ISSUE OF SMOKING

I think the smoking-health issue illustrates how the experts operate. First, the anti-smoking advocates attack the advertising of tobacco products. They firmly state (without credible evidence) that advertisements make people take up smoking. In the mind of the anti-smoking advocates, people are like dogs who respond mindlessly to suggestion. It does not take much thinking to see how such a conclusion—that people are being manipulated into unhealthy behavior—would rile the public. In the case of children, many people feel guilty enough to start with. The public health advocates with the help of some children who are artful at manipulation, make it sound like the hungry-for-the-dollar (standard practice in free enterprise) business people hook children and others on smoking.

Since children and adults are individuals possessing some freedom of choice, the phenomenon of addiction is brought in. There has never been a question in my mind that a person can become addicted to anything, but I have yet to meet an addicting substance. An addicting substance means that anyone who uses it cannot go without it. I know of no such substance.

Let me tell about my own smoking history. I was a pipe smoker while in college and medical school because it was fashionable to smoke a pipe. And as a psychiatrist, smoking a pipe helped me to control my tendency to talk too much. I used my pipe to keep my mouth shut, so I could listen to my patients.

When I became a mover and shaker in government, pipe smoking was impossible. I had to move quickly and often. Meetings, gatherings, and all the hullabaloo that comes with power did not permit the leisure a pipe requires. So I turned to cigarettes and smoked three packs a day.

As I approached the end of my tenure at NIAAA [National Institute on Alcohol Abuse and Alcoholism], one of my sons bet me twenty dollars that I could not go one year without smoking. From the day I left office, I did not smoke for one year, collected the twenty bucks he owed me, and went back to cigarette smoking, but not to three packs a day.

People who were smokers and could not quit told me I must not have been addicted. In other words, if the facts don't fit a preconceived model, you don't throw out the model; you disregard the facts that threaten the model.

It appears to me, therefore, that the anti-smoking advocates think that at first children are hooked by advertising and then when they grow up and become sensible adults, they can't give up the habit because they are physiologically addicted. One question that the anti-smoking advocates have never sought to answer is: does the emphasis on cigarettes being addictive prevent people who would want to from stopping?

I have seen this kind of propaganda in alcoholism treatment as well. People who are recovering from alcohol problems are told their only hope for recovery is total abstinence; if they slip, they'll fail. When they do fail it's because they have been indoctrinated to expect to fail. This corroborates my contention that expectation is as strong a drug as most substances.

Whenever people worry about the effects advertising has on children, I am reminded of the letter a young person wrote to the *New York Times*, "We make our choices even though we know the risks." It's good to remember what Winston Churchill said: "When I get the facts, I twist them to fit my position." Churchill was telling us what the experts do, but he was disarmingly honest about it. Having said that, let us look at what's happening in the tobacco industry.

Public health advocates claim the industry tricks young people to smoke through targeted marketing, advertising, and promotion, and once manipulated (especially when they are not of an age to know better) into smoking, they are physiologically hooked. But methods of manipulation can be artfully unfair, insidious, and omnivorous. Consider the phenomenon called environmental tobacco smoke (ETS).

Studies are legion that link the health risks of second-hand smoke to cancer, sudden infant death syndrome (SIDS), heart disease, and every other ailment imaginable. These studies are flawed because they cannot be controlled, yet they epitomize how science is used to manipulate the public and policy makers. There is no scientific methodology available I know of that will give us the data to determine if a smoker does harm to a nonsmoker. Of course, scientists can come up with statistical models that will provide numbers that will imply certainty where certainty cannot exist.

The *Washington Times* (November 27, 1995) reported on a new service that accuses government and anti-smoking groups of making unsubstantiated claims about the health hazards of second-hand smoke. The Congressional Research Service claims there is no scientific evidence to support the EPA estimate that environmental tobacco smoke (ETS) causes over three thousand lung-cancer deaths among nonsmokers and 150,000 to 300,000 cases of respiratory infection in infants and young children.

Like the anti-alcohol advocates whose exaggerated findings on FAS (Fetal Alcohol Syndrome) led the government to advise pregnant women not to drink alcohol, nonsmoking advocates continue to use unsubstantiated studies to induce the public and policy makers to treat smokers as pariahs.

Crucial to the accuracy of scientific study is controlling for variables. For example, if a person smokes X number of cigarettes around a nonsmoker, the variables to control for would be the setting, the ventilation system, air streams, depth of inhalation and exhalation of both parties, emotional strengths and weaknesses (which affect the immunological system), and hundreds of other variables. Even so the advocates use the flawed studies on ETS to promote their cause, gain power, and feel good about themselves. No better illustration exists than cigarettes to show the tyranny of the experts.

MYTHOLOGY OF SCIENCE

Many of us have a rudimentary familiarity with the scientific method. As children we learn that science is a way of discovering new information about the world through direct observation. We are taught that science performs these observations objectively. Even though a scientific experiment begins with a speculation or hypothesis about the outcome, the goal of scientific experimentation is not the outcome, but the truth.

To a child, the idea of testing reality without having a particular goal in mind sounds highly plausible. Children themselves are natural scientists. When a baby plays with matches, for example, his goal is not to light a fire but to find out what these funny-smelling sticks can do. When children open a cabinet and pull out everything inside, they are experiencing the pure joy of discovery.

Most people's view of science is colored by their visceral memory of this pleasurable and uncomplicated state of learning. Even people who study science as adults often maintain a childlike belief in the objectivity of science and in its ability to sort out the confused messages of the world to find truth.

The basic tenet of science is objectivity. In tests of new drugs, for example, biomedical researchers use "double-blind" studies so that neither the study participants nor the investigators knows who is getting the real treatment and who is getting the placebo. Double-blinding is meant to insulate studies from the expectations of those involved and from self-fulfilling prophecies: for example, the possibility that study participants may consciously or unconsciously try to please the researchers by espousing the desired response; and the expectations of the investigators themselves, who may consciously or unconsciously try to influence the study's outcome to prove their hypothesis.

Double-blinding is one of the procedures that makes science appear "scientific" to everyone, including scientists themselves. But procedures like double-blinding are ultimately part of the mythology of science—the powerful belief system that puts science purportedly above the motivations of the human heart.

Even if scientists were not motivated like the rest of us by personal needs and goals, science by its very nature could not be "objective" or "goalless." Confirming a theory by observation requires the experimenter to devise procedures that will favor the theory's plausibility. Research on anything will yield findings that are a reflection of, and limited by, its procedures for observing or measuring.

This principle is simple to understand. If I am color blind and want to paint a picture of an autumn landscape, for example, my painting will lack the distinctive red hues that characterize certain maple trees. If I am quickly sorting change in my pocket by size and color, I may not notice that I have several Canadian pennies or dimes among my American pennies and dimes. Both of these deviations from "objective reality" are not malicious: in one case, I am prevented from seeing what I miss, and in the other, I simply am not interested in the distinctions. These are what I call "inherent biases": they are not malicious but merely part of the limits of observation.

Understanding the typical blind spots and inattentiveness of the scientific experts is critical. Science will always have a role to play in interpreting the world, but not the role of a soothsayer.

TRENDS OR TRUTH?

The desire to see proof in trends is an ancient human trait. Human beings have always felt there were secret meanings in coincidences. If the rain came when a chant was sung at sunset, for example, our ancestors believed chanting brought the rain.

Children are notorious for misjudging cause and effect. I know a family whose youngest child insisted on visiting the restroom in every restaurant they went to. It became a family joke that the child had been in every bathroom in town. Tired of being teased, the little girl explained that she went to the restroom not because she needed to, but because when she returned to the table her food was always there. She believed that her absence from the table caused the food to arrive.

Unlike the little girl's approach, the experts believe that quantitative research in the sciences is a more sophisticated way of looking for meaningful coincidences. Powerful computers add to the mystique of statistical correlations by evaluating every quantifiable variable in an experiment or research project and calculating the results to as many decimal places as desired. Often those results are accompanied by more numbers announcing the "statistical significance" and "confidence factor" for each conclusion reached.

Nevertheless, these impressive numbers still represent only correlations: coincident facts that may or may not be related. Because a basic characteristic of our minds is the tendency to recognize and recall facts about things we already know, the statistical correlations that interest us tell more about ourselves and our preoccupations than they do about the subjects we study.

For example, when several studies found that young drug experimenters in the 1960s and 1970s tended to use alcohol before they used drugs, researchers concluded that experimentation with alcohol leads to experimentation with drugs. The conclusion seems obvious because we are predisposed to believe it. We could just as well conclude that daily use of alcohol leads to financial well-being, since a study of Harvard's class of 1940 showed that those who drank every day had higher incomes than occasional drinkers or nondrinkers. Based solely on the data, we have no idea whether daily drinking has anything to do with income status. Similarly, we have no idea whether the prior use of alcohol had anything to do with the subsequent use of drugs.

Our minds are biologically programmed to recognize and complete patterns. For this reason, we are more likely to pay attention to numbers that correspond to an existing belief system. For example, the National Academy of Sciences (NAS) used a study showing higher rates of lung cancer deaths among nonsmokers who lived with smokers to come up with an estimate of 3,800 lung-cancer deaths annually caused by passive smoking. Since it has already been established that active smoking causes some lung cancer, the conclusion about passive smoking seemed easy to accept.

But I later learned that the study did not take into account participants, exposure to radon, a naturally produced gas and the deadliest known environmental carcinogen. Radon is believed to cause 20,000 lung-cancer deaths annually. So despite the plausibility of NAS's conclusions, they can't be relied on: radon may have caused some or all of those 3,800 deaths. Many other variables—obvious and measurable, not so obvious and unmeasurable—can cause or prevent lung cancer.

For many years, the tobacco industry argued that there was no proof that cigarette smoking caused lung cancer—just statistical correlations. The industry's argument was deemed self-serving and false: there was strong test-tube evidence that the chemicals in cigarette smoke could initiate cancerous changes in lung tissue. Yet their insistence that the demographic and statistical data did not prove anything was absolutely correct.

The statistical analysis was highly suggestive and pointed researchers in the right direction, but it did not prove—and still does not prove—that cigarette smoking by itself causes lung cancer. As a matter of fact, the *Harvard Health Letter* of August 1995 reports that 85 percent of smokers *never* (emphasis added) develop lung cancer.

LIFE WITHOUT SELF-DELUSION

We want what people have always wanted, protection from our own fallibility, our own weakness, our own mortality. This desire helps to perpetuate our species. Recently I was awed by the raw honesty of my young granddaughter Maria, who glibly summed up the human condition when she stated her life's aspirations: "I want to be a queen; I don't want to die; I want people to do what I tell them to."

Fortunately or unfortunately, I can't grant Maria her wishes, nor can the experts. Whatever advice, warnings, or formulas we follow, no one can make us exceptional, immortal, or omnipotent. By accepting the tenet that the experts cannot give us what we want, I hope we'll be able to give one another the courage to live without self-delusion.

Perhaps the greatest delusion of all is the notion that, individually and collectively, the human race is teetering on the brink of disaster. My common sense tells me that despite the barrage of news each day about the risks of daily life, and despite our many serious social, political, ecological, and economic problems, the earth and the human race are not on the verge of extinction. For every story that says we are running out of time by irreparably damaging our planet, there's another story that tells of an extraordinary scientific discovery, a new drug to treat a formerly intractable condition, a remarkable new movement in painting or sculpture, a groundbreaking new book or symphony or invention.

Whatever goes wrong in the world, we will still retain our most important asset: the infinite creativity and ingenuity of the human mind. I believe these ancient gifts that made man rise above all other animals will steer us through the maze of confusion fostered by the twentieth century's bewildering succession of changes. Our challenge will be to find new ways to tap our wellspring of common sense and instinct for self-preservation. Meeting the challenge requires a commitment to look to ourselves for our own answers, because the spoon-feeding experts lead to our diminishment.

Don't ask me how to proceed once you've made that commitment, because I haven't a clue. What I do know, however, is that it is the journey not the destination that's important. Our search will begin in earnest when we are willing to embark on the journey.

15

The Social Symbolism of Smoking and Health

Joseph R. Gusfield

The mirror images of tobacco as harmful and immoral and smoking as harmless and innocently pleasurable have spiralled through Western history since tobacco was first brought to Europe (Gottsegen, 1940; Best, 1979; Troyer and Markle, 1983). Though our economic, political, and legal institutions have often been dominated by one or another assessment, both positive and negative images of tobacco have been a part of American life. The two concerns of health and morality have appeared in the perception of tobacco and its uses. The pleasures of smoking have been countered at times by claims of its bad effects on health, at times by its perception as an evil habit associated with vicious living. Dual images and dual criteria have been embodied in institutional practices and the recurring interests of various segments of the American population. Neither the rejecting nor the appreciative view of smoking has entirely disappeared from American life.

Health and morality are by no means always, or even often, separate and unconnected domains. In the history of American medicine matters of health and matters of morality have often been interconnected. To be ill has sometimes seemed to be a result of evil living and sometimes its cause (Rosenberg, 1962; Starr, 1982; Tesh, 1988, chs. 1, 2). In recent years, many aspects of illness have been construed as resulting from lifestyle choices—as the direct consequences of chosen behavior (Zola, 1972; Crawford, 1977; Crawford, 1979). How we eat, drive automobiles, accept stress, drink alcohol, exercise, conduct sexual relations, lead sedentary lives, use drugs, and smoke tobacco are widely understood today as important to the health of the individual.

A healthy lifestyle and a moral one might seem unrelated to each other. It is logically possible to see each as separate: as different and distinct frames within which to interpret, assess, and adjudge human actions. However, what is logical is not necessarily sociological. Prescriptions for healthful living, of which nonsmoking is now a part, are also prescriptions for being a particular kind of person leading a particular kind of life (Tesh, 1988; Glassner, 1989).

The frames of morality and health are not as divergent as they appear at first sight. The story of the anti-smoking movement in the past three decades is a story of its leadership by the elite of medical science supported by the official imprimatur of the national government as health agency. The credibility of the scientific research elite is the salient point in any comparison of the current anti-smoking movement with that of the early twentieth century in the United States. The anti-smoking campaigns of the early twentieth century were set in the frame of moral concerns. The present campaigns have been framed in the context of health, an appeal to rational thought devoid of moral judgments. Yet that has not eliminated the moral quality of the issue nor eradicated the significance of emerging social distinctions. The cigarette has been defined in a way different from the earlier twentieth-century move-ment—yet not as different as it first appears. In the context of the health con-sciousness of the past three decades, smoking has taken on a symbolic meaning in which moral and social issues are significant. What began as an appeal to considerations of the smoker's health has accrued meanings that make the smoker an object of moral as well as health concerns. With the rising interest in the environmental smoke produced by smokers, the moral condemnation of smoking has been accentuated.

THE MORAL CONDEMNATION OF SMOKING

The Movement against the "Tyrant in White"

The early campaign against smoking originated in the last twenty years of the nineteenth century. By 1890, twenty-six states had passed legislation pro-hibiting the sale of cigarettes to minors. By the end of 1909, seventeen states had prohibited the sale of cigarettes altogether. By 1917, the movement was clearly in retreat, yet twelve states still maintained prohibitory laws (Gottsegen, 1940, 184; Troyer and Markle, 1983, 34–35).

This early movement was chiefly directed against the cigarette itself, rather than against smoking in general. This first anti-smoking crusade was triggered by a great increase in the consumption of cigarettes, an object that one writer in 1909 referred to as "the tyrant in white" ("A Counterblast Against Tobacco," 1909). Hand-rolled cigarettes had been in use for several centuries, especially in Europe. However, it was not until the 1880s that a mass market was possible in the United States (Sobel, 1978, chs. 1, 2; Schudson, 1984, ch. 5). Three developments made mass consumption feasible. One was the invention of the Bonsack cigarette-rolling machine in 1884 (Wagner, 1971; Sobel, 1978, ch. 2).[1] The second was the invention of the portable and safe matchbook, in use by the 1890s (Sobel, 1978, 66–71; Whelan, 1984, 39–40). The third development was less technological than organizational. James Buchanan Duke organized the cigarette industry when, in the 1880s, he combined several firms to form the American Tobacco Company (Sobel, 1978, ch. 2).

The production and consumption of cigarettes rose dramatically from the mid-1880s, when the estimated per capita consumption of cigarettes was approximately 8.1. By 1900 it was approximately 34.7. By 1920 it had increased to approximately 470.5 (Gottsegen, cited in Troyer and Markle, 1983, 34). Until then, cigars, pipes, and chewing tobacco had been the dominant forms of tobacco consumption in the United States, and adult men had been almost the entire market for tobacco products.

The cigarette introduced a new commodity and made possible a new set of meanings to smoking. It was distinctly smaller, easier to light, and milder than its competitors. As such, it became more accessible to two groups for whom smoking had been under a restrictive taboo: women and young people, especially boys. In this period concerns for the harmful effects of cigarettes on health played a minor role. The moral and social consequences of smoking cigarettes loomed large in the themes that appeared in editorials, in news and magazine stories quoting partisans of the anti-smoking organizations, and in professional medical and scientific journals.[2] Cigarettes were becoming a symbol of moral looseness coupled with a minimized respect for the authority of the male adult—the cigar and pipe smoker.

The following themes appeared in the newspapers and magazines of the period. However, it would be misleading to impute a high level of consensus to this public discussion. Not only were different themes sounded by different people, but there was much disagreement, both within the ranks of nonsmokers and between smokers and nonsmokers.

The Threat to Male Dominance

During the nineteenth century in America, smoking was a major symbol and sign of the adult male in American life. The segregation of the genders and all that it implied was dramatically portrayed in the exclusivity of smoking as a masculine form of pleasure. New technology, however, made it much easier for women to pursue the pleasures of smoking. Cigarettes could be easily hidden in purses, and the newly invented safety match added to convenience and safety. The fact that women were beginning to smoke reinforced the notion that cigarettes posed a social threat. Complaints of women's smoking appeared in the newspapers, opposing so-called continental habits and supporting "good manners" ("A Good Beginning," 1908). A New York assemblyman, introducing his annual bill to prohibit the sale of cigarettes, expressed a sentiment appearing often in the public discourse of the period:

> Do you know that any number of our High School girls, as well as boys, smoke cigarettes, and do you know that many foolish women are beginning to believe that it is real smart to learn to smoke cigarettes? . . . Women in society have taken to smoking cigarettes and persons who are on the ragged edge of society think they have as much right. All roads to ruin are open when [boys and girls] begin to smoke. ("Says Schoolgirls Smoke," 1905).

Although it was not until several years after World War I that public smoking became acceptable for women (Schudson, 1984, ch. 5), cigarettes had already begun to be a symbol of equality between men and women. Whatever the intent of the smoker, the use of cigarettes assumed a political meaning.

As the cigar and pipe were symbolic of male power, the cigarette suffered among male consumers in the 1900s from identification with effeminacy. That impediment to a more rapid development of the cigarette market among men was not to be overcome until after World War I.

The Moral Threat to Youth

With the beginnings of mass marketing of the cigarette, smoking was available to the adolescent. Characteristically, cigarettes were sold in packs of ten and it was sometimes possible to buy one at a time. In marketing them, especially for young men, Duke's advertisers often provided free cards with pictures of alluring young women (Sobel, 1978, ch. 2).

Opponents associated cigarettes with depravity. The cigarette was described as an accompaniment to crime, lust, insobriety, and a general looseness of social obligations. Sometimes this was attributed to the peers with whom the young smoker associated. Sometimes it was seen in the image of the "cigarette fiend" directly affected by the inhalation of smoke. This notion is analogous to more recent discussion of the effects of illegal drugs on the behavior of the addict (Inciardi, 1986, chs. 3, 4). Occasionally the cigarette was portrayed in association with prostitutes, and the woman user seen as a victim of loose morality brought about by the evil weed. Studies were cited establishing an association between cigarette smoking and crime ("Some Cigaret Figures," 1914; Boyers, 1916; Hubbell, 1904). This theme is consistent with the constant fear of the "dangerous classes" and youth, which was common in the nineteenth century and has continued to today (Gusfield, 1991; Kett, 1977; Monkkonen, 1975).

Illustrative of this view was the following from Charles Buckley Hubbell, President of the Board of Education of New York City:

> Boys of ten, twelve and fourteen years of age, naturally bright, were observed to be losing the power of concentration and application of mind. . . . Further investigation disclosed the fact that very many of these boys stole money from their parents, or sold all sorts of articles that they could lay their hands on, in order that they could gratify an appetite that fed on its own indulgence. (Hubbell, 1904, 377)

Loss of Efficiency

The cigarette, some believed, caused a loss of productivity in the work force and led to a decline in mental abilities. Studies indicated most students who smoked did poorly in their school grades (Carter, 1906, 488ff.). Nonsmoking was seen as a prerequisite to an efficient school performance. The smoker was less likely to succeed; the nonsmoker had a headstart in the game of life. (This belief seems to have reappeared [Robb, 1991].)

The themes of immorality, crime, and inefficiency sometimes appear together in the public discussions of cigarettes. Not everyone believed the assertions claiming that cigarettes were responsible for these problems; nevertheless, such associations were sufficiently prominent in the public discussion as "fact" that the cigarette's social meanings were apparent. It represented a challenge to authority, ranging from a mild aura of naughtiness and "continental" sophistication to outright rebelliousness.

Polluting Effects of Smoking

The traditional segregation of the genders when only men smoked had been defended as a concern for the sensibilities of women, for whom smoke was assumed to be distasteful. The same argument, in reverse, was used by the Nonsmoker's Protective League to support laws that banned smoking in public buildings and transportation facilities. Such laws were passed in a number of localities, although their enforcement is less certain. Smoke was, for some, an impure substance and contact with it polluting. The cigarette smoker was portrayed as a physical threat to the nonsmoker.

Medical Harm

Physiologists and professors of medicine had begun to study the effects of smoking at the beginning of the twentieth century. They investigated the effects of smoking on blood pressure and on certain ailments of the eye (tobacco ambylopia) (Dunn, 1906; Bruce et al., 1909; "The Pharmacology of Tobacco Smoke," 1909). Such studies were generally experimental and clinical, and the results were mixed. No large-scale epidemiological study appeared during this period.

Several medical professors were scornful of intuitive judgments about health and morality found in the anti-smoking movements. Most, however, agreed that the prime focus was and should be on the cigarette, if only because the smoker inhaled much more often than with other means of consuming smoke.

But at no time in the early movement were health concerns at the center of the public discussion of cigarette smoking. There was no consensus, among either medical researchers or the lay public, that the physiochemical consequences of cigarette smoking were very harmful to the health of the smoker or the nonsmoker.

By the time the United States entered into World War I, all of the major themes of today's anti-smoking movement were in place in some or most of the population. The popularity of the cigarette in post-World War I America owes little to a changed perception of its healthful or unhealthful properties that new research might have produced. The use of cigarettes increased considerably among women, and American men shifted their habit from cigars, pipes, and chewing tobacco to cigarettes. The total amount of tobacco in use in the United States remained stable between 1918 and 1940, while the sale of cigarettes increased greatly (Schudson, 1984, 182).

The Social Acceptance of the Cigarette

The anti-smoking movement collapsed in the wake of World War I. Many elements are associated with the rise of the cigarette habit and its acceptance by both genders of the American buying public. An adequate social history has not yet appeared, although several elements of the story can be suggested. The carrying convenience of cigarettes, in contrast to pipes and cigars, supported their wide distribution to American soldiers. The association of the soldier with cigarette smoking did much to change the view among men that cigarettes were effeminate and also gave the cigarette an aura of patriotism (Troyer and Markle, 1983, 40-47). The taboo against women smokers, which was weakened by the development of the cigarette, was further weakened as the cigarette came to be identified as a symbol of demand for equality of the sexes (Schudson, 1984, ch. 5). By the early 1920s, all state legislation barring the sale of cigarettes to adults had been repealed.

The mildness of cigarettes, as compared with other forms of tobacco, aided its acceptance among women, as among men. During the 1920s, especially among urban, somewhat cosmopolitan and sophisticated women, smoking became the symbol of the modern. As Schudson expresses it, the cigarette was "connected to the young, the cosmopolitan and the naughty" (Schudson, 1984, 196). It was during the 1920s that smoking in public, although not yet on the streets, became acceptable conduct for women, especially in American cities.

PUBLIC HEALTH: THE CURRENT MOVEMENT AGAINST SMOKING

In understanding the shift in smoking behavior in American life, it becomes clear that health concerns played a small role, if any, before the 1950s.

And until 1964, while some intuitive feeling that smoking was harmful existed among a number of Americans, there was no widely accepted authority that settled the factual question of the healthfulness of smoking. Unlike the moral orientations of the earlier campaigns, the present movement has been directed as an aspect of public health. The earlier movement was largely led by voluntary associations. The present movement has been sparked and directed primarily by public health agencies of government, especially the federal government. It has found its authority in the research of medical science.

For much of its history in Western societies there has been some sense that smoking might be harmful, some hope that it is not, and very little fact to support either claim. How great is the real risk of disease from smoking? The average citizen must look to others—epidemiologists, medical clinicians—to make such determinations. But what others? Who "owns" the cigarette question?

By the late 1940s in the United States, cigarette smoking had become common in all classes and genders. Its possible negative effects on health were not a public issue and cigarette smoking in general was not perceived as a public problem. By the mid-1960s this was no longer the case. A public consensus had developed that smoking cigarettes is harmful to health; that it significantly heightens the risks of developing lung cancer, heart trouble, and other diseases. That consensus is largely the work of scientific research, governmental and news reporting, and the emergence and activism of voluntary medical organizations. It represents the hegemony of medical science over the culture of health.

Divisions often exist not only about the wisdom of public policies but also about the very facts that constitute the conditions that are named as "problems." As it operates in social actions, "reality" is not something given in the nature of things, plain for all to see, and agree upon. Events and conditions have to be attended to and interpreted. The current American birth rate and the gross national product are aggregated facts that cannot be directly perceived by individuals. We depend on institutions and persons that accumulate data and transmit them to an interested audience. It is in this sense that I consider the belief in the harmful effects of cigarettes as an example of "the social construction of reality" (Berger and Luckmann, 1967; Spector and Kitsuse, 1977).

In the early anti-smoking movement the body of research on the negative effects of smoking was too scattered, too conflicting, and too unavailable to the public to serve as an authoritative guide to behavior—a guide that was difficult for the individual to ignore or to impeach. While surveys at the time indicated a public acceptance and appreciation of "science" as an institution and scientists as disinterested investigators, scientific research had little of the institutional structure that has since emerged over the past fifty years (LaFollette, 1990). Nor was the role of government in medical research as central as it became after World War II (Brandt, 1990). But by the time the surgeon general issued the report of 1964, social conditions had become favorable to the transmission and credibility of medical science and the position of the federal government as a source of authoritative advice and activity in the promotion of health.

The Emergence of a Scientific Elite

World War II was an enormous stimulus to the development of science in the United States. The construction of the Lawrence Livermore Laboratory at the University of California and the successful Manhattan Project to create the atomic bomb demonstrated what might be accomplished by governmental subsidization of scientists in large-scale projects (Davis, 1968; Nelkin, 1987). Although there had been earlier instances of such subsidization, as a general policy of the federal government it is largely a recent creation.

By 1964, a structure of science had emerged that made possible the development of a range of medical studies and their dissemination to an attentive public. Large-scale epidemiological research was itself a relatively new development in medical science, addressing the smoking problem in a novel language. The institutions responsible for developing and disseminating knowledge about tobacco use were those charged with the functions of maintaining and improving the health of the nation. Among these, the public health service and the surgeon general's office of the federal government were preeminent.

Research findings were now more easily transmitted to the general public. By 1964, science reporting had become a part of journalism and the science reporter was a specialist on many newspapers and newsmagazines. William Laurence of the *New York Times* and Milton Silverman of the *San Francisco Chronicle,* pioneers in the field, had begun their careers as science reporters in the late 1930s. This meant that some reporters now read certain scientific journals regularly and were attentive to work they saw as significant for their readers.[4] In the medical field this meant that the reports published in the *Journal of the American Medical Association,* the *New England Journal of Medicine, Lancet,* and several other journals for published studies were now accessible to the public. The *Reader's Digest* played a significant role as well in reporting the medical research on smoking, especially in the 1950s. The public was better educated than in the past and was now exposed to television as well as print media (Nelkin, 1987; Pfohl, 1984).

Since the early anti-smoking movement, a nonprofessional medical establishment has developed in the form of organizations that support research and seek to persuade the public of healthful forms of living. Among these are the American Cancer Society (ACS), the American Heart Association, and the American Lung Association. The ACS has been the major source of funds for some of the most widely cited epidemiological studies of smoking both before and after 1964.

Lastly, the federal government became a major player in the game of health promotion. The Department of Health, Education, and Welfare was not established in the United States until the 1950s. Before then, medicine had not been considered a major concern of the federal government, even though government sanitary engineers had played a paramount role in public health activities that greatly improved the country's resistance to major infectious diseases. That the surgeon general's report was received with a high degree of credibility suggests the trust that government and science had gained by 1964.

Of course medical science in the past had often played a large role in affecting personal behavior and public action. The discovery of germ-produced disease, the spread of immunizing vaccinations, and the work of sanitary engineers are all highly significant developments in the relations between medical science, government, and the individual. What is new, however, is the great increase in health consciousness in a public fed a daily diet of newspaper, magazine, and television stories of the latest scientific research, the newest discovery, the most recent advice on how to prevent illness and improve health. Such material is a major part of the more general concern for healthy living characterized as the "health fitness movement."

Medical Science and the Health Effects of Smoking

The modern study of the health effects of smoking might be dated from 1900, from 1925, or from 1938 (Wagner, 1971, 69ff). Such studies, however, made little impression on the public. Yet a sense of harm connected with tobacco smoking in all forms was present in the nineteenth century and earlier

(Wagner, 1971; Best, 1979). That intuition was strengthened by the first anti-smoking movement and continued as an element of American culture after the movement ceased to be an active force in public policy. During the 1930s and 1940s there was a growing consciousness that smoking was unhealthy. Several studies found a strong statistical association between heavy cigarette smoking and the incidence of lung cancer, which was on the rise in the United States (Brandt, 1990). These studies rang alarms, but too softly to be heard. It was finally in the 1950s that a number of prospective epidemiological studies on the risks of smoking were undertaken, especially in the United States, Canada, and England. By the late 1950s these studies had developed in importance so that major news magazines reported their findings in featured studies, sometimes with critiques as well ("Cigarettes," 1958; Cort, 1959; "Do They—or Don't They?" 1959; "Smoking and Cancer," 1955, 1958, 1959; "Latest on Smoking and Cancer," 1955; "What Is Known and Unknown," 1957; "What Britons Are Told," 1957). The demand for a governmental review of this material was growing. In December 1959, Surgeon General Burney issued a statement condemning smoking as unhealthy ("Dr. Burney's Alarm," 1959).

The studies of the 1950s formed the major bases for the conclusions of the surgeon general's report of 1964. Issued in January of that year and accompanied by a televised press conference, the report marked the definitive beginning of a medical and public consensus that tobacco is harmful to health.

The Emergence of Consensus

The alacrity with which the surgeon general's report of 1964, and subsequent reports, were accepted as reality is indicative of the legitimacy of the scientific and the governmental medical agencies in American life. Once issued, the report's conclusions were treated by the mass media as certain and authoritative.

In 1959, *Newsweek,* in its medicine section, described the question of the harmful effects of cigarette smoking as still awaiting "a final, undebatable medical answer" ("Do They—Or Don't They?" 1959, 30). In 1962, the magazine began a story of the announcement that the surgeon general would review the question with the phrase, "No one can say with certainty that cigarettes cause cancer" ("Smoking and Health," 1962a, 74). In a later issue, *Newsweek* described the steps in developing that report as "an attempt to settle one of medicine's most controversial questions" ("Smoking and Health," 1962b). When the report did appear, in January 1964, *Newsweek* gave it two and one-half pages and implicitly criticized the long wait before the government agreed with other countries and American health agencies. However, *Newsweek* now described the belief in the health hazard of smoking as having "the full weight" of U.S. authority. It referred to the report itself as "the official judgment" ("Cigarette Smoking Is a Health Hazard," 1964, 48).

The surgeon general's conclusions were reported elsewhere by the press in similarly definitive terms. The *New York Times* began an editorial with the statement, "Now it is official" ("The Smoking Report," 1964). In the same edition, on the front page, the *Times* stated that the report "found no doubt about the role of cigarette smoking in causing cancer of the lungs" (Sullivan, 1964). *Time* magazine stressed the way in which "the impartial committee of top experts" unanimously supported what was already known about the harmful effects of smoking" ("The Government Report," 1964).

That the report was quickly accepted by public segments is seen by the decline in cigarette sales and numbers of Americans who said, in surveys, that they had stopped smoking. Nineteen sixty-four was a watershed year. Per capita consumption of tobacco in the United States decreased continuously from a high of 4,345 cigarettes in 1963 to 3,971 in 1969 (U.S. Department of Agriculture, 1990, 100, 106). Surveys of the American population also show a continuous decline in percentage of smokers since 1965 (U.S. DHHS, Office of Smoking and Health, 1986, 19–20; U.S. DHHS, Surgeon General, 1988, 565–66).

Medical Knowledge and the American Public

To refer to the hegemony of science is to call attention to the way in which the institution of science, medical science in this instance, creates a believable reality, based on scientific research. Scientists may have to convince each other of the "facts," but they do not have to go too far to be the source of the construction of the "real" character of smoking and health. The very attention of the news media is itself an important element in the definition of truth about smoking. The construction of that reality is an important part of the role that medical science plays.

What is the status of the knowledge of the medical consequences of smoking? David Bloor makes a distinction between "high-status knowledge" and "low-status knowledge" (Bloor, 1992). For much of the public that has been aware of the surgeon general's reports, the condemnation of smoking rests on the certainty of verified knowledge. Such knowledge is the property of those uninvolved in the complexities of the investigations; it is low-status knowledge. For those involved in the production of the knowledge the result of research is more complex; it is high-status knowledge. Probability, revision, and qualification are more the rule in epidemiological studies that depend on talking to human beings or utilizing records produced by human beings. The 1964 surgeon general's report is no different in that respect. Its claims rest heavily on epidemiological studies, although clinical and experimental research were taken into account (U.S. DHEW, 1964a).

The epidemiological studies on which the writers of the report based much of their conclusions were seven prospective studies, in which data on smoking habits were drawn from a population and the same population followed over a period of ten to fifteen years ("longitudinal" studies). Despite consistent findings, the studies presented problems in interpretation. Some of these problems are recognized and dealt with in the report. The authors themselves suggest four major deficiencies in the study populations on which the research was based (U.S. DHEW, 1964a, 94–96). First, the samples were entirely male and were not representative of the total populations of American, British, or Canadian men studied. The samples of respondents were better educated than the total populations from which they were drawn. Second, reporting of deaths was incomplete, especially where they depended on volunteers' reports. Third, even though smokers had higher death rates than nonsmokers, the death rates of both groups, corrected for age, were below the national average, especially so for nonsmokers. As the authors of the report point out, this suggests that the nonsmokers were an especially healthy group. Lastly, the study populations did not include people in hospitals, who probably would have increased the numbers of those who died during the sampled periods. In addition, the almost exclusive use of volunteers in gathering data in two of the largest studies (70 percent of the total populations studied) led to ignorance of the number and character of nonrespondents or how a large part of the population was sampled. A number of other criticisms and qualifications have been made in the medical and other journals where the validity of public health conclusions about smoking have been debated (Burch, 1983, 1984; Eysenck, 1986; Sterling, 1975; Lilienfield, 1983; Weiss, 1975).

What I wish to convey by this discussion is the distinction between conclusions derived from wise, informed judgments and those very rare conclusions in human studies that can be presented with certainty.[4] The authors of the report were aware of many of the defects of the studies. They write, at one point, that "any answer to the question to what general population of men can the results be applied must involve an element of unverifiable judgment" (U.S. DHEW, 1964a, 94).

An essential part of the report's conclusions is developed around a specific perspective toward the concept of causation. Given that most smokers do not develop lung cancer and that some nonsmokers do develop lung cancer, the concept of a single linear cause, necessary or sufficient, is rejected. Indeed, the authors of the report developed a complex view of cause which was itself an innovation in epidemiology (Burch, 1983; Brandt, 1990). It utilized criteria based on consistency, strength, specificity, temporality, and coherence of the statistical associations between smoking and death rates. No single criterion or study is sufficient, but a number of different criteria, taken together, establish a test (U.S. DHEW, 1964a, 181–89).

As already stated, statistical methods cannot establish proof of a causal relationship in an association. The causal significance of an association is a matter
of judgment which goes beyond any statement of statistical probability. (U.S.
DHEW, 1964a, 182)

The authors of the report, aware of the immense difficulties in achieving
certainty, defend their conclusions and recommendations by stressing the
interrelated elements of the consistency, strength, specificity, temporality,
and coherence of the associations found in the various studies (U.S. DHEW,
1964a, 183–86). Thus, despite their differences, all of the studies found similar relative risks for lung cancer. All report a dose-effect phenomenon:
heavy smokers were more likely to die earlier and of lung cancer than were
lighter smokers; lighter smokers more than ex-smokers; and ex-smokers
more than nonsmokers.

Medical researchers operating in the arena of public problems face this
dilemma: if they wait until they possess "certain" proof, they may never have
answers for a public eager to know the best advice. An editorial in the *American Journal of Public Health* makes the case. While the precise importance
of smoking can be debated, wrote the editor, "[T]here can be no question that
widespread cessation of smoking would result in more good than harm. To
dilute the importance of smoking is to foolishly divert us from an important
goal" (Ibrahim, 1976, 133).

The summary of the report, published nine months later, cautiously stated:

On the basis of prolonged study and evaluation of many lines of converging
evidence, the Committee makes the following judgment: CIGARETTE SMOKING IS
A HEALTH HAZARD OF SUFFICIENT IMPORTANCE IN THE UNITED STATES TO WARRANT
APPROPRIATE REMEDIAL ACTION. (U.S. DHEW, 1964b, 6)

In discussing the possible causative role of smoking in coronary disease,
the report's authors finds such a role, though not proven, strongly enough
suspected to warrant countermeasures. They conclude:

IT IS ALSO MORE PRUDENT TO ASSUME THAT THE ESTABLISHED ASSOCIATION
BETWEEN CIGARETTE SMOKING AND CORONARY DISEASE HAS CAUSATIVE MEANING
THAN TO SUSPEND JUDGMENT UNTIL NO UNCERTAINTY REMAINS. (U.S. DHEW,
1964b, 10)

In public discourse, however, the distinction between the guarded character of "judgment" and the certainty of "cause" gets lost. In the arena of
public knowledge, qualifications and conceptual difficulties gave way to
consensus and certainty. The *San Diego Union* began its front-page story on
the 1964 report with the sentence, "Heavy cigarette smoking is the principal
cause of cancer of the lungs" ("Cigarettes Called Peril to Health," 1964, 1).

American Cancer Society materials currently use several different terms. Sometimes they refer to smoking being "responsible" for harm; sometimes to "cause" and sometimes to "may cause" (American Cancer Society, 1982, 1987a, 1987b). A statement mandated to be placed on the walls of California hotels and restaurants that permit smoking reads: "WARNING: This Facility Permits Smoking and Tobacco Smoke is Known to the State of California to Cause Cancer." In these forms, public discourse is informed by a more ordered and certain perception of harm than [that] given by the necessarily fragile and limited character of wise judgment.

THE CULTURE OF HEALTHFUL LIVING

The surgeon general's report and the media's reporting were couched in the language of health. While such language does not disappear, in the three decades since the report a distinct moral tone has been added; the individual's responsibility to follow the advice of medical science becomes a significant element in health or illness. To some extent, we have returned to the moral rhetoric of the earlier movement.

The Meanings of Illness

The surgeon general's reports on smoking, published annually since 1964, do not occur in a vacuum. They are congruent with and add to a more general shift in the perception of health and medicine which is still occurring in American life. In the remainder of this chapter, I want to consider divergent conceptions of health and medicine and the place of smoking in them.

The smoking issue may be described in more general terms to highlight the idea of health as an aspect of morality. Illness may be, and has been, seen as a sign of deficient moral character; epidemics can become symbols of communal malfeasance. This Sodom and Gomorrah story is especially clear in illnesses such as venereal disease and AIDS. Here the transmission of disease depends on human behavior. This viewpoint is to be contrasted with that perspective in which medical science focuses on the nonpurposive, non-human forms of disease instigation. Illness is seen as a result of factors external to individual character or behavior (Tesh, 1988). The individual's health is less a result of harmful living than of chance, genetics, and environment. Attention is thus directed toward treatment of disease rather than toward educating people to change their behavior.

While the search for a cure for cancer is still dominated by the latter view, in the cases of smoking, lung cancer, and coronary disease, lifestyles and personal habits have assumed a great importance as ways of preventing illness.

To see cancer or heart trouble as consequent on a lifestyle is to shift, to some degree, the nature of the disease and responsibility for its occurrence onto the person. In this fashion, medicine comes to emphasize prevention of diseases by proper living, rather than treatment by chemical or physical means.

Who, then, is the healthful person? What is the lifestyle enjoined by the transformation of health from the domain of the medical institution to the domain of the individual? Since the 1970s, the public has been exposed to the idea that the healthful person incorporates the pursuit of good health into his or her daily life, at work and at leisure. He or she eats nutritiously, avoiding excess fats, watching caloric intake, and aiming at weight reduction. Exercise is a part of leisure; jogging, fitness activity, cycling are all aspects of daily routine. Drinking alcohol is risky behavior and should be limited or eliminated. Smoking is a foolish risk and should not be a part of life. "Safe sex" should be the rule. Health is not the absence of illness but something pursued in the very way we behave (Stone, 1986; Zola, 1972; Gusfield, 1992). This emphasis on the adoption of healthful styles of living can be considered a social movement—the health-fitness movement (Goldstein, 1991). It has been advocated and supported by work of the health "establishment," including government and voluntary medical associations such the American Health Association (U.S. DHEW, 1979).

The individual becomes the focus of responsibility for his or her own health. A further example is found in the rise of the nutritional approach to health, which was met with skepticism and resistance by medical science in the 1950s and early 1960s but has become a major element in American orientations toward good health (Belasco, 1989; Gusfield, forthcoming; Schwartz, 1986; Goldstein, 1991). What we eat and how much we eat have come to be viewed as major elements in preventing or developing illness.

The role of government in this endeavor at preventive medicine is furthered by the increased role of federal and state governments in financing medical care and the greatly enhanced costs of physician and hospital services. Preventive medicine has virtues for public finance when compared to the one-on-one costs of treating and hospitalizing ill patients.

The Smoker as Responsible Victim

The advice of the health organizations, including government, has been a major part of the health-fitness movement. That advice includes the underlying "moral message" of the movement. In its focus on preventive behavior, the rhetoric of the advice distinguishes between responsible and irresponsible people. Smokers are foolish, ignorant, or lacking in the kind of character necessary for healthfulness. The reward of a healthful lifestyle is long life; the punishment of unhealthy living is early death. The avoidance of risk is a virtue; the acceptance of risk is vice.

The surgeon general's reports on smoking, from 1964 until the early 1980s, and the news coverage that transmitted them, are largely addressed to a public that is to be persuaded to stop smoking or never to begin to smoke. Their rhetoric makes an appeal to a disciplined self-control. People are asked to act in a rational fashion by developing habits that minimize risk and giving up habits that maximize risk. It is assumed that sensible people will desire a longer and more healthful life. Only fools or addicts will begin smoking or make no efforts to stop. The person who persists in smoking is a victim of his or her own ignorance, stupidity, or lack of self-control. In any case the smoker falls short of the character enjoined by authoritative medical science.

THE HEALTHFUL PUBLIC

In describing the public response to the surgeon general's reports, I have not differentiated parts of the population from one another. The image of the healthful citizen as a model to be followed is, however, more prevalent in some segments of the population than others. Not everyone is a follower of medical news in the popular culture of contemporary America.[5] Not everyone places the trust in science described above. Not everyone makes health the cornerstone of life depicted in the model of the healthful citizen.

Our knowledge of the segments of population that are attuned to medical science and incorporate health recommendations into their lives is still meager. Nevertheless, all studies report that the college-educated public is the prime recipient and appreciator of health news and advice (U.S. DHHS, Surgeon General, 1989, ch. 5; U.S. DHHS, Office of Smoking and Health, 1986; Schoenborn and Boyd, 1989; Pierce et al., 1989; Fiore et al., 1989). Lesser, but significant, differences exist between income levels (Goldstein, 1991; Williams, 1990; Fuchs, 1979).

In the years since 1964, the surgeon general's reports have consistently presented three important findings in respect to smoking:

1. The cessation of smoking and the absence of initiation into smoking is more often found among better educated than less educated persons. This is especially true of the gap between college-educated and non-college-educated persons. It is also truer of men than of women. (This latter finding is reversed in other forms of health behavior in the health-fitness movement, such as alcohol use and dieting, where women are more responsive to health advice.)

2. That difference has been continuous and has increased over the years since 1964. White-collar workers are less likely to smoke than are blue-collar workers and employed workers more likely to smoke than

unemployed workers. High-school students expecting to attend four-year colleges are less likely to smoke than are students not expecting to continue education past high school. These indices of smoking and cessation from smoking show the close association between compliance with health advice and markers of social class and status. While studies indicate a high level of knowledge of the harmful effects of smoking at all social levels, the response to health information is structured along lines of social stratification.

3. While both men and women have decreased their usage of cigarettes, the decrease has been considerably greater among men than women. At present the prevalence of smoking among women is only slightly less than among men. Moreover, as new smokers, women are beginning to smoke in larger percentages than are men.

The Social Symbolism of Commodities

Styles of daily living are part of a person's "cultural capital" (Bourdieu and Passeron, 1977); they are signs of membership in networks of people of similar styles. In Veblen's terms, they are signs that the claimant to a status and to a group membership is a person of worth and not someone of a different and less valuable culture (Veblen, 1934).

Refraining from smoking becomes necessary to the style of health-oriented, rational, risk-aversive people. Following the prescriptions of medical science demonstrates that they are people of virtue. It shows that they take a measured, self-controlled attitude toward their lives and behavior. They are people who have heard the calls of medical research and have the will to avoid the indulgences toward which a consumer-oriented market beckons their participation. To cease smoking demonstrates the capacity for self-control which has so often been a mark of American self-help movements.

Creating Moral Boundaries: Smokers as Victims and Villains

In the health-fitness movement smoking has been described as a habit hurting the smoker. Since the early 1980s, however, this situation has changed. With the research and publicity about passive smoking, the smoker has become troubling to others, to nonsmokers, as well.

The appearance of research on passive smoking, its dissemination to the anti-smoking public, and the recent wave of legislative and administrative polices based on conceptions of passive smoking have widened the distinctions between the smoker and nonsmoker. By the 1990s, the smoker was not only a foolish victim of his or her habit but also an obnoxious and uncivil source of danger, pollution, and illness to others. The early movement against the cigarette and the current movement against smoking take on growing similarities.

Smoking and the Creation of Moral Boundaries

In a recent case challenging the use of gender as a screening device in health insurance rates, the Supreme Court gave voice to the now more common usage of the unhealthy lifestyle as a point of differentiation between Americans:

> [W]hen insurance risks are grouped, the better risks always subsidize the poorer risks. Healthy persons subsidize medical benefits for the less healthy . . . persons who eat, drink, or smoke to excess may subsidize pension benefits for persons whose habits are more temperate. . . . To insure the flabby and the fit as though they were equivalent risks may be more common than treating men and women alike.[6]

What is noteworthy in this opinion is the consciousness of healthful and unhealthful lifestyles as bases for boundaries of significance in American society. "Excess" and "temperate" are used in this context as terms of opprobrium and approval as are "flabby" and "fit."

Before the emergence of the anti-smoking movement, the issue of smoking did not warrant enough significance to make it a part of descriptions of people. While parents may have cautioned their teenaged children against it, smoking occupied the same status as drinking: an adult pleasure which children might be expected to experiment with before adulthood. It might be a chastised act among teenagers, but by itself it was an ambiguous dereliction. This has changed, and smoking has become a matter of note, of distinction. Even in personals ads today modes of eating, drinking and smoking are elements of self-description ("Classified Ads—Personal," 1991). Smoking or nonsmoking has become an issue; a behavior toward which a stand must be taken. As a source of social distinctions it has been given a moral status. "Substance abuse" has added smoking to form a new trinity: alcohol, cigarettes, and drugs.

For Americans in the middle years (25–60), lower-class and less educated people have higher death and illness rates than their opposites (House et al., 1990). There is some evidence that differences in lifestyles, perhaps more than access to medical care, explain such class differences in health (Williams, 1990). It is beyond the scope of this chapter to disentangle the ways in which differences in class affect styles of health behavior. A credible argument can be made for the view that income, education and occupation create a social milieu that deeply influences access to information, dispositions to self-control, and exposure to smoke and to smoking pressures (Navarro, 1976; Tesh, 1988).

I do not want to overstate the differences between lifestyles and social groups. For one thing, according to the National Institute of Health surveys for 1987, in all educational levels today most people are nonsmokers. In 1985 smokers made up approximately 18 percent of those with sixteen or more years of education, but they made up only approximately 34 percent of those with less than twelve years of education (Pierce et al., 1989). Nor are class and education levels fully congruent. In American society, as compared with other nations such as France, the cultures of classes and other groups are only loosely homogeneous (Lamont, forthcoming).

A better way to think about the boundaries developing in American society is to think about health habits and fitness as emergent criteria by which people judge each other, with smoking behavior serving as an important indicator (Troyer and Markle, 1983). In this respect consciousness of smoking as a boundary marker is more likely to be shared in the professional, college-educated, expert-oriented upper middle class than in social classes with opposite attributes.

Passive Smoking: The Smoker as Pariah

During the early 1980s, the public became aware of research on what is known as "involuntary smoking" or "passive smoking." This research, carried out in several countries, has investigated the effect of ambient cigarette smoke on the health of nonsmokers (U.S. DHHS, Surgeon General, 1986, ch. 2; Repace, 1985, ch. 1). The dominant research has consisted of epidemiological studies of the children of smokers and the nonsmoking spouses of smokers.

While the effects on nonsmokers of different periods and different circumstances of exposure to smoke is still undergoing debate, discussion, and further investigation, passive smoking has already had a profound impact on the anti-smoking movement and on the moral meanings of smoking and smokers. Scientific support for belief in the danger of smoking for nonsmokers has been the intellectual basis for legislation and policy to prohibit smoking in many public areas and to segregate smokers from nonsmokers in many public and work areas.[7]

Before the 1980s, smokers had been viewed in public discourse as people who should be troubling to themselves. Now they were becoming people troubling to others as well. In this fashion smokers have become similar in the public eye to users of alcohol and illicit drugs (Gusfield, 1991).

The emergence of research into passive smoking has turned the distaste of smoke into a positive source of exclusion. The smoker is on the defensive as the act of smoking is increasingly banished from many social circles and the smoker so frequently admonished not to smoke. The mandatory exclusion of smoking from public places, including outdoor seating areas in stadia, furthers the public definition of the smoker as pariah.

As we have seen in the materials on the early anti-smoking movement, a belief in the polluting effects of smoking and a distaste for proximity to smoke has been a part of American culture for a long time. In public discourse and policy it remained in the background until recent years. Now it is forcefully and often legally revived. Cigarettes have come to assume the status of "dangerous object." The *New York Times,* in an editorial sounding the theme of the shift in the status of the smoker, wrote

> What a difference a few years and a few surgeon general's reports can make. Only yesterday the nonsmoker was perceived as odd man (or woman) out. Today it's the smoker who stands out. Only 30 percent of adults smoke now, and they may be feeling a bit hounded. ("Clearing the Air for Nonsmokers," 1984, A38)

Public policy cannot wait until scientific criticism has been answered. It draws on the already present sense of the polluting character of smoke to which the twenty-five years of the contemporary anti-smoking movement has been added. The resulting pressure for legal measures to segregate smokers has produced a continuing set of local and state measures banning or limiting smoking in public areas.

In recent years, a variety of policies have been put in place that implicitly and symbolically create the definition of the smoker as pariah: someone to be excluded from casual sociability unless he or she abides by the rules of nonsmoking (Schauffler, 1993; Sugarman, 1993). Individual life insurance and hospitalization health insurance now require higher premiums for the smoker than the nonsmoker (Stone, 1986). The physical segregation of the smoker on airplanes is now supplanted by the elimination of smoking from all domestic flights in the United States. Smoking is bracketed increasingly with other vices such as drinking and drug abuse. When New York City recently outlawed smoking in public places, the law exempted bars from its provisions, again associating smoking with marginally acceptable areas of behavior. Norms of civility in many social circles now restrict the smoker from smoking in the presence of others (Kagan and Skolnick, 1993). Smoking is an indulgence if granted at all by hosts and often requires the smoker to exclude himself or herself temporarily from sociability.

The moral boundaries between smokers and nonsmokers are now widened by actual physical boundaries. Whenever the smoker steps outside to smoke he or she acts out the symbolism of the pariah being cast from the community. As smoking takes on the attributes of social deviance, of unsocial action, it is even more able to play the role of a social divider. It symbolizes the inability to be aware of or to respect medical science—a sign of a less educated person.

Public Health and the Individual

The anti-smoking campaigns and the health-fitness movement have raised again the issues of paternalism and civil liberties. Such issues have always dogged public health efforts to create an environment that would minimize risks to the individual entailed by unhealthy behavior (Beauchamp, 1988). Whether public policy should intervene in the free market of business supply and consumer choice has been a question in the movement against the cigarette as it has in other similar public health activities. The developing norms of smoking act to segregate the smoking act rather than prohibit it entirely (Kagan and Skolnick, 1993). To smoke or not to smoke, to cease or not to cease, are still consumer choices.

The effort to eradicate the cigarette in American life is another stage in the public control and self-control of individual life through science and reason. It is in this sense that the health movement and the component promotion of nonsmoking are a facet of modernization. The extension of discipline and forethought to the body as a continuation of the self presupposes and reinforces an image of the noble person. As eating, drinking, smoking, physical movement, and leisure are objects of expert, professional advice and law, the individual who shuns the hegemony of the health elite risks both early death and social censure.

By contrast, the resistance by some to the advice of medical science and public health reflects a distrust of law, social norms, and other constraints on individual action. This resistance is a facet of the glorification of the uniqueness and expressiveness of the "authentic" person in American culture. It symbolizes an individualism that has long been seen as accentuated in the United States as compared with other democratic and modernized societies (Beauchamp, 1988, ch. 5; Lukes, 1973; Riesman et al., 1950; Bellah et al., 1985).

In the context of that cultural tension between the individual and the public the cigarette becomes a symbol of rebellion and individuality. A recent movie, *The Fabulous Baker Boys,* illustrates the point. This is the story of two brothers who work as a dual piano team playing popular music in nightclubs and cocktail lounges. The film is set in the present. The bourgeois brother lives in the suburbs with his family. The other lives in sleazier quarters in the city. The cigarette smoking of the less conformist brother is an issue between the two of them. A female singer, who hints of a past as a prostitute, joins the duo. Her smoking and that of the more "outcast" brother establishes a contrast to the conventional brother. In the end, the bohemian brother gives up his job playing the kind of popular music he hates to devote himself to the jazz world of his black friends. The "hero" has opted for the authenticity of impulse and risk. Smoking is a sign of his identity; a symbol of his opposition to convention and comfort. The cigarette has been given a "heroic" meaning.

From a standpoint of rational concern with health such attitudes may appear frivolous, foolish, romantic, and hedonistic. What medical science advises is a disciplined orientation toward the body based on avoidance of risk. The rational person seeks to maximize life at an acceptable level of bodily comfort. The costs of indulgence in harmful behavior clearly outweigh whatever may be the transient benefits of bodily neglect. A rational orientation toward life and leisure consists in constant consciousness of how each action contributes to health and longevity. Instant gratification, impulsive behavior, and habit-forming activities are a threat to wellness.

The contrast in perspectives is also illustrated in the necessarily public, aggregated character of the research material on smoking. In almost all of the material on the risks of smoking, the differences in death rates between smokers and nonsmokers are stated in relative rather than absolute terms. Thus we know that the chances of a smoker dying of lung cancer during the ten- to fifteen-year period studied for the 1964 report was approximately ten times that of a nonsmoker. This way of reporting the data tells us nothing about the absolute chance of dying of lung cancer. For example, in the data of the 1964 report, for the sample studied, I have calculated that chance as approximately 1 in 357 for smokers and 1 in 3,807 for nonsmokers.[8] From the standpoint of the total nation that difference in risk is very important. In a large population it adds up to a magnitude of considerable importance. From the standpoint of the individual its significance is less clear (Beauchamp, 1988, ch. 5). Will he or she be that one person who comprises all the elements, known and unknown, that determine who will contract lung cancer? Smoking is a significant addition to those elements, to be sure, but its importance is accentuated from the perspective of the total population. It is the public character of the risk rather than its application to specific persons that forms the basis for environmental control and individual advice.

The contemporary place of the cigarette in American life is a distant shout from its accepted position in the 1950s. Despite the opposition of the tobacco industry, the public health campaigns of the past three decades have brought about a remarkable change in attitudes and meanings toward smoking. The health movement has produced a cultural shift in the meaning of health and patterns of living that would have seemed impossible thirty years ago. A new medical reality conflicts with an older one. The current meaning of smoking is by no means a mirror image of the early twentieth-century anti-smoking movement in the United States, nor is it a complete contrast to the 1950s. But it now includes some important similarities.

Although in the 1960s the findings of medical science reversed the accepted place of smoking in American life, by the 1990s smoking has become a moral as well as a medical issue.

We live in a world of symbols in which commodities can represent ourselves both to others and to ourselves; in which the measures taken to improve or ignore healthful acts occur in a society that defines the virtuous, the villainous, the foolish, and the romantic. Like most acts of human beings, smoking is not aloof from a culture where meanings dilute the boundaries of medicine, morality, and science.

NOTES

1. Both Wagner and Sobel lack adequate documentation. Wagner's book has neither footnotes nor bibliographical references, although there are frequent quotations. Sobel's has a bibliographical note but does not document specific assertions or quotations.

2. Virtually all material on smoking listed in the *Reader's Guide* and in the *Index Medica* before 1945 and available in the University of California, San Diego, library was read for this article. Figures on tobacco production, voting on anticigarette bills in state legislatures, letters to the editors, and articles about other uses of tobacco (e.g., nicotine as a natural insecticide) were excluded. After 1930, the "evils" of tobacco were discounted and almost no information was listed in the *Reader's Guide.*

3. I am indebted to Milton Silverman, formerly of the *San Francisco Chronicle,* and to David Perlman, currently Science Reporter for the *Chronicle,* for informative conversations on the history and current functioning of science reporters.

4. "In sum, *any scientific estimate is likely to be based on incomplete knowledge combined with assumptions, each of which is a source of uncertainty that limits the accuracy that should be assigned to the estimate*" (National Research Council, 1986, 44).

5. As David Perlman, science reporter for the *San Francisco Chronicle* put it in an interview: "If I write an article about AIDS most everyone in the gay community will read it but very few drug users will do so."

6. *City of Los Angeles Dept. of Water and Power* v. *Manhart,* 435 U.S. 702, 710 (1978).

7. This chapter was completed and in press before the appearance of the widely publicized report on passive smoking of the U.S. Environmental Protection Agency in December 1992 (U.S. EPA, 1992). Its general conclusion, that "environmental tobacco smoke in the United States presents a serious and substantial health impact" (1-1), rests chiefly on sources also reviewed for this chapter. The report appears to have already increased support for restrictions on smoking in public places.

8. This figure of absolute risks differs from that of Viscusi, who reported the risk of lung cancer death for smokers in a range of .05–.10. He used lung cancer rates per year and thus a much longer period of time in which outcomes of smoking were manifest. He also assumed that 85 percent of lung cancer deaths were due to smoking. He does not report the absolute rate of lung cancer deaths over the same period for nonsmokers. The research reported in the 1964 surgeon general's report referred to a specific population over a period of approximately ten to fifteen years (Viscusi, 1990). My point is not the "true" rate but the significance of the difference between absolute and relative measurements.

REFERENCES

American Cancer Society. (1982). *The Most Often Asked Questions About Smoking Tobacco and Health and the Answers,* sections 4, 24, 26.

———. (1987a). *Facts on Lung Cancer.*

———. (1987b). *The Truth About Alcohol Use—Statistics, Facts and Figures.*

Beauchamp, Dan. (1988). *The Health of the Republic.* Philadelphia: Temple University Press.

Belasco, Warren. (1989). *Appetite for Change: How the Counterculture Took on the Food Industry, 1966–1988.* New York: Pantheon Books.

Bellah, Robert, Richard Madsen, William Sullivan, Ann Swidler, and Steven Tipton. (1985). *Habits of the Heart: Individualism and Commitment in American Life.* Berkeley and Los Angeles: University of California Press.

Best, Joel. (1979). "Economic Interests and the Vindication of Deviance: Tobacco in Seventeenth Century Europe." *The Sociological Quarterly* 20 (Spring): 171–82.

Bloor, F. (1992). "What Can the Sociologist of Knowledge Say about 2 × 2 = 4?" Unpublished lecture, 13 January, University of California, San Diego.

Bourdieu, Pierre, and Jean-Claude Passeron. (1997). *Reproduction in Education, Society and Culture.* London and Beverley Hills: Sage Publications.

Boyers, Charles. (1916). "A City Fights the Cigarette Habit." *The American City* 14 (April): 369–70.

Brandt, Allen. (1990). "The Cigarette, Risk, and American Culture." *Daedalus* 119: 155–76.

Bruce, James, James Miller, and Donald Hooker. (1909). "The Effect of Smoking upon the Blood Pressures and upon the Volume of the Hand." *American Journal of Psychology* 24: 104–16.

Burch, P. R. J. (1983). "The Surgeon-General's 'Epidemiologic Criteria for Causality': A Critique." *Journal of Chronic Diseases* 36: 821–36.

Carter, R. Brudenell. (1906). "Alcohol and Tobacco." *The Living Age* 32 (25 August): 479–93.

"Cigarette Smoking is a Health Hazard." (1964). *Newsweek,* January 20, pp. 48–50.

"Cigarettes." (1958). *Consumer Reports* December, pp. 628–36.

"Cigarettes Called Peril to Health." (1964). *San Diego Union,* January 12, p. l.

"Classified Ads—Personal." (1991). *New York Review of Books* July 18, p. 47.

"Clearing the Air for Nonsmokers." (editorial) (1984). *New York Times,* December 19, p. A38.

Cort, David. (1959). "Cigarettes, Cancer and the Campus." *The Nation* August 15, pp. 69–71.

"A Counterblast Against Tobacco." (1909). *New York Times,* October 2, p. 17.

Crawford, Robert. (1977). "You Are Dangerous to Your Health: The Ideology and Politics of Victim Blaming." *International Journal of Health Services* 7: 663–80.

———. (1979). "Individual Responsibility and Health Politics in the 1970s." In *Health Care in America,* edited by Susan Reverby and David Rosner. Philadelphia: Temple University Press.

Davis, Noel Pharr. (1968). *Lawrence and Oppenheimer.* New York: Simon and Schuster.

"Do They—or Don't They?" (1959). *Newsweek* 21 December: 80–81.

"Dr. Burney's Alarm." (1959). *Newsweek,* December 7, p. 66.

Dunn, Percy. (1906). "Tobacco Amblyopia." *The Lancet,* December 1, pp. 1491–93.

Eysneck, Hans J. (1986). "Smoking and Health." In *Smoking and Society,* edited by Robert Tollison, pp. 17–87. Lexington, Mass.: Lexington Books.

Fiore, Michael, Thomas Novotny, John Pierce, Evridiki Hatzandrieu, Kantilal Patel, and Ronald Davis. (1989). "Trends in Cigarette Smoking: The Changing Influence of Gender and Race." *Journal of the American Medical Association* 261: 49–55.

Fuchs, Victor. (1979). "Economics, Health and Post-industrial Society." *Milbank Memorial Fund Quarterly/Health and Society* 57: 153–82.

Glassner, Barry. (1989). "Fitness and the Post-Modern Self." *Journal of Health and Social Behavior* 30 (June): 180–91.

Goldstein, Michael. (1991). *The Health Movement: Promoting Fitness in America.* Boston: Twayne Publishers.

"A Good Beginning" (editorial). (1908). *New York Times,* May 5, p. 6.

Gottsegen, Jack J. (1940). *Tobacco: A Study of Its Consumption in the United States.* New York: Pitman.

"The Government Report." (1964). *Time* magazine (n.d.), p. 42.

Gusfield, Joseph. (1991). "Benevolent Repression: Popular Culture, Social Structure and the Control of Drinking." In *Drinking: Behavior and Belief in Modern History,* edited by Susanna Barrows and Robin Room. Berkeley and Los Angeles: University of California Press.

— — —. (1992). "Science and the Textual Culture of Health." Unpublished lecture, 24 March, Princeton University, Princeton, N. J.

— — —. (1992). "Nature's Body and the Metaphors of Food." In *Cultivating Differences,* edited by Michelle Lamont and Michel Fournier. Chicago: University of Chicago Press, chapter 4.

Hubbell, Charles. (1904). "The Cigaret Habit—A New Peril." *The Independent* 56:375–78.

Ibrahim, Michael. (1976). "The Cigarette Smoking/Lung Cancer Hypothesis." *American Journal of Public Health* February: 132–33.

Inciardi, James. (1986). *The War on Drugs: Heroin, Cocaine, Crime and Public Policy.* Mountain View, Calif.: Mayfield Publishing Co.

Kett, Joseph. (1977). *Rites of Passage: Adolescence in America.* New York: Basic Books.

Lamont, Michelle. (1992). *Money, Morals and Manners: The Culture of the French and the American Upper-Middle Class.* Chicago: University of Chicago Press.

Latest on Smoking and Cancer. (1955). *U.S. News and World Report,* June 17, pp. 45–47.

Lillienfeld, Abraham. (1983). "The Surgeon General's Epidemiologic Criteria for Causality: A Criticism of Burch's Critique." *Journal of Chronic Diseases* 36: 837–45.

Lukes, Steven. (1973). *Individualism.* Oxford: Basil Blackwell.

Monkkonen, Eric. (1975). *The Dangerous Class.* Cambridge, Mass.: Harvard University Press.

National Research Council. (1986). *Environmental Tobacco Smoke: Measuring Exposures and Assessing Health Effects.* Washington, D.C.: National Research Council.

Navarro, Vincente. (1976). "The Underdevelopment of Health of Working Americans: Causes, Consequences and Possible Solutions." *American Journal of Public Health* 66: 538–47.

Nelkin, Dorothy. (1987). *Selling Science: How the Press Covers Science and Technology.* New York: W. H. Freeman.

Pfohl, Stephen. (1984). "The Discovery of Child Abuse." *Social Problems* 24: 310–23.

Pierce, John, Michael Fiore, Thomas Novotny, Evridiki Hatzandreu, and Ronald Davis. (1989). "Trends in Cigarette Smoking in the United States: Educational Differences Are Increasing." *Journal of the American Medical Association* 261:56–60.

Repace, James. (1985). Risks of Passive Smoking." In *To Breathe Freely: Risk, Consent, and Air,* edited by Mary Gibson. Totowa, N.J.: Rowman and Allanheld.

Reisman, David, Ruel Denny, and Nathan Glazer. (1950). *The Lonely Crowd.* New Haven, Conn.: Yale University Press.

Robb, Christina. (1991). "Child Deficits Tied to Smoke Breathed by Mothers at Work." *Boston Globe* July 17, pp. 1, 17.

Rosenberg, Charles. (1962). *The Cholera Years.* Chicago, Ill.: University of Chicago Press.

Rosenstock, Irwin M., Andy Stergachis, and Catherine Meany. (1986). "Evaluation of Smoking Prohibition Policy in a Health Maintenance Organization." *American Journal of Public Health* 76: 1014–15.

"Says Schoolgirls Smoke." (1905). *New York Times,* February 20, p. 12.

Schoenborn, Charlotte, and Gayle Boyd. (1989). "Smoking and Other Tobacco Use, 1987." *National Center for Health Statistics: Vital Health Statistics* 10: 69.

Schudson, Michael. (1984). *Advertising: The Uneasy Persuasion.* New York: Basic Books.

Schwartz, Hillel. (1986). *Never Satisfied: The Cultural History of Diets, Fantasies and Fat.* New York: The Free Press.

"Smoking and Cancer." (1955). *Time* magazine, June 13, pp. 67–69.

"Smoking and Cancer (cont'd)." (1958). *Time* magazine, May 5, p. 61.

— — —. (1959). *Time* magazine, April 27, p. 73.

"Smoking and Health." (1962a). *Newsweek,* June 18, pp. 74–75.

"Smoking and Health." (1962b). *Newsweek,* November 19, p. 74.

"The Smoking Report" (editorial). (1964). *New York Times,* January 12, pp. IV–12.

Sobel, Robert. (1978). *They Satisfy: The Cigarette in American Life.* Garden City, N.Y.: Anchor Press.

"Some Cigaret Figures" (editorial). (1914). *Literary Digest,* August 8.

Spector, Malcolm, and John Kitsuse. (1977). *Constructing Social Problems.* Menlo Park, Calif.: Cummings Publishing Co.

Starr, Paul. (1982). *The Social Transformation of American Medicine.* New York: Basic Books.

Sterling, Theodore. (1975). "A Critical Reassessment of the Evidence Bearing on Smoking as the Cause of Lung Cancer." *American Journal of Public Health* 65: 939–53.

Stone, Deborah A. (1986). "The Resistible Rise of Preventive Medicine." *Journal of Health Politics, Policy and Law* 11:671–96.

Sullivan, Walter. (1964). "Cigarettes Peril Health, U.S. Report Concludes." *New York Times,* January 12, p. ll.

Tesh, Sylvia Noble. (1988). *Hidden Arguments: Political Ideology and Disease Prevention Policy.* New Brunswick, N.J.: Rutgers University Press.

Troyer, Ronald J., and Gerald Markle. (1983). *Cigarettes: The Battle over Smoking.* New Brunswick, N.J.: Rutgers University Press.

U.S. Department of Agriculture. (1990). *Agricultural Statistics.* Washington, D.C.: Government Printing Office.

U.S. Department of Health, Education and Welfare (U.S. DHEW). (1964a). *Smoking and Health.* Report of the Advisory Committee to the Surgeon General of the Public Health Service. Washington, D.C.: Government Printing Office.

— — —. (1964b). *Public Health Service Publication No. 1103-D.* Summary of the Report of the Surgeon General's Advisory Committee on Smoking and Health. Washington, D.C.: Government Printing Office.

— — —. (1979). *Healthy People: The Surgeon General's Report on Health Promotion and Disease Prevention.* Washington, D.C.: Government Printing Office.

U.S. Department of Health and Human Services (U.S. DHHS). (1986). *Smoking and Health: A National Status Report.* Rockville, Md.

— — —, Surgeon General. (1986). *The Health Consequences of Involuntary Smoking.* Washington, D.C.: Government Printing Office.

— — —, Surgeon General. (1988). *The Health Consequences of Smoking: Nicotine Addiction.* Washington, D.C.: Government Printing Office.

— — —, Surgeon General. (1989). *Reducing the Health Consequences of Smoking: 25 Years of Progress.* Washington, D.C.: Government Printing Office.

U.S. Environmental Protection Agency (EPA). (1992). *Respiratory Health Effects of Passive Smoking: Lung Cancer and Other Disorders.* Washington, D.C.: Government Printing Office.

Veblen, Thorstein. (1934). *The Theory of the Leisure Class.* New York: The Modern Library, Inc.

Viscusi, W. Kip. (1990). "Do Smokers Underestimate Risks?" *Journal of Political Economy* 98:1253–69.

Wagner, Susan. (1971). *Cigarette Country*. New York: Praeger Publishers.

Weiss, William. (1975). "Smoking and Cancer: A Rebuttal." *American Journal of Public Health* 65: 954–55.

"What Britons Are Told About Lung Cancer and Tobacco." (1957). *U.S. News and World Report* August 2, pp. 84–86.

"What Is Known and Unknown About Smoking and Cancer." (1957). *U.S. News and World Report,* July 26, pp. 56–75.

Whelan, Elizabeth. (1984). *A Smoking Gun: How the Tobacco Industry Gets Away with Murder.* Philadelphia: George F. Stickley Co.

Williams, David. (1990). "Socioeconomic Differentials in Health: A Review and Redirection." *Social Psychology Quarterly* 53: 81–99.

Zola, Irving. (1972). "Medicine as an Institution of Social Control." *Sociological Review* 20: 487–504.

16

Smoking, Human Rights, and Civil Liberties

Douglas J. Den Uyl

> Irrational creatures cannot distinguish between injury and damage, and there-
> fore, as long as they be at ease, they are not offended with their fellows; whereas
> man is then most troublesome when he is most at ease, for then it is that he loves
> to show his wisdom and control the actions of them that govern the common-
> wealth. (Thomas Hobbes)

Nineteen eighty-three was a landmark year for anti-smoking forces. It was in
1983 that Proposition P, otherwise known as the Smoking Pollution Control
Ordinance, was passed in San Francisco. The ordinance, hotly contested and
only narrowly passed, marked the first instance in this country of a government
regulation whose effects are likely to mean the prohibition of all smoking in
many places of work. Prior to Proposition P, legislation such as Connecticut's
Clean Indoor Air Act (1979) was either much more limited in the range of
places covered by the act or required separation of smokers and nonsmokers
rather than prohibition, as in Minnesota's Clean Indoor Air Act of 1975. Even
though the San Francisco ordinance is only a city ordinance, its logical implications are more pervasive than those of preceding pieces of legislation. Furthermore, the media exposure given to the San Francisco ordinance—through
a segment of the popular television news program *60 Minutes* aired on January
29, 1984—has turned an otherwise local affair into a national one. However
one feels about smoking, the more aggressive regulatory posture of the San
Francisco ordinance combined with the national attention the ordinance has
received should give one pause for reflection and concern.

Originally published in *Smoking and Society: Toward a More Balanced Assessment*, edited by
R. D. Tollinson (Lexington, Mass.: Lexington Books, 1986). Reprinted by permission of University Press of America.

In this chapter we shall discuss the propriety of the San Francisco ordinance as well as some criteria that might be used for evaluating the rights of smokers and nonsmokers in "public places." The discussion which follows is formulated in a context that would be most familiar to readers in the United States. However, a brief appendix is provided which discusses the political philosophy exhibited by the World Health Organization's campaign against smoking. For purposes of this chapter we shall assume that smoking is at least offensive and perhaps harmful. We are not *arguing* or *conceding* that smoking is offensive or harmful to smokers or nonsmokers. Rather, we start with this assumption in order to more clearly identify the rights in question and to avoid the accusation that the following analysis depends upon an overly benevolent interpretation of controversial smoking issues. Before discussing smoking directly, however, we must first lay the foundations that will be used in our analysis of the smoking issue. To that task we now turn.

HUMAN RIGHTS, CIVIL LIBERTIES, AND GOVERNMENT INTERVENTION

Rights and Liberty

One of our most treasured national documents is the Declaration of Independence. This document is not simply a historical statement of our desire to break from English rule, but is (perhaps more importantly) an expression of a political and moral philosophy. That philosophy is contained in the following familiar passage:

> We hold these Truths to be self-evident, that all Men are created equal, that they are endowed by their Creator with certain unalienable Rights, that among these are Life, Liberty, and the Pursuit of Happiness—That to secure these Rights, Governments are instituted among Men, deriving their just Powers from the Consent of the Governed, that whenever any Form of Government becomes destructive of these Ends, it is the Right of the People to alter or to abolish it, . . .

This passage has been cited so often in so many speeches and articles that it is now trite and, because of overuse, almost meaningless. Nevertheless, the very triteness of the passage masks the quite substantial theses contained within it. These theses deserve renewed attention because they do say something significant about the role and purpose of government. Moreover, the principles enumerated in the Declaration constitute the framework within which the smoking controversy will be analyzed below. Here are a few of the significant principles mentioned in the passage cited from the Declaration:

1. People, by their very nature, have certain rights which are neither created by government nor alterable by government.

2. These basic rights are foundational—that is, they are not defined in terms of anything but themselves (not, for example, in terms of social utility, public welfare, state security, and so on).

3. All persons have the same rights—not collectively, but individually.

4. The function of government is to protect these rights. Indeed, governments are legitimately established for this end *and no other.*

5. Laws which violate these rights should be abolished or altered so that they no longer violate these rights. The same can be said about governments which systematically violate basic rights.

Jefferson included life, liberty, and the pursuit of happiness among the basic rights. This was a paraphrase of John Locke's triad of life, liberty, and property.[1] There is no disagreement here between Jefferson and Locke. Both saw property as a basic right and as an integral part of the pursuit of happiness.

Of the three terms in the triad of basic rights, "liberty" seems to be the most crucial. Equal pursuit of happiness, for example, is merely the expression of the freedom to pursue individual interests. And given the diversity of human interests, the state would be protecting the right of divergent pursuits of interest in protecting basic rights. Notice that Jefferson does not say that the state should guarantee our happiness nor even that it should outline the paths we should take toward that end. The Declaration also does not say that the government should keep us from falling into unhappiness. The role of the state consists simply in not interfering with our *pursuit* of happiness even if we are mistaken about what will in fact bring us that happiness. Since we possess equal basic rights, the same protection must be provided to all, which usually means protecting us from the interference of others and others from our interference.

The centrality of the concept of liberty with respect to our basic rights indicates that these rights are essentially negative. They impose obligations of noninterference on each of us vis-à-vis others' pursuit of happiness. Interference by the state is legitimate only when some person or group has first crossed the boundaries of noninterference (through a criminal act, for example). Individuals, however, are not the only violators of basic rights. States can violate them, too, and this is why Jefferson was insistent that a Bill of Rights be added to the Constitution. Violations of rights by states are actually more serious than violations by individuals, since states possess a virtual monopoly on the use of force. Rectification of a rights violation perpetrated by the state, thus becomes difficult or impossible.

Clearly, applying these rights in concrete practice can be complicated and can raise numerous questions and difficulties. Nevertheless, the heat of the moment should not make us lose sight of the basic principles involved, especially when it is possible to have our basic rights eroded piecemeal by laws. The Declaration urges us to stand back every now and then from more specific disputes and to reflect upon general principles. We are permitted this detached perspective because our particular laws and social policies are meant to be evaluated in terms of principles more fundamental than themselves—our "unalienable rights."

Traditionally our "unalienable rights" were called "natural rights." That terminology has since gone out of fashion. Today the phraseology is likely to be "human rights." In either case, we are said to possess certain basic rights that cannot be legitimately violated by either our fellow citizens or government and which can be used to evaluate the actions of either. Herein lies the difference between a moral perspective on an issue and other types of approaches. If a lawyer or legal theorist were writing on our topic, for example, he would have to operate within the framework of existing law. The legality of the San Francisco ordinance would have to be challenged or defended in terms of existing law or legal procedures. By the same token, an economist must evaluate social utility in terms of current desires and interests. Jefferson's remarks in the Declaration, however, indicate that an issue can be examined from a point of view that need not pay particular attention to existing law or what will currently maximize social utility. We can instead evaluate an issue from a *moral* point of view.

In matters of public policy, the moral point of view translates into a discussion of basic rights.[2] Since the purpose of the state is to protect people's rights, public policies can be assessed by analyzing whether rights are in fact being protected. No prediction need be made about whether the correct course of action will in fact be taken, nor are we limited to using the term "rights" in a narrowly legalistic fashion. We may instead be concerned with what ought to be the case, even if practical realities are biased in an alternate direction. With Jefferson, therefore, we shall assume that there are basic human rights, that the concept of liberty best expresses the essence of these rights, that these rights are foundational in the sense that they morally override policies that do not respect them, and that the function of government is to protect these basic rights. These values, finally, are not necessarily peculiar to the United States. Many Western liberal democracies claim to be grounded in similar values. Thus it is upon this bit of theoretical scaffolding that we shall build the case that follows.

Legal Paternalism

If we agree that governments are acting legitimately when they keep us from violating each others' rights, do they have a further obligation to insure that we use our liberty in ways that keep us from harming ourselves? The belief that governments ought to protect people from harming themselves is known as legal paternalism, and governments often act in legally paternalistic ways. Because of its intervention under this principle, for example, people have limited access to pornography, marijuana, laetril, and prostitutes. There are also more subtle forms of paternalism, such as Federal Trade Commission regulation of advertising in the name of the most gullible members of society, or Securities and Exchange Commission regulation of the stock market on roughly the same principle. It is hard to know where the authority for such paternalistic acts comes from. I may wish to have my self-harming actions regulated, but it is not clear how I can legitimately impose such restrictions upon you, especially if you can be (or are) made easily aware of the risks you are taking. Furthermore, it is not clear where I would derive the right to use your resources in financing a government program to protect me from self-harm (or vice versa).

Nevertheless, some philosophers have argued for the legitimacy of legal paternalism. Many of these thinkers can be dismissed as having little sympathy for the principle of liberty mentioned above. Others, however, do deserve to be described as civil libertarians in the sense that they give the benefit of the doubt to the principle of liberty. These thinkers would generally hold that there is a prima facie case against government interference with self-harming actions, but allow for certain interferences in appropriate cases. The following principle has been offered by Joel Feinberg to help determine when such interference is justified: "A man can rightly be prevented from harming himself (when other interests are not directly involved) only if his intended action is substantially nonvoluntary or can be presumed to be so in the absence of evidence to the contrary."[3] The key terms here are obviously "other interests," "nonvoluntary," and "absence of evidence to the contrary." But let us resist the temptation to discuss each of these concepts in turn, and instead take the passage as a whole and apply it to the topic at hand—smoking.

At another point in the article from which the preceding passage was taken, Feinberg claims that we would run "serious risks of governmental tyranny" if those who voluntarily chose to smoke were prevented from doing so.[4] However, he also makes the following statement:

> The way for the state to assure itself that such practices [smoking] are truly voluntary is continually to confront smokers with the ugly medical facts so that there is no escaping the knowledge of what the medical risks to health exactly are. Constant reminders of the hazards should be at every hand and with no softening of the gory details. The state might even be justified in using its taxing, regulatory, and persuasive powers to make smoking . . . more difficult or less attractive.[5]

It is hard to imagine how the state could use its "taxing, regulatory, and per-suasive powers" and not seriously threaten individual liberty. Furthermore, it would seem to follow from the desire to make an action "truly voluntary" that the state would have to supply any *contrary* evidence to smokers and nonsmokers alike. And this does not even begin to address the troublesome question of why the resources of voluntary smokers should be expropriated (through taxation and regulation) for a program that will inevitably diminish their freedom and pleasure in smoking.

The chief difficulty, however, with the passage on smoking is that it vio-lates the principle for justified legal paternalism mentioned earlier. Notice that the principle of legal paternalism allows for state interference only when an individual's action is "substantially nonvoluntary." On the other hand, the passage just cited implies that the state may interfere to insure that our actions are "truly voluntary." Obviously "substantially nonvoluntary" and "truly voluntary" are rather different concepts, with the latter concept implying the most complete and rationally correct assessment of the evi-dence that is humanly possible. Indeed, "truly voluntary" is the kind of con-cept that could be used by the state to reject any form of deviant behavior, since any form of deviant behavior can be interpreted as "irrational" according to conventional norms.

Clearly Feinberg is not using "truly voluntary" in a way that would usher in the totalitarian state. It is evident, though, that "substantially nonvolun-tary" is the preferred expression because it is a more manageable concept and because it is more likely to inhibit state intervention. In the smoking contro-versy, then, a substantially nonvoluntary action would be one that was per-formed in ignorance of any medical evidence of the alleged adverse effects of smoking. Moreover, "substantially nonvoluntary" must also mean that information about smoking was significantly inaccessible to the average smoker. In both cases there can be no presumption in favor of legal pater-nalism for smoking. Not only is there a widespread belief that smoking is harmful (continuously reinforced by television advertisements), but in addi-tion a warning is printed on each package. I might add that when Feinberg made these statements about smoking in 1971, which was prior to the ciga-rette labeling law, there was still a widely held belief that smoking was harmful to health. Thus even before the current widespread public contro-versy on smoking, it would not be easy to claim a smoker's actions were sub-stantially nonvoluntary.[6]

What is clear from the foregoing analysis is that there are no grounds for legal paternalism with respect to smoking. Furthermore, the expenditure of public funds on attempts to convince people not to smoke is also an illegiti-mate form of legal paternalism. To ask people to finance campaigns against their own choices, even if those choices are irrational, neither secures the protection of rights nor enhances the prospects of such protection.

Rights and Harms

If the coercive power of the state cannot be legitimately used to protect individuals from any harm to themselves that smoking may cause, perhaps it can be used to prevent harm to others. To answer this question an examination of the relationship between rights and harms is required. Is protecting someone from harm the same thing as protecting someone's rights? Can one be harmed and not have one's rights violated? And alternatively, can one not be harmed and yet still have one's rights violated? These questions must be addressed before an intelligent assessment of the smoking controversy can be made.

Consider the following case: a person is running at full speed. During the run another person steps in front of the runner and throws his body at the runner, breaking the runner's nose. It is clear that the runner has been harmed. Is it also clear that the runner has had his rights violated? The answer to this question must be no, because too little information is provided. Suppose, for example, that the event just described took place during a professional football game. The tackler may regret that the runner's nose was broken, but the runner knowingly and voluntarily agreed to face the risk of such injuries when he agreed to join the football team. Thus, although a harm was certainly the result of the interaction between tackler and runner, no one's rights were violated.

Consider another case: a burglar enters my house by picking the lock. At the time he enters no one is home. The burglar looks around, finds nothing of value, and leaves. I return home later and find nothing out of order. The lock on the front door has not been damaged and nothing inside the house has been disturbed. The only reason I know a burglar has entered my house is that he left a note saying: "Please find a better job so that you can afford to buy something worth stealing—your local cat burglar." My acute embarrassment causes me to finally have the courage to quit my job, and I subsequently find another one at twice the salary. From this case it is clear that I have not been harmed by the burglar's actions. Indeed, I may even have benefited by those actions. Nevertheless, the burglar's trespass violated my rights, because his entry into my house was not gained with my permission.

These two cases indicate that when a person is harmed, his or her rights have not necessarily been violated, and also that one's rights may be violated even if one is not harmed. A recent paper by J. Roger Lee has detailed more sufficiently than we can here the points made by our preceding examples.[7] Lee's basic argument is that it is not the harmfulness of an action per se that ought to concern legislators, but whether the harm was accompanied by a lack of consent by the one who suffers the harm. Lee further points out that consent does not mean what one would *like* to happen but what one *might reasonably expect* to be the risks and benefits of an action. Broken bones are clearly a risk voluntarily incurred by one who plays professional football even though no one who suffers such injuries would *like* to have them and even though football players would *prefer* to play without receiving any injuries. Thus, if the proper concern of legislators ought to be to protect us from violations of our rights (protection from nonconsensual interferences), the regulation of activities to protect us from harms may extend beyond the province of legitimate governmental authority.

Lee's own argument operates within what he calls a framework of rational expectations.[8] We need not explore the technical details of Lee's discussion to see its main point. If a person enters a situation containing possible risks, harms, or other unpleasant features which were known to the person or could reasonably be presumed to be known, then it is plausible to conclude that the person has consented to those risks, harms, or unpleasant features. If those risks, harms, or unpleasant features then do come about, no one's rights have been violated. If, on the other hand, someone introduces a component into the situation which the person could not plausibly have been said to have consented to in the sense just mentioned, then there is evidence that the person's rights have been violated. Although people tend to complain only when the factor to which they did not consent is harmful, it is important to realize that it is not the harm itself that matters here, but rather the fact of lack of consent.

Real-life cases can be complicated, and that to which a person can be reasonably expected to consent (given cultural circumstances and knowledge) can also be unclear or changeable at times. Nevertheless, borderline or complicated cases do not detract from the validity of the position that causing harm does not necessarily violate rights (or vice versa). Given that the proper function of government is to protect rights, it would therefore not necessarily follow that the government should "do something" if being around smokers is either harmful or offensive. But the question of the extent to which government should or should not interfere with smoking needs more exploration. The next two sections are designed to provide the needed additional discussion based upon the principles just discussed.

SMOKING AND PROPERTY RIGHTS

The Nature of the San Francisco Ordinance

Section 1001 of the San Francisco Smoking Pollution Control Ordinance states:

> Because the smoking of tobacco or any other weed or plant is a danger to health
> and is a cause of material annoyance and discomfort to those who are present in

confined places, the Board of Supervisors hereby declares that the purposes of this article are (1) to protect the public health and welfare by regulating smoking in the office workplace and (2) to minimize the toxic effects of smoking in the office workplace by requiring an employer to adopt a policy that will accommodate, insofar as possible, the preferences of nonsmokers and smokers and, if a satisfactory accommodation cannot be reached, to prohibit smoking in the office workplace.

Additional sections of this ordinance spell out the meaning of the points contained in Section 1001. The ordinance is not a complete ban on smoking in the workplace, although in certain cases smoking may have to be banned to accommodate the terms of the ordinance. Rather, the ordinance was intended to institute a two-stage approach. The first phase involves businesses attempting to work out an arrangement that would satisfy both smoking and nonsmoking employees. If that cannot be accomplished, that is, if there is even one nonsmoking employee who remains dissatisfied with the arrangement, then smoking must be banned from the workplace.

The ordinance is explicitly weighted in favor of the nonsmoking employee (section 1003), but there are exemptions to the ordinance. "Public places" such as stadiums, bars, and restaurants are exempted; however, medical waiting rooms, libraries, museums, and hospitals do fall under the ordinance. Offices inhabited exclusively by smokers (even if nonsmokers visit) are exempt, as are offices in private homes and offices rented by a single contractor. The ordinance also states that employers are not required to undertake any expenditures to accommodate smoking or nonsmoking employees. Of course, if an employer fails to undertake expenditures to satisfy a nonsmoking employee, the employer may end up having to ban smoking from the workplace entirely.

A number of anomalies are contained in the statement of purpose (section 1001) cited above. First of all, if smoking is such a "danger to health" it seems inconsistent to "accommodate" smokers at all. In hazardous industries such as the chemical industry, the government tends to regulate exposure by anyone who comes in contact with the chemical. The government certainly does not allow those who may wish to play with toxic chemicals to risk the health of fellow workers and then ask those workers to "accommodate" their more chemically playful colleagues. In a similar fashion, it is hard to understand how one "minimizes toxic effects" by accommodating producers of those effects. It would seem, therefore, that "public health" is more a ploy to gain legal respectability than a substantive feature of the ordinance. That, of course, leaves "annoyance and discomfort" as the chief justification for the ordinance. Secondly, the ordinance repeatedly refers to accommodating smokers; yet it is difficult to understand what accommodating smokers means here, since it is the nonsmoker who is being accommodated. Logically this must be the case, for there would be no purpose to the ordinance if it did not assume that smokers were already being accommodated. "Accommodation" could, of course, mean a *mutually* acceptable arrangement between smokers and nonsmokers, but if this is its meaning, then the bias in favor of the nonsmoker contradicts the intent of the term. The ordinance could have simply required mutual accommodation and left each office to its own devices about how to secure such accommodation; or it could have required relieving any employee (smoker or nonsmoker) of his position if he refused to bargain in good faith. These are not recommendations on my part, but rather indications of the sloppy or incomprehensible logic of the ordinance.

The preceding arguments are merely minor swipes at an ordinance that has much more serious defects. These defects include excessive governmental intrusion into the liberties of citizens and a violation by government of property rights. We have already discussed many of the background principles needed to make such charges stick. But some additional theorizing is needed to insure that the defects of the ordinance are fully clarified.

LIBERTY AND PROPERTY

The connection between liberty and property is one that advocates of governmental power would like to sever. Men like Jefferson and Locke were quite convinced that the surest way for the government to erode the liberty of its citizens was to take control of the property of its citizens. Today the erosion of property rights has gone so far that people no longer associate the right to property with the concept of civil liberties. But as we noted in the first section of this chapter, what a government does and what it ought to do are not always the same. Our contention is that "economic liberties" ought to be respected in the same way and for the same reasons as "civil liberties."

Consider, for example, what a civil liberty like freedom of speech would mean without property rights. It would mean that the microphone, newspaper, magazine, or book that you are using to express yourself would be controlled by the state. The potential thus exists (and is likely to be realized) for censorship of views the state finds unacceptable (usually expressed by such phrases as "against the public interest"). With property rights, however, an individual may "censor" the views of those with whom he/she disagrees by excluding the views from his/her magazine or publishing house, but an individual cannot *generally* exclude contrary opinions from society at large as the state can. The same type of reasoning applies to other standard examples of civil liberties, such as freedom of assembly.[9] Civil liberties divorced from property rights therefore represent simply what will be allowed by the currently dominant social power.

In the United States, the term "civil liberties" has come to mean the rights guaranteed by the amendments to its constitution (primarily amendments one through ten and fourteen). These were rights *against* government interference. There is, however, no amendment that refers explicitly to the right of property. This is because the Founding Fathers believed that the separation of powers and the system of checks and balances would be sufficient to protect private property rights. Recent scholarship further indicates that the Founders intended Article 1, section 10 of the Constitution to prohibit state intervention with the obligations of contracts.[10] In addition, Bernard Siegan has argued that judicial review of economic liberties and the application of substantive due process to economic matters were part of constitutional law until relatively recently.[11] Thus despite present tendencies to conceptually distinguish economic liberties from other civil liberties, the political and social theory advanced here is not without legal precedent.

For our purposes a distinction must be drawn between government regulation of private property and government protection of private property rights. The latter is a legitimate function of government; the former is not. Ordinary discourse often conflates these two notions by calling legitimate protection of private property rights "regulation."[12] For example, if corporation X promises that its product will perform *p*, *q*, and *r* tasks and the product only performs *q*, it is not "regulation" to require the corporation to make good on its promise or offer compensation. Rather, government action in this case is a protection of my property rights which are infringed if my property (my money) is taken under false pretenses. On the other hand, if corporation X informs a consumer that its product performs *p*, *q*, and *r* and the state disapproves of *r*, then it would be regulation to prevent corporation X from selling the product with feature *r*. The difference between the two cases is that in the latter some end other than the protection of rights is being sought. Voluntary exchange (my money for the product) between consenting parties is being limited to enhance some end, such as preventing self-harm, beyond the propriety of the exchange itself. The former case, however, recognizes that *both* parties have property rights and seeks to ensure that the exchange of property was a voluntary one.

Notice that the "protection of property rights" has less to do with things and objects than it does with voluntary exchange or use of those objects. We noted above that the concept of "voluntary" can become complicated in certain cases, but this does not detract from the central point: no (property) rights have been violated if A (either group or person) exchanges with B and B with A something to which each is entitled (that is, was not obtained by force or fraud) and of which A and B understand, or can be presumed to understand, the nature, consequences, or uses. Conversely, a person's property rights have been violated if something to which that person is entitled has been taken under false pretenses or (what amounts to the same thing) has been taken in exchange for something whose uses, nature, or consequences the person could not reasonably be expected to understand. To illustrate these general principles with a controversial example, if I (a cancer victim) agree to exchange some money for your bottle of laetril knowing full well the scientific skepticism about the usefulness of that product and in the absence of any claims on your part that the drug will in fact cure cancer, then no one's property rights have been violated by the exchange. If, on the other hand, I purchase your bottle of laetril because you told me it cures cancer and not only does it not perform as promised but also I could not be expected to know the risks I was taking, then my property rights have been violated.

Furthermore, if the government prevents or restricts my informed purchase of the drug or prevents or restricts your sale of the drug despite your willingness to inform the consumer about the possible risks, then both our property rights have been violated. Lee's concept of rational expectations would obviously have some role to play here, since complicated technology may imply a reasonable presumption of ignorance on the part of consumers with respect to certain products. Nevertheless, a regulatory attitude will tend to imply a different sort of approach to this problem than will a "rights protecting" attitude. A regulatory attitude will tend to decide *for* consumers what they ought or ought not to have or purchase; a rights protecting attitude will instead tend to concern itself with consumer information, leaving it up to the consumer to decide what he ought or ought not have or purchase.

The current government posture is regulatory rather than rights protecting; but that is beside the point for present purposes. The rights protecting posture is the one that is consistent with the traditions of individual liberty on which our argument is based. All that remains, therefore, is the application of these principles to the San Francisco ordinance.

Limiting Governmental Power

In discussing the limitations of governmental power over private property, it is first necessary to be clear about the meaning of private property. Property is private if it is owned by an individual or group of individuals and not by the state. Contrary to the San Francisco ordinance's classification scheme, bars and restaurants are not public property. Opening one's doors to the public does not thereby transform private property into public property. The resources are still being controlled and used for the benefit of the owners who, in such cases, are not the government. Museums and libraries, however, may be public property because they are owned by the state and run with tax dollars. To "open one's doors to the public" simply means that one is advertising the terms of an agreement for an exchange to any and all comers. It does not mean that one has a public responsibility to others beyond living up to the terms of the agreement, nor are the owners of such properties implying by their advertisement that they wish to relinquish control of their property to the state.

Despite commonly misleading terminology, companies whose stock is held by large numbers of persons are also not public companies but private companies. The number of owners does not transform a piece of property from private to public. All such companies are claiming when they sell stock is that a share in the equity of the company can be purchased for a certain price. They are not thereby necessarily inviting the state to become business partners. Clearly, then, workplaces qualify as private property, since such places are owned by and are part of private businesses. The obligation of government would therefore be to protect the property rights of those who own these businesses as well as those who trade with these businesses.

One way to trade with a business is to offer services in exchange for money or other forms of remuneration. Protecting property rights in such cases would mean insuring that both parties live up to the terms of their agreement. It obviously does not mean dictating the terms of that agreement. Employers and employees are thus free to come to whatever terms both find mutually agreeable. "Mutually agreeable" here does not mean what either or both parties *wish* to be the case, but rather what conditions are necessary for an exchange to take place. If no exchange takes place, the presumption must be that the terms were not mutually agreeable. If an exchange does take place, the presumption is that the terms were mutually agreeable. The only remaining question would then be whether it is reasonable to assume that both parties understood the terms in question.

It is important to realize that if both parties understood the terms of the agreement, it is quite irrelevant whether one or both parties are harmed by the agreement. A theory which respects rights and liberty must also respect the possibility, even likelihood, that people might willingly undertake risks that could result in harm to them. Since a reasonable presumption exists that people do not wish to harm themselves without an understanding of the risks they are taking, parties to an exchange can expect to be informed of the risks about which they could not reasonably be expected to know. The state may intercede in an exchange on behalf of one party if the other has hidden certain pertinent facts or misled the other party about such facts. If, on the other hand, the risks are understood and an exchange takes place, the person(s) subject to those risks can be understood as having consented to them, leaving no ground for state action.

According to the standards just enumerated, the San Francisco ordinance is a clear violation of property rights and an illegitimate extension of governmental power. It is the employer who has the right to decide the smoking policy of the firm and not the city of San Francisco. If the working conditions with respect to smoking are known to the employee when he or she considers a job offer, then that person has accepted those working conditions in accepting the job. The state's (here the city of San Francisco) imposition of additional restraints upon the employer turns a voluntary agreement into an involuntary one, since state action would be unnecessary if the employer would have voluntarily offered terms like those stated by the ordinance.

One might object that either a) the employees cannot be presumed to understand the claimed health or discomfort effects of working in an environment with smokers, or b) the employees cannot be presumed to understand that there would be smokers in their work environment. Assuming the employer gave no information to the employee about a or b, I find both quite implausible. Smoking has been common enough in workplaces that a person can expect to have coworkers who smoke. Moreover, smoking is common enough for a person to have experienced the "discomforts" of being around smokers. And finally, the possible "negative" health effects of smoking have been sufficiently publicized to warrant the presumption that being around smokers might be risky. Of course, if some of the essays in this volume and elsewhere about the lack of sufficient evidence on the alleged detrimental effects of ambient smoke are true, then the case for government intervention is removed entirely.[13]

Someone may doubt the accuracy of my statements about the cultural expectations of employees accepting jobs in environments with smokers. However, even if I am wrong about these expectations, it affects the argument in only a minor way. If people cannot be expected to know they will be working with smokers, that problem could be solved by an ordinance requiring that firms clearly state their policy on smoking to prospective employees (current employees already know what that policy is).[14] To require that firms inform prospective employees about its smoking policy is in no way similar to the current San Francisco ordinance. Under the proposed "information ordinance," a firm could tell a prospective employee that no smoking anywhere will be allowed, or that it requires smokers and nonsmokers to share desks and that smokers must blow smoke in the nonsmoker's face every five minutes (or anything in between). Although it seems to me that this "information ordinance" would be a superfluous bit of legal posturing, it is at least not inconsistent with individual freedom of choice. The present ordinance, on the contrary, *requires* a certain form of behavior or policy.

It might also be thought that the San Francisco ordinance is not as pernicious as I have implied since its main intention is to accommodate both smokers and nonsmokers. This objection fails to understand the principle involved, which is that employers *have* no social obligation to accommodate either smokers or nonsmokers. Obviously a firm which discriminates completely against smokers or nonsmokers pays an economic cost if more qualified job candidates are sacrificed for adherence to a smoking policy; but that is the firm's business and not the state's. This is all we need show as far as the political nature of smoking in the workplace is concerned.

Private Alternatives

Although companies have the right to adopt whatever smoking policies they choose, it is likely that the market will tend to reflect the desires of prospective employees. In an article in the *San Francisco Chronicle* explaining the smoking ordinance, it was noted that many firms have already adopted smoking policies.[15] In many cases, these were more "anti" or "restrictive" smoking policies than permissive ones, but the general point is worth noting. If most employers have employees who object to working around smokers, the market will begin to reflect this. Not only will employers find ways to satisfy the desires of their employees, but prospective employees will begin looking for firms whose policies best reflect their own smoking habits.

State intervention in market processes such as the San Francisco ordinance is almost always detrimental for reasons other than the ones given above. Because laws must be universal and essentially static, and because actors in the market never universally fall into one behavior pattern or necessarily have the same desires over time, restrictive legislation such as the San Francisco ordinance is invariably inconvenient to many people. Given the general effectiveness with which the market tends to respond to changing desires and attitudes, it seems quite unnecessary and excessive for coercive state action to intervene in that process. Moreover, it is almost comical to observe that those workplaces most plausibly subject to government control—"any property owned or leased by state or federal governmental entities"—are exempt from the San Francisco ordinance.[16]

SMOKING AND PUBLIC PROPERTY

Harm and Ambient Tobacco Smoke

Since a restrictive case for state control of smoking on private property cannot be made, our attention must be turned to smoking on public property. Public property differs significantly from private property because it is owned by the public and controlled by the state. Unlike private ownership, the owners of public property cannot exclude each other or transfer their shares of the property. Moreover, the resources of the owners are forcibly expropriated to support the management of the public property. In a sense, then, the rules that would govern use of public property would be rules that apply to people who are "stuck" together whether they wish to be or not. And the significant difference between public and private property may make a difference in how we evaluate smoking in such places.

One thing, however, does not seem to change in our movement from private to public property: paternalism seems no more justified in the public case than in the private. To ban smoking in public places simply because the state has decided its citizens should not smoke is to manage a piece of property against the interests of some of its owners. Unless one can show that people utilize public property for paternalistic purposes, there is no reason to believe that paternalism suddenly becomes a function of government on public property.

On the other hand, the concept of harm does seem to factor in more significantly with respect to public property than with private property. Since owners cannot exclude each other or transfer ownership rights there is virtually no choice about one's associates or possibility of avoiding (or accepting) the potential harms one may face. Thus, preventing harmful or risky behavior on public property would be a legitimate function of the state. If exposure to ambient tobacco smoke is in fact harmful, it could be legitimately banned from public places. We must therefore devote a moment to the question of whether ambient tobacco smoke is harmful.

Although public discussion may proceed as if the negative health effects of ambient tobacco smoke were solidly established, the evidence for such effects is either weak or nonexistent. Certain studies, such as those by White and Froeb, claim to show negative health effects of ambient tobacco smoke.[17] But such studies have been seriously criticized on both methodological and substantive grounds.[18] Furthermore, a number of other studies showing contrary results have been conducted.[19] Statements and supporting evidence to this effect can be found in other essays in this volume, and we are in no position in this chapter to judge the validity of the scientific claims and counterclaims on this issue. Nevertheless, a fair reading of *all* evidence on ambient tobacco smoke should generate, even in the layperson, a high degree of skepticism that there is sufficient evidence to support claims that ambient tobacco smoke is harmful.

In this section of the chapter, therefore, we shall operate under the assumption that ambient tobacco smoke is not a health hazard. Instead we shall assume that a significant number of people find it annoying to be around smokers. On the basis of this assumption we shall discuss the principles that might apply to offensive behavior on public property.

The Balance of Interests Approach

One of the remarkable aspects of the San Francisco ordinance is that it does not cover hallways, lobbies and office lounges.[20] On the face of it, it would seem more plausible for the state to regulate such "public places" than it would for it to control the activities of private offices. Of course, the argument could be made that, unlike an office, the limited exposure to tobacco

smoke one would face in lounges and hallways does not justify state regulation of smoking in such places (beyond what the Fire Marshall may require).
This argument may be true, but it concedes a great deal. Since public buildings are analogous to lounges and hallways with respect to public usage, this
argument suggests that smoking should be permitted on similar terms in
public buildings. Secondly, the argument admits that at least limited exposure
to ambient smoke is not a health problem. And finally, the argument seems
to imply that smoking is sufficiently inoffensive to most other people that the
state need not concern itself with smoking in such "public places."

We cannot, however, assume that all regulators will use the same type of
logic that seems to be exhibited by the San Francisco ordinance. Therefore let
us keep our assumption that smoking offends a significant number of people
even if it does not harm them. Remembering that all citizens are technically co-
owners of public property with the government serving as their trustee, the
question now is what principles might be advanced for determining when the
government can legitimately ban "offensive" behavior from public places?

In a well known essay Feinberg outlines the principles that ought to
apply to offense behavior in public places.[21] Feinberg's purpose was to derive
a set of principles that would mediate between reasonable and unreasonable
offense. Some people, for example, might be "unreasonably" offended by the
sight of an interracial couple kissing in a public place. It does not seem to
Feinberg that the state should prevent such "offenses." On the other hand,
erecting pornographic billboards in Times Square does seem to be a form of
behavior that the state might "reasonably" prevent. Thus Feinberg sought to
develop a set of principles that would not call for state intervention in the first
case but would in the second.

Feinberg selects three principles which are designed to solve the aforementioned problem.[22] The first of these is the "standard of universality,"
under which the behavior in question must be offensive to a vast majority of
people, with "vast majority of people" meaning "any person chosen at
random, taking the nation as a whole, and not because the individual selected
belongs to some faction, clique, or party."[23] The second standard is the "standard of reasonable avoidability." If an action qualifies as offensive under the
first principle, there may still not be sufficient grounds to prevent it if individuals can avoid experiencing the offensive act without undue inconvenience. As Feinberg points out, thrusting pornographic pictures into people's
hands on a public street violates this second principle; but if those same pictures are contained in a book that one neither has to purchase nor open, the
second principle does not permit state intervention. It is important to note
that this second principle should be concerned with normal people: "No
respect should be shown for *abnormal susceptibilities*," Feinberg states.[24]
Finally, if a person is constrained by law for offensive behavior, such a
person "must be granted an allowable alternative outlet or mode of expres-

sion."[25] We shall assume that this third principle applies only if a behavior can be shown to be offensive by the first two principles. This assumption is justified because the third principle begins with the notion that someone's behavior was restricted for [being] offensive behavior.

If we apply these principles to public smoking, we see that the first principle does not justify state intervention with smoking. Since we can safely assume a) that smokers do not mind being around other smokers, b) that there is a significantly large population of smokers, and c) that many nonsmokers have no objection to being around smokers, there is no reason to suppose that any normal adult picked at random from the nation at large would object to smoking in public places.[26] Given this answer to the first principle, it would seem that there is little reason to call upon the second. Nevertheless, to avoid any biases and to account for the possibility that some random samples would not suggest anything definitive, let us consider the second principle.

The second principle would seem to support anti-smoking advocates. After all, it is not easy to avoid cigarette smoke once it is in the air. However, given our assumption that ambient tobacco smoke is not harmful, the burden of proof under this balancing of interests approach rests with the anti-smoker and not the smoker. The anti-smoker is the one calling upon intervention with an activity that is a common occurrence. Thus, the anti-smoker must show that there are no reasonable ways to avoid smokers. If this can be shown, then the state is obligated not to ban smoking in most places, but only to provide alternatives for anti-smokers. Further, providing alternatives for anti-smokers is not the same as providing alternatives for nonsmokers, since not all non-smokers can be presumed to be anti-smokers. It is only under a condition where most of society is filled with anti-smokers that public property may have to make special provisions for the smoker. Thus under current conditions smoking should be permitted in public places.

One may still wish to argue that although most nonsmokers may not mind that much being around smokers, they would, given a choice, prefer not to be around smokers. It should be remembered, however, that smokers are legitimate owners of public property also. Mere preference therefore is not sufficient grounds for restricting their liberty. I, for example, would *prefer* not to be around people with body odor or loud and ill-mannered individuals in public places, or children on field trips to the museum as I seek to contemplate the artifacts in silence. My preferences do not, however, justify a claim to exclude such individuals or groups, especially if I can find alternate times to visit a public place when the likelihood of confronting such individuals is lessened. The bias must always be in favor of freedom of action, and this bias places the burden of proof squarely on the shoulders of those who would restrict another's actions—not the other way around.

Some may claim that the foregoing argument gives the benefit of the doubt to the smoker when really it should be the other way around. After all, the "natural" state of things is for there not to be smoke in the air. Since the smoker initiates an action against others of which they may disapprove, this places the burden of proof on the smoker. Of course, erecting a building is not "natural" either; but this argument may be saying that individuals have a right to clean air and that the smoker is someone who pollutes that air. Hence a moment must be spent discussing this type of argument.

The Rights Approach

Pollution need not be harmful to qualify as pollution. If I dump my trash on your yard, I have "polluted" your yard even though the type of trash involved may only be papers so that no issue of a health hazard arises. Public smoking might be viewed in a similar vein. Even though the smoke from my cigarette may not harm you, it does enter your airspace and thus could be seen as a form of "pollution." Of course, I have the right to "pollute" my own airspace provided I do not infringe upon yours (and vice versa).

As some recent work has suggested, the rights approach remains unmoved in the face of pleas to consider the costs or inconveniences to polluters.[27] Polluters must refrain or be made to refrain from polluting regardless of costs or inconvenience. But the rights approach is not as simplistic as first appearances might suggest. The preceding sentences do not imply that all pollution must be halted. Rather, the implication is that pollution can occur on one's own property provided it does not spread to the property of others without their consent. What is needed, therefore, are unambiguous rights claims—not necessarily the cessation of all pollution. Since private property establishes relatively unambiguous rights claims, a solution to the pollution problem consistent with individual rights is to privatize unowned or public resources. Oddly enough, a certain "meeting of the minds" is now occurring on this issue between philosophers (who argue from a theory of individual rights) and economists (who tend to view matters in cost/benefit terms). A number of thinkers in both groups are calling for the privatization of public resources as a means of solving the pollution problem.[28]

It can safely be assumed that privatization is already established in places that are now private. Consequently, our section on smoking and private property shows that there is no significant pollution problem with respect to smoking and private business establishments. As we noted above, firms have the right to make whatever arrangements they wish regarding smoking. Although privatization will go a long way toward removing the ambiguities involved in solving conflicts of interest over public resources, we must assume that there will always be some public property, since the government will, at the very least, need buildings from which to operate.[29] What, then, can be said about an alleged form of nonharmful pollution in areas that must remain public?

Ostensibly the rights approach would not answer the foregoing question by an appeal to cost-benefit (or "risk-benefit") analysis or by an appeal to "balancing interests." This is because a theory of individual rights such as the one outlined in this chapter tends to see such approaches as subsuming the individual into some sort of social aggregate. The sphere of permissible behavior for the individual is thus defined in terms of some overall social good (for example, that the benefits to society exceed the costs), rather than the social good being a function of the protection of individual rights. Under the aggregating method an individual's interest will be respected only to the extent that a sufficient number of others have the same or similar interest. If only a few have the same interest, then that interest will tend to lose in the face of an overwhelming majority of contrary interests. But if there are sufficient numbers on both sides of an issue, some procedure for balancing the interests would have to be found.

The rights approach, on the other hand, places little or no emphasis on how many people line up on one side or the other of an issue. Hence, if an individual has a right to a certain resource, his freedom to use that resource cannot be restricted (assuming that his use does not violate any one else's rights) *even if society would be "worse off" by that individual's use of his property.* With respect to the public smoking issue, then, someone might argue that if ambient smoke violates the airspace of even one individual, the inconvenience to smokers is irrelevant to the legitimacy of requiring that they refrain from such activities. Certainly this argument places the burden of proof on the smoker's shoulders in a way that the argument of the preceding section may not have.

The rights argument works if the premise about violating another's airspace can be established. Keeping in mind, however, that the resource in question here is necessarily public and cannot be subject to privatization, both the smoker and nonsmoker can lay equally justified claims to exactly the same airspace. The nonsmoker has no more right to say that the air must be free of smoke than the smoker has the right to say it can be full of smoke, since both are owners of the same air.[30] Here we have a true and irreconcilable conflict of interest, for without clearly distinguishable rights claims (allowing exclusion and transferability), there is no basis to decide in favor of one interest to the exclusion of the other. The only way to handle such a case, therefore, is to employ the "second best" solution of trying to balance interests as discussed in the last section. In essence, public property is not amenable to analysis in terms of individual rights.[31] Given our assumption that the property in question is necessarily public and that no impending threat of serious harm exists, something like the balancing of interests approach discussed above is all that can be used in conflict of interest cases.

It is interesting to note that the foregoing argument has something significant to say about broader problems of pollution. Except perhaps in cases where an obvious, immediate and serious threat to health is present, those who wish to solve the pollution problem by turning over more and more resources to the state are in essence asking that more and more resources become subject to irreconcilable conflicts of interest. Recent trends in the politics of pollution seem to bear this point out.[32] In contrast, the establishment of private property rights in the marketplace provides a system whereby individuals can express their true values on how much pollution they wish to avoid or be exposed to. Of course, if public smoking were taken to be a form of pollution, it would be on a much more limited and minor scale than externalities such as acid rain or toxic wastes.

We can now conclude this section by noting that, since the balance of interests approach must be employed in situations of necessarily public property, no case can be made for banning smoking from public property at this time. Indeed, only under certain limited conditions — conditions where the anti-smoker must be given an outlet — can a case be made for segregating smokers and nonsmokers. Of course the particulars of this analysis may change if the vast majority of people become anti-smokers or if they become pro-smokers. If the pendulum swings significantly in either of these directions, the minority of advocates left on the other side will be losers. That is the inherent difficulty with public property, as we noted above.

CONCLUSION: MARKETS, MANNERS, AND PUBLIC POLICY

In this chapter we have tried to discuss the limits of governmental intervention in the smoking controversy. We have assumed that smoking is either harmful or offensive in order to clarify the role of government under a "worst case" scenario. Of course, if smoking is neither harmful nor offensive, especially to others, then the case for government involvement is weakened considerably. "Offense," however, is a rather subjective concept and it is doubtful that smoking (or any other adult pleasure) will ever be free from being offensive to somebody. Furthermore, however misguided the San Francisco ordinance may be, its even marginal political acceptability does indicate some significant disapproval of smoking by many people.[33] Significant disapproval does not, on the other hand, mandate a public policy on smoking, and herein lies one of the chief problems with current thinking about public policy.

Since the ultimate weapon of the state is the use of coercive physical force, one would expect a civilized society to call upon such a weapon only as a last resort and only when evidence of nonconsensual risk is beyond reasonable doubt. As we noted at the end of the second section, state action tends to be universal and inflexible and thus tends to ignore differences of desire and circumstance. A law such as the San Francisco ordinance may speak of accommodation, but everyone knows that the bottom line has more to do with obedience than accommodation. It is unfortunate, therefore, that instead of calling upon the state last, people today look to the state first to reform behavior which some find objectionable. The hysterical claims and missionary-like zeal exhibited by groups who wish to impose their vision of the good upon others is symptomatic of certain asocializing forces in our society.

The reasons for this disturbing trend could range from the theory that members of wealthy urbanized cultures have the proximity and leisure to concern themselves with the behavior of others, to the idea that vocal publicity is an effective means of tapping public resources for one's own ends. Speculation about such causes is best left to sociologists and economists, but there is one consideration we can offer in this context—the widespread ignorance of the meaning of political liberty and its practical correlate, the free market. Despite the rhetoric about competition, we need to understand that the marketplace is an instrument of accommodation and socialization and not, as its critics charge, a vehicle for asocialization. On the other hand, state power that extends beyond what is necessary for individuals to enjoy peace and security is destructive of social life.

Because a free market is defined by freedom of exchange, the benefits of exchange can only be enjoyed if individuals find mutually agreeable terms according to which they make their exchanges. Thus the incentives of the marketplace are all towards accommodation. Joseph Schumpeter noted long ago that one of the reasons it would be unlikely for businessmen to lead the fight against the erosion of economic liberties is that such people develop habits of accommodation instead of conflict. Businessmen cannot afford to alienate potential customers, and although this may not generate the kinds of feelings one finds in a family, it will tend to diminish dogmatic and self-righteous attitudes.

If, on the other hand, the value of political liberty is unappreciated, the social benefits of market processes will be ignored or rejected. Problems will then become politicized, creating incentives opposite to the ones just mentioned. Apart from the inherent moral problems that arise from a disrespect of liberty, reliance upon state-imposed solutions will tend to generate rather than alleviate social alienation. If social winners and losers are defined by the extent to which their policies can be imposed upon others through state action, it is clear that some gain *at the expense of others,* rather than by agreement with others. The public smoking controversy is a good case in point. Both smokers and nonsmokers feel victimized by whatever public policy is adopted. If no policy against smoking in public is issued by the state, nonsmokers believe that they are not being protected. If restrictive smoking policies are adopted, smokers believe that they are being unfairly abused. It seldom occurs to either side that maybe the public smoking question is not an issue that should be conceived in public policy terms at all.

Under the assumption that the case for the negative health effects of ambient tobacco smoke is negligible or nonexistent, the market and good manners are more than adequate to solve any problems between smokers and nonsmokers. Businesses can try various smoking policies to meet the needs of their customers, clients, and employees. These policies will tend to reflect the desires of those customers, clients, and employees without generalizing to the circumstances of other businesses. For example, one restaurant may find that most of its customers are nonsmokers and therefore adopt more restrictive smoking rules than another restaurant whose customers are mostly smokers. Why, in all fairness and justice, should the policies of one of the businesses have to apply to another? Similarly, private individuals in their own personal relations will function in a market-like manner as well. The value a person places on being around smokers or nonsmokers will tend to influence the choices that person makes in social contexts.

Leaving the issue to the marketplace might seem like a submission to pro-smoking forces. A little reflection, however, will indicate that there is nothing in the preceding suggestion that formally supports either smoking or nonsmoking forces. That would depend on social attitudes at any given moment. It is interesting to note that despite the reputation the tobacco industry has for being all-powerful, it has not been that effective in reversing the trend towards negative attitudes about smoking, even among many smokers. And as one might expect, the market is beginning to reflect these attitudes without the help of the state.

Finally, a word must be said in defense of good manners. However well the market works, we often find ourselves in situations where the smoking preferences of those around us are unknown or different from our own. In general, good manners suggest that we consider the interests of others and defer our own desires to theirs if the demands for doing so are not too excessive. It seems quite rude for a smoker to light up in a room full of nonsmokers who have made their distaste of smoking known. By the same token, it is excessively boorish for a nonsmoker to hysterically demand that a room full of smokers put out their cigarettes or to lecture them on the "evils" of smoking. Both parties can excuse themselves periodically or suffer some inconvenience for a time. Certainly the state cannot serve as a surrogate for good manners, since rules of etiquette are useful in precisely those cases which the general perspective of the state can never anticipate or comprehend.

Perhaps the general point of this chapter, then, is that the habit of calling upon the state to relieve any inconvenience is more dangerous than current presumptions about the habit of smoking itself. To ask public authorities to take responsibility for what can and should be the responsibility of individuals is always a threat to liberty. Thus although the factual assertions about the smoking controversy may dominate public discussion, deeper issues of political and social philosophy may lie beneath those more visible disputes.

And in the end, the deeper issues may be more significant for public policy than the factual assertions will ever be.

NOTES

1. See Saul K. Padover, *Jefferson* (New York: Mentor Books, 1952), p. 35.

2. The moral point of view per se is broader than the rights issue, however. It should also be mentioned that even if one does not adopt a natural rights perspective, the argument of the following pages holds, because it depends on a commitment to the central value of liberty which some may arrive at by means other than a natural rights approach. However, it is my view that the natural rights approach best secures the central value of liberty. Moreover, this is still the language of much political debate on moral and political values.

3. Joel Feinberg, "Legal Paternalism," in *Rights, Justice, and the Bounds of Liberty* (Princeton: Princeton University Press, 1980), p. 129.

4. Ibid., p. 121.

5. Ibid.

6. Someone might wish to argue that the allegedly "addictive" character of smoking makes the action substantially nonvoluntary. The thesis that smoking is addictive, however, is thoroughly discredited by the large and ever growing number of people who quit smoking. Smoking is at most a habit (perhaps a strong one). But habits are not "substantially nonvoluntary" actions. Indeed, one of the first great moralists—Aristotle—claimed that the whole purpose of morality was to "habituate oneself to virtue." Thus "habit" and "voluntariness" are not in conflict. All the term "habit" implies is a degree of difficulty in altering behavior.

7. J. Roger Lee, "Choice and Harms," in T. Machan and M. B. Johnson, eds., *Rights and Regulation* (Cambridge, Mass.: Ballinger, 1983), pp. 157–73.

8. Technically defined by Lee as: "if a person truly and knowingly enters into situation A, which has the rational-expectation framework (p,q,r,s, not-t), then if that person objects to the consequence of an event described by 'p', that person owes an explanation why p is objectionable and further, why, knowing that p would eventuate, he/she entered into situation A. The fact that he/she entered into situation A is strong evidence that the occurrence of p does not violate his/her rights. Similarly, if the rational-expectation framework for situation A clearly excludes t, then if t occurs when a person B enters into A and if t was a consequence of an act of a second person C toward B in situation A, then there is evidence that C has violated B's rights" (p. 169).

9. See Tibor R. Machan, *Human Rights and Human Liberties* (Chicago: Nelson Hall, 1975).

10. Bernard H. Siegan, *Economic Liberties and the Constitution* (Chicago: University of Chicago Press, 1980), p. 5 and ch. 2.

11. Ibid., ch. 1ff.

12. See Tibor Machan, "Should Business Be Regulated?" in T. Regan, ed., *Just Business: New Introductory Essays in Business Ethics* (New York: Random House, 1984), pp. 202–234.

13. Of course, some nonsmokers may still find being around smokers "offensive." But if the government has no business dictating acceptable risk, it surely has no business dictating acceptable offenses.

14. This parenthetical remark may seem too facile for some. It must be remembered, however, that the smoking case is not comparable to a situation where a substance previously thought to be harmless has suddenly been discovered to be toxic. In such emergency situations the state might intervene temporarily to insure that people understand the risks involved.

Claims against smoking (even exposure to ambient smoke), on the other hand, have been around for a long time. Most nonsmokers have grown up around parents or peers who smoke. Continued association by nonsmokers with smokers suggests a degree of skepticism about the hyperbolic claims made against exposure to ambient smoke. Thus it is unlikely that employment patterns would change significantly even if some minor long term risks could in fact be established. In any case, if a thoroughly substantiated risk were discovered, employers could give current employees a reasonable period of time to decide whether they wish to accept the firm's smoking policy.

15. Marshall Kilduff, "How Smoking Law Will Affect Firms and S.F. Workers," *San Francisco Chronicle,* 10 November 1983.

16. Section 1004 of the Smoking Pollution Control Ordinance.

17. J. White and H. Froeb, "Small-Airways Dysfunction in Nonsmokers Chronically Exposed to Tobacco Smoke," *New England Journal of Medicine,* 1980 (302): 720–23.

18. A summary of such criticisms is contained in the *Congressional Record,* 16 December 1982, submitted by The Honorable L. H. Fountain.

19. Statement by Michael D. Lebowitz to Public Health Commission, County of Los Angeles.

20. Kilduff, "Smoking Law."

21. Joel Feinberg, "Harmless Immoralities," in *Rights, Justice, and the Bounds of Liberty* (Princeton: Princeton University Press, 1980), pp. 69–95.

22. Ibid., pp. 88–92.

23. Ibid., p. 88.

24. Ibid., p. 90.

25. Ibid., p. 91.

26. Remember, that those who have a vested interest in seeing smoking increased or banned are excluded from Feinberg's random selection.

27. Tibor Machan, "Pollution and Political Theory," in Tom Regan, ed., *Earthbound: New Introductory Essays in Environmental Ethics* (New York: Random House, 1984), pp. 74–106.

28. For a good discussion of this point and the whole pollution question, see Peter H. Aranson, "Pollution Control: The Case for Competition," in *Instead of Regulation* (Lexington, Mass.: D.C. Heath and Company, 1982), pp. 339–393.

29. Nevertheless, in a rightly ordered society, the amount of public property would be negligible. Even streets and roads need not be public. For example, see Walter Block, "A Free Market in Roads," in *The Libertarian Reader* (Totowa, N.J.: Rowman and Littlefield, 1982), pp. 164–83.

30. It might be argued that the nonsmoker has a clear right to his lungs and what goes into them even if he does not have the same right with respect to the air. But of course the smoker has the same right. And since it is the same air that must be used to exercise either right, the conflict of interest remains.

31. Even in the case of harm, it is not individual rights that justifies state action, but rather that balancing interests and excluding harm cannot be reconciled, so excluding harm is given priority.

32. See B. Peter Pashigian, "The Political Economy of the Clean Air Act: Regional Self-Interest in Environmental Legislation," *Center for the Study of American Business,* Formal Publication Number 51, October 1982.

33. The point is not limited to the San Francisco area. California has had statewide referendums on smoking similar to the San Francisco ordinance. Although these were defeated, opponents of smoking did not fail to generate some significant support.

17

Tobacco and Public Policy: A Constitutionalist Perspective

Robert D. Tollison and Richard E. Wagner

In the traditional, pre-public-choice approach to public policy, the creation of public policy was seen as exogenous to the economic process. Within this exogenous perspective, there was no scope for a theory of economic policy or political choice as such. The analytical task was not to explain the central characteristics of the policy choices that emerge from a political process, but rather to advise the policymaker on the characteristics of desirable policy measures. To this day, the central core of what is called welfare economics has consisted of specifying the characteristics of "good" policy measures. Whoever is the creator of public policy stands outside the economic process, and the task for the economic analyst is to suggest ways for the policymaker to improve the operation of the economic process. Presumably, the more benevolent or public-spirited the policymaker, the more fully the policy measures actually enacted will advance the economic welfare of the nation.

But once the production of public policy is itself treated as an ordinary economic activity, as the public choice approach treats it and as the Founding Fathers did, public policy becomes endogenous to the economic process, and the characteristics of public policy measures become objects of explanation. In this case, what primarily governs those characteristics are the incentives that politicians face. For a given set of incentives, there will tend to be a particular set of policy measures that will represent a political equilibrium. This statement is equivalent to the proposition that for a given set of preferences, resource availabilities, technologies, and property rights, there will exist an

Originally published in *Smoking and the State: Social Costs, Rent Seeking, and Public Policy* (Lexington, Mass.: Lexington Books, 1988). Reprinted by permission of University Press of America.

economic equilibrium. In the familiar economic case, we say that for changes in the structure of production to take place, there must be preceding changes in such things as preferences, resource availabilities, technologies, and property rights. But in similar fashion, we can say that changes in the characteristic outcomes of the political process require changes in the same things, but in this case, "property rights" refer to the whole set of institutional rules constraining the operation of political processes.

A constitution, then, is a set of social institutions or rules within which individuals operate and interact with one another. All societies must have some sort of constitution under which social interaction is regulated and disputes between individuals with competing ends are resolved. A society without a constitution is not really a society at all; it is a jumble of individuals at best and a mob at worst. The social constitution is analogous to the rules of the game in sports. Brennan and Buchanan (1980) developed this analogy:

> A game is described by its rules—its constitution. These rules establish the framework within which the playing of the game proceeds; they set boundaries on what activities are legitimate, as well as describing the objects of the game and how to determine who wins. It is clear intuitively that the choice among alternative strategies that a player might make in the course of a game is categorically quite distinct from his prior choice among alternative sets of rules. A tennis player after hitting a particular shot may reasonably wish that the net was lower, yet prior to the game he may have agreed to a set of rules in which the height of the net was specified. (p. 3)

It is important to emphasize that all social orders are ultimately based on some sort of constitution. Hence, the social constitution is not necessarily related to the document by that name that often serves as the legal basis for government; the constitution of society in America may be thought to include, but is not the same as, the U.S. Constitution. The social constitution refers to all of the "rules of the game" that affect social interaction and regulate disputes among individuals—not just laws, but also all other relevant social conventions that constrain individual behavior.

A constitutionalist perspective implies that since the production of public policy conforms to an economic logic, "improvement" in the type of policy measures produced is much more a matter of changing the incentives constraining political processes than it is a matter of giving policymakers better advice. For this reason, a constitutionalist perspective focuses on an analysis of social interaction that explicitly takes into account the constitutional constraints affecting social behavior and pays particular attention to the effects resulting from changes in these constraints over time. Constitutions are not the result of divine intervention, nor are they laid upon us by exogenous but benevolent despots. Rather, they arise from interactions among utility-maximizing individuals pursuing their self-interest, each of whom must accommodate to the fact of others' similar actions. Constitutions arise from the purposive action of rational, self-interested individuals, not from selfless lawgivers. For this reason, constitutions may change over time in ways that serve the interests of restricted subsets of society at the expense of the common interest, as represented by the substitution of rules and policies that emphasize the transfer of wealth for rules and policies that emphasize the creation of wealth.

PRINCIPLES OF CONSTITUTIONAL POLITICAL ECONOMY

Constitutions form the basis for all social activity. Therefore, all economic production is ultimately a function of the constitutional order in place in a given society. Economists have traditionally maintained that production, in order to take place, requires some combination of three basic inputs: land (that is, all natural resources), labor, and capital (the result itself of a combination of land and labor over time). In fact, however, the constitution is another basic and vital "factor of production." The extent to which economic activity can be conducted efficiently is limited by the nature of the constitution. Regardless of the stock of labor and natural resources available within a country, the degree of freedom and economic opportunity available to its citizens and the rates of economic growth and development it is capable of achieving depend upon the constitutional constraints in place, for these govern the relative incentives of wealth-creating and wealth-transferring activities. There are many examples of unfree and undeveloped countries that have anemic economies but are nevertheless endowed with abundant labor, land, and natural resources (for example, the [former] Soviet Union or the People's Republic of China), as well as of free, rapidly developing countries that have robust and energetic economies but meager endowments of natural resources and land (for example, Japan and Hong Kong). The difference in economic performance arises, to an important extent, because countries such as Japan have social constitutions that encourage and nurture freedom and economic opportunity for individual consumers and producers, whereas countries such as the People's Republic of China have constitutions that stifle and repress freedom and economic activity.

As previously noted, however, constitutions do not result from divine intervention. The same factor that dominates the determination of outcomes in private markets—the driving force of rational self-interest—is also the primary factor determining outcomes in constitutional "markets." Laws, conventions, and all other forms of social regulation are the outcome of the competition between various individuals, each seeking to maximize his or her own utility.

However, there is a vital difference between two kinds of constitutional competition. This difference reflects the fact that the social constitution can be separated into two fundamentally different parts. The first part is composed of those rules that are the result of a voluntary agreement between all participants; they are, in a strict sense, analogous to rules in sports. Everyone who plays baseball, for example, has agreed, of his or her own volition, to obey a certain set of rules of that game. Otherwise, they would not agree to play in the first place. The "voluntary" rules are the result of spontaneous agreement among all participants and represent a quite literal "social contract." As with ordinary contracts in private markets, no coercion is involved in securing agreement. Everyone involved agrees to abide by the rules in question because, in each individual case, they perceive themselves to be better off by so doing. Most customs, social conventions, and informal rules of social interaction—such as manners—are examples of the "sportslike" portion of the social constitution.

The other part of the constitution is determined and enforced through political processes. This includes laws, government regulations, and the actual, written constitution of the government in question. Unlike the "sportslike" portion of the constitution, this portion is not formulated as the result of completely voluntary agreement among all participants across free markets. Rather, it is the result of decisions made in the political sector and imposed on society whether all individuals agree or not. This portion of the constitution is based on coercion.

Despite this major distinction, the two portions of the constitution of a society are not, by their nature, fundamentally incompatible. The use of some coercion may be necessary in order to provide for the efficient operation— and even the existence—of a free society. For example, in the case of certain public goods, such as national defense, voluntary market exchange may not provide optimal quantities. A modification of the social constitution in such a way as to allow for a government to provide such necessary goods may represent an efficient solution. The protection of property rights by means of the formulation and enforcement of criminal law may be another similar example of a necessary governmental function requiring modifications to the social constitution in order to allow a certain and precisely delimited amount of coercion by government. Such forms of "coercive constitutionalism" may actually *increase* the level of individual liberty in society by protecting and extending the functioning of the free marketplace. Such coercive, political portions of the social constitution may form a necessary bulwark for a free market and a free society by serving to protect the rights of individuals from force and fraud.

However, there is another, darker side to the political constitution. What Caesar gives, Caesar can also take away. Because modifications to the political portion of the social constitution do not require the consent of all participants in the social order, modifications can occur that do not improve the welfare of all individuals. This is not the case with voluntary, "sportslike" constitutional rules: if changes in the rules did not benefit all participants, they would not voluntarily agree to those changes. But for changes in the political constitution, voluntary agreement on the part of all participants is irrelevant. Even if a large minority vigorously object to a given rule (whether statute, regulation, or other form), their objections are irrelevant so long as the measure in question has sufficient political support—in a democracy, a majority of the voters; in a nondemocracy, like most countries in the world today, perhaps much less—to ensure its passage. Those who object will simply be coerced into acceptance.

Hence, the major difference between the two types of constitutional change is obvious. Changes in the voluntary, spontaneous, "sportslike" constitution must, by definition, benefit all participants; otherwise, they would refuse to agree to the changes. By contrast, changes in the political portion of the constitution *do not* necessarily benefit all participants. They may benefit only the relatively small subset of society that is sufficient to ensure enactment of the changes, because the rest will be forced to accept them at the point of a gun. In both constitutional realms, individual actors are assumed to be rational and self-interested and to be seeking to maximize their own utility within a process in which they are competing with other individuals with similar motivations. The same economic principles describe the operation of competition in the market for rules with equal validity. The only important difference is that in the first realm, the competition is limited to the pursuit of voluntary agreement by means of persuading others; in the latter, competition extends to the use of force to provide the means to coerce compliance.

THE SELF-OWNERSHIP FOUNDATIONS OF A DEMOCRATIC POLITY

There is a logical dichotomy at the base of all discussions of political obligation that is very simple but that can be ignored only at our peril. It is an economic principle that all resources that have value are owned by someone. Extending this simple maxim to individuals provides the basis for this dichotomy: either individuals own themselves or someone else owns them.

The United States was founded on the premise—clearly expressed in both the Declaration of Independence and the Constitution—that each individual in society owns himself. This implies that individuals are free to pursue their own unique goals and, at the same time, that they are responsible for the consequences of their own actions. One of the most important of these responsibilities is respecting the equal freedom of other individuals to pursue their own ends similarly.

Other nations in the world today are founded on a different premise: that individuals do not own themselves but are, in effect, owned by the state. The state makes all important decisions regarding economic and social affairs, and individuals have no rights at all. Individuals have only the privileges that those who control the state deign to grant them, for as long as those in control find convenient.

Unfortunately, in the real world, the line of demarcation between these two extremes can become blurred. This is particularly the case in free societies with constitutions that have established democratic decision-making structures. There is a necessary tension between individual liberty and democracy that can tend to dilute the power of self-ownership of free individuals if it is not carefully controlled.

A free society does not necessarily require democratic governmental structures, but such structures are probably the best available for ensuring that the power of government is effectively constrained by the preferences of citizens. But democracy is like a fire. Carefully constrained and limited, it can be a valuable tool for accomplishing productive ends, as in clearing farmland of useless brush or in controlling floods. When it is not carefully constrained and limited, however, it can be immensely destructive of life, limb, and property.

Democracy only necessarily protects the freedom and property of the *majority*; without express protection, minority interests will be unprotected from the depredations of the majority. But even worse, the majority that is protected today may be a different group of people from that protected yesterday or that protected next week. In other words, majorities are not likely to be stable over time. This week, A and B may gang up on C and steal him blind; next week, B and C might do the same to A; and on and on. In the absence of effective constitutional constraints on the actions of government—bounds that clearly establish which uses of political coercion are legitimate and acceptable and which are illegitimate and unacceptable—democracy can be transformed from a useful social decision-making device to a kind of majoritarian tyranny based on the unrestrained hunt for plunder of vulnerable minority interests.

There is sometimes a tendency to use the term *democracy* as a synonym for *free society*. This is dangerously misleading. Even though free societies commonly find some variant of democratic decision making the most efficient means for controlling government, democracy in the absence of effective limits is just another form of tyranny.

The Founding Fathers worked long and hard on the thorny problem of how to establish a democratic form of government that would be effectively restrained from running roughshod over the rights of minorities (a term, as noted earlier, that refers to those unfortunate enough to be outside the majority coalition at the time in question). The U.S. Constitution was designed as a strong leash on a form of government that the Founding Fathers envisaged as a powerful, vicious dog—dangerous if allowed to roam free, but potentially an effective protector of the rights and property of the individuals who constitute the society.

CONSIDERATIONS FROM THE ECONOMIC THEORY OF LEGISLATION

. . . The modern economic theory of legislation has as its basis the fact that competition for legislation and regulation is affected by the same forces that affect competition across ordinary markets for other goods and services, and that the outcomes of political competition are as much the outcomes of market processes as those that flow from the ordinary, private marketplace. The same rational, self-interested, utility-maximizing individuals inhabit both worlds. One implication of this analysis is that legislative outcomes normally tend to be the result of intense competition among competing interest groups that expect either to gain or to lose tangible and significant amounts of income from the passage (or nonpassage) of a law or regulation. In the real world, legislatures are unlikely to pass a law for the simple and altruistic reason that they expect that it will somehow make "society" better off. Legislatures typically act as a kind of brokerage firm, supplying wealth transfers to competing interest groups, thereby making some people in society better off at the expense of others.

It should be noted that this process of rent-seeking competition among interest groups is perfectly consistent with democracy. In one way or another, interest groups must purchase the votes of a majority in order to have the measures that benefit themselves passed. Democracy, by itself, places little constraint on the process of rent-seeking competition in the political sector, for it means only that policy measures must receive majority approval in a legislative assembly. However, it is fully possible for measures that would be rejected overwhelmingly in a referendum or plebiscite to receive majority approval in a legislature.

All political processes will necessarily be vulnerable to increasing control by rent-seeking interest groups unless there are effective constraints on what government coercion can be used to do and on what it is prohibited from doing. Otherwise, activity by government that reduces the welfare of society at large and tramples on the rights and liberties of individuals is not only possible but probable, if such activity would tend to benefit some interest group.

The political portion of the social constitution in general, not just laws passed by legislatures, will be determined in such an environment. Under ordinary circumstances, we should expect that changes are advocated in the political constitution of society primarily by groups that are seeking rents that they expect to flow to themselves as a result. Constitutions are a battlefield on which rent-seeking interest groups compete for coercive wealth transfers that they expect to result from the operation of the political process.

This has two major implications in terms of the constitution of society discussed here. First, any tendency toward shifting matters from the voluntary, "sportslike" constitutional arena to the political and coercive portion of the constitution will necessarily involve subjecting those matters to rent-seeking competition by interest groups that are striving for wealth transfers. Fantasies of disinterested, public-spirited politicians and regulators with a single-minded determination to enhance the welfare of society by enacting enlightened legislation and regulation disintegrate after exposure to the real world. If government's power to intervene in society is kept tightly limited, this rent-seeking competition will be held in tight check as well. But in the absence of such constitutional limits on government, rent-seeking interest groups will almost inevitably come to dominate the process in their pursuit of wealth transfers. Second, although there is a natural tendency for matters left in the former realm to be resolved in a manner consistent with the rights and preferences of all, there is no such tendency in the latter. The former is the world of peaceful persuasion and cooperative competition; the latter is that of coercion and conflict.

IMPLICATIONS FOR PUBLIC POLICY TOWARD TOBACCO

The implications of the constitutionalist perspective on social decision making for public policy with respect to tobacco products should also be obvious. . . . There is no valid scientific basis for claiming that smokers impose costs on nonsmokers. . . . With respect to environmental tobacco smoke, there is no valid scientific basis for asserting that smokers impose uncompensated costs on nonsmokers. . . . Whatever harm smokers impose upon themselves by smoking is also borne economically by those smokers, not by nonsmokers.

Suppose that, sometime in the future, evidence becomes available that indicates that smoking seriously harms the health of both the smoker and those exposed to tobacco smoke in the environment. Would this fact make any difference in terms of restrictions by government on tobacco consumption by adults? Unless one is willing to reject the basis of the free society of self-owning and self-responsible individuals, it should not. Adults who smoke do so of their own free will and bear, voluntarily, whatever risks are associated with that activity. A case could always be made that smokers who do not understand the risks should be protected by government, because government possesses better information. However, such claims about knowledge seem far-fetched in the case of tobacco products. For twenty years, the federal government has engaged in a widely publicized, concerted campaign to convince the general public that smoking is dangerous. If there is any misinformation on the part of smokers, it is likely to be a substantially *exaggerated* idea of the riskiness of smoking. . . . The same may be true for nonsmokers, many of whom may be nonsmokers only because the same informational bias leads them to hold exaggerated perceptions of the risks associated with smoking.

The fact remains that tobacco consumers smoke because the value they place on the benefits they receive from smoking exceeds the cost of smoking to them, including their perceived risk of health consequences. Similarly, nonsmokers who choose to expose themselves to ETS for extended periods do so because the benefits they receive from relationships with smokers exceed the costs of those relationships. To pretend that it is proper and necessary, in the case of either smokers or nonsmokers, for government to protect the public from cigarettes is tantamount to assuming that normal adults are incapable of making rational and coherent decisions regarding the conduct of their own lives. Even if smoking could be proved to generate significantly increased health risks either for smokers or for nonsmokers through ETS, mandatory restrictions on the behavior of smokers, ostensibly based on grounds of "protecting the public health," would imply that adult individuals in general were somehow unable to assess risks rationally and to make responsible decisions.

Of course, . . . political events do not just fall from the sky. Much antismoking rhetoric is likely to be rhetorical window-dressing, instrumental in the pursuit of rents through politics. Nonsmokers can be expected to gain higher wages as the result of clean indoor air acts at the expense of smokers, as the mandatory regulations act as a barrier to entry that generates monopoly rents. Politicians who view tax revenue as the raw material for wealth transfers that they can supply to favored interest groups will gain from the proceeds from tobacco taxes ostensibly enacted to improve the public health. Large restaurants may favor mandatory segregation of smokers and nonsmokers in order to impose relatively high costs on small restaurants, thereby reducing the competition they face. But whatever the real motivation behind the movement to restrict the consumption of tobacco products, it represents a fundamental rejection of the principles of individual liberty upon which a free society is ultimately founded.

IMPLICATIONS FOR PUBLIC POLICY MORE BROADLY CONSIDERED

If adults cannot be expected to make rational and responsible decisions about tobacco products without coercive government supervision, how can they be expected to make rational decisions concerning nutrition, child rearing, job selection, gardening, or house painting, among the myriad decisions they must make? Indeed, how can democracy be trusted to work well if people are such poor judges of their own self-interest? If government has the power to protect people from making choices that involve relatively high risks, why stop at tobacco consumption? What about skiing, mountain climbing, hang gliding, drinking alcohol, and working long hours? Are the risks "too high"? By whose standard? Some people are so risk-averse that they rarely venture out of their own homes.

As important as questions are involving the liberty of tobacco consumers to act on their free choice and mind their own business, there is another, much more important aspect to the tobacco question that extends far beyond cigarettes. Put simply, if government is going to be allowed to enact coercive measures that arbitrarily restrict the liberties and trample the rights of smokers, where will employment of this restrictive power end?

If government is not expressly prohibited from interfering with the free expression of voluntary choice by peaceful adults in the case of tobacco, what is to restrain the government from similarly imposing restrictions on political expression or religious practice? What is to prevent a conservative government from making liberal speech illegal, or vice versa? Sadly, the First Amendment to the Constitution may not be a sufficient answer. The First Amendment did not prevent the exclusion of tobacco advertising from television. The point is not that amendments to the written Constitution are necessarily without effect—surely, they can be vitally important—but rather than the one-time passage of such an amendment, no matter how stringent it sounds, may not be enough. If the general public is unwilling to oppose the tendency of the political sector, driven by the demands of rent-seeking interest groups, to expand beyond its necessary and proper domain, even a seemingly strong, written constitutional constraint enacted sometime in the past may prove ineffective.

If a broad social consensus exists that acquiesces to the legitimacy of governmental intrusions into the liberties and rights of individuals, further intrusions are much more likely. The liberty of all depends on drawing a line beyond which government may not cross. That line must represent the rejection by the general public of the principle of unlimited government intervention into the peaceful domain of social life. Tobacco regulation is only one example. Every time governmental power extends beyond the realm of the simple protection of individuals against force and fraud, the very existence of the free and competitive social order is increasingly threatened. Tobacco regulation may not itself constitute Pandora's box, but to the extent that the liberties of tobacco consumers are increasingly whittled away, the Pandora's box of statism is cracked open a little bit more.

REFERENCES

Atkinson, Anthony B., and Joy L. Townsend. (1977). "Economic Aspects of Reduced Smoking." *Lancet* 3: 492–95.

Blank, R. M., and A. S. Blinder. (1986). "Macroeconomics, Income Distribution, and Poverty." In *Fighting Poverty: What Works and What Doesn't,* eds. H. Danziger and D. H. Weinberg, pp. 180–208. Cambridge, Mass.: Harvard University Press.

Boadway, Robin W. (1979). *Public Sector Economics.* Cambridge, Mass.: Winthrop.

Brennan, H. Geoffrey, and James M. Buchanan. (1980). *The Power to Tax.* Cambridge: Cambridge University Press.

Buchanan, James M. (1963). "The Economics of Earmarked Taxes." *Journal of Political Economy* 71 (October): 457–69.

———. (1969). *Cost and Choice.* Chicago: Markham.

———. (1986). "Politics and Meddlesome Preferences." In *Smoking and Society: Toward a More Balanced Assessment,* ed. Robert D. Tollison, pp. 335–42. Lexington, Mass.: Lexington Books.

Buchanan, James M., and Gordon Tullock. (1962). *The Calculus of Consent.* Ann Arbor: University of Michigan Press.

Coase, R. H. (1960). "The Problem of Social Cost." *Journal of Law and Economics* 3 (October): 1–44.

Committee on Ways and Means. (1986). *Hearings on User Fees, Revenue Proposals Contained in President Reagan's 1986 Budget, and Other Revenue Measures.* Washington, D.C.: U.S. Government Printing Office.

Cowell, M. J., and B. L. Hirst. (1980). "Mortality Differences between Smokers and Nonsmokers." *Transactions of the Society of Actuaries* 32: 185–261.

Dahl, Tor, Barbara Gunderson, and Kathleen Kuehnast. (1984). "The Influence of Health Improvement Programs on White Collar Productivity." Working paper, University of Minnesota, Minneapolis.

Danziger, S. H., and P. Gottschalk. (1985). "The Impact of Budget Cuts and Economic Conditions on Poverty." *Journal of Policy Analysis and Management* 5: 587–93.

Den Uyl, Douglas J. (1986). "Smoking, Human Rights, and Civil Liberties." In *Smoking and Society: Toward a More Balanced Assessment,* ed. Robert D. Tollison, pp. 189–216. Lexington, Mass.: Lexington Books.

Doll, Richard, and Richard Peto. (1981). "The Causes of Cancer: Quantitative Estimates of Avoidable Risks of Cancer in the United States Today." *Journal of the National Cancer Institute* 66 (June): 1193–1308.

Efron, Edith. (1984). *The Apocalyptics: Cancer and the Big Lie.* New York: Simon and Schuster.

Egger, Garry. (1978). "Increasing Health Costs from Smoking." Health Commission of New South Wales, Australia, May.

Epstein, Richard A. (1985). *Taxings: Private Property and the Power of Eminent Domain.* Cambridge: Harvard University Press.

Ferrara, Peter J. (1980). *Social Security: The Inherent Contradiction.* Washington, D.C.: Cato Institute.

Hammond, E. C. (1966). "Smoking in Relation to the Death Rates of One Million Men and Women." In *Epidemiological Study of Cancer and Other Chronic Diseases,* National Cancer Institute Monograph No. 19, pp. 127–204. Washington, D.C.: U.S. Government Printing Office.

Holcomb, Harry S., III, and J. Wister Meigs. (1972). "Medical Absenteeism among Cigarette, Cigar, and Pipe Smokers." *Archives of Environmental Health* 25 (October): 295–300.

Kristein, Marvin M. (1977). "Economic Issues in Prevention." *Preventive Medicine* 6: 252–64.

Lee, Dwight R., and Robert D. Tollison. (1985). "Towards a True Measure of Excess Burden." Working paper, Center for Study of Public Choice, Fairfax, Va.

Leu, Robert E. (1984). "Anti-Smoking Publicity, Taxation, and the Demand for Cigarettes." *Journal of Health Economics* 3: 101–16.

Leu, Robert E., and Thomas Schaub. (1983). "Does Smoking Increase Medical Care Expenditure?" *Social Science and Medicine* 17: 1907–14.

Lewit, E. M., and D. Coate. (1982). "The Potential for Using Excise Taxes to Reduce Smoking." *Journal of Health Economics* 1: 121–45.

Luce, Bryan R., and Stuart O. Schweitzer. (1977). "The Economic Costs of Smoking-Induced Illness." National Institute of Drug Abuse Research Monograph Series, No. 7, Department of Health, Education, and Welfare, December.

———. (1978). "Smoking and Alcohol Abuse: A Comparison of Their Economic Consequences." *New England Journal of Medicine* 9 (March): 569–71.

McCormick, Robert E., and Robert D. Tollison. (1981). *Politicians, Legislation, and the Economy.* Boston: Martinus Nijhoff.

McMahon, Walter W., and Case M. Sprenkle. (1970). "A Theory of Earmarking." *National Tax Journal* 23 (September): 255–61.

Minarik, Joseph J. (1985). *Making Tax Choices.* Washington, D.C.: Urban Institute Press.

Musgrave, Richard A. (1959). *The Theory of Public Finance.* New York: McGraw-Hill.

National Research Council, Committee on Passive Smoking, Board on Environmental Studies and Toxicology. (1986). *Environmental Tobacco Smoke: Measuring Exposures and Assessing Health Effects.* Washington, D.C.: National Academy Press.

Niskanen, William A., Jr. (1971). *Bureaucracy and Representative Government.* Chicago: Aldine-Atherton.

Office of Management and Budget. (1984). *Budget of the United States Government, Fiscal 1985.* Washington, D.C.: U.S. Government Printing Office.

Office of Technology Assessment Staff Memorandum. (1985). *Smoking-Related Deaths and Financial Costs.* Washington, D.C.: Office of Technology Assessment.

Oster, Gerry, Graham A. Colditz, and Nancy L. Kelly. (1984). *The Economic Costs of Smoking and Benefits of Quitting.* Lexington, Mass.: Lexington Books.

Pechman, Joseph A. (1985). *Who Pays the Taxes?* Washington, D.C.: Brookings Institution.

Peltzman, Sam. (1984). "Constituent Interest and Congressional Voting." *Journal of Law and Economics* 27 (April): 181–210.

Peston, M. H. (1971). "Economics and Cigarette Smoking." *The Second World Conference on Smoking and Health*: Proceedings of a Conference Organized by the Health Education Council, ed. R. Richardson. Imperial College of London: London, England.

Ravenholt, R. T. (1984). "Addiction Mortality in the United States, 1980: Tobacco, Alcohol, and Other Substances." *Population and Development Review* 10 (December): 697–724.

Robertson, A. Haeworth. (1981). *The Coming Revolution in Social Security.* Reston, Va.: Reston.

Seltzer, Carl C. (1980). "Smoking and Coronary Heart Disease: What Are We to Believe?" *American Heart Journal* 100 (September): 275–80.

Shillington, E. Richard. (1977). *Selected Economic Consequences of Cigarette Smoking.* Ottawa, Canada: National Ministry of Health and Welfare.

Shughart, William F., II, and James M. Savarese. (1986). "The Incidence of Taxes on Tobacco." In *Smoking and Society: Toward a More Balanced Assessment,* ed. Robert D. Tollison, pp. 285–307. Lexington, Mass.: Lexington Books.

Shughart, William F., II, and Robert D. Tollison. (1986). "Smokers versus Nonsmokers." In *Smoking and Society: Toward a More Balanced Assessment,* ed. Robert D. Tollison, pp. 217–24. Lexington, Mass.: Lexington Books.

Solmon, Lewis C. (1983). "The Other Side of the Smoking Worker Controversy." *Personnel Administrator* 28 (March): 72ff.

Spielberger, Charles D. (1966). "Psychological Determinants of Smoking Behavior." In *Smoking and Society: Toward a More Balanced Assessment,* ed. Robert D. Tollison, pp. 89–134. Lexington, Mass.: Lexington Books.

Sterling, T., and J. Weinkam. (1976). "Smoking Characteristics by Type of Employment." *Journal of Occupational Medicine* 18: 743–54.

Stoddart, Greg L., et al. (1986). "Tobacco Taxes and Health Care Costs: Do Canadian Smokers Pay Their Way?" *Journal of Health Economics* 5: 63–80.

Survey of Businesses and Eating Establishments in Montgomery County, Maryland. Hamilton and Associates, 1982.

Szasz, Thomas. (1978). *The Theology of Medicine.* New York: Colophon Books.

Taylor, Daniel T. (1979). "Absent Workers and Lost Work Hours, May 1978." *Monthly Labor Review* 402 (August): 49–53.

Tobacco Institute. (1985). *The Tax Burden on Tobacco, Vol. 19, 1984.* Washington: Tobacco Institute.

Tullock, Gordon. (1965). The Politics of Bureaucracy. Washington, D.C.: Public Affairs Press.

U.S. Department of Labor, Bureau of Labor Statistics. (1983). *Consumer Expenditure Survey: Diary Survey, 1980–81.* Washington, D.C.: U.S. Government Printing Office, September.

Vogel, Alfred. (1985). "Are Smokers Really Less Productive than Nonsmokers?" *Legislative Policy* (Summer): 6–8.

Wagner, Richard E. (1983). *Public Finance: Revenues and Expenditures in a Democratic Society.* Boston: Little, Brown.

Weaver, Carolyn L. (1982). *The Crisis in Social Security: Economic and Political Origins.* Durham, N.C.: Duke University Press.

18

Cigarettes and Property Rights

Walter E. Williams

The kind of man who demands that government enforce his ideas is always the kind whose ideas are idiotic.

—Henry Louis Mencken

Waiting in a long reservation line for a flight from San Francisco to Philadelphia, I lit a cigarette. After a few puffs, a middle-aged woman in front of me said, "Sir, would you mind putting that cigarette out?" Being bored and willing to converse, I asked, "Do you own the air?" "What does that have to do with putting out that cigarette which is causing a nuisance?" she replied. "It has a lot to do with it," I admonished. Little did she know that she was about to receive a minilesson on property rights. The complex property rights issue is one ignored by both smokers and anti-smokers.

Anti-tobacco campaigns have waxed and waned for several centuries. King James I, who saw smoking as a pernicious habit borrowed from wild, uncivilized Indians, was among the first prohibitionists. French Cardinal Richelieu objected to smoking and thought a tobacco tax would not only check its spread but be a great source of government revenue as well. During the Napoleonic period, Vienna, Paris, Berlin, and parts of Switzerland passed laws prohibiting smoking in the streets. Queen Victoria hated smoking; she made royal guests at Windsor Castle smoke into fireplaces so the smoke could go out the chimney.

In the United States, Lucy Page Gasten led the first anti-tobacco movement around the time the Women's Christian Temperance Union movement

Originally published in *Clearing the Air: Perspectives on Environmental Tobacco Smoke*, edited by Robert D. Tollison (Lexington, Mass.: Lexington Books, 1988). Reprinted by permission of University Press of America.

was campaigning against alcohol consumption. Her movement was followed by Dr. Charles Pease of the Nonsmokers' Protection League of America. Henry Ford, the automobile industrialist, was a fanatic anti-smoker who tried in vain to get his employees to stop smoking. The early anti-tobacco campaign had modest success. Twelve states had statutes that either banned or restricted the sale or use of cigarettes; however, along with the demise of the Eighteenth Amendment, these statutes were repealed.

Early anti-tobacco campaigns centered their attention on how cigarette smoking harms the smoker. Experts of the time alleged that smoking was not only harmful to physical and mental health but led to a breakdown in morals, leading first to alcoholism and then to opium addiction. Moreover, they said, adult smoking would lead increasing numbers of children and young adults to take up the habit. Their message and efforts fell on deaf public ears as cigarette smoking grew in America.[1] But early medical experts were not in full agreement. Cornelius Bontekoe, a celebrated Dutch physician, said, "There is nothing so good, nothing so estimable, so profitable and necessary for life and health as the smoke of tobacco, that royal plant that kings themselves are not ashamed to smoke."

SMOKING HARMS THE SMOKER

At the outset, let me be clear. Although I possess no special expertise, I accept the medical evidence that cigarette smoking is a major contributor to several health disorders, such as lung cancer, heart disease, and respiratory distress. On the other hand, not everyone who smokes suffers from these disorders. Whether an activity such as cigarette smoking is harmful to the individual is not the relevant criterion for law in a free society.

Many human activities can result in personal harm. Skiing, football, boxing, skydiving, and swimming are activities where a person puts safety at risk. Soft drink consumption by children may lead to hyperactivity and aggravate allergies. Medical experts agree there is no dietary reason for adding salt to foods. Yet many people do so and subsequently increase their risk of hypertension and other circulatory diseases. Sunbathing often leads to skin cancer. A higher risk of coronary disease is associated with high cholesterol consumption. Automobile driving, mining, and bridge construction often result in injuries and fatalities. These are but a few ways we take risks with the length and quality of our own lives. Yet no one, I suspect, would advocate legal prohibitions against sunbathing, salt, red meat consumption, and other harmful and risky activities. Instead we simply leave it up to education and persuasion, but otherwise leave the individual free to choose.

In a free society, each individual owns himself or herself. That means and requires that each person be permitted to take chances with his or her own life. If this person were to be prevented from engaging in every behavior that risked health and safety, he or she would not be free. He or she would be like a caged canary—safe but a prisoner. I have posed the following question to class after class over twenty years: Would you be satisfied if government had the power to prevent you from doing everything that might cause you harm? I have yet to receive an affirmative answer.

There is the frequent assertion that people who place themselves at risk by smoking, riding a motorcycle without a helmet, or engaging in dangerous activities may become medically indigent and hence a financial burden to society. The conclusion reached by this observation is that since society has the ultimate responsibility of paying the bill, it has a right to restrict people's right to take risks with their health and safety. Such a position raises an important question: if intervention, for this reason, is deemed legitimate in the case of cigarette smoking or motorcycling, is it not a logical extension of the same principle to regulate other activities, such as sunbathing and salt consumption, that may jeopardize health and safety and cause people to become a financial burden on society?

The argument that if people are permitted to take chances with their life and good health may lead to circumstances where they become a financial burden to society is not a good one against individual freedom. Instead it is a better argument against socialism. In a free society, when an individual harms himself or herself and is thereby unable to make a contribution to the productive output of society, he or she is penalized by having no wages and hence no ability to make claims on goods and services produced by society unless he or she had foresight to purchase disability insurance, had caring family or friends, or was lucky enough to receive charity. In a free society, individuals bear most of the cost of harming themselves, or the people who bear the cost do so voluntarily. Who bears the cost of mistakes is one way to distinguish between free markets and socialism. In free markets, costs of mistakes are borne by the individual who makes them. Under socialism, costs of people's mistakes are politically spread among the society at large.

Having failed in their efforts to persuade people to give up cigarette smoking voluntarily for health reasons, the anti-smoking campaign has focused its attention on the claim that others, being in the presence of smokers, or what they call involuntary smoking, risk adverse health effects. Anti-smokers now concede that cigarette smokers have the right to harm themselves but not others. The medical evidence on the effects of "secondary" cigarette smoke is less clear, and there is considerable controversy.[2] But it seems that some people with allergies, asthma, bronchitis, and other respiratory problems suffer in the presence of cigarette smoke. Moreover, just the odor of cigarette smoke is highly offensive to many people. These factors do not make cigarette smoke unique. Some people suffer the same allergic and respiratory distress in the presence of fumes or vapors from household cleaners, hair sprays, perfumes, deodorants, after-shave lotions, and other toiletry items.

Harm to Others

Harmful or beneficial side effects may arise in the course of consuming some commodities and affect people not directly involved in the consumption of the good in question. Economists refer to these side effects as externalities. External economics of consumption occur when one person's consumption indirectly benefits another. When one home owner makes increased expenditures to maintain property, he or she unavoidably raises the attractiveness and hence the value of neighbors' property. A person wearing a lotion pleasing to others unavoidably benefits them. External diseconomies of consumption occur when one person's consumption indirectly harms another, as in the case of an airplane flying over a property or a person dressed in displeasing attire. In either externality case, there is no compensation for the harm or benefit.

When external diseconomies of production or consumption occur where A's activities harm B, it is intellectually shallow to ask how we can stop A from harming B. The reason is that externalities are always reciprocal. That is, to prevent B from being harmed automatically harms A. For example, a motorcyclist riding down an otherwise quiet road momentarily disturbs, and hence harms, the residents. Shortsighted inquiry would ask how we can prevent the cyclist from harming the residents. But such a question fails to evaluate and consider the harm that can come to the motorcyclist by preventing him or her from using the road.

We can think of other nuisances, such as airplanes flying over congested areas, traffic noises, or schools adjacent to residential areas. In each case a home owner may be harmed by the consumptive activities of others; however, to prevent the nuisance imposes a harm on those participating in those consumptive activities. Although superficial analysis might suggest that home owners are harmed by these nuisances, it is not always clear they are harmed on balance. The presence of neighborhood schools may raise property values. The presence of a nearby airport may stimulate economic activity and in turn raise property values of the people annoyed. In other words, the same externality may simultaneously produce both harmful and beneficial effects.

It is difficult to conceive of a world where all harm has been outlawed. In such a world, activities we normally take for granted could not occur. Marriage is one of them. When a man or a woman marries, he or she unavoidably harms other people. In other words, he takes a woman who might have been the apple of some other man's eye, and she takes the man who might have been the apple of some other woman's eye. The more attractive the marriage partners are, the more widespread is the harm in terms of the prospective mates they had to say no to.

The same reciprocal externalities apply to the smoking controversy. Some nonsmokers are harmed by smokers. Public debate centers around ways to prevent smokers from causing harm to nonsmokers. This is intellectually shallow because it ignores the potential harm done to smokers. The harm done to smokers is that of denying them the opportunity to engage in an activity they enjoy.

In the case of externalities, there is no way of unambiguously assessing which harm is more devastating or more important to prevent. To attempt to do so is to make interpersonal utility comparisons that economic theory proves impossible. In other words, there is no way to establish whether having a noisy school in a neighborhood is intrinsically more, or less, valuable than having quiet in the neighborhood. It is a matter of personal values. Similarly, there is no way to assess whether the harm done to a nonsmoker is more important than the benefit gained by the smoker or whether the gain to the nonsmoker through smoking bans is more important than losses to the smoker.

Moreover, the nonsmoker, as well as the smoker, places subjective values and trade-offs on the harm or benefit he or she is willing to accept. Consider the following: Would all nonsmokers turn down an invitation to a White House dinner knowing they would be seated at the table with a president who smokes? Would a nonsmoker faced with a disabled car refuse the offer of a passing motorist who smoked? Would a nonsmoker turn down an interview for a job he has always wanted because the employer smoked?

The Right to Clean Air

Some people in the anti-smoking movement have argued that a basic unenumerated constitutional right is the right to breathe clean air. Taken at face value, such a statement would produce ludicrous results. Pollution of one form or another is the by-product of all consumption or production. The production of dresses, soap, medicine, and everything else uses energy. A by-product of energy consumption is pollution. The consumption of auto services, use of hydrocarbons, and even the act of life itself (taking in air and expelling carbon dioxide) produces pollution. Hence, what is the meaning of the statement that people have a constitutional right to clean air? Obviously anyone who makes such an assertion must be prepared to offer a trail of modifiers or call for the absolute curtailment of production and consumption.

At least one court has recognized this in *Gasper* v. *Louisiana Stadium and Exposition District* (577 F.2d 897 [1978]). The court disagreed with the right to clean air argument saying, "To hold that the First, Fifth, Ninth, or

Fourteenth Amendment recognize as fundamental the right to be free from cigarette smoke would be to mock the lofty purposes of such amendments and broaden their penumbral protections to unheard-of boundaries."

PROPERTY RIGHTS

At the core of the smoking controversy lies the property rights issue. Property rights have to do with who makes decisions to acquire, use, and dispose of resources. Property rights are said to be held privately when the person deemed the owner has (1) exclusive rights to use, (2) rights to receive all benefits and duty to pay all costs, and (3) rights to transfer these property rights (sell). When property rights are well defined and transactions costs (costs associated with information and contract enforcement) are zero, external costs and benefits are internalized regardless of the property rights assignment. In other words, the person whose consumptive activity confers an indirect benefit on another is compensated, and the person whose consumptive activity imposes an indirect cost on another compensates that person. If I break a person's window while playing baseball, I compensate the owner; if I collide into your car, I compensate you for the damages. Alternatively, if I confer a benefit through mowing another's lawn, which imposes a cost on me through sacrificed leisure, I am compensated by receiving wages. In the case of well-defined property rights, there are no externalities.

Smoking in Homes

The common law presumption is that the decision whether smoking is allowed in private homes is left in the hands of the person(s) deemed the owner(s). This means, regardless of the external effects, that nonsmokers have the right to restrict smoking in their homes but not in somebody else's house. I suspect even the most zealous anti-smoker would be offended by a law banning smoking in private homes even though smoking in private homes may pose the same risks to the smoker and those around him or her, such as family members and guests, as it would on airlines and in restaurants.

I imagine the counsel to a person who complained about being in the presence of smokers at another's house would be a suggestion to leave the premises. Similarly, a person who complained about others smoking in his house would receive similar counsel: tell the smoking guests to refrain or leave. Resolution of conflict over smoking is straightforward and reasonably simple where clearly defined property rights prevail. I imagine a defendant in a tort case in which the plaintiff claims injury by cigarette smoke would use the affirmative defense of assumption of risks; the defendant would claim that the plaintiff had knowledge of a condition or situation that was dangerous and yet exposed himself or herself to the hazard created by the defendant.

Smoking in Publicly Owned Places

The conflict of wishes between smokers and nonsmokers becomes a more contentious issue in publicly owned places because property rights are defined in the sense of who owns what. Publicly owned places include municipal airports, parks, schools, and state and federal buildings. Presumably smokers as well as nonsmokers pay taxes and both can claim partial ownership of publicly owned places. There is nothing in principle that says whose rights should prevail: the right to smoke and have cigarette-polluted air or the right to ban smoking and have nonpolluted air in publicly owned places. More often than not, whose wishes prevail is a result of which group has the dominant political power at the moment.

Smoking in Privately Owned Establishments

Smoking in factories, offices, restaurants, airlines, and department stores, which cater to the public as workers or customers, is the current focus of the anti-smoking movement. These establishments are clearly privately owned. The fact that they do business with the general public does not make them publicly owned. In their cases, private property rights are well defined and should resolve the smoking controversy just as it does in the case of privately owned homes. The owner makes the decision whether smoking is to be permitted on the premises and accepts the economic consequences.

What are the options available to the nonsmoker or anti-smoker worker under these circumstances? The most obvious is for the worker to withhold his or her productive services from employers who permit smoking on their work sites. Another option is to try to convince, cajole, or embarrass smoking coworkers into abstention.

Employers have a common law duty, given the state of technology, to ensure a safe workplace. There is a similar common law expectation that home owners must take reasonable precautions to ensure safety for their visitors. At the same time the common law holds employers and home owners accountable to take reasonable measures to ensure the safety of employees and visitors, it also places a burden on the latter to take reasonable measures to protect themselves.

Unlike the cases of slippery stairs, radioactivity, and certain noxious fumes, the fact that coworkers and others are smoking is visible, apparent, and cheap to detect. Therefore a person who might suffer injuries from being in the presence of smokers knowingly assumes the risk of harm. The remedies available to a worker in a workplace where the employer permits smoking are identical to those available to a nonsmoker who visits a house where the owner permits smoking: avoid the danger by leaving. To rejoin to this remedy by saying the visitor has choices while the worker does not is the same as asserting the intersection of two improbable events: there are no other jobs available, and all employers permit smoking.

Obviously similar remedies are available to nonsmokers in choice of restaurants, bars, and other places of entertainment. They are free to withhold patronage from establishments that permit smoking. To facilitate non-smokers' options or, for that matter, smokers' as well, all that is necessary is for owners to make readily available information about whether smoking is permitted at their establishments.

Abrogation of Private Property Rights

Under private property rights, and implications for resource usage, some people may bear costs that can be avoided with government allocation of resources. One experience can demonstrate this principle. The hotel bellman summoned a taxi for me. Upon entering the taxi, I noticed a sign saying, "No Smoking." I told the driver that since he did not permit smoking, I would get another taxi. The driver used abusive language to exhibit considerable dis-pleasure when I got into another taxi.

The driver's displeasure might have resulted from any one of several fac-tors. First, he had to get out of the taxi waiting line for naught. Second, he lost a fare and had to wait for another. Third, he might have objected to my rejecting his services solely because of his prohibition of smoking in his vehicle. There were some costs borne by me as well, namely those associated with finding another taxi. In this instance, they were low since there was a taxi queue.

The taxi driver would have not encountered the inconvenience and lost earnings if there had been a law against smoking in taxis because there would have been no alternative to a no-smoking taxi. On the other hand, if there were a law mandating the right to smoke in taxis, the experience would have been cheaper for me; I would not have to search for another taxi.

One of us would have gained from the abrogation of the property rights of the other. Abrogation of property rights has become the most popular route in the anti-smokers' drive for prohibition. They have realized the age-old prac-tice of using the legislature to accomplish what they deem more costly through voluntary market transactions. Their agenda is to use the legislature to take away part of the owner's decision on how his or her property is used.

A similar scenario emerged in California. In April 1986 the Beverly Hills city council enacted a ban on smoking in restaurants. By August, Beverly Hills restaurants had lost 30 percent of their customers to restaurants in nearby towns, which allowed smoking. The city council then adopted new rules, permitting smoking in restaurants provided there were no-smoking areas and adequate ventilation.[3]

The problem for the Beverly Hills restaurants was that the city council had the power to ban smoking in Beverly Hills but not elsewhere. Moreover, there was a loophole in the law exempting bars and cocktail lounges from the smoking ban, and some Beverly Hills restaurants "became" lounges. The combined effect was losses to no-smoking restaurants resulting from customers taking their business elsewhere.

Beverly Hills restaurateurs would have benefited from a similar ordinance abrogating the property rights of restaurateurs in adjacent towns. Broader smoking restrictions would have reduced their revenue losses by denying customers alternatives. This suggests that if businesspeople perceive a high probability of enactment of smoking bans, they can be expected to join the lobby for the enactment of the ban. This is true whether or not individual businesspeople are against it. It is in their financial interests to make the application of the smoking ban as broad as possible so they do not experience losses like those experienced by the Beverly Hills restaurants. Therefore, we would not expect one private airline to enact smoking bans on its aircraft, even if its owners were anti-smokers; they would fear the revenue loss. We would expect them to seek legislation outlawing smoking on aircraft altogether so as to avoid revenue losses from customers "voting on their feet."

USE OF THE STATE FOR WINDFALL GAIN

People often seek to use state powers to redistribute wealth from one class of citizens to another. An example from housing will be used to illustrate the process. Consider the person who purchases a house for $100,000 in a neighborhood where identical houses across the road sell for $125,000. The reason why houses on his side of the road sell at a discount is because a railroad runs behind the properties, causing noise and vibration. For this nuisance, home owners with property adjacent to the railroad have been compensated, through the market, by a property discount of $25,000.

The home owners on the noisy side of the road might form a political coalition and appeal to the legislature to enact a law forcing the railroad to relocate its tracks or invest resources in noise- and vibration-abatement equipment. They might buttress their complaint by bringing scientific evidence that the train nuisance harms their children by having their sleep disturbed by passing trains.

If the state legislature ruled in favor of the home owners, the railroad company would have to incur the costs of noise abatement or track relocation. As a result, not only would home owners now have undisturbed sleep, they would receive windfall gains in the form of a wealth transfer from the railroad. Their homes, which differed from their across-the-road neighbors only by the nuisance of passing trains, would begin to appreciate in price. Assuming the train nuisance was the only difference, after its removal, their houses would sell for $125,000, the price of other houses not encumbered by the railroad nuisance.

Obviously similar use of state power can be employed in many other ways to confer windfall gains at the expense of windfall losses to others who are not as politically strong. This principle can be applied to the issue of smoking bans in the workplace. A nonsmoker might take employment in a business establishment knowing the employer permits smoking on the premises. Rather than not take the job in the first place or quitting if the smoke becomes intolerable, he or she can use the legislature to abrogate property rights of the owner by outlawing cigarette smoking. The non-smoker's windfall gains are not monetary but are nonetheless state-acquired gains resulting from wealth redistribution that raises his or her sense of well-being at the expense of another.

The Market and Conflict Resolution

People exhibit many likes and dislikes. Often these likes and dislikes lead to conflict. Political allocation of resources raises the potential for conflict because one person benefits only at the expense of another. Political alloca-tion of resources is a zero-sum game where the gain to one person necessarily comes as a loss to another. Market allocation reduces the potential for con-flict because it is a process where all parties to the exchange benefit, a posi-tive-sum game.

Smoking may be an annoyance and possibly harmful to those around the smoker. Such an observation does not place smoking in a category by itself. Loud music, featured at discotheques and bars, is said to lead to hearing loss and headaches. Typically the person who is offended by the loud music either leaves the establishment or does not enter in the first place. As long as loud discotheque music is contained within the establishment, most people offended by it would not descend on the state legislators lobbying for enact-ment of a law specifying a particular decibel range. There is no ugly con-frontation. People who like loud music go to discos, and those who do not go elsewhere. It appears as though a similar response is available to people who find smoking distasteful.

Efficiency Gains through the Market

Most human conduct is regulated not by law but by force of social custom, etiquette, and ostracism. Behavior regulated in this way includes, or included, men giving up their seat for women, boisterous behavior, child rearing, foul body odor, coughing around others, and dress codes. Violation of these customs is met with social sanctions leading to general compliance without their being regulated by threat of state violence or punishment. Customs and etiquette are ways we internalize externalities in the presence of nonzero transactions cost.

A reasonable question is whether efficiency gains can be realized using social norms, as opposed to the threat of state violence, as a regulator of annoyances related to smoking. Clearly one source of efficiency is the case where nonsmokers have neutral preferences about being around smokers. If there is a law prohibiting smoking, it is more likely that some people will be worse off without the benefit of anybody else being better off.

Such a principle is a subject of considerable study in the area of economics known as welfare economics. Welfare economics studies the conditions under which society is made better or worse off. The maximization of society's well-being requires the optimal allocation of resources in production, consumption, and exchange.

The efficiency rule, a cornerstone of modern economics, is known as Pareto optimality named after Vilfredo Pareto, its turn-of-the-century Italian discoverer. According to Pareto-optimality criteria, any change that improves the well-being of some individuals (in their own estimation) without reducing the well-being of other individuals (in their own estimation) clearly improves the welfare of the group as a whole. Such a change will move the group from a Pareto-nonoptimal position to a Pareto-optimal position.

Applying Pareto criteria to the smoking controversy, if a set of conditions prevails where some people will derive increased enjoyment from smoking and others around them are not made worse off (in their own estimation), then the group is made better off if smoking is permitted. Under such circumstances, anti-smoking laws serve no purpose other than preventing greater enjoyment for the group. Etiquette, in the form of "Do you mind if I smoke?" would be a better regulator.

Common Law and Smoking

In traditional common law of torts, there appears to be no actionable remedy for a plaintiff bringing a nuisance or injury case against a home owner, restaurateur, cafe owner, or manufactory owner defendant claiming injury by the secondary effects of cigarette smoke in the defendant's establishment. It would appear that the defendant would have several common law doctrines for defense.

First, though controversial, is the coming-to-the-nuisance doctrine cited in *Bove* v. *Donner-Hanna Coke Corporation* where the court rejected the plaintiff's request for an injunction saying:

> With all the dirt, smoke and gas which necessarily come from factory chimneys, trains and boats, and with full knowledge that this region was especially adapted for industrial rather than residential purposes, and that factories would increase in the future, plaintiff selected this locality as the site of her future home. She voluntarily moved into this district, fully aware of the fact that the atmosphere would be contaminated by dirt, gas and foul odors and she could not hope to find in this locality the pure air of a strictly residential zone. She evidently saw certain advantages in living in this congested center.[4]

There is considerable equivocation on the issue of coming to the nuisance. In the *Restatement of Torts* on nuisance provisions, it is argued that assumption of the risks should be a defense in nuisance actions to the same extent it is a defense in other tort actions. Also, in coming to the nuisance, *Restatement of Torts* holds that "the fact that a plaintiff has acquired or improved his land after a nuisance interfering with it has come into existence is not in itself sufficient to bar his action, but is a factor to be considered in determining whether the nuisance is actionable."

Another common law doctrine almost wholly ignored in nuisance law is the duty to mitigate damages. In some cases, the parties to a conflict can avoid or reduce damages leading to litigation by taking reasonable low-cost steps. For example, if a nonsmoker sees or knows that the owner of a private establishment permits smoking, which the nonsmoker perceives as hazardous, he or she may simply leave or not enter the premises.[6] This duty to mitigate damages seems to be related to court decisions where people come to the nuisance and are thereby held to have assumed the attendant risks. None of this argument suggests that property owners do not have a duty to ensure the safety of their premises. But it would appear that the safety obligation applies to hazards that cannot be reasonably known or anticipated by others entering the premises.

The tradition of common law respect for private property may explain why people who wish to abrogate the private property rights of others choose statutory relief rather than appeal to civil courts.

CONCLUSION

Cigarette smoking is a private act that produces external diseconomics for some people. For that reason anti-smokers call for government regulation. However, it is possible to prove that every private act has external effects of one sort or another. The list of private acts that can reduce the physical and psychological well-being of other people is enormous and includes loud music, rambunctious behavior, poor table manners, barking dogs, disheveled appearance, sexual promiscuity, obscene language, trespass, obesity, meat eating, and flatulence. Therefore to call government regulation of private acts solely because they produce external costs and reduce the welfare of other people is to call for government regulation of everything.

Social costs or external diseconomies are a politician's dream. It gives them what they consider the moral justification for having government play a larger and larger regulatory role in our lives. For political gain, it gives them power to grant favors and privileges to one group of citizens at the expense of another group of citizens. The smoking controversy is no exception to the ongoing efforts of politicians, promoting class interests, to grab power. While a case might be made for political regulation of smoking in publicly owned places, no case can be made, and simultaneously respect private property rights, for political intervention to regulate smoking on private property.

NOTES

1. See S. Wagner, *Cigarette County: Tobacco in American History and Politics* (New York: Praeger, 1971).

2. We must always be alert to people using science as a means to accomplish hidden agendas. See Edith Efrom, *The Apocalyptics: Cancer and the Big Lie* (New York: Simon & Schuster, 1984), chaps. 1, 2.

3. *Time*, August 3, 1986, p. 23.

4. Cited by Charles O. Gregory, Harry Kalven, Jr., and Richard A. Epstein, *Cases and Material on Torts*, 3d ed. (Boston: Little, Brown, 1977), p. 535.

5. Ibid. p. 535.

6. See Bruce Ackerman, ed., *Economic Foundation of Property Law* (Boston: Little, Brown, 1975), pp. 293–94.

BIBLIOGRAPHY

Ackerman, Bruce, ed. *Economic Foundation of Property Law.* Boston: Little, Brown, 1975.
Chung, Steven N. S. *The Myth of Social Cost.* Menlo Park, Calif.: Cato Institute, 1980.
Count Corti. *A History of Smoking.* London: George G. Harrop & Co., Ltd., 1931.
Gregory, Charles O., et al. *Cases and Material on Torts.* 3d ed. Boston: Little, Brown, 1977.
Trayer, Ronald, and Gerald Marble. *Cigarettes and the Battle over Smoking.* New Brunswick, NJ.: Rutgers University Press, 1983.
Wagner, S. *Cigarette Country: Tobacco in American History and Politics.* New York: Praeger, 1971.

19

Smokers' Rights to Health Care

Rajendra Persaud

INTRODUCTION

Underwood and Bailey, two cardiothoracic surgeons, launched the recent controversy with a *British Medical Journal* paper[1] which begins: "... when resources are restricted and some form of rationing of health care is effectively taking place, is it ethical to restrict access of patients to particular treatments if there are alterable factors in their lifestyle which make the treatment less likely to work?" A fierce debate then began within the profession,[2] crystallized around the slogan: "Should smokers be offered coronary bypass surgery?" (the title of Underwood and Bailey's paper).

Subsequently, surgeons at two separate U.K. medical centers were reported to have withdrawn non-urgent coronary bypass operations from those refusing to give up smoking,[3] and later that month the *Times* newspaper found four other hospitals where this practice was widespread.[4] When asked to comment, British government ministers tacitly supported this new method of health-rationing, declaring these decisions should be left to doctors, even if "they were now playing God."[5]

R. Persaud, "Smokers' Rights to Health Care." This article was first published in the *Journal of Medical Ethics* 21 (1995): 281–87, and is reprinted by permission of the BMJ Publishing Group.

THE WIDER ISSUE

The issue has implications well beyond the smoker; if individuals wilfully endanger their health, it may be unreasonable for the state to pay for the consequences. Hence the question: Should health service budgets be "squandered" on those whose drinking, diet and poor compliance with medication damages their health in contrast to those whose illnesses arise *despite* efforts to remain healthy?

By extension those who take part in dangerous sports could also find themselves without state health care in the event of injury. One estimate of the cost to the British National Health Service [NHS] of road traffic accidents is about 90 million pounds per annum.[6] Would those who are willing to withdraw treatment from smokers also consider doing so from those who do not wear seat belts?

Alternatively, the fact that people still smoke could be viewed as a failure of public health campaigns. Preventative health makes good economic sense, but when public education campaigns fail, the state frequently *forces* us to look after our health, for example road safety laws compel us to wear motor vehicle seat belts. These measures followed the failure of such road safety education campaigns as the "clunk-click" campaign, which had not significantly influenced public attitudes toward seat belts.[7]

Before the 1983 legislation only 40 percent of drivers wore them. Since then, however, it has been estimated that 95 percent of motorists obey the new law and that as a result, calculations are that seven hundred deaths and six thousand serious injuries have been avoided in a single year.[8] At no point did anyone suggest surgery should not be offered to those not wearing belts. Furthermore, well before that stage could ever have been reached, legislation has been used to coerce "healthful" behavior. It would follow that if smoking is a serious enough behavior to affect health rights, then a rational first step to take before this situation arises might be to legislate against the behavior itself, to ban smoking.

Doctors concerned with health care implications of smoking may want to consider campaigns to influence state legislation of this behavior as an alternative to withdrawing care from smokers.

WHY DO SMOKERS CONTINUE TO SMOKE?

It could be argued that wearing seat belts is significantly different from smoking; doctors rarely advise patients on driving safety, but they persistently and forcefully forewarn on the dangers of smoking. If patients knowingly ignore their doctor's advice, does that alter their future claims on their physicians, and hence their health rights?

The argument partly rests on the notion that smokers choose to smoke of their own free will, in full cognizance of the facts, and could give up if they placed the same value on health as they expect their surgeons to. There would appear to be an ethical world of difference between the harms that others inflict upon you, those you inadvertently administer to yourself, and harms that you *knowingly and freely* wreak upon your own body.

Yet there are many risks which smokers are not explicitly warned of in health education campaigns. While much stress is laid on lung cancer, the risk of circulatory diseases such as Buerger's disease, is seldom emphasized.[9] Ironically, this area, of circulatory diseases, is precisely the area within which cardiothoracic surgeons operate, and from which they seek to exclude smokers. In one poll, while most smokers were aware of the links with lung cancer, 63 percent did not know that smoking causes most cases of bronchitis, and 85 percent were unaware that it causes most cases of emphysema.[10]

Another ethically relevant issue is how free smokers are to give up. If they were suffering from an addiction, this could excuse them from failure to give up. Receptors for the active ingredients of tobacco have been discovered in the brain, while nicotine dependence has been classified as an addiction by the American Psychiatric Association[11] and the World Health Organization.[12] Surveys suggest that 90 percent of regular smokers have tried to quit on at least one occasion; one study found that only 36 percent had succeeded in maintaining abstinence for a whole year, while relapse rates after a given period of time are almost the same for nicotine as for heroin.[13]

This is not to say giving up is *impossible,* just that it may be *difficult.* But no matter how difficult: do smokers have an ethical obligation to their cardiothoracic surgeons to try giving up, or even to *succeed* in giving up?

ARE THERE ETHICAL OBLIGATIONS TO GIVE UP SMOKING?

If there is a moral obligation for doctors to promote their patients' health—do patients have a corresponding ethical duty to seek their own health? In other words, are doctors and patients engaged in a common moral enterprise which legitimately claims the allegiance of both parties?

Parsons[14] delineated the existence of a "sick role" (ill persons are viewed as having social obligations), to positively value health and cooperate with doctors in order to regain it. In coming under the care of doctors, it appears patients enter a relationship defined and oriented by the importance of health values.[15] Not to value health while seeking help and advice from doctors might represent an attempt to enter such a relationship under false pretenses.

Hence, implicit in the very act of any medical consultation could be the agreement that both parties, doctor and patient, value health.[16] But smoking would seem to suggest, at the very least, that other values, such as pleasure, have a higher priority than health. Do not doctors have the right, when this implicit contract within which they attempt to work meaningfully with patients has been violated, to withdraw care?[17]

The problem with this argument is that patients rarely value health as much as doctors do (except possibly in the case of hypochondriacs). Doctors, by their personal orientation and professional training, probably value health more than anyone else in society. For most people, other values, such as those to do with money or pleasure, frequently take priority over health. In fact it could be argued that patients often do not see doctors because they value health—they avoid doctors so as to *avoid suffering*. Hence their tendency to make appointments after experiencing pain or discomfort, rather than attending for health checkups or preventative health advice.

If this is the case, the notion of shared values between doctor and patient becomes questionable, and equally so would any ethical obligations based on such values. While doctors may value health, they could not meaningfully make their medical practice contingent on these values being found in their patients. Among other problems this would automatically exclude many, such as the suicidal and the mentally handicapped, from rights to medical care.

On the other hand, the suicidal and the mentally handicapped are presumed not to value health for reasons other than fully conscious rational choice. If patients in full possession of their faculties and the facts choose a hierarchy of values which represents a relative depreciation of health, should doctors' contrasting set of priorities be relied on to come to the rescue?

It seems morally inconsistent to expect to be helped precisely because those who provide the help hold a set of values you have rejected. The individual can maintain moral consistency only by relinquishing expectations of help in the context of behavior which does not value health, or by accepting the set of values which provides the context in which help is provided, and hence changing his/her behavior.

ARE SMOKERS' HEALTH RIGHTS A MEDICAL ISSUE?

The gap in health values between doctors and patients means that if doctors had their way, patients might be subject to much more restrictive legislation than at present, for example, the freedom to box, or drink in public houses or bars at any time of the day could be limited.[18] Given the tension in values between profession and public, primarily ethical decisions such as those to do with smokers' rights, should perhaps be left to the state and not to doctors. While doctors have ethical obligations to provide good treatment for patients—*who* should actually receive health care is possibly not a *medical* decision but instead one society and its elected representatives should resolve.[19]

For example, in many countries, if they cannot afford it, people do not receive medical care. This is not a decision taken by doctors, but by those who constructed that health care system. The public, via their governments, have decided that medical care should largely be rationed through the free market. Even in the British National Health Service (NHS) there are many treatments which are no longer offered—much dental care, for example. Again these are not rationing decisions taken by health professionals, but by those who administer the health service, and therefore it could be argued that it is they who ought to wrestle with the ethics of whether doctors should treat smokers, and not doctors.[20]

While this is the line taken by some of the correspondents involved in the debate over smokers' health care rights in the *British Medical Journal,*[21] it seems an inadequate response for, among others, British fundholding general practitioners. These have a budget allocated by the state, with the precise undertaking that they will be responsible for rationing decisions within the constraints of that budget.[22]

Part of the power of fundholding was always intended to be the product of bringing together medical expertise with wider management and administration skills under the same roof.[23] While this has undoubted efficiency advantages, it does also push fundholders into the front line of ethical rationing dilemmas precisely of the kind: "Should smokers be referred for expensive treatments?"

Even doctors who are not fundholders are morally implicated in these questions—frequent attempts are made to disguise the ethical dilemma as a clinical one. In Underwood and Bailey's original *British Medical Journal* paper, the emphasis was on the poorer prognosis of smokers receiving coronary bypass surgery.[24] The problem with this perspective is that while a *terminal* prognosis is often the basis of a decision to withhold treatment on the grounds of mercy, a poor prognosis is not necessarily a good clinical reason for withholding treatment—in fact often the contrary applies: very ill people often attract more care from doctors, not less.

SMOKERS' RIGHTS TO HEALTH

Another way of looking at the dilemma is: Do some people lose their right to equal access to health care as a result of their behavior? After all, we readily accept that while everyone has a right to liberty, that right is lost in committing a serious crime.

Just as we all have obligations to obey the law, ill people can also be viewed as having certain social obligations, for example, to positively value health, and to cooperate with doctors in order to regain it. Those who do not fulfill these obligations should surely lose their claims on others. For example, patients who are violent to general practitioners have long been considered as relinquishing the obligation of being kept on the practice list.

However, these examples also illustrate the principle that while we are used to giving people many social and economic rights, and also taking them away in certain circumstances, there is a distinction between these and even more fundamental rights—*human* rights—rights to life, for example, often considered as worth preserving under almost any circumstances.[25] For example, however heinous the crime, criminals have a right to trial, and to certain basic conditions in prison. Might not health be considered such a *basic human right?*

Another ethical principle which comes to bear on the dilemma over smokers and their rights to health care, is the general acknowledgement that our individual actions should not endanger others, and that where necessary this principle should be enforced by law. The smoker who uses up the health service budget on expensive operations could be seen as endangering the life of others, since their health resources get squeezed as a result.[26]

This leads to a utilitarian question: does the doctor have less of an ethical responsibility for the *individual* patient sitting in front of his desk, and a more primary obligation to the *group* of patients on his list? Should he not make decisions which maximize the well-being of the *group,* even if that is at the expense of the smoking minority?

A characteristic feature of an individual "right" is its regulation of how individuals may be treated, however desirable the collective goal. For example, individual rights to freedom take precedence over the well-being of the population at large. Utilitarianism conflicts with rights theory precisely at this point. Utilitarianism allows significant individual interests to be sacrificed in order to attain collective benefits.

Any nationalized health system is likely to exhibit a compromise between principles of individual responsibility and community solidarity, as it assumes that the financial risks of ill-health should be borne by society at large. The risk in doing this is that individuals are no longer penalized for overeating, drinking, and smoking. Yet any lifestyle involves an implicit valuation of one's own health. Average health under such a system becomes rather like a public good, such as clean air or uncongested roads, from which everyone benefits, but toward which none have an incentive to contribute.

The problem is that this very discouragement of personal responsibility for health may eventually become detrimental to the individual herself in the long term. Hence, another aspect of the dilemma over smokers' right to health: if smokers are denied rights to health care this may in itself act as a forceful incentive to give up smoking. This becomes an empirical question for which there is currently inadequate data. However, if one long-term consequence of denying smokers' rights is to reduce the number of smokers, enabling those who have given up to have access to health care, a utilitarian argument may then supervene, namely, do more smokers benefit in the long run from depriving a minority of rights to health care? This argument resonates with several key elements of the legislation-over-seat-belt-wearing debate.

A NATIONALIZED HEALTH SERVICE AND SMOKERS' HEALTH RIGHTS

Perhaps one thing this debate about smokers' health rights has made clear is that the ethical principles on which the British National Health Service were founded, have been forgotten. The possible referral strategies for smokers which are being contemplated, contravene these principles.

The welfare state is based on the assumption of "each according to his ability, to each according to his need." This is sympathetic both to the *right* to be unhealthy and to a duty to care for the unhealth of others, paid for through heavy taxation.[27] In other words those who cannot look after themselves should be looked after by those who are more able. It is important to remember this in the current smoking debate, as wealthy smokers will always be able to afford bypass surgery: the issue is really one of the rights of *poor* smokers to health care.

The nationalized health service was founded to ensure wealth should not make a difference (whether it succeeds or not the intention still stands) and refusing to refer the smoker for health care returns to the days when affluence did matter. The rich smoker will always be able to obtain his operation, while the poor smoker will not.

Yet if the wealthy smoker is forced to pay for his own treatment because he smokes, this will save the health service money, which can be used to treat many others—a solid utilitarian argument. The potential savings to the health service seem unlimited if the same principle is applied to other medical problems—drinkers in need of liver transplantation, HIV patients who acquired the infection through drug addiction or promiscuous sex, heart patients who are overweight, accident victims who had been driving carelessly or under the influence of drink, and those with sports injuries.

In fact the very best economics might be to *encourage* people to smoke. This is because no matter how much a patient does exactly what his doctor advises, everyone dies of something sooner or later. Doctors tend to forget that the medical costs of smoking-related diseases can only be calculated after the costs that *would have been incurred* had the people killed by smoking died of something else later, are subtracted.[28] In fact, in terms of overall medical expenditure over the course of their lives as a whole, there is some evidence that there may be *no significant difference* between smokers and nonsmokers in medical costs to society.[29] Smokers even save the state money by dying early.

Smoking tends to cause few problems during a person's productive years, and then kills them before social security and pensions payments are made. In fact, it is the nonsmoking pensioner who benefits financially from the contributions his smoker counterpart never lives to claim. And then, let us not forget the billions in tax revenue cigarettes contribute to the exchequer: 8 percent of total British government revenue.[30]

Denying the smoker treatment on the utilitarian/economic grounds of costs to society ignores hazardous behaviors smokers might replace smoking with if it did not exist, and the health problems they would live to develop if they did not die of smoking. Utilitarianism taken to this extreme always extinguishes individual rights. If a health service were founded on principles of maximum economic utility, then it might even make sense to encourage smoking!

WHEN CAN RIGHTS TO HEALTH CARE BE CHANGED?

Part of the force behind many of the arguments over smokers' rights to health care is the unfairness of "changing the rules after the game has begun." For doctors to practice medicine within a health service which embodies certain implicit values, only then to attempt to change their personal practice in a way which becomes inconsistent with that health service, demonstrates an inconsistency which requires these doctors either to leave that form of employment, or reform their personal practice.

There is another sense in which "changing the rules after the game has begun," applies to smokers' rights to health care. If smokers were informed before their decision to start smoking that such behavior would jeopardize their rights to health care, then there is a sense in which such decisions to smoke, taken on that understanding, appear to reduce these smokers' entitlement to demand health care as a right.

AN IMPORTANT DISTINCTION

If this argument is accepted it should also be apparent that starting smoking with no awareness that such behavior would reduce rights to health care, does not permit the smoker the chance to change his behavior in the light of this information. Therefore subsequently to enforce such a restriction on rights to health care appears unfair. This contention suggests that rights to health embodied in a society or a health care system, whatever they might be, cannot be made up or changed "on the hoof," and that patients have the right to know how their behavior will affect entitlements to health care *before* they make decisions about such behavior. Hence, attempts to reduce smokers' rights to health care should only be made with generations who have yet to take up smoking. This should logically apply to all hazardous-to-health behaviors.

Here then we have an important distinction: while it may be possible to hold a smoker at least partly culpable for subsequent ill health (as it is common knowledge that smoking is injurious to health) it appears less fair to withhold *treatment* unless the smoker was also aware that such treatment would be withheld before she began smoking, or aware in sufficient time after she had begun smoking to give her the chance to change her behavior in the light of such information.

This point also has a bearing on doctors' and patients' responsibilities for health. If a doctor withholds a treatment and consequently a patient dies from an illness that the patient could not have reasonably prevented, then that doctor would be seen as responsible for the patient's death. If, however, the illness was partly produced by the patient's behavior, which the patient knew would be self-injurious, then although the doctor still has some responsibility for the patient's death if treatment is withheld, it now appears that as the patient could also have prevented death by a prior change in personal behavior, the patient now also shares some responsibility for her own demise.

The patient appears to have even more responsibility for her death if she further knew also that her behavior would lead to the doctor deciding to withhold treatment. If by withholding treatment from one patient the doctor instead saves another, then the doctor is no longer responsible for a death, but merely for who dies. Supposing that someone had to be treated and therefore someone else had to go without treatment, the fact that in this situation a smoker dies could be seen as being even more that smoker's responsibility, if she had prior knowledge such a choice would be made, and she could have prevented that death by not smoking.

Looked at from the perspective of varying patient and doctor responsibilities for death, and therefore conversely health, although there is always some medical responsibility for the outcome of withholding treatment, as patient responsibility waxes and wanes depending on the patient's ability to avoid death by choice of behavior, it is possible that the responsibility for the death of the smoker by the withholding of treatment, should be placed less at the door of a surgeon, than if similar treatment is withheld from the non-smoker. What I am suggesting is that there is some diminution of the responsibility of the surgeon for the smoker's death if treatment is withheld.

On the other hand, just because a particular set of circumstances makes a doctor less responsible for the death of a patient, does that mean these circumstances produce any less of a moral obligation on the doctor to *attempt to save* the patient's life?

In fact, it is acknowledged that while doctors do have moral obligations to save their patients' lives this does not appear to be significantly different from the obligation we all have to save life if we find ourselves able to do so.[31] Doctors may possess special skills which enable them to rescue others more frequently than the rest of us, but the reasons *why* they should do so are the same as the reasons why we should all do so. If doctors' moral obligation to save life is no different from anyone else's, it follows that doctors should not be expected to value life any more than the community within which they function values life.

However, if doctors find themselves working in a community which does not appear to value health or life as highly as the profession may feel it ought to, then doctors may wish to attempt to alter the community's views by health campaigns or individual patient counseling. However, if doctors should not impose their own values of health on a community, similarly a community must abide by the decisions of its doctors, if these merely reflect the values of that society.

Difficulties

While doctors may be expected to value life more than particular individuals they care for may choose to do, such as the suicidal or drug abusers, they cannot be expected by the community in which they work, to value life more or less than the culture in which they function. Hence, it also follows they cannot be expected by their patients to value life in a way not required by the values of the system of medicine constructed by the society (and hence their patients) within which they function.

Difficulties for doctors occur when they appear to be expected by patients to value life or health more or less than the health service constructed by the society in which the doctors live and work. For example, in a democratically approved, strict fee-for-service system for nonemergency health care, it would appear odd for the general public to expect doctors still to have a moral obligation to provide nonemergency medical care for those who could not afford it.

The system that society evolves for distributing health care embodies within it values which apportion moral obligations to doctors. However, individuals within that society, even large groups, may disagree with the majority view of the moral obligations of doctors to provide nonemergency health care, and may campaign to change that system. Yet this does not mean they can expect doctors to practice medicine in ways which radically depart from the views shared by the rest of society. Their disagreement is not, then, with doctors, but with the rest of society.

It is important to remember that there are other circumstances which convey society's estimations of the moral obligation to save lives. For instance, once someone engages in a hazardous behavior, an implicit value is placed on the life put in danger by the amount society is willing to invest in a rescue attempt. It appears inconsistent to expect doctors to place a higher or lower value on a life than that conveyed by society's general attempts at rescue.

However, there are several different ways of interpreting the value society puts on life and these may not be entirely consistent. For example, the amount spent on making roads safer may not place the same value on human life as that invested in rescue services.

Hence, if as a society we choose not to invest a great deal in warning smokers of the dangers to their health of that behavior, it appears we have made a collective and implicit decision as to the value of smokers' lives. On the other hand, if much more is spent in providing health care for the same smokers once they become ill, this might lead to a different calculation as to the value of smokers' lives. Hence it appears possible to ascertain the value society places on life by certain policy decisions, and by the way it organizes and funds its health service.

Not just societies, but also individuals, may appear inconsistent in the degree to which they value health. Patients who make, but then fail to attend, appointments represent a significant cost in doctors' time and resources,[32] and doctors may wonder how obligated they are to push health care onto those who fail to attend by vigorously pursuing them. Given that some patients may not want to be pestered by doctors, it appears patients may also have a *right* not to value health care as much as their doctors. This right is enshrined in the Mental Health Act of 1983 which allows medical treatment against a conscious patient's wishes in only very narrowly defined circumstances; usually only when there is a significant risk to the safety of self or society as a result of a severe mental illness.[33]

Therefore, even if doctors do value health more than their patients this does not mean they can usually force these values on their patients. Patients appear to have the right to place their own value on health in circumstances when this conflicts with doctors'. Given the various circumstances in which doctors' and patients' values on health may conflict, we are left to ask what should guide behavior in these situations. If patients are not to be dictated to by doctors or vice versa, it appears the only remaining resort is to an inspection of the generally held values of health in the society within which doctors and patients live and work.

COMPLEX INTERPLAY

It therefore follows that the outcome of a procedure to save a life is the product not merely of an interaction between an individual doctor and an individual patient, but the result of a complex interplay between the values placed on life by an individual, a society, a health care system and a doctor. It thus follows that it is in fact discrepancies which arise between these different values which account for the moral difficulties created by the rights to health care of those who indulge in hazardous behavior.

Such difficulties could not arise if hazardous behavior did not lead to controversy over what constitutes an unreasonable risk to personal health, implying contrasting health values in different sections of society. At an individual level a confusion over values also frequently exists. For example, the very fact smokers demand health care means that two behaviors, smoking and seeking health care, which place a very different value on health, can originate within the same person.

Highlighting the contradictory nature, in terms of health values, of such requests for health care might lead society at large to begin resolving these contradictions, one way or the other. As doctors tend to be more knowledgeable about the health implications of various behaviors it might fall to them to draw attention to conflicts between healthful behaviors and other values; conflicts which would not otherwise occur to those choosing how to behave.

While it seems fairly uncontentious that doctors should play a role in fostering this discussion, it is less obvious that they should determine the outcome. Withholding treatment seems to be taking a firm position before the dispute has had a chance to get off the ground. On the other hand, in taking a controversial stand, those doctors who attempted to withhold treatment from smokers put the debate on the front pages of national newspapers, which probably catalyzed the controversy and engaged the public far more than the back pages of academic journals ever could.

CONCLUSION

This chapter has attempted to marshal the main arguments involved in the debate over whether hazardous behaviors, especially smoking, should affect rights to health care. The particular context of the health care system in which this debate occurs is crucial, as this determines implicit "rights-to-health" assumptions which underpin doctors' behavior. In an extreme free-market health care system whether smokers receive treatment will depend solely on whether they can afford it; smoking itself will be an irrelevancy.

If an alternative health care system is constructed which attempts to assign certain basic human rights to health care, and hence to ensure that personal financial considerations are irrelevant to treatment, decision making within that system should attempt to be consistent with the principles underpinning such a service.

Hence, it would follow that denying smokers health care *because they smoke* would be inconsistent with the principles on which that health service was founded.

An interesting implication of this argument is that one test of whether a nationalized health care system, based on universal and equal rights to health, has become terminally underfunded, is when debates of this kind begin to occur.

NOTES

1. M. J, Underwood and J S. Bailey, "Should Smokers Be Offered Coronary Bypass Surgery?" *British Medical Journal* 306 (1993): 1047–50.

2. M. I. Khalid, "Denying Treatment Is Indefensible," *British Medical Journal* 306 (1993): 1408; N. Mamode, "Denying Access Is More Costly," *British Medical Journal* 306 (1993): 1408.

3. M. Dean, "London Perspective: Self-Inflicted rationing," *Lancet* 341 (1993): 1525.

4. Ibid.

5. Ibid.

6. B. J. Houghton, "Compulsory Health and Safety in a Free Society," *Journal of Medical Ethics* 10 (1984): 186–90.

7. Ibid.

8. Ibid.

9. R. E. Goodin, "The Ethics of Smoking," Ethics 99 (1989): 574–624.

10. Ibid.

11. American Psychiatric Association, *Diagnostic and Statistical Manual of Mental Disorders,* 3d ed. (Washington, D.C.: APA, 1987).

12. World Health Organization. *International Classification of Disease,* 9th ed. (Geneva: WHO, 1978).

13. J. A. Winsten, "Nicotine Dependency and Compulsive Tobacco Use: A Research Status Report of the Center for Health Communication, Harvard School of Public Health," reprinted in *Tobacco Product Liability* Reporter 1 (1986): 7.

14. T. Parsons, "Health and Disease: A Sociological and Action Perspective. In W. T. Reich, ed. *Encyclopedia of Bioethics* (New York: The Free Press, 1978), pp. 590–99.

15. R. C. Sider and C. D. Clements, "Patients' Ethical Obligation for Their Health," *Journal of Medical Ethics* 10 (1984): 138–42.

16. Ibid.

17. Ibid.

18. H. Hayry and M. Hayry, "Utilitarianism, Human Rights and the Redistribution of Health through Preventative Medical Measures," *Journal of Applied Philosophy* 6, no. 1 (1989): 43–51.

19. J. Garfield, "Let the Health Authority Take the Responsibility," *British Medical Journal* 306 (1993): 1050.

20. Ibid.

21. Ibid.

22. R. Persaud, "Winning the War on Waiting Lists," *Fundholding* 1, no. 22 (1992): 18–19.

23. Ibid.

24. Underwood and Bailey, "Should Smokers Be Offered Coronary Bypass Surgery?" pp. 1047–50.

25. H. Powell, "Human Rights," *Journal of Medical Ethics* 3 (1977): 160–62.

26. A. Weale, "Statistical Lives and the Principle of Maximum Benefit," *Journal of Medical Ethics* 5 (1979): 185–95.

27. R. Persaud, "What Future for Ethical Medical Practice in the New National Health Service?" *Journal of Medical Ethics* 17, no. 1 (1991): 10–18.

28. D. Wikler, "Persuasion and Coercion for Health: Ethical Issues in Government Efforts to Change Lifestyles," *Health and Society* (now *Milbank Quarterly*) 56 (1978): 303–308.

29. J. J. Weinkam, W. Rosenbaum, and E. D. Sterling, "Smoking and Hospital Utilization," *Social Science and Medicine* 24 (1987): 983–86.

30. M. H. Preston, "Economics of Cigarette Smoking," in R. G. Richardson, ed., *Proceedings of the Second World Conference on Smoking and Health* (London: Pitman Medical, 1971), pp. 100–10.

31. J. Harris, "Must Doctors Save Their Patients?" *Journal of Medical Ethics* 9 (1983): 211–18.

32. K. J. McGlade, T. Bradley, G. J. J. Murphy, G. P. Lundy, "Referrals to Hospital by General Practitioners: A Study of Compliance and Communication," *British Medical Journal* 297 (1988): 1246–48.

33. R. Jones, *Mental Health Act Manual* (London: Sweet and Maxwell, 1991).

20

Smoking Right and Responsibility

Jeffrey A. Schaler

"I am not advocating restrictions on personal choices that are currently legal. Smoking is a choice, but it is a bad one." (Sullivan, 1990, p. 1582)

The increasing attempt to hold tobacco companies responsible for the consequences of smoking behavior poses a greater threat to liberty in a free society than nicotine ever could (Hansen, 1997). Despite the fact addiction is not listed in standard textbooks of pathology (because it does not meet the nosological criteria for disease classification), anti-smoking propagandists define the behavior of smokers as if it were some kind of epileptic seizure. Their attempts to absolve people of responsibility for their behavior are the obvious consequence. Yet attributing smoking entirely to addiction is not based on the facts and has inevitably led to a legal policy based on fiction. Here are the facts about smoking and responsibility.

There's a difference between what smoking does to a person's body and how smoke gets into his body. The U.S. Food and Drug Administration (FDA), in cooperation with the public-health industry and with attorneys who argue smokers get sick because they have "lost the ability to choose" not to smoke, clouds that distinction. Concurrently, these groups suggest a person's body (as opposed to the person himself) causes a particular vice and its consequences, i.e., smoking behavior doesn't exist apart from physiological processes. Nothing could be further from the truth.

While their intentions may be compassionate (Is compassion a body product like smoking, i.e., caused?), the net effect of their thinking is to

J. A. Schaler (1997). Smoking right and responsibility. *Psychnews International* 2, no. 2, section B, February–March. (http://userpage.fu-berlin.de/~expert/FTP_2_2/PN12_2.b)

reduce human beings to machines—chemical and electrical interactions, soulless animals—lacking free will and moral agency, the very qualities we characterize as distinctly human. And, remember machines don't operate by themselves. They are operated by people.

Does a car "drive" the driver? Does a pencil "write" the writer? Does a body "run" the person? Of course not. People run their bodies, not the other way around. Yet those who assert nicotine addiction causes smoking are engaging in just such illogical thinking.

Consider the dangerous legal precedent that could be set by such thinking: If smokers physical addiction to nicotine causes them to smoke, one might just as easily argue rapists' bodies cause them to commit rape, murderers' bodies cause them to commit murder, child abusers' bodies cause them to abuse. What kind of world would we live in if those theories were upheld by the courts? If we attribute responsibility for the harm people do to themselves to physiological processes, don't we necessarily have to remove people's responsibility for the harm they cause to others to justly apply the rule of law? And then we must remove moral agency and responsibility for good behaviors, too: Heroism, courage and other virtuous acts such as loving and praying, academic achievement and creativity must also be viewed as having nothing to do with ethical human action. They're simply products of biology. We all know that's inaccurate reasoning.

Nevertheless, it is exactly the kind of argument used by people who are suing tobacco companies for injuries the plaintiffs may have caused themselves by smoking. Tobacco caused them to smoke, they claim, as if tobacco had a will of its own. Cigarettes, renamed "nicotine-delivery systems" by the FDA, render smokers incapable of abstinence. Any reasons for smoking thereby become irrelevant.

This doublespeak contradicts the scientific evidence: smokers quit all the time—when it is important to them to do so. They moderate their smoking at will, too. For example, a study of over five thousand Minnesota workers published in the September 1996 issue of the *American Journal of Public Health* showed "a substantial proportion of smokers are low-rate users and suggest[s] that the proportion may be rising" (Hennrikus et al., 1996). This finding supports the idea that psychological factors play a part in smokers' decisions to smoke or not to smoke. It contradicts the claim that people become physiologically enslaved by nicotine addiction once they start smoking.

Moreover, studies published in the *Journal of the American Medical Association* (*JAMA*) have long shown smokers can quit on their own (Fiore et al., 1990; Glynn, 1990). This finding undoubtedly upsets the manufacturers of nicotine patches and gum, as well as those who make money on smoking cessation clinics and programs. Indeed, these groups are economically addicted to convincing the public that smokers cannot quit on their own, that willpower won't work. So they spread the lie smokers have an addiction disease, caused by a physiological dependency on nicotine, one they can never manage on their own. They want the public to believe their products are necessary for curing the disease. Yet scientific studies have long shown that treatment programs for smoking addiction don't work for most people (Fiore et al., 1990; Glynn, 1990).

Choosing to quit is a simple statement of intention. Whether people are heavy or light smokers has nothing to do with the ability to quit. The best predictor of smoking and cessation of smoking is level of education (Escobedo et al., 1990). Plaintiffs' lawyers in the numerous liability cases directed at British and American tobacco companies rely on public ignorance in order to make money. They know less educated persons on the jury are less likely to reason out the facts and more likely to be swayed in their attitudes by "authorities" who obscure the difference between behavior and disease.

Most of us know people who smoked for years then quit abruptly. Their bodies had adapted to nicotine and since they chose to quit, they did. Question: What do we attribute that behavior to? Answer: Free will.

And what of people who do not want to quit? Why explain their behavior using terms such as weak will and physiological addiction? Those people simply choose to continue smoking, even if a doctor or loved one has suggested they quit. They aren't suffering from a weak will. They have an iron will: They choose to continue smoking against medical advice. And ironically, they are often the ones who transform their iron will into an iron fist, demanding they be financially compensated for the consequences of their own behavior.

There's nothing particularly unusual about noncompliance with medical advice or blaming others for one's own behavior. Many people continue to engage in certain behaviors against medical advice. How many people continue to eat a high-fat diet when their doctor recommends against it? If they develop cardiovascular disease, will they blame McDonald's and Burger King for hooking them on hamburgers and french fries? Why not?

Smoking and quitting, like eating and dieting or exercising and being a couch potato, are matters of free will and personal choice. Yes, habits may cause disease—but habits aren't diseases in and of themselves. Cancer is a disease. Smoking is a habitual behavior. Moreover, likening a behavior to a disease seems especially cruel to people with real diseases. A person cannot choose to quit or moderate diabetes.

The price of freedom in a free society is responsibility for the consequences of one's actions. Liberty and responsibility are positively correlated. That's a fact. People who claim addiction causes people to smoke say the two are negatively correlated. That's fiction. We cannot increase freedom by decreasing personal responsibility. That's the road to serfdom.

REFERENCES

Escobedo, L. G., R. F. Anda, P. F. Smith, P. L. Remington, and E. E. Mast. (1990). "Sociodemographic Characteristics of Cigarette Smoking Initiation in the United States. Implications for Smoking Prevention Policy." *Journal of the American Medical Association* 264: 1550–55.

Fiore, M. C., T. E. Novotny, J. P. Pierce, A. Giovino, E. J. Hatziandreu, P. A. Newcomb, T. S. Surawicz, R. M. Davis. (1990). "Methods Used to Quit Smoking in the United States. Do Cessation Programs Help?" *Journal of the American Medical Association* 263: 2760–65.

Glynn, T. J. (1990). "Methods of Smoking Cessation—Finally, Some Answers." (Editorial). *Journal of the American Medical Association* 263: 2795–96.

Hansen, M. (1997). "Capitol Offensives." *American Bar Association Journal* (January): 50–56.

Hennrikus, D. J., R. W. Jeffrey, and H. A. Lando. (1996). "Occasional Smoking in a Minnesota Working Population." *American Journal of Public Health* 86: 1260–66.

Sullivan, L. (1990). "An Opportunity to Oppose: Physicians' Role in the Campaign against Tobacco." (Editorial). *Journal of the American Medical Association* 264: 1581–82.

21

Passive Smoking, Scientific Method, and Corrupted Science

Antony Flew

PART ONE: THE ETS QUESTION: A PHILOSOPHER'S VIEW

Some years ago, I made a prediction. I mention this with pride, since social scientists rarely make predictions that come true. I made it in a paper that I wrote when I first became interested in the politics of health. I said that the anti-smoking movement had a big problem, at least in the Western democracies. Even if smoking really were so harmful to smokers as was claimed, the natural response would be to call it a matter of individual choice . . . The only solution to this problem available to the anti-smoking movement, I said, would be for it to find (and this was my term) an 'innocent bystander'. I suggested that one means of doing this would be to convince people that they could be harmed by the smoking of others. This is exactly what happened, and on the basis of scientific evidence which strikes even me, a non-natural scientist, as very dubious indeed. Professor Peter Berger[1]

Respiratory Health Effects of Passive Smoking: Lung Cancer and Other Disorders was issued in December 1992 by the Office of Research and Development of the Office of Health and Environmental Assessment of the US Environmental Protection Agency (EPA). This document constitutes the latest and perhaps the most specious of many such attempts "to convince people that they could be harmed by the smoking of others." Detailed critical examination of the evidence which it deploys is, of course, a job for scientists. Nevertheless, especially since the ultimate if not the primary objection

Originally published in *Forest (Promoting Equal Rights for Smokers)* (1993). Reprinted by permission of the publisher and author.

of the EPA is to convince the general public, it will perhaps be worthwhile to spell out some of the reasons why lay people ought to feel uneasy about epidemiological evidence of the sort presented and discussed here.

I. The Statistical Basis of Epidemiology

The first reason is the essentially statistical character of epidemiology. The epidemiological evidence which is offered about not only passive but also active smoking is evidence of the proportion of all the members of such and such a "set"[2] which can reasonably be expected to die of lung cancer or some other smoking-related condition, and hence of the probability that any particular member of that set will become a victim. The evidence for the harmful effects of passive smoking is of course even more probabilistic. For the degree of exposure to ETS of the sets of people studied is never actually measured but only estimated, while further estimates have to be made of the proportion of these supposed never-smokers who have not been telling the truth because they were in fact active as well as passive smokers.

In itself, and until and unless such evidence of probabilities can be supplemented and supported by evidence of causal connections, such statistical facts are an inadequate and unsatisfactory guide to conduct. Yet it appears that there is still no evidence of any other kind making it possible to determine that any particular death was caused by the patient's persistent heavy smoking. For, in all countries from which adequate information is available, there are minorities or even majorities of smokers who continue to die of something other than lung cancer, and that at a ripe old age.

Dr. Tage Voss in his lively polemic *Smoking and Common Sense: One Doctor's View*[3] gives the figures for his country:

> Many nonsmokers (in Denmark 800 a year) die from lung cancer . . . There are 1.8 million smokers in Denmark. Each year 55,000 people die, 25,000 of them smokers; 3,200 deaths are due to lung cancer. If we accept the worst case estimate that 80 per cent of the annual cases of lung cancer afflict smokers, then the figure is 2,400 out of the 25,000 smokers dead—less than one tenth. Finally, it is unlikely that all those smokers who die from lung cancer have contracted it from their smoking. There are many other important factors that may cause lung cancer, the same ones, presumably, that cause the disease in nonsmokers.[4]

No one knows, and few if any are even asking, what it is which is working to ensure that these fortunate smokers escape what anti-smoking campaigners consider to be their deserts. It is this fact, that no one has sufficient warrant to pick out any particular patients whose lung cancer was caused by their smoking, which explains why, even in America, no plaintiff has so far succeeded in winning a product liability case against a tobacco company. It also appears that there is no correlation across countries between high consumption of tobacco and high mortality from lung cancer. In Japan in the 1950s 85 percent of all men smoked, yet it had the world's lowest lung cancer mortality: 15 per 1,000. But the younger generation, which is tending to smoke less than its elders, seems nevertheless to be generating an increase estimated to reach 100 per 1,000 by the end of the century.

The absence of any such transnational correlations, together with the inability to determine in any particular cases that lung cancers were actually caused by smoking, surely ought to induce epidemiologists: either to rethink the question whether the correlations between smoking and lung cancer may not after all be a product of confounding[5]; and/or to make really strenuous efforts to discover what it is which saves so many Greeks (see below) and older Japanese men from the lung cancer to which they would otherwise have been doomed.

It is, I suggest, significant of the policy, and in that sense political, commitments of the EPA that the authors of *Respiratory Effects of Passive Smoking* show so little interest in prophylactic possibilities. The nearest they come is in Appendix 4.17.4, where they note that their findings about passive smoking in Greece:

> are compatible with the relatively low incidence of lung cancer in the Greek population—a population with the highest per capita tobacco consumption in the world, but with a very high fruit consumption as well . . .
> *Dietary data indicated that high consumption of fruits was inversely related to the risk of lung cancer.* Neither vegetables nor any other food group had any additional protective effect. (p. A-87; emphasis added).

But the authors do not recommend further investigation of what might turn out to be a modestly effective prophylactic: "Eat more fruit!"

II. Misdiagnosis and Misidentification of Causes of Death

A second reason for unease about epidemiological evidence is misdiagnosis with the consequent misidentification of the causes of deaths. Given that the medical profession has become strongly persuaded of the dangers of smoking, this is bound to result in an increase in the number of deaths mistakenly recorded as due to smoking-related diseases. The most extensive study ever performed in the U.K. was started in 1951 and reported in 1964.[6] It is therefore somewhat ancient.

But the latest report from the Office of Population Censuses and Surveys in the Government Statistical Service finds the situation still unsatisfactory[7]; and we may be sure, in view of the changing convictions of the profession, that whatever mistakes are made in diagnosing the conditions of patients known to be smokers are now more likely than in that earlier period to be in the direction of incorrectly inferring that those patients are suffering from smoking-related diseases.

In 1959 the researchers surveyed reports from seventy-five National Health Service hospitals in England and Wales, comparing diagnoses made in the patients' lifetimes with the results of post-mortem examinations. For cancer of the lung they found that doctors had diagnosed 338 cases when the pathologists found 417; in only 227 cases did the doctors and the pathologists agree. Thus 111 (33 percent) of the cases diagnosed as lung cancer were not in fact cases of lung cancer, while the pathologists found that in 190 cases what had been put down as something else was actually lung cancer.

If error on this scale is going to infect the statistical data on what is in everyone's view at worst the very weak effect of passive smoking then it must surely render the results of significance calculations meaningless? Yet in their first study of "Mortality in Relation to Smoking," which appeared in the same year as the work from which these figures of relevant diagnostic errors were drawn, Doll and Hill merely state that they sought confirmation for the cause of death from the doctor who certified the death and, when necessary, from the consultant to whom the patient had been referred. What mention of post mortems there is is very brief, and curiously inconclusive: ". . . in more than half of the deaths (56 percent) there was histological, cytological, or necropsy evidence together with x-ray or bronchoscopic confirmation. . . ."[8]

III. Exposure Rates to ETS

A third reason why lay people, and surely not lay people only, should feel uneasy about evidence of the kind so triumphantly presented in *Respiratory Health Effects of Passive Smoking* is the extreme smallness of the exposure of the passive relative to that of the active smoker. Everyone apparently agrees that smokers need to smoke fairly intensively and/or for a considerable period of time in order to be at serious risk of succumbing to lung cancer or other smoking-related disease. Yet we read in this EPA report that, although the available measures are far from perfect:

> Nevertheless, nicotine and cotinine levels in ETS-exposed nonsmokers measured in laboratory and field studies have been used to estimate cigarette equivalent exposures and to equate ETS exposures with active smoker exposures . . . On an equivalent cigarette basis, an upper-bound estimate of nicotine dose of 2.5 mg/day for a passive smoke exposure has been proposed . . . This would translate into the equivalent of about one-fifth of a cigarette per day or about 0.7 percent of the average smoker's dose of nicotine (cigarette equivalent dose of other toxins or carcinogens would be different . . .). (pp. 3–46)

These figures are, surely, sufficiently small to warrant the conclusion that, if passive smoking does indeed have some nosogenic effect, then that effect is likely to be exceedingly weak and, consequently, exceedingly difficult to establish? If research appeared to show a strong effect here, then, in the light of these figures, a reasonable first reaction would be to suspect the findings. If those findings were nevertheless confirmed then we should, paradoxically, have to begin to look for the nosogenic effect of passive smoking on active smokers. For it is known both that smokers tend to marry or otherwise cohabit with smokers and that much non-matrimonial smoking is done, or should we say performed, in company.

Small though the figures given in this EPA report are, they are still very large compared with those estimated by others. Thus one 1986 study[9] "estimated that, for the average nonsmoker, the retained dose of particulate material is 0.069 milligrams per kilogram for men and 0.033 milligrams per kilogram for women. These doses represent only 0.02 percent and 0.01 percent of the doses estimated to be retained by the average active smoker."[10] Given these retention ratios, and assuming both that active smoking increases the relative risk of lung cancer tenfold and that the relationship between the number of cigarettes smoked and the risk of lung cancer is approximately linear, then it must follow "that the risk to the exposed nonsmoker would be increased by a factor of about 1.002 for men and 1.001 for women, a very small increase indeed."[11]

In order to appreciate how small are these estimates based on relative retention ratios, we may compare them: both with the far larger risks which the EPA has here derived from a meta-analysis of epidemiological studies; and with the still larger ones which the EPA has allowed to be perfectly tolerable in areas where it did not have prevention policies and did not wish to develop any. Thus the final finding from the meta-analysis of all the studies selected for such analysis here, the estimate of the increased risk which is construed as warranting ETS to be a "Group A: Known Human Carcinogen," is 1.28; while the highest ever reported from any single study was 2.55.[12] By contrast, when the EPA investigated diesel emissions in 1989 it estimated that here the risk ratio was 2.6. Despite the seemingly graver threat, the EPA rated diesel only as a "Group B: Probable Human Carcinogen." An EPA review of the carcinogenic properties of electromagnetic fields in 1990 found several risk ratios over 3.0, as well as a "consistently repeated pattern of lymphoma, leukemia, nervous system cancer and lymphoma in childhood studies."[13] But electromagnetic fields were not deemed sufficiently perilous even to classify.

Finally, under the present subheading, there is one other finding which should not go unmentioned. For it suggests the presence in, it seems, up to 10 percent of all homes of another, different factor increasing risk at over five times the rate which the EPA takes to be sufficient to warrant rating ETS a "Group A: Known Human Carcinogen." This 1988 finding,[14] which so far

neither the EPA nor anyone else has attempted either to confirm or discon-
firm, is that, after taking smoking into account, people who keep pet birds in
their homes have a 6.7 times higher risk of developing lung cancer than those
who do not. The most plausible explanation, if this finding is confirmed,
would be that detritus in the birds' cages getting into the ambient air as par-
ticles of dust causes pathological fibrotic changes which in turn predispose
to cancer.

IV. The Corruption of "Official" Science

The first 3 parts of the present chapter enumerated and expounded reasons
why lay people ought to feel uneasy about epidemiological evidence of the
sort presented and discussed in *Respiratory Health Effects of Passive
Smoking*. This part offers a justification for a suspiciously critical approach to
all categorical and unqualified pronouncements from official bodies about the,
allegedly, rock-solid scientific foundations of their policies. This justification
is that official bodies, and indeed all bodies having policies to promote, must
be tempted, and all too often in fact succumb to temptations, to be misguided
by what has now been usefully nicknamed the "Lalonde Doctrine."

This doctrine was openly advocated by Marc Lalonde, sometime Minister of National Health and Welfare in the Government of Canada, in *A New
Perspective on the Health of Canadians* (Information Canada, Ottawa,
1974). Chapter 9, significantly entitled "Science versus Health Promotion,"
makes the crucial point clearly:

> *Science is full of 'ifs', 'buts' and 'maybes' while messages designed to influence
> the public must be loud, clear and unequivocal.* (Emphasis mine)

Noting that scientists are divided on issues like the bearing of exercise and
diet on coronary heart disease, it goes on to say that, such indeterminacy
notwithstanding:

> action has to be taken . . . even if all the scientific evidence is not in. (p. 57)

The conclusion is:

> The scientific "yes, but" is essential to research but for modifying the behavior
> of the human population it sometimes produces the "uncertain sound" which is
> all the excuse needed by many to cultivate and tolerate an environmental and
> lifestyle that is hazardous to health. (p. 58)[15]

But now, if and when the available scientific evidence is thus insufficient
and/or ambiguous in its implications, how can the politicians promoting their
particular policies of behavioral modification nevertheless pretend them-

selves to know what the problems actually are and what are the right ways of solving those problems, in what directions; that is, whose behavior has to be modified? Aficionados of the Lalonde Doctrine thereby become committed to making policy bets on behalf of and at the expense of a public from which they are at the same time committed to concealing the uncertainties of the betting issues. They are also inclined, as is indicated by the passage just quoted, to dispose of recalcitrants by simply assuming that all they have to offer in their defense is irrational rationalization rather than objections deserving of serious discussion.

The Australian Institute of Health, in its 1988 biennial report *Australia's Health,* acknowledged that Lalonde's *A New Perspective* had had "a major impact on thinking about health, health services and illness prevention"(p. 17). However extensive or however limited the direct influence of that book, there is no question but that a great many individuals and organizations in several different countries have been and still are misguided by the substance of the doctrine nicknamed for its author.

For instance: in 1986 the Surgeon General of the United States and the National Health and Medical Research Council of Australia reached the conclusions, respectively, that the evidence against 'passive smoking' was "strongly suggestive," even "compelling." This was on the basis primarily if not exclusively of T. Hirayama's "Nonsmoking Wives of Heavy Smokers Have Higher Risk of Lung Cancer: A Study From Japan" and of D. Trichopolous, A. Kalindi, L. Sparros and B. MacMahon "Lung Cancer and Passive Smoking." But, as J. R. Johnstone has so devastatingly argued, they contrived to reach these confident conclusions only by ignoring all published criticism of those seminal papers:

> The NHIMRC in its Report grasped the nettle firmly. Only the original and incorrect calculations of risk ratios given by Trichopolous et al. were quoted: no mention was made of the total recalculation of risk-ratios made by Heller and accepted by Trichopolous. The surgeon general of the USA gave the corrected values but attributed them to "Trichopolous et al., 1983," where they do not appear, rather than to Heller . . . For his trouble Heller does not even get mentioned. . . .[16]

Commenting that this "avoidance of published corrections leads to a quite natural sense of security in the acceptance of erroneous published conclusions" Johnstone proceeds to review the treatment of Hirayama:

> The surgeon general in a discussion of Hirayama's critics made no mention of the errors in Hirayama's 1981 paper. On the contrary, he said that in response to Lee's criticism "the calculations were later confirmed," but did not mention the fact that Hirayama himself admitted making errors of a magnitude which put them more in the realm of cosmology than of epidemiology. The NHMRC

Report on the other hand simplified the issue by not even mentioning the question of error.[17]

V. The Scandal of the EPA

Our immediate concern is with the EPA. Europeans need to be warned that "almost throughout its entire history, there have been cries of horror and charges of scandal over the scientific performance of the EPA, so many they cannot be summarized."[18] So the following paragraph will have to suffice as support:

> In response to one series of hearings investigating reportedly fraudulent EPA research, Congress passed the Environmental Research, Development Demonstration Authorization Act, which accorded to the Science Advisory Board the job of overseeing EPA's research and development. In 1977, the board repeatedly clashed with the EPA's judgment, and Dr. James I. Whitteberger, chairman of the Department of Physiology of Harvard School of Public Health and chairman of the Science Advisory Board Subcommittee, said that EPA's 'health risk assessments are largely speculative, incomplete, and heavily dependent on studies of questionable validity'. In 1978, John Walsh of *Science,* reporting on EPA's difficulties in 'dealing with uncertainty', said that 'the validity of its scientific information is the make or break factor for the agency'. And EPA's scientific capabilities are seen by knowledgeable critics as chronically weak . . . There are persistent complaints that many of [EPA's] labs have not kept pace scientifically or developed sufficient competencies. . . .[19]

In its earlier treatment of the putative dangers of ETS the EPA certainly ran true to its general past form. In 1990 its Scientific Advisory Board leaked the findings of a draft report claiming that ETS is a Group A: Known Human Carcinogen. But that report, although it had been compiled by well-known anti-tobacco activists, had not been subjected to any kind of peer review. Indeed, within a month the Chairman of the Scientific Advisory Board, Dr. Morton Lippmann, pooh-poohed it, stating that the risk from ETS was "probably much less than you took to get here through Washington traffic."[20]

It is of course always possible that this time the EPA is crying "Wolf!" when it actually has at last succeeded in establishing that passive smoking is after all a serious health hazard. I must leave it to my scientist colleagues to determine whether or not *Respiratory Effects of Passive Smoking* has in truth what it claims to have proved. But, unless it has, there is good reason to suggest that the drive "to convince people that they could be harmed by the smoking of others" has led and continues to lead to a misdirection of research effort. That the effort has been substantial is seen from the fact that "As late as November 1988 a major WHO review of everything then published about passive smoking concluded that, until then, there were not sufficient studies (there were at the time more than 1,000) to prove a connection between passive smoking and lung cancer."[21] Peter N. Lee reached the same negative conclusion in a thorough and exhaustive 1992 study described as "A Detailed Review of Epidemiological Evidence Relating Environmental Tobacco Smoke to the Risk of Cancer, Heart Disease and Other Causes of Death in Adults Who Have Never Smoked." Its last words were:

> Taken as a whole, the evidence does not demonstrate that exposure to environmental tobacco smoke increases risk of cancer, heart disease or other diseases among adult nonsmokers.[22]

VI. "Inconvenient" Science Vs "Official" Science

Already I have noticed and regretted the apparent lack of concern to investigate such possible prophylactics against lung cancer as fruit eating. There is now some reason to believe that smoking itself may constitute some sort of prophylactic against Alzheimer's disease.[23] The researchers appear to have been embarrassed by the "political incorrectness" of this finding. For they write:

> Although the association is compatible with a protective effect of smoking for familial Alzheimer's disease, it has no relevance for prevention of Alzheimer's disease because of the adverse health effects of smoking.

We have here one of those occasions on which talk of saving lives by stopping smoking can be seriously misleading. For it tempts us to overlook that everyone who is saved from dying of lung cancer will die later of something else.[24] If these first findings were to be confirmed, and smoking was proved to be an effective prophylactic against Alzheimer's, then I for one, as a never-smoker who has seen cases of both Alzheimer's and lung cancer, would unhesitatingly opt to reduce my risks of the one by opting to take up smoking and thus increase my risks of the other.

NOTES TO PART ONE

1. Peter Berger, "Toward a Religion of Health Activism," in Peter Berger et al., *Health, Lifestyle and Environment* (Social Affairs Unit, London/Manhattan Institute, New York, 1991), p. 29.

2. By Canto's Axiom for Sets the sole essential feature of a set is that its members must have at least one common characteristic, any kind of characteristic.

3. Peter Owen, London, 1992.

4. Ibid, p. 39.

5. See, for instance, George Davey Smith and Andrew N. Phillips, "Confounding in Epidemiological Studies: Why 'Independent' Effects May Not Be All They Seem," *British Medical Journal*, no. 2 (1992): 757–59.

6. M. A. Heasman and L. Lipworth, *Accuracy of Certification of Cause of Death.* This was Number 20 of the Studies on Medical and Population Subjects produced by the General Register Office (HMSO, London, 1964).

7. John Ashley and Tim Davis, "Death Certification from the Point of View of the Epidemiologist," *Population Trends* (Spring 1992): 22–28.

8. R. Doll and A. B. Hill, "Mortality in Relation to Smoking: Ten Years' Observation of British Doctors," *British Medical Journal,* 1964, I, pp. 1402–1403.

9. A. Arundel, T. Irwin and T. Sterling, "Nonsmoker Lung Cancer Risks From Tobacco and Smoke Exposure," *Journal of Environmental Science and Health* (1968), 4, Part C: 93–118. I owe this reference to George Leslie, "Environmental Tobacco Smoke and Lung Cancer," in A. K. Armitage, ed., *Other People's Tobacco Smoke* (Yorkshire: Galen, Beverley, 1991), pp. 81–98.

10. Leslie, "Environmental Tobacco Smoke and Lung Cancer," pp. 84–85.

11. Ibid., p. 85.

12. R. Inoue and T. Hirayama, "Passive Smoking and Lung Cancer in Women,"in M. Aoki, S. Hisamichi, and S. Tominaga, eds., *Smoking and Health* (Amsterdam: Elsevier, 1988), pp. 283–85. I owe this reference to Christopher Caldwell, "Smoke Gets in Your Eyes," *The American Spectator* (May 1992): 25–38.

13. Caldwell, "Smoke Gets in Your Eyes," p. 27.

14. P. A. Holst, D, Kromhout and R. Brand, "For Debate: Pet Birds as an Independent Risk Factor for Lung Cancer," *British Medical Journal* 1 (1988): 1319–21. This reference is given both in Leslie, "Environmental Tobacco Smoke and Lung Cancer," and in F. J. C. Roe, "How Inadequate Ventilation May Impair Health and Well-Being," in A. K. Armitage, *Other People's Tobacco Smoke,* pp. 5–20.

15. I owe these quotations from Lalonde and also a later reference to the 1988 report on *Australia's Health* to Professor Peter Finch of Monash University. See Peter Finch, "The 'Lalonde Doctrine' and Passive Smoking," *Policy* 6, no. 2 (Winter 1990); Idem, "Misleading Claims on Smoking and Health," *Policy* 6, no. 3 (Spring 1990), reprinted as *Lies, Damned Lies . . . A Close Look at the Statistics on Smoking and Health* (London: Forest, 1991).

16. The quotation can be found at p. 65 of J. R. Johnstone's "Scientific Fact or Scientific Self-Delusion: Passive Smoking, Exercise and the New Puritanism," in Peter Berger et al., *Health, Lifestyle, and Environment,* pp. 57–77, which also provides all the relevant references.

17. Ibid, p. 65. This is perhaps as good a place as any to point out an oddity at page A-63 of the present EPA report on *Respiratory Health.* We read there that "Macdonald (1981) contended that the six prefectures from which the sample was drawn are relatively industry-heavy. Hirayama (1983a) presented data showing that 40,390 of the cohort's wives were married to agricultural workers, 19,264 to industry workers, and 31,886 to 'others,' indicating some over-representation of agricultural areas." But now, 40,390 out of 91,540 is 44 percent. So unless Japan is in this respect not just quite substantially but really enormously different from other heavily industrial countries this over-representation is not merely modest but gross. If the cooking practices of Japanese farm workers' wives differ from those of their urban sisters then their over-representation might perhaps turn out to be relevant. Otherwise it can only provide yet another indication of Hirayama's somewhat slap-happy approach to questions quantitative. (Subsequent to writing this I have been informed by Judith Hatton that, according to *The Economist Book of Vital World Statistics,* 7.2 percent of the Japanese labor force is in agriculture.)

18. Edith Efron, *The Apocalyptics: How Environmental Politics Controls What We Know about Cancer* (New York: Simon and Schuster, 1984), p. 263.

19. Ibid., pp. 263–64.

20. *EPA Watch* 1, no. 2 (16 March 1992): 2.

21. Tage Voss, *Smoking and Common Sense: One Doctor's View* (London: Peter Owen, 1992), p. 106.

22. Peter N. Lee, *Environmental Tobacco Smoke and Mortality* (Basel: Karger, 1992), p. 209.

23. Cornelia M. van Duijn and Albert Hofman, "Relation between Nicotine Intake and Alzheimer's Disease," *British Medical Journal,* June 22, 1991, pp. 1491–94.

24. Peter Skrabanek claims, but without displaying his calculations, that "Even if all lung cancer disappeared by magic, average life expectancy would be extended by six months at most." See Armitage, *Other People's Tobacco Smoke,* p. 174

PART TWO: TOWARD TRUTH, THROUGH FALSIFICATION

"The Editor's Dilemma," it has been explained in the journal *Indoor Environment,*[1] is that "It is difficult to think of an area of work that is more prone to political influences, and it is not always easy to distinguish between articles of this type and the more straightforward contributions." The reason why this area of work is so exposed is, of course, that those more straightforward contributions will typically report finding that elements in some indoor environments either are or are not potentially harmful to the inhabitants of those environments. Indeed a main reason both for funding and for doing the research will presumably have been that it was believed that the results would be practically relevant in that way.

This is where political influences are bound to come in—political influences, that is, in the most general sense of pressures for or against policies of acting or refraining from acting in particular sorts of ways. For precisely that is what practical relevance is relevant to. The editor-in-chief, acknowledging a debt to Wittgenstein's *Philosophical Investigations,*[2] proceeded to offer one or two tips for distinguishing pure scientific sheep from impure political goats. "Political writers are seemingly unable to resist using the word 'issues', whereas scientists deal, or attempt to deal, with 'problems'." Again, "to a scientist the word 'significant' is usually associated with the result of a statistical test, whereas to the politician or lobbyist it is a euphemism for 'important', or rather for what he or she would like the audience to think is 'important'."

All this is very much to the point; as is the insistence that *Indoor Environment* must include "two kinds of article: reports of research findings and interpretations of findings, which in some cases are aimed at influencing what and how scientists, the general public and governments think about problems."[3] (Surely in this context the word should have been not 'problems' but 'issues'?) The final statement in that Editorial was that "New methods, new data and new insights might at any time lead to different conclusions."[4]

I. The Method of Science: Conjectures, Refutations and Criticism

These emphases upon ever-continuing critical inquiry, and upon the consequent permanent possibilities of radical revisings of previously accepted conclusions, suggest that there is also something relevant to be learned from *Conjectures and Refutations* and other works by Sir Karl Popper.[3] For it is he who has insisted that the scientific enterprise essentially involves the exposing of every hypothesis to persistent, radical, truth-directed criticism. Only when and in as much as hypotheses have survived and continue to survive such criticism, remaining still unfalsified, do we become rationally entitled to feel confident that, even if these have not yet reached the final truth, then they do at least constitute the nearest approaches presently available.

II. Politicized Science and Its Tactics

In contrasting science with politics we have to recognize and to remember that there is not always and everywhere a sharp, clear line separating detached and neutral scientists from involved and committed lobbyists. Most important perhaps today is the international movement of self-styled 'progressive' scientists, identified by Aaron Wildavsky and others.[4] This movement is dedicated to revealing, denouncing and opposing the 'corporate greed' which is supposedly responsible for wantonly distributing all manner of what are alleged to be unacceptably dangerous substances. Anyone who dares to challenge the pronouncements of this movement, especially if they have ever accepted research funding from any private corporation, is likely to be dismissed as a "kept scientist," one of "the hired guns of the scientific world" or the like.[5]

Such abrupt and insulting dismissals of unwelcome criticism should be altogether unacceptable; in the first place because they prejudicially assume the critics' guilt. If there is a suitable occasion for investigating someone's motives in raising false, incoherent, irrelevant or otherwise worthless objections it must be after those objections have been duly discredited by evidence and argument; and not before.

Such dismissals are distracting and diversionary in another and more extensive way. By their concentration upon the exclusively mercenary motives thus attributed to commercial and industrial corporations and their shareholders and employees they withdraw attention from the facts, both that similarly sordid and material motives can be and sometimes are harbored by other participants in these debates, and, more important, that there are innumerable other possible motives which may and often do tempt fallible human beings into intellectual errors and misdemeanors.

Thus the fact that an organisation was supposedly established to serve some supposed public interest does not guarantee that its employees will have no private interests in the survival and expansion of that organisation. On the contrary: they very naturally and obviously will. Again, such disinterestedly ideological commitments as a "progressive" animosity against capitalist corporations or a crusading concern to promote public health can constitute temptations to self-deceiving error as strong as any material interest. Nor should we be human if we did not all hope that the findings of research would tend to confirm our own beliefs and, if we are scientists, our own hypotheses.

III. The Importance of Criticism

It is, surely, a recognition both of the difficulties of doing fault-free scientific work and of the strength and variety of the temptations to self-deceiving error which has led to the institutionalization of sustained and systematic criticism throughout the entire scientific world. To achieve scientific respectability papers have to be published; and published in a refereed journal. They have, that is to say, to be subjected to the criticism of referees before they can be published at all in a scientific journal; and then, by that publication, they are exposed to further criticism from all the other peers of their writers. Only the findings which have survived such criticism, which have not been disconfirmed by other workers, and which have been shown to be intelligibly related to what else is already known can be accounted truly scientific; and then only until and unless "New methods, new data and new insights . . . lead to different conclusions."

IV. . . . and the Case of "Passive Smoking"

Readers of *Indoor Environment* will no doubt be only too aware that in this and other countries various authorities which ought to know better have been and still are proclaiming in the name of science, and offering as the bases of public policy, much of what by these criteria is not truly scientific. Take, for instance, the question of the harmfulness or otherwise of ETS. All persons and organizations campaigning against smoking have a compelling reason for wanting to establish that ETS is harmful; and the more extensive and substantial that harm the better. For this is precisely the discovery which they need in order to undermine principled libertarian opposition to the introduction of laws against smoking and/or restrictions upon the production and sale of tobacco products.

The motive here, and the consequent temptations to error, may well be ideally disinterested and benevolent—a desire to prevent people suffering and dying from smoking-related diseases. These temptations are nevertheless temptations to commit what should be seen as serious scientific offenses. Many of those who ought to have known and done better have in fact succumbed. Thus in Australia in 1986 the National Health and Medical Research Council concluded—on the basis primarily if not exclusively of 1981 studies by Hirayama[6] and by Trichopolous et al.[7]—that the case against 'passive smoking' was "strongly suggestive," even "compelling." But the Council quoted only the original and incorrect calculations of risk-ratios from Trichopolous, making no mention of his acceptance of Heller's systematic recalculations.[8] And about errors in Hirayama's paper it said nothing whatever.[9]

In the same year the surgeon general of the United States, in a report on *The Health Consequences of Involuntary Smoking,*[10] gave the corrected values but attributed them to "Trichopolous et al., 1983,"[11] where they do not appear, rather than to Heller,[8] who is not so much as mentioned. In discussing Hirayama the Surgeon General similarly neglected to mention the monumental miscalculations which were pointed out by Lee[12] and later admitted by Hirayama himself.[13] On the contrary: for the Surgeon General's response to Lee's criticism was apparently to maintain that "the calculations were later confirmed."[9]

Most recently, and nearest to home, Veronica Bland sued her former employer, Stockport Council, in Greater Manchester, for compensation for illnesses allegedly caused by the smoking of fellow employees. Ms Bland should surely count herself lucky to have been awarded in January 1993 £15,000 in an out of court settlement. For she ought to have expected that, had the case been brought to court, her causal contention would have been exposed to devastating defense criticism.

With an eye to encouraging further cases of the same kind ASH[14] obtained a Counsel's Opinion. It was to the effect that plaintiffs could hope to succeed only if they were able to establish a causal connection between their own injuries or illnesses and their own exposure to ETS. The awkward crux is that it thus appears to be legally essential to prove causal connection in the particular case. That is sufficiently difficult if not impossible with respect to active smoking and lung cancer, since many if not most heavy smokers in fact die without contracting lung cancer, and since many of those who do contract it are never-smokers. So far no plaintiff has succeeded, not even in the USA where the courts are notoriously ready to find justifications for extracting tort compensatory awards from "deep pocket" defendants.[15] But whereas we can take it as established that active smoking is one of the possible causes of lung cancer, as well as of some other afflictions, the conclusion of the latest and most comprehensive critical survey of the research findings on ETS is "that the epidemiological evidence has not convincingly demonstrated that ETS increases the risk of mortality."[16]

V. . . . and Even Active Smoking

In the U.K. both the most striking and the most amusing examples of uncrit-
icized assertions presented as the revelations of scientific experts are provided by campaigners against active smoking. Despite their insistence that
the risk of suffering from smoking-related diseases is reduced to that of a
nonsmoker a few years after giving up smoking, the campaigning authorities
appear never to notice, and much less to venture any suggested saving explanation for, the fact that reductions in the proportion of smokers in the populations seem to be being rewarded not by decreases but by actual increases in
the numbers of deaths from smoking-related diseases. Thus, according to the
National No Smoking Day Fact File, the percentage of smokers for 1972 and
1988 were, respectively, 52 and 33; while in November 1991 *Social and
Community Research* reported a further fall to 27. Yet, whereas in 1983 the
Royal College of Medicine maintained that there were 50,000 smoking-
related deaths a year, by 1991 they had upped their figure to 110,000. A year
later the Royal Society for Medicine managed to find an extra 5,000.

Popper, as was noted earlier, sees the progress of science as consisting in
the development of bold conjectures challenging critical refutation. The
reason for thus seeking not confirmation but falsification is, in the oft-quoted
words of Francis Bacon, "that the force of the negative instance is greater."
For conclusively to falsify any unrestricted universal generalization—any
proposition, that is, of the form 'All so-and-sos, without restriction of time or
place, are such-and-such'—it is sufficient to produce a single counter-
example, a single case, that is, of a so-and-so which is not a such-and-such.
It is, however, impossible equally conclusively to verify a proposition of this
form. For there remains always, no matter how many so-and-sos are found to
be such-and-such, at least the theoretical and conceptual if not the live practical possibility of eventually discovering a counter-example. It can be illu-
minating to see this insistence upon the imperative need for criticism, and for
attention to that criticism, as one especially important application of a general principle which has many other related applications. It is that, if anyone
with even modest pretensions to rationality is to be allowed to be sincerely
pursuing any purpose whatsoever, then they must be constantly concerned to
discover whether and how far that purpose has been and is being achieved.

The overriding aim of all scientific inquiry is to discover both what the
facts truly are and the true reasons why they are what they are. Both because
there are so many possible interests and inclinations tempting and misleading
people to adopt and defend beliefs which, although congenial to them, are not
in fact true, and because even the most dedicated and disinterested investigators are still liable to make mistakes, it becomes exceedingly difficult to
ensure that what we have got is indeed the truth. Yet to the extent that we
really are sincerely devoted to the discovery and assertion of truth, we cannot

accommodate any substitutes, however seductively appealing. Why criticism is needed in the present context, and what it is for, is to detect such substitutes; and, consequently, to reject them.

A corollary of the same general principle is that, if and in so far as agents become aware that their professed aims are not being achieved by the policies supposedly adopted and pursued for those purposes, then—unless they show themselves ready to respond by adopting alternative and hopefully more successful tactics—we have to conclude that, whether or not those originally professed aims were then professed sincerely, they are surely not the present purposes of those agents in pursuing those policies.

NOTES TO PART TWO

1. Donald F. Weetman (School of Health Sciences, University of Sunderland), "The Editor's Dilemma," *Indoor Environment* 1, no. 3 (March/April 1992): 129–30.

2. L. Wittgenstein, *Philosophical Investigations,* 2d. ed., (Oxford: Blackwell, 1958).

3. Karl Popper, *Conjectures and Refutations: The Growth of Scientific Knowledge,* 4th ed. (Routledge, 1972). And see also his *The Logic of Scientific Discovery* (1959) (London: Hutchinson, 1976), and *Objective Knowledge: An Evoilutionary Approach* (Oxford: Clarendon Press, 1972). P. A. Schilpp, ed., *The Philosophy of Karl Popper,* 2 vols. (La Salle: Open Court, 1974), contains papers by different authors on Popper's work, together with Popper's "Replies to My Critics" and a full bibliography of his work to that date.

4. Aaron Wildavsky, "If Claims of Harm from Technology are False, Mostly False, or Unproven What Does That Tell Us about Science?" in Peter Berger et al., *Health, Lifestyle and Environment* (Social Affairs Unit, London/Manhattan Institute, New York, 1992), pp. 11–45.

5. For this and many similar charges, see Edith Efron, *The Apocalyptics: How Environmental Politics Controls What We Know about Cancer* (New York: Simon and Schuster, 1984), pp. 231–383.

6. T. Hirayama, "Nonsmoking Wives of Heavy Smokers Have Higher Risk of Lung Cancer: A Study From Japan," *British Medical Journal* 282 (1981): 183–85.

7. D. Trichopolous, A. Kalandidi, L. Sparros, B. MacMahon, "Lung Cancer and Passive Smoking," *International Journal of Cancer* 27 (1981): 1–4.

8. W. D. Heller, "Lung Cancer and Passive Smoking," *The Lancet* 4 (1984): 1309.

9. J. R. Johnstone, "Scientific Fact or Scientific Self-Delusion: Passive Smoking, Exercise and the New Puritanism," in Peter Berger et al., *Health, Lifestyle and Environment: Countering the Panic* (The Social Affairs Unit, London/The Manhattan Institute, New York, 1991), pp. 57–77.

10. *The Health Consequences of Involuntary Smoking—A Report of the Surgeon General* (Washington, D.C.: U.S. Department of Health and Human Services, 1986).

11. D. Trichopolous, A. Kalandidi, L. Sparros, "Lung Cancer and Passive Smoking: Conclusion of the Greek Study," *The Lancet* 2 (1938): 677–78.

12. Peter N. Lee, "Untitled Letter," *British Medical Journal* 283 (1981): 1465–66.

13. T. Hirayama, "Untitled Letter," *British Medical Journal* 283 (1981): 1466.

14. Since this organization is ever eager to emphasize that FOREST (Freedom Organisation for the Right to Enjoy Tobacco) is funded to the tune of "£300,000 per year by the tobacco industry," it is only fair to point out that ASH itself receives a annual quarter of a million pounds of public, i.e., taxpayers', money.

15. See Peter Huber, *Liability—The Legal Revolution and its Consequences* (New York: Basic Books, 1988), and *Galileo's Revenge: Junk Science in the Courtroom* (New York: Basic Books, 1991).

16. Peter N. Lee, *Environmental,Tobacco Smoke and Mortality: A Detailed Review of Epidemiological Evidence Relating Environmental Tobacco Smoke to the Risk of Cancer, Heart Disease and Other Causes of Death in Adults Who Have Never Smoked* (Basel: Karger, 1992), p. 207.

Suggestions for Further Reading

Alexander, B. K. (1993). "Mark Twain and the American Drug 'Literature.' " Paper presented at the American Psychological Association Meetings, Division 28 (Psychopharmacology), Toronto, Ontario, Canada, August 20. Available from the author, Department of Psychology, Simon Fraser University, Burnaby, B.C., Canada, V5A IS6.

Becker, G. S., M. Grossman, and K. M. Murphy. (1994). "An Empirical Analysis of Cigarette Addiction." *The American Economic Review* 84: 396–418.

— — —. (1991). "Rational Addiction and the Effect of Price on Consumption." *The American Economic Review* 81: 237–41.

Becker, G. S., and K. Murphy. (1988). "A Theory of Rational Addiction." *Journal of Political Economy* 96: 675–700.

Boot, M. (1996). "A Texas-Xized Class Action Fraud." *The Wall Street Journal,* May 22, A23.

— — —. (1996). "On the Trail of the Cigarette Papers." *The Wall Street Journal,* April 10, A17.

— — —. (1996). "The Plaintiff's Bar Targets Tobacco Companies." *The Wall Street Journal,* March 20, A15.

Buchanan, J. M. (1988). "Politics and Meddlesome Preferences." In R. D. Tollison, ed., *Clearing the Air: Perspectives on Environmental Tobacco Smoke,* pp. 107–15. Lexington, Mass.: Lexington Books.

Geyelin, M., and S. L. Hwang. (1997). "What Brought Big Tobacco to the Table." *The Wall Street Journal,* April 18, Bl.

Goodin, R. E. (1989). *No Smoking: The Ethical Issues,* pp. 7–56. Chicago: University of Chicago Press.

Halpin Schauffler, H. (1993). "Health Insurance Policy and the Politics of Tobacco." In R. Rabin and S. Sugarman, eds., *Smoking Policy: Law, Politics and Culture.* New York: Oxford University Press.

Hennrikus, D. J., R. W. Jeffery, and H. A. Lando. (1996). "Occasional Smoking in a Minnesota Working Population." *American Journal of Public Health* 86: 1260–66.

Hersch, J., and W. K. Viscusi. (1990). "Cigarette Smoking, Seatbelt Use, and Differences in Wage-Risk Tradeoffs." *The Journal of Human Resources* 25: 202–27.

Hilts, P. (1996). *The Truth behind the Tobacco Industry Coverup.* New York: Addison-Wesley.

Howard, G. (1996). "Tobacco and the Law: The State of the Art." *British Medical Bulletin* 52: 143–56.

Lammi, G. G. "States Face Many Pitfalls When Hiring Contingency Fee Lawyers." *Legal Backgrounder* 12, no. 6 (March 7).

Leventhal, H., and P. D. Cleary. (1980). "The Smoking Problem: A Review of the Research and Theory in Behavioral Risk Modification." *Psychological Bulletin* 88: 370–405.

Littlechild, S. C. (1986). "Smoking and Market Failure." In R. D. Tollison, ed., *Smoking and Society: Toward a More Balanced Assessment,* pp. 271–84. Lexington, Mass.: Lexington Books.

Marsh, A. (1984). "Smoking: Habit or Choice?" *Population Trends* 37: 20.

McLachlan, H. (1995). "Smokers, Virgins, Equity and Health Care Costs." *Journal of Medical Ethics* 21: 209–13.

Postrel, V. (1994). "The Other Drug War." *Reason* 28, no. 6: 4.

Rabin, R., and S. Sugarman. (1993). *Smoking Policy: Law, Politics, and Culture.* New York: Oxford University Press.

Russell, M. A. H. (1993). "Reduction of Smoking-Related Harm: The Scope for Nicotine Replacement." In N. Heather, A. Wodak, E. Nadelmann, and P. O'Hare, eds., *Psychoactive Drugs and Harm Reduction: From Faith to Science,* pp. 153–67. London: Whurr.

Sullum, J. (1998). *For Your Own Good: The Anti-Smoking Crusade and the Tyranny of Public Health.* New York: Simon & Schuster.

Szasz, T. S. (1988). "The Ethics of Addiction." Adapted from "The Ethics of Addiction," *Harper's Magazine,* April 1972, 74–79. In *The Theology of Medicine.* Syracuse, N.Y.: Syracuse University Press.

Szasz, T. S. (1978, May 29). "New Addictions for Old." *Inquiry,* pp. 4–5.

Tollison, R. D. and R. E. Wagner. (1988). "Social Cost, Rent Seeking, and Smoking: A Public Choice Perspective." *Journal of Public Finance and Public Choice* 3: 171–86.

Tollison, R. (1986). *Smoking and Society.* Lexington, Mass.: Lexington Books.

———. (1988). *Clearing the Air.* Lexington, Mass.: Lexington Books.

Tollison, R., and R. Wagner. (1988). *Smoking and the State.* Lexington, Mass.: Lexington Books.

Wagner, R., and R. Tollison. (1992). *Economics of Smoking.* Norwell, Mass.: Kluwer Academic Publishers.

Viscusi, W. Kip. (1992). *Smoking: The Risky Decision.* New York: Oxford University Press.

———. (1990). "Do Smokers Underestimate Risks?" *Journal of Political Economy* 98: 1253–69.

Contributors

George J. Annas, J.D., M.P.H., is Professor of Health Law at Boston University Schools of Medicine and Public Health.

Peter L. Berger, Ph.D., is a distinguished sociologist and University Professor at Boston University honored with doctor of laws, Loyola University and University of Notre Dame; doctor of humane letters, Wagner College; and as a U.S. representative, United Nations Working Group on the Right to Development.

Lowell Bergman, a longtime television investigative reporter now working as a correspondent for FRONTLINE in Boston, was a founder of the Center for Investigative Reporting in 1977.

Morris E. Chafetz, M.D., was the founding director of the National Institute on Alcohol Abuse and Alcoholism and is currently founder and president of Health Education Foundation, an organization that relates health to lifestyle, in Washington, D.C.

Douglas J. Den Uyl, Ph.D., is an Assistant Professor of Philosophy at Bellarmine College, in Louisville, Kentucky.

Antony Flew is Professor Emeritus of Philosophy at the University of Reading (UK), has held numerous visiting lectureships and professorships, and is the author of many books and articles on philosophy.

Linda Goldman, BDS, LLB, is a barrister in a common-law chambers, Lincoln's Inn, London.

Joseph R. Gusfield, Ph.D., is Professor Emeritus of Sociology, University of California, San Diego, and the author of many books and articles on sociology.

Peter D. Jacobson, J.D., M.P.H., is Assistant Professor in the School of Public Health, University of Michigan, where he teaches courses on health law and policy.

Graham E. Kelder Jr., J.D., Managing Attorney of the Tobacco Law and Policy Project, is the author of numerous journal articles on tobacco control and tobacco litigation, and co-instructor (with Professor Richard Daynard) of "Toxic Torts and Complex Litigation" at Northeastern University School of Law.

David A. Kessler, M.D., J.D., the former Commissioner of the U.S. Food and Drug Administration, is currently Dean of the School of Medicine at Yale University.

Mark Edward Lender, Ph.D., co-authored *Drinking in America: A History* for Free Press/Macmillan in 1982, and since 1986 has been Director of Advanced Study and Research at Kean College in Union, New Jersey.

Rajendra Persaud, M.D., MPhil, MRCPsych, MSc, is Consultant Psychiatrist at the Bethlem and Maudsley Hospital Trust in London.

Blake D. Poland, Ph.D., teaches in the Department of Public Health Sciences, Faculty of Medicine, at the University of Toronto.

Robert N. Proctor, Ph.D. is Professor of the History of Science at Pennsylvania State University.

David Ryder, M.S., teaches at Edith Cowan University in Perth, Western Australia, and is completing his Ph.D. at the University of Western Australia.

Jeffrey A. Schaler, Ph.D., a psychologist, is adjunct professor of justice, law, and society at American University's School of Public Affairs and is currently writing a book entitled *Addiction Is a Choice* for Open Court Publishers in Chicago. He teaches psychology at Johns Hopkins University and is a member of the faculty at the institute for Humane Studies, George Mason University, Fairfax, Virginia.

Magda E. Schaler, M.P.H., received her B.A. degree in sociology with a program concentration in Law, Medicine and Health Policy from Brandeis University; and her M.P.H. degree from the Division of Health Policy and Management at Columbia University's School of Public Health. She is currently a law student at Columbia University School of Law.

Edward L. Sweda Jr. is Senior Attorney at the Tobacco Control Resource Center.

Thomas S. Szasz, M.D., is Professor Emeritus of Psychiatry at the State University of New York Health Sciences Center in Syracuse and author, most recently, of *The Fatal Freedom: The Ethics and Politics of Suicide* (Praeger, 1999).

Robert D. Tollison, Ph.D., is Professor of Economics and Director of the Center for Study of Public Choice at George Mason University, Fairfax, Virginia.

Walter E. Williams, Ph.D., is John M. Olin Distinguished Professor of Economics at George Mason University, Fairfax, Virgina.